C & C++
Code Capsules

ISBN 0-13-591785-9

90000

**Prentice Hall Series
on Programming Tools and Methodologies**

P.J. Plauger   *Series Advisor*

Allison   *C & C++ Code Capsules:*
                               A Guide for Practitioners

Lipkin   *String Processing and Text Manipulation in C:*
                               Selected Data Structures and Techniques

Plauger   *Programming on Purpose I:*
                               Essays on Programming Design

                               Programming on Purpose II:
                               Essays on Software People

                               Programming on Purpose III:
                               Essays on Software Technology

                               The Standard C Library

                               The Standard C++ Library

Plauger/Brodie   *Standard C: A Reference*

Rogers   *Framework-Based Software*
                               Development in C++

Van Sickle   *Reusable Software Components: Object-Oriented*
                               Embedded Systems Programming in C

C & C++ Code Capsules:
A Guide for Practitioners

Chuck Allison
Fresh Sources
http://www.freshsources.com

To join a Prentice Hall PTR Internet mailing list, point to
http://www.prenhall.com/mail_lists/

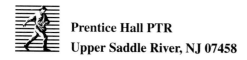

Prentice Hall PTR
Upper Saddle River, NJ 07458

Editorial/Production Supervision: *Precision Graphics*
Acquisitions Editor: *Bernard M. Goodwin*
Marketing Manager: *Dan Rush*
Cover Design: *Wee Design*
Cover Design Direction: *Jerry Votta*
Art Director: *Gail Cocker-Bogusz*
Manufacturing Manager: *Alexis R. Heydt*

 © 1998 Prentice Hall PTR
Prentice-Hall, Inc.
A Simon & Schuster Company
Upper Saddle River, NJ 07458

Prentice Hall books are widely used by corporations and government agencies for training, marketing, and resale.

The publisher offers discounts on this book when ordered in bulk quantities.
For more information, contact Corporate Sales Department, phone: 800-382-3419;
fax: 201-236-7141; e-mail: corpsales@prenhall.com
Or write: Prentice Hall PTR
      Corporate Sales Department
      One Lake Street
      Upper Saddle River, NJ 07458

Printed in the United States of America
10 9 8 7 6 5 4 3 2 1

ISBN 0-13-591785-9

Prentice-Hall International (UK) Limited, **London**
Prentice-Hall of Australia Pty. Limited, **Sydney**
Prentice-Hall Canada Inc., **Toronto**
Prentice-Hall Hispanoamericana, S.A., **Mexico**
Prentice-Hall of India Private Limited, **New Delhi**
Prentice-Hall of Japan, Inc., **Tokyo**
Simon & Schuster Asia Pte. Ltd., **Singapore**
Editora Prentice-Hall do Brasil, Ltda., **Rio de Janeiro**

To the Humble Programmer

Contents

Foreword

Bruce Eckel

Ifirst heard about Chuck when his bit handling classes, `bitset` and `bitstring`, were accepted into the standard C++ library in March 1993 (`bitstring` was later absorbed when the STL was added). While I myself did add a couple of tiny bits to the C++ standard here and there, the idea of successfully running an entire class through the terrible gauntlet of the ANSI/ISO C++ committee (on which we were both participants, so we knew) impressed me greatly.

But in the world of computers, which is so full of overstatement that I must ironically rely on my intuition rather than my intellect to discern truth, what impresses me more is someone who can explain things in a simple, clear, and non-overblown way. That is, a great teacher. Chuck is a great teacher. You can see it in the activities he finds himself compelled to do: writing, teaching, editing, explaining. When I find someone like this—and I know for sure when I see them speak to an audience—I convince them to speak at the Software Development (SD) conference (where I chair the C++ and Java tracks). Chuck has become a regular fixture at the conference, satisfying audiences on both coasts.

At the last SD conference (Fall 1997 in Washington, DC), it was Chuck's birthday, and when we found this out a group of us took him out to dinner. It was only after we were finally seated that I looked around and realized we were all authors: Bjarne Stroustrup (creator of C++ and author of *The C++ Programming Language*), Dan Saks (C++ columnist, speaker, consultant, and long-time secretary of the ANSI/ISO C++ committee), Bobby Schmidt (CUJ columnist, speaker), Marco Cantu (author of the "Mastering Delphi" books as well as C++ books), Tim Gooch (editor of the Cobb Group publications on C++ and now Java), and myself. These are the folks who respect Chuck enough to buy him dinner.

There are, of course, lots of "introduction to C++" books. Sometimes I feel like I keep trying to write a book on that subject over and over (my—I hope—final effort was *Thinking in C++*). But what happens when you've understood the basics and you want more depth? Books exist, but they can often be written in the tongue of the experts (a language that leaves me gasping) or they cover topics that are too esoteric or advanced. This book provides a bridge to the world of advanced topics; it gives you what you need but it won't overwhelm you in the process.

Chuck has made his book both clear and accurate, and accuracy is something else I'm exceptionally fond of. When a book has too many flaws I grow tired of it (in the early days we had to put up with such things, but now there are enough carefully created C++ books that there's no reason to waste your time). Another thing I like a lot about this book is the brevity of the chapters, and the way each one is focused on a single topic, so I can pick it up and get an entire concept at once (I have a somewhat short attention span). This is a book that you will enjoy over time as it hands you one insight after another.

Bruce Eckel
http://www.EckelObjects.com
October 1997

Preface

This book is for people who program in C and C++ for a living. It assumes that you are already familiar with the syntax and basic constructs of both languages, and it offers practical wisdom for creating effective, real-world programs. Each code capsule, or sample program, contains working code illustrating proven idioms and techniques that leverage the power of these important programming languages.

This book serves as a voice of experience for those who wish to strengthen their skills and improve their effectiveness in the workplace. Despite current fervor for the object-oriented paradigm (which this book abundantly embraces), I make no excuse for paying homage to the C foundations of C++. I have found too many developers ill-prepared to master C++ because they lack a thorough understanding of basic concepts such as pointers, scope, linkage, and static type checking. Perhaps the biggest deficiency of all is a lack of familiarity with the standard C library. It is sad indeed when developers waste time reinventing what the library functions already provide so well. The C++ novice is often too eager to abandon (i.e., gloss over) simple C in favor of the "exciting" features of C++, such as inheritance, exceptions, or overriding operator new, even when such are not warranted. I feel confident that everyone will learn something from these pages. Chapters 1 and 13 through 16 are strictly C++ chapters, and Chapters 4 through 6 apply only to the C language. All other chapters cover both the C and C++ aspects of their respective topic.

That said, this is primarily a C++ book. As it goes to press, the C++ standardization effort is in its home stretch. The second public committee draft (CD2) has completed its cycle and only minor edits remain. As a member of this committee since early 1991, I have seen its document grow from 200 to over 750 pages. We have added exceptions, templates, namespaces, runtime type identification (RTTI) and other features to the language, and a sophisticated, templatized system of interrelated algorithms, containers, and iteration constructs to the library (commonly known as the Standard Template Library, or STL). Unlike other standards efforts, this committee has concentrated as much on invention as on standardizing existing practice. The overwhelming intricacies of C++ caused one Internet surfer to post this message: "If C gives you enough rope to hang yourself, then C++ gives you enough rope to hang everyone in your neighborhood, hoist the riggings of a small sailing ship, and still have enough left over to hang yourself." I have labored to illustrate and motivate standard C++ and its library in such a way that you might use your rope more wisely.

The first chapter (Chapter 0), an excerpt from an interview I conducted with Bjarne Stroustrup, records his feelings about the state of C++ as it becomes a standard. The rest of the book is divided into three parts.

Part I: Preliminaries

After a brief tour of C++, these chapters close some of the gaps a typical C programmer might have before s/he prepares to tackle C++. Chapter 2, "Pointers," is based on a well-received three-part series I ran in the *C Users Journal* in 1993. Chapters 4 through 6 cover what every professional should know about the standard C library, which is a crucial part of standard C++.

Part II: Key Concepts

This section thoroughly motivates and illustrates the concepts and features of the C++ language. Chapter 7 introduces data abstraction through classes, and Chapter 8 covers type abstraction as implemented by the C++ template mechanism. Templates are every bit as crucial to the effective use of C++ as objects are, perhaps even more so. Chapter 14 not only treats inheritance and polymorphism, but also illustrates object-oriented design and reuse as it presents a framework for object persistence that works with today's relational database management systems. The chapters in between give the reader depth in important fundamental concepts that too many developers tend to overlook.

Part III: Leveraging the Standard Library

Chapters 15 through 20 show how to use and appreciate the notable components of the standard C++ library, as well as elucidate some of the more sophisticated features of the standard C library that went beyond the scope of Chapters 4, 5, and 6. Chapters 15 and 16 explain why the STL subset of the library is what it is, and how to use it effectively. Chapter 19 contains a useful date component that can even handle partial dates, a common business data processing requirement.

In summary, this is book about what works. I've attempted to steer the reader away from the "gotchas" by illustrating "best practices" with a reasonable balance of breadth and depth. Why another C++ book in 1998? Because the language and library haven't stabilized until now. This book goes to press just one week after the standards committee met to approve the final draft of ISO C++, and I have taken care to steer clear of any dark corners that remain (all languages and environment have them). I am confident that all the material in this book will be timely for years to come.

Acknowledgments

This book has actually been in the making for more years than I care to admit. It began in 1984 when I chaired the Computer Science department at Pima Community College in Tucson, Arizona, and my colleague Claire Hamlet persuaded me to pursue a grant to develop the first course in C programming there. Thereafter I started collecting C program examples and shared them with my fellow employees at Hughes Aircraft Company and at the World Headquarters of the Church of Jesus Christ of Latter-day Saints in Salt Lake City. The "code capsule" idea, short vignettes with examples on particular topics, grew from my effort to make learning C fun and relatively painless for COBOL refugees. I was fortunate enough for a time to have management support in chairing an internal C Language Support Committee, a first-rate team of experienced programmers (David Coombs, John Pearson, Lorin Lords, Kent Olsen, Bill Owens, Drew Terry, and Mike Terrazas) that developed an outstanding curriculum and effectively trained over 100 Church employees.

The name "code capsules" occurred to me over breakfast with Lee Copeland in the Church cafeteria (he has a way of keeping me on my toes). Mike Terrazas reviewed early versions of these vignettes, and suggested that I present them to the *C Users Journal,* which I unwittingly did by showing them to P. J. "Bill" Plauger in London at the March 1992 meeting of the C++ Standards Committee. As senior editor, he proposed that I become a columnist for the *Journal*. The *Code Capsule* column ran from October 1992 until May 1995, when time commitments forced me to resign. A valued mentor and friend, Bill has also been instrumental in encouraging me to put these capsules in book form. Bruce Eckel was very kind to review portions of the book, and Pete Becker scoured the entire manuscript, uncovering a number of errors and inconsistencies. When it comes to "support," however, that necessary intangible that keeps one going, I must follow the example of almost every author who has ever written by thanking my family. Only Sandy, James, and Kim have a feel for the magnitude of the effort that has brought these pages to press. As 21-year-old James recently wrote from England, where he is spending two years, "So, Dad is finally finishing his book! He's been working on that for as long as I can remember."

Chuck Allison
http://www.freshsources.com
Novemver 1997

C++: The Making of a Standard

(An Interview with Bjarne Stroustrup)

As this book goes to press, the second official committee draft (CD2) has been released, and national standards bodies have given their comments to the joint ISO/ANSI standards committee (X3J16/WG21). The features of the language have been stable for some time. Shortly before the committee met to approve CD2 in Stockholm in July 1996, I had the opportunity to interview Bjarne Stroustrup for the *C/C++ Users Journal*. I was interested in getting his feelings on the state of the language and his thoughts on the future of C++. This chapter is an excerpt from that interview.

To appreciate the work that has gone into the standard, as well as the interview that follows, a little history is in order. For a detailed technical and anecdotal history of C++, see Stroustrup's *The Design and Evolution of C++* (Addison-Wesley, 1994).

Bjarne Stroustrup, a Dane with a Ph.D. from Cambridge University (England), had used the Simula language for distributed systems simulations in his research. He was disappointed with its poor performance, however, so in 1979 when his new employer, AT&T Bell Labs, invited him to "do something interesting," he decided to infuse the C language with some Simula features he had grown accustomed to—most notably classes. Thus C with Classes was born. It caught on at AT&T, was dubbed "C++," and then proceeded to become a support burden for its inventor. After the first edition of Stroustrup's *The C++ Programming Language* (Addison-Wesley, 1985) hit the shelves, however, there was no turning back; the language became too popular. And as you might expect, multiple implementations appeared, each with its own special features. About the time the C standard became official, the major players in the C++ community were pushing for a C++ standard. ANSI committee X3J16 met for the first time in December 1989, with Dmitry Lenkov of Hewlett-Packard as chair. Steve Clamage of Sun Microsystems, himself an early implementor of C++, became chair in 1996.

The base documents for the committee included the ISO C standard, as well as Ellis and Stroustrup's *The Annotated C++ Reference Manual* (ARM). The latter pretty much reflected

AT&T C++ 2.0, along with Bjarne's ideas for extensions (mainly templates and exceptions). The main goals at the outset were to standardize IOStreams, and to add templates and exceptions to the language. Due to the large number of non-U.S. participants, the committee voted to work jointly with ISO Working Group 21 beginning at the June 1991 meeting in Lund, Sweden. It looked like things were winding down at the end of 1993, yet there was still some uneasiness about a lack of robustness in the standard library. At the San Jose meeting in November 1993, Alex Stepanov, then of Hewlett-Packard, gave a presentation on generic programming that really put templates to good use. By the San Diego meeting the next March, he had refined his and Meng Lee's standard template library (STL) to the point that the committee was ready to consider it seriously, even if it meant delaying the completion of the standard. I remember being one of the conservative skeptics at the time, yet my hand went up in favor of STL, which, along with IOStreams, is now the centerpiece of the standard C++ library.

The major features added since C++ 2.0 include templates, exceptions, user namespaces, and runtime type identification (RTTI). They are "major" because they directly affect the overall structure of your programs. Minor features, which are less intrusive but very powerful in their own right, include new-style casts, a new boolean data type (`bool`), a capacity to overload on enumerated types, support for wide characters, and alternative tokens to support foreign keyboards (e.g., `or` for `||`). In addition to STL, the standard library includes renovated stream classes, a string class template with specializations for wide and narrow characters, and the infrastructure for RTTI and for overloading and overriding `operator new` and `operator delete`.

Chuck Allison: I know you have a Ph.D. in Applied Math. What were your other degrees?

Bjarne Stroustrup: Not quite; my Masters degree (Cand.Scient.) from the University of Aarhus (Denmark) is in "Mathematics with computer science." I took the math part because that was the only way to do computer science there in those days. My Ph.D. from Cambridge (England, of course) is in Computer Science. I'm a very poor mathematician, but I guess that's better than not being one at all.

CA: How did you get into computing?

BS: By signing up for math and computer science in university. I have tried to remember why I did that, but I really don't know. I certainly hadn't seen a computer by the time I signed up. I guess the combination of scientific and practical aspects attracted me.

CA: When did you notice that C with Classes was becoming something that was going to consume much of your time, if not your career, and not just a temporary interest?

BS: Somewhere in 1982 I realized that support of the C with Classes user community was becoming an unacceptable drain on me. As I saw it, the user population had become too large for one person to serve well while also doing research, but too small to support an infrastructure. I had to decide whether to develop C with Classes into a more flexible and expressive language, or to drop it. Fortunately, I didn't think of a third alternative—which people point out is the conventional solution—which is to gather more users through hype.

Through C with Classes, I decided to further develop the combination of valuable ideas from C and Simula that I had experienced. The result was C++. I tried to escape to other work on several later occasions, but always the growth of the C++ community and the challenges of new applications kept me involved.

CA: What do you do for your day job now?

BS: I'm trying to build up a research group to focus on large-scale programming, that is, to do research on the use of programming in large programs rather than just language design, just the study of small (student) programs, or the exclusive focus on design and/or process. I think that programming technique, programming language, and the individual programmer have a central role in the development of large systems. Too often, either the scale of industrial projects or the role of programming is ignored.

This research will involve work on libraries and tools. Naturally, C++ will play a major role here, but I have no plans to limit my interests to just C++.

My department is part of AT&T Research. In the breakup of AT&T, AT&T kept half of the information sciences research of the old AT&T Bell Labs (the other half and the name went to Lucent Technologies). The AT&T part is now called AT&T Research and we aim to be a research organization second to none.

To a considerable degree, C++ is still my "day job." I work on standards issues, help users, write papers, give talks, write books, etc. Occasionally, I even get to write some code, though not as much as I'd like.

CA: What would you like to accomplish before you "retire."

BS: Retire from C++ development, or for real? I'm too young to retire, so I'll assume that you mean from C++. I consider the language and its standard library complete and sound, so that phase of the evolution is over with. ISO C++ is a better approximation of my ideals than any earlier version. The improvements to templates and the inclusion of the STL into the standard library were the key to getting C++ to where I wanted it.

CA: How would you summarize the impact/benefit of STL?

BS: My greatest hope is that it will teach many more people to use C++ as a high-level language rather than as a glorified assembler. My aim with C++ was and is to raise the level of abstraction in code so that the program text directly reflects the concepts of the application and general computer science concepts wherever reasonable. Yet, far too many people get lost fiddling with bits and pointers. The standard library allows people to take `string`, `vector`, `list`, and `map` as given and delay worrying about C-style strings and the pointer-level implementation of basic data structures until necessary.

CA: You have often used the story of the *Vasa* to encourage taking the simple route in defining the C++ language. But it is pretty much common public opinion that C++ is one of the most complicated languages in existence. Any comment on that? If there are different levels of C++ usage, how would you characterize them?

BS: Clearly there was a danger; why else would I bother telling a cautionary tale?

Construction of the *Vasa* started in 1625, at the request of King Gustav. It was originally intended to be a regular warship, but during the construction the king saw bigger and better ships elsewhere and changed his mind. He insisted on a flagship with two gundecks; he also insisted on a lot of statues suitable for a Royal flagship. The result was (and is) very impressive. Rather top-heavy, though. On its maiden voyage the *Vasa* only made it half way across Stockholm harbor before a gust of wind blew it over; it sank killing about 50 people. It has been raised and you can now see it in a museum in Stockholm. It is a beauty to behold—far more beautiful at the time than its unextended first design and far more beautiful today than if it had suffered the usual fate of a 17th century battleship—but that is no consolation to its designer, builders, and intended users.

So far, C++ has escaped the fate of the *Vasa;* it has not keeled over and disappeared, despite much wishful thinking and many dire predictions. Some of the newer extensions are seen as generalizations that actually make life easier for C++ programmers. My programs have certainly become shorter, clearer, and easier to write over the years. I simply don't have to go through as many contortions to express good design notions as I used to. Naturally, if your view is that the best programming language is the one that lets a novice get a demo running fastest, C++ doesn't fare so well, because it certainly takes longer to master. However, my primary concern is production code, and in competent hands C++ is a delight. ISO C++ is a closer approximation to my ideas than the C++ described in the ARM.

It might be worth noting that in one respect King Gustav was right: had the *Vasa* as originally designed come alongside a "modern" two-gundeck battleship, it would have reached the bottom almost as fast as the actual *Vasa* did. The flaw wasn't to add a gundeck; that gundeck was essential for the *Vasa* to fulfill its mission. The fault was to add the gundeck in the wrong way. Given this perspective, we might also take a kinder view of the extra time the committee took to make sure that the extensions to C++ were properly designed and tried out.

C++ is of course quite complex when compared to, say, the original Pascal, but so is every other modern programming language. Compared to the programming environments we use and the systems we program for, however, C++ is still simple.

For a novice, it would be a serious mistake to try to first learn all of C++ and then start using it. Instead, it is best to start with a subset and expand one's repertoire as needed. I recommend starting with a C-like subset, but using the standard `vector`, `list`, `map`, and `string` classes instead of fiddling with C-style arrays and strings. Naturally, macros should be avoided and also unions and bitfields. However, you can write very nice code with that subset of C and C++ plus the four standard library classes I mentioned.

Soon after, one can start experimenting with simple classes, simple templates, and simple class hierarchies. I recommend focusing on abstract classes before designing any nontrivial class hierarchy. Very simple exception handling can also be useful early on. The most important thing to keep in mind is to focus on the problem to be solved, rather than on the language-technical aspects of C++. It is always easier to learn a language if you have an experienced and nonprejudiced friend or colleague to help.

CA: What is the next step in the evolution of C++?

BS: Tools/environments and library design. I'd like to see incremental compilers and linkers for C++. Something like two seconds is a suitable time for recompiling and relinking a medium-sized C++ program after a change that is localized to a few functions. I'd like to see browsers and analysis tools that know not only syntax but also the type of every entity of a program. I'd like to see optimizers that actually take notice of C++ constructs and do a decent job of optimizing them, rather than simply throwing most of the useful information away and giving the rest to an optimizer that basically understands only C. I'd like to see debuggers integrated with the incremental compiler so that the result approximates a C++ interpreter. (I'd also like to see a good portable C++ interpreter.) None of this is science fiction; in fact, I have seen experimental versions of most of what I suggest—and more. We still suffer from first-generation C++ environments and tools.

CA: Certainly a large part of C++'s success is that it was built on C. (We're all familiar with the phrase, "as close as possible to C, but no closer," which is a twist on Einstein's, "as simple as possible, but no simpler.") But C compatibility has certainly been a challenge and has brought about a number of compromises as the upcoming ISO standard has evolved. What are the major compromises that you recall?

BS: I think most of the compromises were in place long before the standards committee was convened. (See my answer to the next question.) The C++ specific major features, such as classes, namespaces, templates, and exceptions, were constrained by a wish to be able to generate very compact and efficient code and to coexist with code written in other languages, rather than by anything C-specific.

Actually, most "compromises" can be seen as driven by the "zero-overhead principle," which says that any feature you don't use shouldn't cost you anything in time or space. That's what keeps C++ a viable systems programming language, and what has kept it from evolving toward something more convenient for toy examples, but less useful as a tool for everyday programming.

CA: Suppose for a moment that C compatibility was not an issue. How would C++ be different, in your view?

BS: That is not really a fair question because "as close to C as possible, but no closer" really was a basic design aim, delivering definite technical benefits to C++ users. It was not just a political or commercial (advertising) decision. Had C not been there and been more than adequate for my needs, I would have found some other language to be compatible with. I see no virtue in designing yet another Algol-family language. Also, the sheer effort of finding and maintaining the appropriate degree of C compatibility is not to be underestimated. C compatibility was one of the hardest decisions to make and put into practice, in addition to being one of the most important.

However, there are many aspects of C that I'm no fan of, so had there been a language as efficient, flexible, and available as C without those features, I would have chosen to be compatible with that. For example, I consider the C declaration syntax an experiment that failed, and in general, the C syntax for declarations is too lenient. Note that C++ has dropped the "implicit int rule":

```
static T;
```

is no longer valid C++; you must write

```
static int T;
```

if you really mean to declare an integer.

There are many such details that make life unnecessarily hard for the compiler writer and for the casual reader of real-life C and C++ code (as opposed to trivial examples like the one above).

I suspect that my dislike for the preprocessor is well known. Cpp is essential in C programming and is still important in conventional C++ implementations, but it is a hack and so are most of the techniques that rely on it. It has been my long-term aim to make Cpp redundant. However, I wouldn't dream of banning it until long after it had been made genuinely redundant, and that hasn't happened yet. Templates, const, inline, and namespaces make most uses of macros redundant (and counterproductive), but we have no widely available alternative to several common uses of #ifdef (so far). The preprocessor is one of the main factors that has led to the lack of more sophisticated C program-development environments; the fact that the source text seen by the programmer isn't the text seen by the compiler is a crippling handicap. I think the time has come to be serious about macro-free C++ programming.

I also find C-style arrays too low level for most uses. However, I don't consider C's success an accident. It was and often still is superior to alternatives in enough ways to be the right choice for many projects—except, of course, when the alternative is C++. I have never found an application where C was a better choice than C++ for any reason but the lack of availability of a C++ compiler. If there is some non-C feature of C++ that someone finds unsuitable for a project, it can simply go unused there.

CA: What is your take on the Java revolution?

BS: What Java revolution? Java is (at least) two distinct things: A fairly standard modern programming language with a superficial resemblance to C++, and a rather interesting system for downloading code into other people's computers when prompted through their web browsers. The latter addresses hard, interesting, and important problems. If the serious security problems with Java and Javascript can be solved, this could be very important. It could be very important even if the security holes are left open, because it seems that most people generally don't care about security anyway.

I guess you meant to ask me about Java as a programming language and its relationship to C++, but I'd rather not say too much about that, because language comparisons that are not based on significant user experience are rarely fair. In light of your previous question, I will point out, though, that Java is certainly not the language I would have designed if I had had no compatibility constraints.

If people insist on comparing C++ and Java—as they seem to do—I suggest they look through D&E to see why C++ is the way it is, and consider both languages in the light of the design criteria I set for C++. The differences between C++ and Java are more than skin-deep, and not every advantage goes to the same language.

CA: In your inaugural address to X3J16 in December 1989, you stated that if the committee took more than five years to come up with a standard, it would have failed. It looks as if it's going to be almost nine years when all is said and done. Any comment?

BS: I guess some "weasel wording" is in order because I think that the committee has done a great job—even if it has taken too long to do it. I seriously underestimated the time it takes to create a consensus among the impressively diverse membership.

However, look back a couple of years, say to March 1995, when my five-year time allotment ran out. Every major language feature and every major standard library part were in place. Unless something nasty happens with template compilation, we could—if we wanted to take a sympathetic view—write the last three years off to polishing and ISO rules.

One thing that I had hoped for, and that actually happened, was that the implementations started reflecting the standard long before the ink was dry. Much of the good work of the standards effort is already in the hands of C++ programmers.

CA: How will the existence of a standard change things in the C++ community? And for you personally?

BS: For the community: greater stability, better compilers, better tools, better libraries, better teaching materials, and better techniques. For me: finally a chance to use C++ as I meant to use it, without being distracted by standards work and language design concerns. The important and interesting topic is programming, not programming languages.

I find far too many people belonging to one of two camps: those who think that programming languages are of no importance and only get in the way of systems builders (many C programmers are in this camp), and those who think that a programming language can perform miracles for them if only some very specific, language-technical aspects are "just right." (They never are, so all efforts are expended on designing *the* perfect programming language.)

I belong to a third camp: I know that a good language can be most helpful for an individual programmer and for a group, but I also know that much more good code has been written in languages deemed bad than in languages proclaimed great!

What matters most of all is the programmer's understanding of the problem to be solved and the techniques needed to solve it. A programming language can help express clear ideas and even help clarify ideas that are almost right by providing a suitable framework. I think C++ does that for a wider range of applications than any other current language, and that C++ will become an even better tool if people do themselves the favor of taking the time to learn the techniques made possible by the features provided by ISO C++. However, without a clear idea of what you are doing and how, you're lost in whatever language you choose to program in.

Preliminaries

A Better C

A Tale Of Two Languages

C++ had its beginnings at AT&T in the early 1980s with C with Classes, Bjarne Stroustrup's successful attempt to speed up his simulations written in Simula-67. "Class" is the Simula term for a user-defined type, and being able to define objects that mirror reality is a key to good simulations. What better way to get fast simulations than to add classes to C, the fastest procedural language? Choosing C not only provided an efficient vehicle for classes, but a portable one as well. Although other languages supported data abstraction through classes long before C++, it is now the most widespread. Almost every major platform that has a C compiler also supports C++.

A first look at C++ can be overwhelming. If you're coming from C, you'll need to add the following (and then some) to your vocabulary:

abstract class, access specifier, adaptor, allocator, base class, class, class scope, constructor, copy constructor, default argument, default constructor, delete operator, derived class, destructor, exception, exception handler, exception specification, explicit constructor, explicit specialization, export, facet, friend, function object, inheritance, inline function, iterator, manipulator, member function, member template, multiple inheritance, mutable, namespace, nested class, new handler, new operator, new-style cast, one-definition rule, operator function, overloading, partial specialization, pointer to member, polymorphism, private, protected, public, pure virtual function, reference, runtime type identification, static member, stream, template, template specialization, this pointer, traits, try block, typeid, type-safe linkage, using, virtual base class, virtual destructor, virtual function.

The good news is that C++ is a powerful, efficient, object-oriented language able to handle complex applications. The bad news is that the language itself must therefore be somewhat complex, and is more difficult to master than C. And C itself is part of the problem. C++ is a hybrid, a blending of object-oriented features with a popular systems programming language. It is impossible to introduce such a rich set of new features without the host language having to bend a little. Yet compatibility with C was a major goal of the design of C++. As Bjarne stated in his keynote address to the ANSI C++ committee in 1989, C++ is an "engineering compromise," and must be kept "as close as possible to C, but no closer."

C++ is in fact a *multiparadigm* language. It supports the traditional procedural style of programming, like C and Pascal do; like Ada it supports data abstraction and generics (templates); and it supports inheritance and polymorphism, as do all the other object-oriented languages. All this may make for a somewhat "impure" programming language, but it also makes C++ the more practical choice for production programming. C++ unquestionably gives the best performance; it functions well in mixed-language environments (not just with C, but with other languages, too) and does not require the enormous runtime resources that Smalltalk and LISP do (the latter being *environments*, not just compile-and-link processes).

And there is more good news.

Incremental Journey

You can use C++ effectively without having to master all of it. In fact, object-oriented technology promises that if vendors do their job of providing well-designed class libraries crafted for reuse and extensibility, then your job of building applications will be easier. Current development environments, with their application frameworks and visual components, are proving this to be true.

If you feel you must master the language, you can do it in steps and still be productive on the way. Three "plateaus" have emerged:

1. A Better C
2. Data Abstraction
3. Object-oriented programming

You can use C++ as a better C because it is safer and more expressive than C. Features on this plateau include type-safe linkage, mandatory function prototypes, inline functions, the const qualifier (yes, C borrowed it from C++), function overloading, default arguments, references, and direct language support for dynamic memory management. You will also need to be aware of the incompatibilities that exist between C++ and its predecessor. In this chapter I will explore these non–object-oriented features that make C++ a better C. Because it is difficult to motivate some of the better-C features without showing their class-based origins, I will also illustrate the class mechanism of C++.

The Type System

Perhaps the most important thing to understand about C++ is its devotion to *type safety*. The other object-oriented languages mentioned above are essentially untyped, or at best very weakly typed, because they perform error checking mainly during execution. C++, on the other hand, requires you to declare the type of every program entity, and it fastidiously checks your usage of the same at *compile time*. It is type safety, more than anything else, that makes C++ a better C and the most reasonable choice for common programming tasks. Features of the type system include function prototypes, type-safe linkage, new-style casts and runtime type identification (RTTI). (See Chap. 10 for casts and RTTI.)

Function Prototypes

Function prototypes are not optional in C++. In fact, the prototype mechanism was invented for C++ before the ANSI C committee adopted it. You must either declare or fully define each function before its first use. The compiler will check each function invocation for the correct number and type of arguments. In addition, it will perform automatic conversions where they apply. The following program reveals a common error that occurs in C when you don't use prototypes.

```
/* convert1.c */
#include <stdio.h>

main()
{
    dprint(123);
    dprint(123.0);
    return 0;
}

dprint(d)
double d;              // old-style function definition
{
    printf("%f\n",d);
}

/* Output:
0.000000          Oops!
123.000000
*/
```

The function dprint expects a double argument. Without knowing dprint's prototype, the compiler doesn't know that the call dprint(123) is an error. When you provide the prototype for dprint, the compiler automatically converts 123 to a double for you:

```
/* convert2.c */
#include <stdio.h>

void dprint(double);  /* prototype */
```

```
main()
{
    dprint(123);
    dprint(123.0);
    return 0;
}

void dprint(double d)
{
    printf("%f\n",d);
}

/* Output:
123.000000
123.000000
*/
```

Next to type safety, the key new feature in C++ is the *class*, which extends the struct mechanism to allow function members in addition to data members (but we call them *member functions*). A member function with the same name as the structure tag is a *constructor*, and is used to initialize a class object when you declare it. Since C++ allows types that you define to behave like built-in types, it allows implicit conversions for user-defined types. The program below defines a new type, A, which contains a double data member, and a constructor that takes a double argument.

```
// convert3.cpp
#include <stdio.h>

struct A
{
    double x;
    A(double d)
    {
        printf("A::A(double)\n");
        x = d;
    }
};

void f(const A& a)
{
    printf("f: %f\n", a.x);
}

main()
{
    A a(1);
    f(a);
    f(2);
}
```

```
// Output:
A::A(double)
f: 1
A::A(double)
f: 2
```

Since the constructor for struct A expects a double argument, the compiler automatically converts the integer 1 to a double in the definition for a. The call f(2) in the first line of main generates the following actions:

1. Convert 2 to a double.
2. Initialize a temporary A object with the value 2.0.
3. Pass that object to f.

In other words, the compiler generates code equivalent to

```
f(A(double(2)));
```

Note C++'s function-style cast syntax. The expression

```
double(2)
```

is equivalent to

```
(double) 2
```

Only one implicit user-defined conversion is allowed in any one conversion sequence, however. The program in Listing 1.1 requires a B object to initialize an A object. A B object in turn requires a double, because its only constructor is B::B(double). The expression

```
A a(1)
```

becomes

```
a(B(double(1)))
```

which has only one user-defined conversion. The expression f(3), however, is illegal because it would require the compiler to provide two automatic user-defined conversions:

```
// Can't do both an A and a B conversion implicitly
f(A(B(double(3))))     // illegal
```

The expression f(B(3)) is okay, because it explicitly requests the conversion B(double(3)), so the compiler provides only the remaining conversion to A.

Implicit conversions via single-argument constructors are convenient for mixed-mode expressions. For example, the standard string class allows you to mix strings and character arrays, as in

```
string s1 = "Read my lips...";     // Initialize s1
string s2 = s1 + " no new taxes."; // Concatenate s1 with a const char*
```

Listing 1.1   Shows that only one user-defined conversion is allowed

```
// convert4.cpp
#include <stdio.h>

struct B;

struct A
{
    double x;
    A(const B& b);
};

void f(const A& a)
{
    printf("f: %f\n", a.x);
}

struct B
{
    double y;
    B(double d)  : y(d)
    {
        printf("B::B(double)\n");
    }
};

A::A(const B& b)  : x(b.y)
{
    printf("A::A(const B&)\n");
}

main()
{
    A a(1);
    f(a);

    B b(2);
    f(b);

//  f(3);                  // Won't compile!

    f(B(3));          // Implicit B-to-A conversion
    f(A(4));
}
```

Listing 1.1   (continued)

```
// Output:
B::B(double)
A::A(const B&)
f: 1
B::B(double)
A::A(const B&)
f: 2
B::B(double)
A::A(const B&)
f: 3
B::B(double)
A::A(const B&)
f: 4
```

The second line is equivalent to

```
string s2 = s1 + string(" no new taxes,");
```

because the standard string class provides a constructor that takes a single const char* argument. But sometimes you may not want the compiler to be so accommodating. For example, if there were a string constructor taking a single numeric argument (which there is not), say to initialize a string to a specific number of blanks, then what would be the result of the following expression?

```
string s2 = s1 + 5;
```

The right-hand side becomes s1 + string(5), which adds five blanks to s1, a somewhat confusing "feature." You can prevent such implicit conversions by declaring the single-argument constructor explicit. With our hypothetical string constructor so declared, the statement above is ill-formed, but the declaration string s(5) would be legal, since it explicitly calls the constructor. Similarly, if you replace the declaration of A's constructor in Listing 1.3 with

```
explicit A(double d)
```

the compiler will diagnose the expression f(2) as an error.

Type-safe Linkage

C++ can even detect improper function calls across compilation units. The program in Listing 1.2 calls a function in Listing 1.3. When compiled as a C program it gives the erroneous output:

```
f: 0.000000
```

Listing 1.2 Illustrates program linkage (see also Listing 1.3)

```
void f(int);

main()
{
    f(1);
}
```

Listing 1.3 A function intended to link with Listing 1.2

```
#include <stdio.h>

void f(double x)
{
    printf("f: %f\n",x);
}
```

C has no way of knowing that the f's are different. The conventional work-around is to put the correct prototype in a header file that all compilation units include. In C++, however, a function call will only link with a function definition of the same *signature*, which is the combination of the function name and its sequence of argument types. When compiled as a C++ program, the output of Listing 1.2 and 1.3 from one popular compiler is

```
Error: Undefined symbol f(int) in module safe1.cpp
```

Most compilers achieve this *type-safe linkage* by encoding the function's signature along with its name, a technique often referred to as *function name encoding*, *name decorating*, or (my favorite) *name mangling*. For example, the function f(int) might appear to the linker as

```
f__Fi           // f is a function taking an int
```

but f(double) would be

```
f__Fd           // f is a function taking a double
```

Since the names are different, the linker won't find f(int) in this example, and reports an error.

References

Since C passes function parameters by value, passing large structures to functions can waste time and stack space. Most C programmers pass a pointer instead. For example, if struct Foo is a large record structure, you can do something like the following:

```
void f(struct Foo *fp)
{
    /* Access the structure through fp */
    fp->x = ...
    etc.
}
```

You have to pass the address of a `struct Foo` in order to use this function, of course:

```
struct Foo a;
...
f(&a);
```

The C++ reference mechanism is a notational convenience that saves you the bother of providing explicit indirection of pointer variables. In C++, you can render the above code as

```
void f(Foo &fr)
{
    /* Access members directly */
    fr.x = ...
    etc.
}
```

You can now call f without using the *address-of* operator, like this:

```
Foo a;
...
f(a);
```

The ampersand in the prototype for f instructs the compiler to pass its argument by reference, which in effect takes care of all the indirection for you. (For you Pascal programmers, reference parameters are equivalent to Var parameters.)

Call-by-reference means that any changes you make to a function parameter also affect the original argument in the calling program. This means that you can write a swap function (not a macro) that actually works (see Listing 1.4). If you don't plan on modifying a reference argument, declare it a *reference-to*-const, as I did in Listing 1.1. A reference-to-const argument has the safety and notational convenience of call-by-value, and the efficiency of call-by-reference.

As Listing 1.5 illustrates, you can also return an object from a function by reference. It may look strange to have a function call on the left-hand side of an assignment, but this comes in handy when overloading operators (especially `operator=` and `operator[]`).

Type-safe I/O

Certainly every C programmer has at sometime used incorrect format descriptors with `printf`. There is no way for `printf` to check whether the data items you pass match your format string.

Listing 1.4   A swap function that illustrates call-by-reference

```
// swap.cpp
#include <stdio.h>

void swap(int &, int &);

main()
{
    int i = 1, j = 2;

    swap(i,j);
    printf("i == %d, j == %d\n", i, j);
}

void swap(int &x, int &y)
{
    int temp = x;
    x = y;
    y = temp;
}

// Output:
i == 2, j == 1
```

How often have you done something like the following, only to discover the problem at run-time?

```
double d;
...
printf("%d\n",d);              /* Oops! Should've used %f */
```

The C++ streams library, on the other hand, uses the type of an object to determine the proper formatting:

```
double d;
...
cout << d << endl;        // can't fail
```

The expression cout << d translates into a call to a function that takes a stream and a double argument (viz. operator<<stream&, double), so there is no way for the output processing to misinterpret your value. If you want to print floating-point numbers with a fixed precision, you can say so just once:

```
double x = 1.5, y = 2.5;
cout.precision(2);                      // Show 2 decimals from now on
cout.setf(ios::showpoint);              // Preserve trailing 0's
cout << x << '\n';                      // prints 1.50
cout << y << '\n';                      // prints 2.50
```

Standard Streams

There are four predefined streams: cin (standard input), cout (standard output), cerr (standard error), and clog (standard error). All but cerr are fully buffered streams. Like stderr, cerr behaves as if it is unbuffered, but it is actually *unit buffered*, meaning that it flushes its buffer automatically after processing each object, not after each byte. For example, with unit buffering, the statement

```
cerr << "hello";
```

buffers the five characters and then flushes the buffer. An unbuffered stream sends each character immediately to its final destination.

Listing 1.5   Returns an object from a function by reference

```
//retref.cpp:   Returning a reference
#include <stdio.h>

int & current();   // Returns a reference
int a[4] = {0,1,2,3};
int index = 0;

main()
{
    current() = 10;
    index = 3;
    current() = 20;
    for (int i = 0; i < 4; ++i)
        printf("%d ",a[i]);
    putchar('\n');
}

int & current()
{
    return a[index];
}

// Output:
10 1 2 20
```

The following program copies standard input to standard output:

```
// copy1.cpp: Copy standard input to standard output
#include <iostream>
using namespace std;

main()
{
    char c;

    while (cin.get(c))
        cout.put(c);
}
```

Note that standard header names (viz. iostream) no longer take a .h suffix. Almost everything in the standard C++ library, including streams, resides in the *namespace* std. A namespace is just a named scope containing declarations. The using directive in the second line above instructs the compiler to search std when looking for declarations of names it encounters during translation. The standard C headers are also in the std namespace in C++ programs, and are prefixed with the letter c. To include <stdio.h>, you can do the following:

```
#include <cstdio>
using namespace std;
```

or just the usual #include <stdio.h>, if you like.

A function that reads from a stream is called an *extractor*, and an output function an *inserter*. The get extractor stores the next byte from a stream into its char reference parameter. Like most stream member functions, get returns the stream itself. When a stream appears in a boolean context like in the while loop above, it tests true if the data transferred successfully, and false if there was an error, such as an attempt to read beyond end-of-file. Although such simple boolean tests suffice most of the time, you can query the state of a stream any time with the following boolean member functions:

bad()	severe error (stream is corrupted)
fail()	conversion error (bad data but stream is OK)
eof()	end-of-file
good()	none of the above

The following program copies text line by line:

```
// copy2.cpp: Copy input lines
#include <iostream>
using namespace std;
```

```
main()
{
    const size_t BUFSIZ = 128;
    char s[BUFSIZ];
    while (cin.getline(s,BUFSIZ))
        cout << s << '\n';
}
```

The getline extractor reads up to BUFSIZ−1 characters into s, stopping if it finds a new-line character, appends a null byte, and discards the newline. Output streams use the left-shift operator as an inserter. Any object, built in or user defined, can be part of a chain of insertions into a stream. You must overload operator<< yourself for your own classes.

Listing 1.6 contains a program that illustrates extraction with operator>>. Since in C you normally use stderr for prompts (because it is unbuffered), you might want to use cerr in C++:

```
cerr << "Please enter an integer: ";
cin >> i;
```

This is not necessary in C++ because cout is *tied* to cin. An output stream tied to an input stream is automatically flushed when input is requested of its partner. There is a flush member function if you ever need to force a flush.

Listing 1.6   Prompts for an integer, echoes its value and address

```
// int.cpp: Prompt for an integer
#include <iostream>
using namespace std;

main()
{
    int i;
    cout << "Please enter an integer: ";
    cin >> i;
    cout << "i == " << i << '\n';
    cout << "&i == " << &i << '\n';
}

// Sample execution:
Please enter an integer: 10
i == 10
&i == 0xfff4
```

Machine addresses print in an implementation-defined format, usually hexadecimal. Character arrays are, of course, an exception: The string value is printed, not the address. To print the address of a C-style string, cast it to a `void*`:

```
char s[] = ...;
cout << (void *) s << '\n';      // prints address
```

The `operator>>` skips whitespace by default. The program in Listing 1.7 uses this feature to count the "words" in a text file. Extracting into a character string behaves like the `%s` format specifier in `scanf`. It is possible to turn off the skipping of whitespace when reading characters (see Listing 1.8).

Formatting

In Listing 1.8 `ios::skipws` is an example of a *format flag*. Format flags are bit-mask values that you can set with the member function `setf`, and reset with `unsetf`. (See Table 1.1 for a complete description.)

The program in Listing 1.9 illustrates numeric formatting. The standard stream member function `precision` dictates the number of decimal places to display for floating-point values. Unless the `ios::showpoint` flag is set, however, trailing zeroes will not appear. To print positive numbers with a leading plus sign, use `ios::showpos`. To display the *x* in hexadecimal values and the e in exponential in upper case, use `ios::uppercase`.

Listing 1.7   Counts the words in a text file

```cpp
// wc.cpp: Display word count
#include <iostream>
using namespace std;

main()
{
    const size_t BUFSIZ = 128;
    char s[BUFSIZ];
    size_t wc = 0;

    while (cin >> s)
        ++wc;
    cout << wc << '\n';
}

// Output from the command "wc < wc.cpp"
34
```

Listing 1.8 Identical to program `copy1.cpp`, but uses the extraction operator to read whitespace

```
// copy3.cpp:  Reads whitespace with >>
#include <iostream>
using namespace std;

main()
{
    char c;

    // Don't skip whitespace
    cin.unsetf(ios::skipws);

    while (cin >> c)
        cout << c;
}
```

Table 1.1 Format flags

Flag	Meaning	Default
boolalpha	do bool I/O in alpha format	
showbase	shows octal or hex prefix	off
showpoint	shows trailing zero decimals	off
showpos	show plus sign when positive	off
skipws	>> skips whitespace	on
uppercase	0X for hex, E for scientific	off
unitbuf	enables unit buffering	off

Some formatting options can take on a range of values. For example, `ios::basefield`, which determines the numeric base for displaying integers, can be set to decimal, octal, or hexadecimal. (See Table 1.2 for a description of the three format fields available.) Since these are bitfields and not single bits, you set them with a two-parameter version of `setf`. For example, the program in Listing 1.10 changes to octal mode with the statement

```
cout.setf(ios::oct,ios::basefield);
```

With the flag `ios::showbase` set, octals print with a leading 0 and hexadecimals with a leading 0x (or 0X if `ios::uppercase` is also set).

Listing 1.9   Illustrates numeric formatting

```cpp
// float.cpp:   Format real numbers
#include <iostream>
using namespace std;

main()
{
    float x = 12345.6789, y = 12345;
    cout << x << ' ' << y << '\n';

    // Show two decimals
    cout.precision(2);
    cout << x << ' ' << y << '\n';

    // Show trailing zeroes
    cout.setf(ios::showpoint);
    cout << x << ' ' << y << '\n';

    // Show sign
    cout.setf(ios::showpos);
    cout << x << ' ' << y << '\n';

    // Return sign and precision to defaults
    cout.unsetf(ios::showpos);
    cout.precision(0);

    // Use scientific notation
    cout.setf(ios::scientific,ios::floatfield);
    float z = 1234567890.123456;
    cout << z << '\n';
    cout.setf(ios::uppercase);
    cout << z << '\n';
}

// Output:
12345.678711 12345
12345.68 12345
12345.68 12345.00
+12345.68 +12345.00
1.234568e+09
1.234568E+09
```

Table 1.2 Format fields

Field	Values	Default
adjustfield	left, right, internal	right
basefield	dec, oct, hex	dec
floatfield	fixed, scientific	fixed

Listing 1.10 Shows the bases of integers

```
// base1.cpp:  Shows the bases of integers
#include <iostream>
using namespace std;

main()
{
    int x, y, z;

    cout << "Enter three ints: ";
    cin >> x >> y >> z;
    cout << x << ',' << y << ',' << z << endl;

    // Print in different bases
    cout << x << ',';
    cout.setf(ios::oct,ios::basefield);
    cout << y << ',';
    cout.setf(ios::hex,ios::basefield);
    cout << z << endl;

    // Show the base prefix
    cout.setf(ios::showbase);
    cout << x << ',';
    cout.setf(ios::oct,ios::basefield);
    cout << y << ',';
    cout.setf(ios::hex,ios::basefield);
    cout << z << endl;
}

// Sample Execution:
Enter three ints: 10 010 0x10
10,8,16
10,10,10
0xa,010,0x10
```

Manipulators

When the identifier `endl` appears in an output stream, a newline character is inserted and the stream is flushed. The identifier `endl` is an example of a *manipulator*, an object which you insert into a stream for a side effect. The built-in manipulators declared in `<iostream>` are listed in Table 1.3. The program in Listing 1.11 is functionally equivalent to the one in Listing 1.10 but it uses manipulators instead of explicit calls to `setf`. Manipulators often allow for more streamlined code.

Table 1.3 Simple manipulators (`<iostream>`)

Manipulator	Effect
[fmtflags Group]	
boolalpha	setf(boolalpha)
noboolalpha	unsetf(boolalpha)
showbase	setf(showbase)
noshowbase	unsetf(showbase)
showpoint	setf(showpoint)
noshowpoint	unsetf(showpoint)
showpos	setf(showpos)
noshowpos	unsetf(showpos)
skipws	setf(skipws)
noskipws	unsetf(skipws)
uuppercase	setf(uppercase)
nouppercase	unsetf(uppercase)
unitbuf	setf(unitbuf)
nounitbuf	unsetf(unitbuf)
[adjustfield Group]	
internal	setf(internal, adjustfield)
left	setf(left, adjustfield)
right	setf(right, adjustfield)
[basefield Group]	
dec	setf(dec, basefield)
oct	setf(oct, basefield)
hex	setf(hex, basefield)
[floatfield Group]	
fixed	setf(fixed, floatfield)
scientific	setf(scientific, floatfield)
[other]	
endl	Inserts a newline and calls flush()
ends	Inserts a '\0'
flush	Flushes the stream

Listing 1.11 Changes numeric base with manipulators

```
// base2.cpp:  Shows the bases of integers
//             (Uses manipulators)
#include <iostream>
using namespace std;

main()
{
    int x, y, z;
    cout << "Enter three ints: ";
    cin >> x >> y >> z;
    cout << x << ',' << y << ',' << z << endl;

    // Print in different bases
    cout << dec << x << ','
         << oct << y << ','
         << hex << z << endl;

    // Show the base prefix
    cout.setf(ios::showbase);
    cout << dec << x << ','
         << oct << y << ','
         << hex << z << endl;
}
```

Other manipulators take parameters (see Table 1.4). The program in Listing 1.12 uses the setw(n) manipulator to set the output width directly in the insertion sequence, so you don't need a separate call to width. The field ios::width is special: It is reset to 0 immediately after every insertion. When ios::width is 0, values print with the minimum number of characters necessary. As usual, numbers are not truncated, even if you don't allow enough space for them.

Table 1.4 Parameterized manipulators (iomanip)

Manipulator	Meaning flush
resetioflags(n)	Reset all the flags that are set in n
setioflags(n)	Set all the flags that are set in n
setbase(n)	Same as setf(n, ios::basefield)
setfill(n)	Same as fill(c)
setprecision(n)	Same as precision(n)
setw(n)	Same as width(n)

Listing 1.12   Sets the output field width with `setw`

```
// adjust.cpp: Justify output
#include <iostream>
#include <iomanip>
using namespace std;

main()
{
    cout << '|' << setw(10) << "hello" << '|' << endl;

    cout.setf(ios::left,ios::adjustfield);
    cout << '|' << setw(10) << "hello" << '|' << endl;

    cout.fill('#');
    cout << '|' << setw(10) << "hello" << '|' << endl;
}

// Output:
|     hello|
|hello     |
|hello#####|
```

You could replace the statement

`cout.fill('#');`

with the in-sequence manipulator

`... << setfill('#') << ...`

but it seems cumbersome to do so in this case.

Extractors usually ignore width settings. An exception is C-style string input. You should set the width field to the size of a character array before extracting into it in order to avoid overflow. When processing the input line

`nowisthetimeforall`

the program in Listing 1.13 produces

`nowisthet,im,eforall`

Remember that extractors by default use whitespace as a delimiter, so if the input is

`now is the time for all`

then the output is

`now,is,the`

Listing 1.13   Controls the width of input strings

```
// width.cpp:   Control width of input strings
#include <iostream>
#include <iomanip>
using namespace std;

main()
{
    char s1[10], s2[3], s3[20];
    cin >> setw(10) >> s1
        >> setw(3) >> s2
        >> s3;
    cout << s1 << ',' << s2 << ',' << s3 << endl;
}
```

Input and output streams also support the new boolean data type, bool, along with format flags and manipulators for either numeric or alphabetic text:

```
bool b = true;
cout << b << endl;          // prints "1"
cout.setf(ios::boolalpha);  // (or just insert the manipulator
                            // boolalpha)
cout << b << endl;          // prints "true"
```

You can create your own manipulators by simply defining a function that takes a stream reference parameter and returns that same reference. For example, here is a manipulator that rings the bell at an ASCII console when you insert it into any output stream:

```
// A manipulator that beeps
#include <iostream>

ostream& beep(ostream& os)
{
    os << char(7); // ASCII BEL
    return os;
}
```

To use this, just insert it:

```
cout <<... << beep << ...
```

Function Overloading and Function Templates

The swap function in Listing 1.4 is useful only if you want to swap integers. What if you want to swap two objects of any built-in type? C++ allows you to define multiple functions of the same name, as long as their signatures are different. Therefore you can define a swap for all built-in types:

```
void swap(char &, char &);
void swap(int &, int &);
void swap(long &, long &);
void swap(float &, float &);
void swap(double &, double &);
etc.
```

You can then call swap for any two objects of the same built-in type. If you were to implement each of these functions, however, it wouldn't take long to discover that you're doing the same thing over and over—the only thing that changes is the type of the objects you want to swap. To save tedium and the chance of making a silly mistake, you can define a single *function template* instead. See Chapter 8 for more about templates.

Operator Overloading

You can also overload operators in C++. For example, suppose you define a complex number data type as:

```
struct complex
{
    double real, imag;
};
```

It would be quite convenient if you could use infix notation for adding complex numbers, such as:

```
complex c1, c2;
...
complex c3 = c1 + c2;
```

When the compiler encounters an expression such as `c1 + c2`, it looks for one of the following two functions (only one of which must exist):

```
operator+(const complex &, const complex &);      // global
complex::operator+(const complex &);               // member
```

The `operator` keyword is part of the function name. You could define a global `operator+` for adding two complex numbers like this:

```
complex operator+(const complex &c1, const complex &c2)
{
    complex r;
    r.real = c1.real + c2.real;
    r.imag = c1.imag + c2.imag;
    return r;
}
```

Listing 1.14   `operator+` and `operator<<` for complex numbers

```cpp
#include <iostream>
using namespace std;

struct complex
{
    double real, imag;
    complex(double = 0.0, double = 0.0);
};

complex::complex(double r, double i)
{
    real = r;
    imag = i;
}

inline ostream& operator<<(ostream &os, const complex &c)
{
    os << '(' << c.real << ',' << c.imag << ')';
    return os;
}

inline complex operator+(const complex &c1, const complex &c2)
{
    return complex(c1.real+c2.real,c1.imag+c2.imag);
}
```

You are not allowed to overload built-in operations, such as addition of two `int`s, therefore at least one of the operands needs to be of a user-defined type.

The streams library "knows" how to format the various built-in types through operator overloading. For example, the `ostream` class, of which `cout` is an instance, overloads `operator<<` for all the built-in types. When the compiler sees the expression

```cpp
cout << i;
```

where `i` is an `int`, it generates the following function invocation

```cpp
cout.operator<<(i);     // ostream::operator<<(ostream&, int)
```

which formats the number correctly.

Listing 1.14 shows how to extend the standard streams by overloading `operator<<` for complex numbers (sample output in Listing 1.15). The compiler transforms the expression

```cpp
cout << c
```

where c is a complex number into the function call

```
operator<<(cout, c)
```

which invokes operator<<(ostream&, const complex&) to, in turn, break the operation down into formatting objects of built-in types. This function also returns the stream so that you can chain multiple stream insertions in a single statement. For example, the expression

```
cout << c1 << c2
```

becomes

```
operator<<(operator<<(cout,c1), c2)
```

which requires that operator<<(ostream&, const complex&) return the stream, which it does by reference for efficiency.

Inline Functions

The inline keyword, seen in Listing 1.14, is a hint to the compiler that you want the code "inlined," that is, placed directly into the calling context without the overhead of an actual function call. If the compiler chooses to grant your request, it replaces each call to such a function with the appropriate code in place, avoiding the usual overhead of an actual function call. This mechanism is different from a function-like macro, which performs text substitution before program translation. Inline functions have all the type checking and semantics of true functions, without the overhead and without the sensitivity to side effects that macros have. For example, were you to define a macro to find the smaller of two numbers as

```
#define min(x,y) ((x) < (y) ? (x) : (y))
```

it would fail miserably with an incremented argument, such as

```
min(x++,y++)
```

Inline functions don't have this problem, since they behave like real functions.

Listing 1.15   Uses the complex number data type

```
#include <iostream>
#include "complex.h"
using namespace std;

main()
{
    complex c1(1,2), c2(3,4);
    cout << c1 << " + " << c2 << " == " << c1+c2 << endl;
}

// Output:
(1,2) + (3,4) == (4,6)
```

Not all functions can or should be inlined, however. Certainly a recursive function doesn't qualify for inlining. Large functions can increase code size substantially when inlined. Inlining is mainly for small, simple functions.

Default Arguments

Default arguments in a function's declaration instruct it to infer values from its prototype. The program in Listing 1.16 has a function with the prototype:

```
int minutes(int hrs, int min = 0);
```

The "= 0" after the last parameter instructs the compiler to supply the value 0 for the second argument when you omit it in a call to minutes. This mechanism is essentially a shorthand for defining related overloaded functions. In this case, it is equivalent to the following:

```
int minutes(int hrs, int min);
int minutes(int hrs);                 // ignores minutes
```

The complex constructor in Listing 1.14 uses default arguments to allow you to define a complex number with 0, 1, or 2 arguments; for example,

```
complex c1;          // (0,0)
complex c2(1);       // (1,0)
complex c3(2,3)      // (2,3)
```

It is the third form that is used in the return statement of operator+ in Listing 1.14.

Listing 1.16   Illustrates default arguments

```
// minutes.cpp

#include <iostream>
using namespace std;

inline int minutes(int hrs, int mins = 0)
{
    return hrs * 60 + mins;
}

main()
{
    cout << "3 hrs == " << minutes(3) << " minutes" << endl;
    cout << "3 hrs, 26 min == " << minutes(3,26) << " minutes" << endl;
}

// Output:
3 hrs == 180 minutes
3 hrs, 26 min == 206 minutes
```

new and delete

To use the heap in C, you need to compute the size of the object you want to create:

```
struct Foo *fp = malloc(sizeof(struct Foo));
```

In C++, the new operator computes the size of an object for you:

```
Foo *fp = new Foo;
```

To allocate an array in C, you call a different function:

```
struct Foo *fpa = calloc(n,sizeof(struct Foo));
```

In C++, new knows about arrays:

```
Foo *fpa = new Foo[n];
```

In addition, the new operator automatically invokes the appropriate constructor to initialize the object(s) before it returns you the pointer. For example, creating complex numbers on the heap automatically initializes them, as in

```
complex *cp1 = new complex;          // -> (0,0)
complex *cp2 = new complex(1);       // -> (1,0)
complex *cp3 = new complex(2,3);     // -> (2,3)
```

To return dynamic memory to the heap, you use one of two forms of the delete operator. For singleton objects you do this:

```
delete fp;
delete cp1;
```

but deleting arrays requires a different syntax:

```
delete [] fpa;          // array-delete syntax
```

Like other C++ features, new and delete improve the type safety of your programs: You aren't just asking for an amount of memory, you are requesting objects, with the appropriate type-checking and initialization. See Chapter 20 for more on memory management.

Statement Declarations

In C++, a declaration can appear anywhere a statement can. This means that instead of having to group declarations at the beginning of a block, you can define objects at their point of first use. For example, in Listing 1.17 the array a is visible throughout the function body, but n is not valid until its declaration, and i not until the next line. Note that i is redeclared in the second for loop, which illustrates that the scope of variables declared in a loop is the loop itself.

Listing 1.17   Shows that declarations are statements

```cpp
// declare.cpp
#include <iostream>
using namespace std;

main()
{
    int a[] = {0,1,2,3,4};

    // Print address and size
    cout << "a == " << (void *) a << endl;
    cout << "sizeof a == " << sizeof a << endl;

    // Print forwards
    size_t n = sizeof a / sizeof a[0];
    for (int i = 0; i < n; ++i)
        cout << a[i] << ' ';
    cout << endl;

    // Then backwards
    for (int i = n-1; i >= 0; --i)
        cout << a[i] << ' ';
    cout << endl;
}

// Output:
a == 0xffec
sizeof(a) == 10
0 1 2 3 4
4 3 2 1 0
```

Standard Library Features

Part III of this book illustrates the standard C++ library in great detail. In addition to streams, the library provides a number of useful concrete types and container classes. Although earlier I defined my own complex type to illustrate some features of classes and operator overloading, the standard library provides a complex type with a robust set of complex arithmetic operations. As Listing 1.18 shows, complex is a *class template*, which you instantiate with the desired underlying numeric type (either float, double, or long double).

C Compatibility

To accommodate strong type checking and object orientation, C++ has had to part ways with C on a few language issues. If you are going to use C++ as a better C, you should be aware of those features that behave differently in the two languages.

Listing 1.18 Illustrates the `complex` template

```
#include <iostream>
#include <complex>
using namespace std;

main()
{
    complex<double> x(1.0, 2.0), y(3.0, 4.0);

    cout << "x + y == " << x + y << endl;
    cout << "x * y == " << x * y << endl;
    cout << "conjugate of x == " << conj(x) << endl;
    cout << "normof x == " << norm(x) << endl;
}

// Output:
x + y == (4,6)
x * y == (-5,10)
conjugate of x == (1,-2)
normof x == 5
```

First of all, there are more keywords in C++ than in C. You must avoid using any of the tokens in Table 1.5 as identifiers in your programs. You can use `const` integer objects and enumerated constants as array dimensions in C++, as in

```
const int SIZE = 100;
enum {BIGGER = 1000};
int a[SIZE], b[BIGGER];
```

Global `const` declarations have internal linkage by default, whereas in C they have external linkage. This means that you can use `const` definitions at file scope in place of #define macros in header files. If you want a `const` object to have external linkage, you must use the `extern` keyword.

In C you can assign any type of pointer to and from a `void*`. This allows you to use `malloc` without a cast, as in

```
#include <stdlib.h>
...
char *p = malloc(strlen(s) + 1);
```

The C++ type system will not allow you to assign from a `void` pointer without a cast. For the example above, you should use the new operator anyway.

If you omit arguments in a function definition in C, the compiler does not check how you use that function (i.e., you can pass any number and type of arguments to it). In C++, the prototype `f` is equivalent to `f(void)`. If you insist upon the unsafe C behavior, use `f(...)`.

Table 1.5 C++ keywords and reserved words

and	dynamic_cast	not_eq	throw
and_eq	else	operator	true
asm	enum	or	try
auto	explicit	or_eq	typedef
bitand	export	private	typename
bitor	extern	protected	typeid
bool	false	public	union
break	float	register	unsigned
case	for	reinterpret_cast	using
catch	friend	return	virtual
char	goto	short	void
class	if	signed	volatile
compl	inline	sizeof	wchar_t
const_cast	int	static	while
continue	long	static_cast	xor
default	mutable	struct	xor_eq
delete	namespace	switch	
do	new	template	
double	not	this	

And finally, single-quoted character constants are of type `char` in C++, not `int`. Otherwise, the expression

```
cout << 'a'
```

would print the internal character code (e.g., 97 in ASCII) instead of the letter "a."

For more on C/C++ compatibility see Appendix A.

Summary

- As a multiparadigm language, C++
  1. is a better C,
  2. supports data abstraction,
  3. supports object-oriented programming,
- C++ is type-safe.
- All functions must be declared or defined before first use.
- Reference parameters directly support call-by-reference semantics.
- You can overload functions and operators.
- Templates allow you to create generic functions.
- Inline functions combine the efficiency of function-like macros with the safety of real functions.
- The free store operators `new` and `delete` are type smart.
- A declaration can appear anywhere a function can.

Pointers

Programming on the Edge

"Segmentation Violation"

"Access Violation"

"Suspicious Pointer Conversion"

"Non-portable Pointer Conversion"

"Null Pointer Assignment"

Do any of these messages sound familiar? Pointers gone awry are the nastiest bugs a C++ programmer has to contend with. Indeed, pointers and the raw power they give the developer have long been a popular criticism of C. It's just too dangerous, people say. The philosophy of C, and to a somewhat lesser degree C++, however, is to trust the programmer. The truth is not so much that these languages are dangerous, but simply that some programmers aren't quite ready to be trusted. Mastering pointers is essential to use C and C++ productively and safely. Fortunately, mastery follows naturally from a few basic principles and techniques.

The Basics

All objects in a program other than register variables reside somewhere in memory. That "somewhere" has an address. On platforms that number each byte of memory in sequence starting from zero, an address is simply the sequence number of a byte. The following program shows how to find the address of program variables:

```
// address.cpp
#include <cstdio>
#include <iostream>
using namespace std;
```

```
main()
{
    int i = 7, j = 8;
    printf("i == %d, &i == %p\n",i,&i);
    cout << "j == " << j << "&j == " << &j << endl;
}

/* Output:
i == 7, &i == 0012FF88
j == 8, &j == 0x0012ff84
*/
```

The & unary operator returns the address of a data object. The %p format specifier displays an address in a compiler-dependent format usually hexadecimal. For all the examples in this book, both integers and addresses are 32-bit quantities (your output may vary).

The memory layout for i and j above looks like this:

```
     j          i
    ┌───────┬───────┐
... │ 0008  │ 0007  │   ...
    └───────┴───────┘
    12FF88   12FF84
```

It is not important that i and j happen to be adjacent in memory (some architectures have gaps between objects due to alignment requirements). Notice that my compiler allocated i after (i.e., at a higher address than) j in memory; this isn't important either. How the computer actually stores the bits of a number is also system dependent. In fact, on the PC, the 7 in i is not really stored in the rightmost portion of i's memory. We can pretend it is most of the time, though, because it is *logically* 0x00000007, no matter how the bits are physically laid out.

A *pointer* is nothing more than a variable that holds the address of another program entity. Most often we are not concerned with the actual numeric value of an address. We usually just want to use it to refer to an object of interest. The program in Listing 2.1 illustrates the use of pointers. A pointer always points to an object of some type, so the referenced type must always appear in the declaration. Thus we speak of "pointer to int" or "pointer to char," etc. The declaration

```
int *ip;
```

indicates that *ip is an int, therefore ip is a pointer to an int. When an asterisk precedes a pointer variable in an expression outside of a declaration, the result refers to the value pointed at. The process of referring to memory indirectly through a pointer is called *indirection* or *dereferencing* and can occur on either side of an assignment statement. With the declarations in Listing 2.1, the statement

```
*ip = 9;
```

has the same effect as

```
i = 9;
```

Listing 2.1   Illustrates pointers and indirection

```cpp
// pointer.cpp
#include <iostream>
using namespace std;

main()
{
    int  i = 7, j = 8;
    int* ip = &i;
    int* jp = &j;

    cout << "Address " << ip
         << " contains " << *ip << endl;
    cout << "Address " << jp
         << " contains " << *jp << endl;

    *ip = 9;
    cout << "Now Address " << ip
         << " contains " << i << endl;
    *jp = 10;
    cout << "Now Address " << jp
         << " contains " << j << endl;
}

// Output:
Address 0x0012ff88 contains 7
Address 0x0012ff84 contains 8
Now Address 0x0012ff88 contains 9
Now Address 0x0012ff84 contains 10
```

If you could define a pointer without mentioning the referenced type, the expression *ip would be meaningless and indirection would be impossible. Never forget that a pointer doesn't just point somewhere in memory; it points to an entity of some type. The only exception to this rule is when a pointer points "nowhere." This happens when you assign a pointer the special value 0 (called the *null* pointer, and represented by the macro NULL in C). You cannot dereference a null pointer; you can only compare it to other pointers.

The memory layout for Listing 2.1 is:

```
        jp      ip        j       i
      ┌──────┬──────┐   ┌──────┬──────┐
 . . .│12ff84│12ff88│   │    8 │    7 │ . . .
      └──────┴──────┘   └──────┴──────┘
        ????    ????     12ff84  12ff88
```

Although addresses usually appear as numbers, you should not assume that there is any relation between pointer types and integral data types. Pointers are a unique data type and should be treated as such. The only things you can do with a pointer are:

1. Store in it the address of an object of the referenced type and retrieve the same;
2. Alter or retrieve the contents at that address (indirection);
3. Add or subtract an integer (staying within array limits);
4. Subtract it from or compare it to another pointer (when both point into the same array);
5. Assign to it or compare it to the null pointer;
6. Pass it as an argument to a function expecting a pointer to the referenced type.

Since the relative memory position of objects is not important (except for array elements, of course), it is usually better to depict the logical layout of memory, as follows:

One usually says "ip points to i" or "jp points at j".

The notion of a pointer is so simple that novices often send themselves into a real snit by looking beyond the mark. If you want to avoid needless hours of frustration and confusion, just remember this:

Grand Pointer Principle 1: A pointer is an address.

Notice that I said "is an address" instead of "holds an address." Both are true, of course. A pointer *is* an address like an `int` *is* an integer. One usually doesn't say that an `int` "holds" an integer. I just want to emphasize that when you use a pointer, think "address of something." What could be simpler?

Since all objects have an address, you can define pointers to any kind of object, including another pointer. The program in Listing 2.2 shows how to define a pointer to a pointer to an integer. The pointer topology for this program is

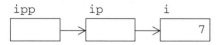

If `ipp` is a pointer to a pointer to an integer, then `*ipp` is the pointer it points at. To finally arrive at the integer 7 in `i` requires another level of indirection, hence the expression `**ipp`. In other words,

```
**ipp == *ip == i      // all refer to same object, in fact
```

Listing 2.2   Illustrates pointers to pointers

```cpp
/* ptr2ptr.cpp: Pointers to pointers */
#include <iostream>
using namespace std;

main()
{
    int   i = 7;
    int*  ip = &i;
    int** ipp = &ip;

    cout << "Address " << ip << " contains " << *ip << endl;
    cout << "Address " << ipp << " contains " << *ipp << endl;
    cout << "**ipp == " << **ipp << endl;
}

// Output:
Address 0x0012ff88 contains 7
Address 0x0012ff84 contains 0x0012ff88
**ipp == 7
```

Pointer Arithmetic

When a pointer references an array element, you can add or subtract an integer to it to point to elements of the same array. Adding 1 to such a pointer increases its value by the number of bytes in the referenced type, so that it points to the next array element. The program in Listing 2.3 performs integer arithmetic within an array of floats. The array looks like this:

a

1.0	2.0	3.0

12ff80

On my platform a `float` occupies four bytes. Incrementing p by 1 actually increases its value by 4. Subtracting two pointers to array elements performs the expected complementary operation: it yields the number of array elements between the two addresses. In other words, if p and q are pointers to the same referenced type, then the statement q = p + n implies q - p == n, and vice versa. The portable way to store the difference between two pointers is in a `ptrdiff_t`, which is defined in `stddef.h`, and which is included by `<iostream>`.

    The rules of pointer arithmetic can be summarized by the following formulas:

    1. p ± n == (char *) p ± n * sizeof(*p)

Listing 2.3   Illustrates pointer arithmetic

```
/* arith.cpp: Illustrate pointer arithmetic */
#include <iostream>
using namespace std;

main()
{
    float a[] = {1.0, 2.0, 3.0};

    // Increment a pointer:
    cout << "sizeof(float) == " << sizeof(float) << endl;
    float* p = &a[0];
    cout << "p == " << p << ", *p == " << *p << endl;
    ++p;
    cout << "p == " << p << ", *p == " << *p << endl;

    // Subtract two pointers:
    ptrdiff_t diff = (p+1) - p;
    cout << "diff == " << diff << endl;
    diff = (char *)(p+1) - (char *)p;
    cout << "diff == " << diff << endl;
}

// Output:
sizeof(float) == 4
p == 0x0012ff80, *p == 1
p == 0x0012ff84, *p == 2
diff == 1
diff == 4
```

which says "adding (subtracting) an integer n to (from) a pointer moves the pointer up (down) in memory n elements of the referenced type," and

   2. $p - q == \pm n$

where n is the number of elements between p and q. **Caution:** Remember that n in Formula 2 is a special type (`ptrdiff_t`). On some architectures, you can only use it as an offset in pointer arithmetic, and in no other way (e.g., you may not even be able to print it).

Pointer arithmetic can only be meaningful within arrays, since the formulas assume a sequence of equally sized objects. However, you can interpret any single object as an array of bytes. The program in Listing 2.4 dissects an integer by storing its address in a pointer to `char`,

Listing 2.4   Illustrates pointer conversions

```
// convert.cpp: char* and pointer casts
#include <iostream>
using namespace std;

main()
{
    int i = 7;
    char* cp = (char*) &i;

    cout << "The integer at " << &i
         << " == " << i << endl;

    // Print each byte value individually:
    for (int n = 0; n < sizeof i; ++n)
        cout << "The byte at " << (void*)(cp + n)
             << " == " << int(*(cp+n)) << endl;
}

// Output:
The integer at 0x0012ff88 == 7
The byte at 0x0012ff88 == 7
The byte at 0x0012ff89 == 0
The byte at 0x0012ff8a == 0
The byte at 0x0012ff8b == 0
```

then visits each byte by pointer arithmetic. Note the cast in the initialization of cp. Assigning pointers of different types requires a cast to convince the compiler that you know what you're doing; otherwise it will tell you that it suspects that you don't—hence the warning, "Suspicious pointer conversion." You don't need casts, however, when converting to void pointers (see the section "Generic Pointers" below).

The output in Listing 2.4 reveals an interesting fact: The Intel processor in my PC stores things "backwards" in that the least significant values of an object are stored at the lower memory addresses. This storage scheme is called "little-endian," because as you move up through memory, you encounter the "little end" of a multibyte integer first. VAX machines are also little-endian, but IBM mainframes are "big-endian." This is not usually a concern in common data processing applications, but sometimes it can make a difference.

Suppose, for example, that you want to store a date from within a single century efficiently. You'll need storage as follows:

```
Year  (0-99)          7 bits
Month (1-12)          4 bits
Day   (1-31)          5 bits
```

Fortunately, this combines to 16 bits, the size of a short integer on a PC. One obvious way, then, to store a date in a `short` is to use bitwise operations as follows:

```cpp
// bit1.cpp: Pack a date into an integer
#include <iostream>
#include <iomanip>
using namespace std;

main()
{
    unsigned short date, year = 92, mon = 8, day = 2;

    date = (year << 9) | (mon << 5) | day;
    cout << hex << date << endl;
}

// Output:
b902
```

The logical layout of bits for the date August 2, 1992 (b902) is as expected:

1011100	1000	00010
(92)	(8)	(2)

But a little-endian machine physically stores it backwards, like this:

01000	0001	0011101

Using the following bitfield structure makes for a more readable program (see Listing 2.5):

```cpp
struct Date
{
    unsigned day: 5;
    unsigned mon: 4;
    unsigned year: 7;
};
```

This structure reflects the reversed layout. To interpret an integer as a bitfield structure, simply cast a pointer to it to a pointer to `Date`. Now you can access the date components by name without the shifting and masking. To access a structure member via a pointer you need first to dereference the pointer and then name the member:

```cpp
(*dp).mon
```

Since this is unwieldy syntax there is a shorthand:

```cpp
dp->mon
```

Listing 2.5   Packs a `short` via a bitfield structure

```
// bit2.cpp: Overlay an integer with a bit field structure
#include <iostream>
#include <iomanip>

struct Date
{
    unsigned day: 5;
    unsigned mon: 4;
    unsigned year: 7;
};

main()
{
    unsigned short date, year = 92, mon = 8, day = 2;
    Date* dp = (Date*) &date;

    dp->mon = mon;
    dp->day = day;
    dp->year = year;
    cout << hex << date << endl;
}

// Output:
b902
```

which I've heard pronounced "dp arrow mon," "dp pointing to mon," and a few other ways not worth mentioning.

Pass-By-Reference Semantics

Unless told to do otherwise, C++ always passes arguments to functions by value. This means that functions use a copy of each argument locally. The result of this approach is that a function can't change the corresponding value of a parameter in the calling program. Consider the following naïve attempt at swapping two integers:

```
void swap(int x, int y)
{
    int temp = x;
    x = y;
    y = temp;
}
```

A call such as `swap(a, b)` will have no effect whatsoever on a and b. A scheme that allows changes in function arguments to persist after leaving a function is called "pass-by-reference."

Listing 2.6 Swaps function arguments through pointers

```
// swap2.cpp: A working swap function
#include <iostream>
using namespace std;

void swap(int*, int*);

main()
{
    int i = 7, j = 8;

    swap(&i,&j);
    cout << "i == " << i << ", j == " << j << endl;
}

void swap(int* xp, int* yp)
{
    int temp = *xp;
    *xp = *yp;
    *yp = temp;
}

// Output:
i == 8, j == 7
```

You can simulate pass-by-reference semantics in C by passing pointers to the arguments that you want to change. You alter the values in the calling program indirectly through those pointers (see Listing 2.6). Passing by reference is common for large objects and in object-oriented systems where a pointer to an object acts as its "handle." As Chapter 1 explains, C++ also supports pass-by-reference directly via references.

Generic Pointers

It is often convenient to write functions that can accept parameters that point to any type. This is necessary, for example, with the standard library function memcpy, which copies a block of memory from one address to another. You might want to call memcpy to copy structures of your own making:

```
struct mystruct a, b;
/* ... */
memcpy(&a, &b, sizeof (struct mystruct));
```

To handle a pointer of any type, memcpy declares its first two arguments as pointers to void. You can assign a pointer of any type to a void* without a cast. You can also assign a void* to any other type of pointer in C but not in C++. Here is a portable implementation of memcpy that illustrates void pointers:

```
void* memcpy(void* target, const void* source, size_t n)
{
    char* targetp = (char*) target;
    const char* sourcep = (const char*) source;
    while (n--)
        *targetp++ = *sourcep++;
    return target;
}
```

This version of memcpy must assign the pointers to void to pointers to char so that it can traverse the memory blocks a byte at a time, copying as it goes. It makes no sense to try to dereference a void*, since its size is unknown.

const Pointers

Note the const keyword in memcpy's second parameter. This tells the compiler that the function will not be changing any of the values that source points to (not without a cast, anyway).
When passing pointers as parameters, it is good practice always to use the const qualifier when
it applies. It protects you not only from inadvertently making an incorrect assignment, but even
from passing pointers whose objects you don't want to change as arguments to functions that
might change them. For example, if the declaration in Listing 2.6 had been

```
const int i = 7, j = 8;
```

you would get a warning for the statement

```
swap(&i,&j);
```

because swap actually does change the values its arguments point to.

If you browse the standard header files provided with your compiler you will see generous
use of const. When const appears anywhere before the asterisk in a declaration, it indicates
that the referenced contents will not change:

```
const char *p;      // pointer to const char
char const *q;      // likewise, pointer to const char
char c;
c = *p;             // OK (assuming p and q are initialized)
*q = c;             // Error; can't modify referent
```

You can also declare that the pointer itself cannot change by putting the const after the
asterisk:

```
char* const p;
*p = 'a';           // OK, only the pointer is const
++p;                // Error, can't modify pointer
```

To disallow modification of both the pointer and the contents referenced, use `const` in both places:

```
const char* const p;
char c;
c = *p;              // OK - can read contents
*p = 'a';            // Error
++p;                 // Error
```

The function `inspect` in Listing 2.7 shows how to print the individual bytes of any object. Since I don't alter the contents of the object, the first parameter is a pointer to `const`, and I am careful to convert it to a pointer to a `const` character before using it.

Listing 2.7   A function that inspects any object

```
// inspect.cpp:    Inspect the bytes of an object
#include <iostream>
#include <iomanip>
using namespace std;

void inspect(const void* ptr, size_t nbytes)
{
    const unsigned char* p = (const unsigned char*) ptr;

    cout.setf(ios::hex, ios::basefield);
    for (int i = 0; i < nbytes; ++i)
        cout << "byte " << setw(2) << setfill(' ') << i
             << ":     " << setw(2) << setfill('0') << int(p[i])
             << endl;
}

main()
{
    char c = 'a';
    short i = 100;
    long n = 100000L;
    double pi = 3.141529;
    char s[] = "hello";

    inspect(&c, sizeof c);    cout << endl;
    inspect(&i, sizeof i);    cout << endl;
    inspect(&n, sizeof n);    cout << endl;
    inspect(&pi, sizeof pi);  cout << endl;
    inspect(s, sizeof s);     cout << endl;
}
```

continued

Listing 2.7   (continued)

```
// Output:
byte  0:     61

byte  0:     64
byte  1:     00

byte  0:     a0
byte  1:     86
byte  2:     01
byte  3:     00

byte  0:     13
byte  1:     7c
byte  2:     d3
byte  3:     f4
byte  4:     d9
byte  5:     21
byte  6:     09
byte  7:     40

byte  0:     68
byte  1:     65
byte  2:     6c
byte  3:     6c
byte  4:     6f
byte  5:     00
```

Pointers and One-Dimensional Arrays

You will notice in Listing 2.7 that I pass the array s without taking its address. This is because C and C++ convert an array name to a pointer to its first element in most expressions. Having taught C and C++ to hundreds of students since 1984, I have noticed that the relationship between pointers and arrays, especially multidimensional arrays, causes much confusion.

It may seem strange to say, but C++ does not really support arrays, at least not in the same way that it does first-class types such as integers or even structures. Consider the following statements:

```
int i = 1, j;
int a[4] = {0,1,2,3}, b[4];
struct pair {int x; int y;};
pair p = {1,2}, q;

j = i;        // OK: integer assignment
q = p;        // OK: structure assignment
b = a;        // No can do!
```

Not all operations are legal with arrays. We could do the following, but it isn't a "real" assignment:

```
int a[4] = {0,1,2,3}, *p;
p = a;                    /* Only stores &a[0] in p */
```

The compiler interprets an array name as a pointer to its first element. except in declarations or when an array name is the operand to the `sizeof` or `&` operators). You can express this principle as

```
a == &a[0]
```

or equivalently as

```
*a == a[0]
```

By the rules of pointer arithmetic, then, if you add an integer `i` to an array name, the result is a pointer to the `i`th element of the array; that is,

```
a + i == &a[i]
```

or, as I like to express it,

Grand Pointer Principle 2: `*(a + i) == a[i]`

The program in Listing 2.8 illustrates Principle 2 and those leading up to it.

Since all array subscripting is really pointer arithmetic, you can use the expression `i[a]` in place of `a[i]`. This follows directly from Principle 2:

```
a[i] == *(a + i) == *(i + a) == i[a]
```

Of course, any program that uses such banalities should be shot instead of executed, and the programmer should be severely dealt with, too. It is not altogether unreasonable, however, to use negative subscripts. If a pointer `p` traverses an array, you can retrieve the element preceding `*p` with the expression `p[-1]`, since

```
p[-1] == *(p - 1)
```

Listing 2.9 contains an ample mixture of pointer and array notation. It also employs a useful formula for the number of elements in an array:

```
size_t n = sizeof a / sizeof a[0];
```

You can use any other valid subscript in the divisor, but 0 is the safest because every array has a 0th element. This idiom only applies when the original array declaration is in scope, of course.

For those of you who like to use C-style strings, a popular idiom that follows from the interaction of pointer and array notation is

```
strncpy(s,t,n)[n] = '\0';
```

Listing 2.8　Shows that an array name is pointer

```cpp
// array1.cpp: Uses an array name as a pointer
#include <iostream>
using namespace std;

main()
{
    int a[] = {0,1,2,3,4};
    int* p = a;

    cout << "sizeof a == " << sizeof a << endl;
    cout << "sizeof p == " << sizeof p << endl;
    cout << "p == " << p << ", &a[0] == " << &a[0] << endl;
    cout << "*p == " << *p << ", a[0] == " << a[0] << endl;

    p = a + 2;
    cout << "p == " << p << ", &a[2] == " << &a[2] << endl;
    cout << "*p == " << *p << ", a[2] == " << a[2] << endl;
}

// Output:
sizeof a == 20
sizeof p == 4
p == 0x0012ff78, &a[0] == 0x0012ff78
*p == 0, a[0] == 0
p == 0x0012ff80, &a[2] == 0x0012ff80
*p == 2, a[2] == 2
```

Listing 2.9　Uses both an index and a pointer to traverse an array

```cpp
// array2.cpp: Traverses an array with an index and a pointer
#include <iostream>
using namespace std;

main()
{
    int a[] = {0,1,2,3,4};
    size_t n = sizeof a / sizeof a[0];

    // Print using array index:
    for (int i = 0; i < n; ++i)
        cout << a[i] << ' ';
    cout << endl;
```

Listing 2.9 (continued)

```
    // You can even swap a and i (but don't YOU do it!)
    for (int i = 0; i < n; ++i)
        cout << i[a] << ' ';
    cout << endl;

    // Print using a pointer:
    int* p = a;
    while (p < a+n)
        cout << *p++ << ' ';
    cout << endl;

    // Using index notation with pointer is OK:
    p = a;
    for (int i = 0; i < n; ++i)
        cout << p[i] << ' ';
    cout << endl;

    // Using pointer notation with array is OK:
    for (int i = 0; i < n; ++i)
        cout << *(a+i) << ' ';
    cout << endl;

    // Print backwards using pointer:
    p = a + n-1;
    while (p >= a)
        cout << *p-- << ' ';
    cout << endl;

    // Negative subscripts are allowed:
    p = a + n-1;
    for (int i = 0; i < n; ++i)
        cout << p[-i] << ' ';
    cout << endl;
}

// Output:
0 1 2 3 4
0 1 2 3 4
0 1 2 3 4
0 1 2 3 4
0 1 2 3 4
4 3 2 1 0
4 3 2 1 0
```

This copies one string to another while guaranteeing that there is no overflow and that the string is null delimited (provided n is not out of bounds)—all in one compact statement.

There is one other difference between pointers and array names to remember: an array name is *not a modifiable lvalue*. This means that the address to which an array name is bound cannot be changed, as the following example attempts to do:

```
int a[5], b[5], *p;
/* All the following are illegal */
a++;
a = p + 5;
b = a;
```

If you could make such assignments, you could easily lose track of where an array resides in memory (not a good idea!).

String literals are arrays of characters that don't have names. You can find their size with sizeof and you even can subscript them (see Listings 2.10 and 2.11). Note that my compiler treats each occurrence of "hello" in Listing 2.10 as a separate object, returning a different address each time. Some compilers can "pool" equivalent string literals into a single occurrence to save space.

Exercise 2.1

Given the declarations

```
int a[] = {10,15,4,25,3,-4};
int *p = &a[2];
```

what is the result of each of the following expressions?

a. *(p + 1)
b. p[-1]
c. p - a
d. a[*p++]
e. *(a + a[2])

Arrays as Parameters

When you pass an array as a parameter to a function, a pointer to its first element is passed, as you would expect. For this reason you can permanently change elements of an array while in the called function. In the function f in Listing 2.12, the address &a[0] is passed by value to the pointer b, so the expression b[i] behaves identically to the expression a[i]. There is no way to pass an entire built-in array by value.

Even though I defined the parameter b with array notation, namely,

```
int b[]
```

it is the same as if I had written

```
int *b
```

Listing 2.10 Shows that a string literal is an anonymous array

```
// array3.cpp
#include <iostream>
using namespace std;

main()
{
    char  a[] = "hello";
    char* p = a;

    cout << "a == " << &a << ", sizeof a == " << sizeof a << endl;
    cout << "p == " << (void*)p << ", sizeof p == " << sizeof p << endl;
    cout << "sizeof \"hello\" == " << sizeof "hello" << endl;
    cout << "address of \"hello\" == " << (void*)"hello" << endl;
    cout << "address of \"hello\" == " << (void*)"hello" << endl;
}

// Output:
a == 0x0012ff84, sizeof a == 6
p == 0x0012ff84, sizeof p == 4
sizeof "hello" == 6
address of "hello" == 0x004090d4
address of "hello" == 0x004090f1
```

Listing 2.11 Indexes a string literal

```
// array4.cpp: Indexing a string literal
#include <iostream>
using namespace std;

main()
{
    for (int i = 0; i < 10; i += 2)
        cout << "0123456789"[i];
}

// Output:
02468
```

Listing 2.12   Shows that array parameters are pointers

```cpp
// array5.cpp: Arrays as parameters
#include <iostream>
using namespace std;

void f(int b[], size_t n)
{
    cout << "\n*** Entering function f() ***\n";
    cout << "b == " << b << endl;
    cout << "sizeof b == " << sizeof b << endl;
    for (int i = 0; i < n; ++i)
        cout << b[i] << ' ';
    b[2] = 99;
    cout << "\n*** Leaving function f() ***\n\n";
}

main()
{
    int a[] = {0,1,2,3,4};
    size_t n = sizeof a / sizeof a[0];

    cout << "a == " << a << endl;
    cout << "sizeof a == " << sizeof a << endl;
    f(a,n);
    for (int i = 0; i < n; ++i)
        cout << a[i] << ' ';
}

// Output:
a == 0x0012ff78
sizeof a == 20

*** Entering function f() ***
b == 0x0012ff78
sizeof b == 4
0 1 2 3 4
*** Leaving function f() ***

0 1 99 3 4
```

Moreover, sizeof(b) == 4, the size of a pointer on my platform. There is no way to determine automatically the compile-time size of an array from within another function.

Pointer parameters that refer to array elements are common in text processing. Here is a function (str_cpy) that copies one string to another (like strcpy, except it doesn't return anything):

```
void str_cpy(char *s1, const char *s2)
{
    while (*s1++ = *s2++)
        ;
}
```

The while loop test is not for equality, but for the value in s1 after the assignment (but before the increment). The loop stops after copying the terminating '\0'. The expression *p++ is a very common C/C++ idiom.

Exercise 2.2

The following statements modify the string s through a sequence of pointer expressions. What character is retrieved by each expression when executed in succession, and what is the final value of s?

```
char s[] = "desolate", *p = s;

*p++     == ?
*(p++)   == ?
(*p)++   == ?
*++p     == ?
*(++p)   == ?
++*p     == ?
++(*p)   == ?

strcmp(s,?) == 0
```

(Thanks to Chet Small of Lincoln Laboratories for this very clever example).

Arrays of Strings

There are two ways to represent arrays of C-style strings: (1) arrays of pointers, and (2) two-dimensional arrays. The program in Listing 2.13 illustrates the first approach. The memory layout looks like this:

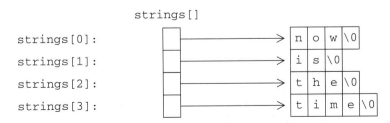

This type of array is sometimes called a *ragged array* because the strings can be of different lengths. This scheme uses only the amount of memory required to hold the data, plus one pointer

Listing 2.13   Implements strings as arrays of pointers to `char`

```
// array6.cpp: Ragged arrays
#include <iostream>
#include <cstring>
using namespace std;

main()
{
    char*  strings[] = {"now","is","the","time"};
    size_t n = sizeof strings / sizeof strings[0];

    // Print from ragged array:
    for (int i = 0; i < n; ++i)
        cout << "String " << i  <<" == \"" << strings[i]
             << "\",\tsize == " << sizeof strings[i]
             << ",\tlength == " << strlen(strings[i])
             << endl;
}

// Output:
String 0 == "now",   size == 4,   length == 3
String 1 == "is",    size == 4,   length == 2
String 2 == "the",   size == 4,   length == 3
String 3 == "time",  size == 4,   length == 4
```

per string. The `argv` array of command-line parameters that the runtime system passes to `main` is a ragged array.

A disadvantage to the ragged array approach is that in most circumstances you need to dynamically allocate memory for each string (see Chap. 20). If you don't mind wasting a little bit of space and if you know the length of the longest string you will encounter, you can use a fixed-size region of storage as a two-dimensional array of characters (one string per row). The memory layout for the array in Listing 2.14 is:

array[] [5]

array[0]:	n	o	w	\0	?
array[1]:	i	s	\0	?	?
array[2]:	t	h	e	\0	?
array[3]:	t	i	m	e	\0

As this program illustrates, you don't have to specify the first dimension of a multidimensional array if it can be inferred from its initializer.

Listing 2.14   Implements strings as rows in a 2-d array of `char`

```cpp
// array7.cpp: Stores strings in 2-d char arrays
#include <iostream>
#include <cstring>
using namespace std;

main()
{
    char array[][5] = {"now","is","the","time"};
    size_t n = sizeof array / sizeof array[0];

    for (int i = 0; i < n; ++i)
        cout << "array[" << i << "] == \"" << array[i]
             << "\",\tsize == " << sizeof array[i]
             << ",\tlength == " << strlen(array[i])
             << endl;
}

// Output:
array[0] == "now",    size == 5,    length == 3
array[1] == "is",     size == 5,    length == 2
array[2] == "the",    size == 5,    length == 3
array[3] == "time",   size == 5,    length == 4
```

C++ is somewhat unique among programming languages in that you can use an array with only some of its subscripts. As the program in Listing 2.14 suggests, the expression `array[i]` is a pointer to the `i`th row. For an array defined as `int a[2][3][4]`, what do you suppose `a[i]` represents? How about `a[i][j]`? Read on.

Pointers and Multidimensional Arrays

Actually, there is no such a thing as a multidimensional array in C++! At least, there is no direct support for such. One usually thinks of a one-dimensional array as a vector, a 2-d array as a table or matrix, and a 3-d array as a rectangular solid. A geometric model for arrays, however, makes it difficult to use higher-dimensional arrays intelligently. C++ supports instead the notion of "arrays of arrays." For example, if a one-dimensional array of integers, say

`int a[4] = {0,1,2,3};`

is an indexed collection of integers:

```
0   1   2   3
```

which we usually depict as a single vector:

0	1	2	3

then a two-dimensional array of integers, such as

```
int a[3][4] = {{0,1,2,3},{4,5,6,7},{8,9,0,1}};
```

is a collection that looks like this:

or, if you like,

a[0]	0	1	2	3
a[1]	4	5	6	7
a[2]	8	9	0	1

which is a collection of *arrays*. So this a is an "array of three arrays of four ints", and a[0] is one of those arrays of four ints. Since an array name always resolves to a pointer to its first element when used in an expression, an expression like a+1 is of type "pointer to array of four ints" and would point in this case to the second row (i.e., a[1]). The program in Listing 2.15 shows how to declare a pointer to an array. Such a pointer can replace the array name with no change in indexing syntax. Novices mistakenly assume that since a pointer to int can substitute for the name of an integer array, as in

```
int a[] = {0,1,2,3}, *p = a;
/* ... */
p[i] = ...
```

then a pointer to pointer to int will do the same thing for a two-dimensional array, like

```
int a[][4] = {{0,2,3,4},{4,5,6,7},{8,9,0,1}};
int **p = a;     /* Suspicious pointer conversion */
/* ... */
p[i][j] = ...
```

To see why this is not correct, consider the expression p[i][j]. By Grand Pointer Principle 2, this is equivalent to:

```
*(p[i] + j)
```

which is equivalent to

```
*(*(p + i) + j)
```

Listing 2.15 Illustrates a pointer to a 1-d array within a 2-d array

```
// array8.cpp:     Uses a pointer to a 1-d array
#include <iostream>

main()
{
    int a[][4] = {{0,1,2,3},{4,5,6,7},{8,9,0,1}};
    int (*p)[4] = a;          // Pointer to array of 4 ints
    size_t nrows = sizeof a / sizeof a[0];
    size_t ncols = sizeof a[0] / sizeof a[0][0];

    cout << "sizeof(*p) == " << sizeof *p << endl;
    for (int i = 0; i < nrows; ++i)
    {
        for (int j = 0; j < ncols; ++j)
            cout << p[i][j] << ' ';
        cout << endl;
    }
}

// Output:
sizeof(*p) == 16
0 1 2 3
4 5 6 7
8 9 0 1
```

Since p is a pointer to pointer to int, the expression p + i advances past p a distance equal to the size of i *pointers*, not i *rows* (we want to advance i rows). Clearly we want the type to which p points to have the size of a row, so p must be a pointer to a row, that is, an array of the appropriate size, hence the interesting but logically consistent syntax:

```
int (*p)[4] = a;
```

With this definition of p, a compiler observes the following steps to evaluate the expression *(*(p + i) + j):

1. p + i

   This computes a pointer to the row which is i rows beyond the row p currently points at.

2. *(p + i)

   This is that row (which is an array).

3. Since the array *(p + i) is not the operand of a sizeof or & operation, it is replaced with a pointer to its first element, namely, &a[i][0], which is a pointer to an int.

4. `&a[i][0] + j`

   Since `&a[i][0]` is a pointer to an `int`, adding `j` advances it by `j` integers, resulting in `&a[i][j]`.

5. `*&a[i][j]`

   This is the integer `a[i][j]`.

Table 2.1 summarizes this relationship between pointers and two-dimensional arrays. Don't let the fact that `a+1` and `a[1]` have the same value (0x8) tempt you to conclude that

```
a[i] == a + i      // Nope!
```

They are only equal in value, not in type, because `sizeof(a+1)` == 2 (a pointer), and `sizeof(a[1])` == 8 (an array of four integers).

Higher and Deeper

It naturally follows that a three-dimensional array is a collection of two-dimensional arrays:

```
int a[2][3][4] = {{{0,1,2,3},{4,5,6,7},{8,9,0,1}},
                  {{2,3,4,5},{6,7,8,9},{0,1,2,3}}};
```

0	1	2	3
4	5	6	7
8	9	0	1

a[0]

2	3	4	5
6	7	8	9
0	1	2	3

a[1]

The first element of this array is the "two-dimensional" array `a[0]` (technically, `a[0]` is an "array of three arrays of four `int`s"). To use a pointer compatible with the array name a, define:

```
int (*p)[3][4] = a;
```

Listing 2.16 has a sample program using such a pointer, and Table 2.2 is the 3-d analogue of Table 2.1.

Table 2.1   Array-to-pointer conversions for a two-dimensional array[1]

Expression	Type	Value
a	array of 3 arrays of 4 `int`s	0x0
a + 1	pointer to array of 4 `int`s	0x10
a[1]	array of 4 `int`s	0x10
a[1] + 1	pointer to `int`	0x14
a[1][1]	int	5

[1] Hexadecimal values are address offsets relative to a.

Listing 2.16   Illustrates a pointer to a 2-d array within a 3-d array

```
// array9.c:      Uses a pointer to a 2-d array
#include <iostream>
using namespace std;

main()
{
    int a[][3][4] = {{{0,1,2,3},{4,5,6,7},{8,9,0,1}},
                     {{2,3,4,5},{6,7,8,9},{0,1,2,3}}};
    int (*p)[3][4] = a;
    size_t ntables = sizeof a / sizeof a[0];
    size_t nrows   = sizeof a[0] / sizeof a[0][0];
    size_t ncols   = sizeof a[0][0] / sizeof a[0][0][0];

    cout << "sizeof(*p) == " << sizeof *p << endl;
    cout << "sizeof(a[0][0]) == " << sizeof a[0][0] << endl;
    for (int i = 0; i < ntables; ++i)
    {
        for (int j = 0; j < nrows; ++j)
        {
            for (int k = 0; k < ncols; ++k)
                cout << p[i][j][k] << ' ';
            cout << endl;
        }
        cout << endl;
    }
}

// Output:
sizeof(*p) == 48
sizeof(a[0][0]) == 16
0 1 2 3
4 5 6 7
8 9 0 1

2 3 4 5
6 7 8 9
0 1 2 3
```

Table 2.2   Array-to-pointer conversions for a three-dimensional array[1]

Expression	Type	Value
a	array of 2 arrays of 3 arrays of 4 ints	0x0
a + 1	pointer to array of 3 arrays of 4 ints	0x30
a[1]	array of 3 arrays of 4 ints	0x30
a[1] + 1	pointer to array of 4 ints	0x40
a[1][1]	array of 4 ints	0x40
a[1][1] + 1	pointer to int	0x44
a[1][1][1]	int	7

[1] Hexadecimal values are address offsets relative to a.

The programs in both Listing 2.15 and Listing 2.16 show how to determine the *rank* (i.e., the dimension) of an array and all of its subarrays. For the two-dimensional array a in Listing 2.15, the rank is the number of rows (one-dimensional objects) it contains, which is

```
sizeof a / sizeof a[0]
```

and the rank of each row is the number of integers (zero-dimensional objects) in each row of a, namely

```
sizeof a[0] / sizeof a[0][0]
```

In general, if a is an n-dimensional array, then a is a collection of

```
sizeof a / sizeof a[0]
```

(n−1)-dimensional objects, and each (n−1)-dimensional object in a contains

```
sizeof a[0] / sizeof a[0][0]
```

(n−2)-dimensional objects, each of which in turn contains

```
sizeof a[0][0] / sizeof a[0][0][0]
```

(n−3)-dimensional objects, and so on, until the number of zero-dimensional objects (e.g., integers) in each one-dimensional object is

```
sizeof a[0][0]...[0]   /   sizeof a[0][0]...[0][0]
    {n-1 subscripts}             {n subscripts}
```

Exercise 2.3

Fill in the array-to-pointer conversion table below, as I did in Tables 2.1 and 2.2, for the four-dimensional array:

```
int a[2][3][4][5] =
{
  {
    {{0,1,2,3,4},{5,6,7,8,9},{0,1,2,3,4},{5,6,7,8,9}},
    {{0,1,2,3,4},{5,6,7,8,9},{0,1,2,3,4},{5,6,7,8,9}},
    {{0,1,2,3,4},{5,6,7,8,9},{0,1,2,3,4},{5,6,7,8,9}},
  },
  {
    {{0,1,2,3,4},{5,6,7,8,9},{0,1,2,3,4},{5,6,7,8,9}},
    {{0,1,2,3,4},{5,6,7,8,9},{0,1,2,3,4},{5,6,7,8,9}},
    {{0,1,2,3,4},{5,6,7,8,9},{0,1,2,3,4},{5,6,7,8,9}},
  }
};
```

0	1	2	3	4		0	1	2	3	4		0	1	2	3	4				
5	6	7	8	9		5	6	7	8	9		5	6	7	8	9		== a[0]		
0	1	2	3	4		0	1	2	3	4		0	1	2	3	4				
5	6	7	8	9		5	6	7	8	9		5	6	7	8	9				

0	1	2	3	4		0	1	2	3	4		0	1	2	3	4				
5	6	7	8	9		5	6	7	8	9		5	6	7	8	9		== a[1]		
0	1	2	3	4		0	1	2	3	4		0	1	2	3	4				
5	6	7	8	9		5	6	7	8	9		5	6	7	8	9				

Expression	Type	Value
a		
a + 1		
a[1]		
a[1] + 1		
a[1][1]		
a[1][1] + 1		
a[1][1][1]		
a[1][1][1] + 1		
a[1][1][1][1]		

Pointers to Functions

A pointer can refer to functions as well as to stored objects. The following statement declares fp to be a pointer to a function that returns an int:

```
int (*fp)();
```

The parentheses around *fp are necessary. Without them the statement

```
int *fp();
```

declares fp as a function that returns a pointer to an int. This is one of the reasons for the increasingly popular style guideline to place asterisks immediately adjacent to the type in a declarator:

```
int* fp();      // Style clarifies fp() returns an int*
```

Of course, this style suggests that you should usually declare only one entity per statement, else the following could be confusing

```
int* ip, jp;    // jp is not a pointer!
```

If you want to specify that the function fp points at must take certain arguments, a float and a string, say, then write

```
int (*fp)(float, char *);
```

You can then store the address of such a function in fp:

```
extern int g(float, char *);
fp = g;
```

The name of a function in an expression resolves to an address that you can think of as pointing to the beginning of the code for that function. The following "hello, world" program shows how to execute a function through a pointer:

```
/* hello.c: Say hello via a function pointer */
#include <stdio.h>

main()
{
    void (*fp)() = printf;
    fp("hello, world\n");
}
```

To execute a function via a pointer, you might think you have to write

```
(*fp)("hello world\n");
```

to dereference the pointer. In fact, you had to do this in pre-ANSI C, but the ANSI C committee decided to allow normal function call syntax as I used in *hello.c* above. Since the compiler knows it is a pointer to a function, it knows that the only thing you can do under the circumstances is invoke the function, so there is no ambiguity.

When you pass a function name as a parameter to another function, the compiler actually passes a pointer to the function (analogous to array names). But why would you ever want to pass a function pointer to another function? One example is the use of the standard C library sort function qsort, which can sort an array of elements of any type, with either simple or compound sort keys. The program in Listing 2.17 shows how to sort command-line argument strings. All you need to do in this case is pass to qsort a function that knows how to compare strings. The action of a function (like qsort) calling another function (like comp) through a pointer determined at runtime is known as a *callback*.

An array of function pointers can come in handy in menu-driven applications. Suppose you want to present the following menu to the user:

1. Retrieve
2. Insert
3. Update
4. Quit

The program in Listing 2.18 uses keyboard input directly as an index into an array of pointers to the functions that process each of the menu choices.

Pointers to Member Functions

What if a callback function is a member function of some class? Obtaining a pointer to a class member works similarly to pointers to nonmember entities, with a little alteration in syntax. For example, consider the following class definition:

```
class C
{
public:
    void f() {cout << "C::f\n";}
    void g() {cout << "C::g\n";}
};
```

You define a pointer to a C member function like this:

```
void (C::*pmf)();          // pmf is a pointer to a member function
                           // of C taking void and returning void.
```

Listing 2.17 Sorts command-line arguments with qsort

```
// sortargs.cpp:  Sorts command-line arguments
#include <iostream>
#include <cstring>
#include <cstdlib>
using namespace std;

int comp(const void*, const void*);

main(int argc, char *argv[])
{
    qsort(argv+1, argc-1, sizeof argv[0], comp);
    while (--argc)
        cout << *++argv << endl;
}

int comp(const void* p1, const void* p2)
{
    const char *ps1 = * (const char**) p1;
    const char *ps2 = * (char**) p2;
    return strcmp(ps1,ps2);
}

// Output from the command "sortargs *.cpp":
address.cpp
arith.cpp
array1.cpp
array2.cpp
array3.cpp
array4.cpp
array5.cpp
array6.cpp
array7.cpp
array8.cpp
array9.cpp
bit1.cpp
bit2.cpp
convert.cpp
inspect.cpp
pointer.cpp
ptr2ptr.cpp
sortargs.cpp
swap1.cpp
swap2.cpp
```

Listing 2.18   Uses an array of function pointers to process menu choices

```c
/* menu.c:   Illustrates arrays of functions */
#include <stdio.h>

/* You must provide definitions for these */
extern void retrieve(void);
extern void insert(void);
extern void update(void);
extern int show_menu(void);               /* Returns keypress */

main()
{
    int choice;
    void (*farray[])(void) = {retrieve,insert,update};

    for (;;)
    {
        choice = show_menu();
        if (choice >= 1 && choice <= 3)
            farray[choice-1]();            /* Process request */
        else if (choice == 4)
            break;
    }
    return 0;
}
```

You can initialize pmf to the different member functions of C as needed, as the following program illustrates:

```cpp
main()
{
    C c;
    void (C::*pmf)() = &C::f;
    (c.*pmf)();
    pmf = &C::g;
    (c.*pmf)();
}

// Output:
C::f
C::g
```

Listing 2.19   Illustrates pointers to members

```cpp
// menu2.cpp: Uses pointers to member functions
#include <iostream>
using namespace std;

class Object
{
public:
    void retrieve() {cout << "Object::retrieve\n";}
    void insert() {cout << "Object::insert\n";}
    void update() {cout << "Object::update\n";}
    void process(int choice);

private:
    typedef void (Object::*Omf)();
    static Omf farray[3];
};

Object::Omf Object::farray[3] =
    {
        &Object::retrieve,
        &Object::insert,
        &Object::update
    };

void Object::process(int choice)
{
    if (0 <= choice && choice <= 2)
        (this->*farray[choice])();
}

main()
{
    int show_menu();      // You provide!
    Object o;

    for (;;)
    {
        int choice = show_menu();
        if (1 <= choice && choice <= 3)
            o.process(choice-1);
        else if (choice == 4)
            break;
    }
}
```

The .* operator calls a member function on behalf of the object that its left operand points to. If cp is a pointer to C, then you use the ->* operator, as in

```
(cp->*pmf)();
```

Because of the way C++ defines operator precedence, the parentheses are needed to fully identify the function to call. See Listing 2.19 for a pointer-to-member version of the menu example from Listing 2.18.

Encapsulation and Incomplete Types

Good programming practice calls for you to hide from the user details of implementation that he or she doesn't need to know. For example, to implement a stack of integers you might provide the user the following include file:

```
// mystack.h
class StackOfInt
{
public:
    StackOfInt();
    void push(int);
    int pop();
    int top() const;
    int size() const;

private:
    enum {MAX_STACK = 100};
    int data[MAX_STACK];
    int stkPtr;
};
```

Because the underlying array and stack pointer are private, the user is forced to do things your way through your public interface (see Listing 2.20 for an example). Even though the implementation of the member functions is hidden from the user, he or she can easily infer something similar to Listing 2.21 from a glance at the header file. If it is important to you to conceal all implementation details, you can add an extra layer of protection by using an *incomplete type*.

An incomplete type is a type whose size cannot be determined at compile time. One example is in the declaration

```
extern int a[];
```

This says that a is an array of unknown size, so don't use sizeof or you'll get an error message. This definition is quite different from

```
extern int *a;
```

which has the size of a pointer. You can strengthen the encapsulation of the stack type above by hiding its implementation in another class. In Listing 2.22, only a pointer to StackImp appears in the private section of StackOfInt. The statement

```
class StackImp;
```

is an incomplete declaration of StackImp; it merely states that the class exists. As long as only a pointer or reference to a StackImp appears in stack2.h, the user has no need of stkimp.h. The member functions of StackOfInt now just pass requests on to StackImp (see Listings 2.23 and 2.24).

Listing 2.20   The definition of StackOfInt

```
// tstack.cpp: Uses the StackOfInt class
#include <iostream>
#include "mystack.h"
using namespace std;

main()
{
    StackOfInt s;

    s.push(10);
    s.push(20);
    s.push(30);
    while (s.size())
        cout << s.pop() << endl;
}

// Output:
30
20
10
```

Listing 2.21   The StackOfInt implementation

```
// stack.cpp:       The StackOfInt implementation
#include "stack.h"

StackOfInt::StackOfInt()
{
    stkPtr = 0;
}
```

Listing 2.21   (continued)

```cpp
void StackOfInt::push(int i)
{
    if (stkPtr == MAX_STACK)
        throw "overflow";
    data[stkPtr++] = i;
}

int StackOfInt::pop()
{
    if (stkPtr == 0)
        throw "underflow";
    return data[--stkPtr];
}

int StackOfInt::top() const
{
    if (stkPtr == 0)
        throw "underflow";
    return data[stkPtr - 1];
}

int StackOfInt::size() const
{
    return stkPtr;
}
```

Listing 2.22   Using an incomplete type for better encapsulation

```cpp
// stack2.h:     Hides the stack implementation
class StackImp;

class StackOfInt
{
public:
    StackOfInt();
    ~StackOfInt();
    void push(int);
    int pop();
    int top() const;
    int size() const;

private:
    StackImp* imp;
};
```

Listing 2.23   Implementation of the `StackOfInt` class

```cpp
// stack2.cpp
#include "stack2.h"
#include "stkimp.h"

StackOfInt::StackOfInt()
            : imp(new StackImp)
{}

StackOfInt::~StackOfInt()
{
    delete imp;
}

void StackOfInt::push(int i)
{
    imp->push(i);
}

int StackOfInt::pop()
{
    return imp->pop();
}

int StackOfInt::top() const
{
    return imp->top();
}

int StackOfInt::size() const
{
    return imp->size();
}
```

Summary

- C and C++ are only as dangerous as those who use them
- A pointer is an address
- You can assign any pointer to a `void*`
- Remember to differentiate between a const pointer and a pointer-to-const
- `p ± n == (char*) p ± n * sizeof(*p)`
- `p - q == ±n`
- `*(a + i) == a[i]`

Listing 2.24   Stack implementation

```cpp
// stkimp.cpp
#include "stkimp.h"

StackImp::StackImp()
{
    stkPtr = 0;
}

void StackImp::push(int i)
{
    if (stkPtr == MAX_STACK)
        throw "overflow";
    data[stkPtr++] = i;
}

int StackImp::pop()
{
    if (stkPtr == 0)
        throw "underflow";
    return data[--stkPtr];
}

int StackImp::top() const
{
    if (stkPtr == 0)
        throw "underflow";
    return data[stkPtr - 1];
}

int StackImp::size() const
{
    return stkPtr;
}
```

- Except in the context of sizeof and &, an array name becomes a pointer to its first element
- There are no multidimensional arrays, only arrays of arrays
- The mere existence of a pointer does not require the availability of the implementation of its referent type (this is an *incomplete type*).

If you understand these concepts, you are on your way to becoming a responsible C++ programmer. Now go tell your boss she can trust you to write real programs.

Answers to Exercises

Ex. 2.1. Given the declarations

```
int a[] = {10,15,4,25,3,-4};
int *p = &a[2];
```

what is the result of each of the following expressions?

```
a. *(p + 1)      25
b. p[-1]         15
c. p - a          2
d. a[*p++]        3
e. *(a + a[2])    3
```

Ex. 2.2. The following statements modify the string s through a sequence of pointer expressions. What character is retrieved by each expression when executed in succession, and what is the final value of s?

```
char s[] = "desolate", *p = s;

*p++     == d
*(p++)   == e
(*p)++   == s
*++p     == o
*(++p)   == l
++*p     == m
++(*p)   == n

strcmp(s,"detonate") == 0
```

Ex. 2.3

Expression	Type	Value[1]
a	array of 2 arrays of 3 arrays of 4 arrays of 5 ints	0x0
a + 1	pointer to array of 3 arrays of 4 arrays of 5 ints	0x0f0
a[1]	array of 3 arrays of 4 arrays of 5 ints	0x0f0
a[1] + 1	pointer to array of 4 arrays of 5 ints	0x140
a[1][1]	array of 4 arrays of 5 ints	0x140
a[1][1] + 1	pointer to array of 5 ints	0x154
a[1][1][1]	array of 5 ints	0x154
a[1][1][1] + 1	pointer to int	0x158
a[1][1][1][1]	int	6

[1]Hexadecimal values are address offsets relative to a.

```
0x0f0 == 240
0x140 == 320
0x154 == 340
0x158 == 344
```

The Preprocessor

Before a compiler begins the usual chores of syntax checking and instruction translation, it submits your program to a preliminary phase called *pre-processing*, which alters the text of the program that the compiler sees according to your instructions. The altered text that the compiler sees is called a *translation unit*. In particular, the preprocessor performs the following three functions for you:

1. Header/source file inclusion
2. Macro expansion
3. Conditional compilation.

The #include Directive

One of the first source lines any C programmer sees or composes is

```
#include <stdio.h>
```

If you're feeling adventurous, take a moment right now and jot down everything you know about this statement.

Let's see how you did. Of course stdio.h is a standard library *header*, so-called because such directives usually appear near the beginning of a source file so that their definitions will be in force throughout the rest of the compilation. We commonly think of it as a header *file*, but there is no requirement that the definitions and declarations in the standard library reside in a file. The C and C++ standards only require that the needed definitions replace the include directive in the text of the program before translation. They could reside in tables internal to the preprocessor. Most PC compilers, for example, install header files in a suitable subdirectory. But implementations are not obliged to supply header information in physical files, nor need they name the files after the include directive. How, for instance, can a compiler supply a file named `stdio.h` on a platform whose file system doesn't allow periods in a file name?

Conforming compilers also support include directives delimited by quotation marks:

```
#include "mydefs.h"
```

The string must represent a name recognized by the local file system. The corresponding file must be a valid C/C++ source file, and, like the standard headers, should contain class declarations, function prototypes, macro definitions, and other declarations. An implementation must document the mechanism it uses to locate the requested source file. On platforms with hierarchical file systems, most compilers search the current directory first, and failing that, try the same place where the standard headers are. Because standard header names are special preprocessing tokens and not strings, any backslashes in a header name are not escape characters:

```
#include <sys\stat.h>                   /* \, not \\ */
#include "\project\include\mydefs.h"    /* ditto */
```

Included files may themselves contain other include directives, nested up to an implementation-defined limit (check your documentation). Since some definitions, such as `typedef`s, must only appear once during a compilation, you must guard against the possibility of a file being included more than once. The customary technique is to define a symbol associated with the file and to exclude the text of the file from the compilation if the symbol has already been seen by the compiler:

```
// mydefs.h
#ifndef MYDEFS_H
#define MYDEFS_H

<declarations/definitions go here>

#endif
```

Other Preprocessor Directives

As you can see, there's more to the `#include` directive than meets the eye. There are eleven other preprocessor directives you can use to alter your source text in meaningful ways (see Table 3.1). All begin with the # character, which must be the first nonspace character on its source line.

The `#define` directive creates *macro* definitions. A macro is a name for a sequence of zero or more preprocessing tokens. Valid preprocessing tokens include valid C++ language tokens like identifiers, strings, numbers, and operators, preprocessing directives, header names, and any single character. For example, the line

```
#define MAXLINES 500
```

Table 3.1   Preprocessor directives

Directive	Description
`#include`	Includes text of header or source file.
`#define`	Enters a symbol into the symbol table for the current compilation unit, with an optional value.
`#undef`	Removes a symbol from the symbol table.

`#if`
`#elif`
`#else`
`#endif`
	Control flow directives for conditional compilation.

`#ifdef` `#ifndef`	Symbol table query directives. (Also used for conditional compilation).
`#error`	Prints a message to `stderr` and aborts.
`#line`	Renumbers the current source line. Utilities, such as code generators, use this to synchronize generated lines with original source lines in error messages.
`#pragma`	Compiler-dependent actions.

associates the text "500" (without the quotes) with the symbol MAXLINES. The preprocessor keeps a table of all symbols created by the #define directive, along with the corresponding replacement text. Whenever it encounters the token MAXLINES outside of a comment or a quoted string, it replaces it with the token 500. It is important to remember that this is *text replacement*. In later phases of compilation it appears to the compiler as if you actually typed 500 instead of MAXLINES. No semantic analysis occurs during preprocessing.

A macro without parameters like MAXLINES above is sometimes called an *object-like* macro, because it defines a program constant that looks like an object. Because object-like macros are like constants, it is customary to type them in upper case as a hint to the reader. There is little reason to define object-like macros, however. You should use const variable definitions instead. The statement

```
const int MAXLINES = 500;
```

has a couple of advantages over

```
#define MAXLINES 500
```

Since the compiler knows the semantics of the object, you get stronger compile-time type checking. You can also inspect const objects with a symbolic debugger. Global const objects have internal linkage unless you explicitly declare them extern, so you can safely replace all your object-like macros with const definitions.

You can also define *function-like* macros with zero or more parameters, such as

```
#define beep()    putc('\a',stderr)
#define abs(x)    ((x) >= 0 ? (x) : (-(x)))
#define max(x,y) (((x) > (y)) ? (x) : (y))
```

There must be no whitespace between the macro name and the first left parenthesis. The expression

```
abs(-4)
```

expands to

```
((-4) >= 0 ? (-4) : (-(-4)))
```

just as if you had typed it that way. It is important that macro parameters (like x above) are parenthesized in the replacement text. This avoids precedence surprises with complex argument expressions. For example, if you had naively used the mathematical definition for absolute value without parentheses:

```
x >= 0 ? x : -x
```

then the expression abs(a - 1) would expand to

```
a - 1 >= 0 ? a - 1 : -a - 1
```

which is incorrect when a - 1 < 0 (it should be -(a - 1)).

Even if you put parentheses around all arguments, you should also parenthesize the entire replacement expression as well to avoid surprises with respect to the surrounding text. To see this, define abs without outer parentheses:

```
#define abs(x) (x) >= 0 ? (x) : (-x)
```

Then abs(a) - 1 expands to

```
(a) >= 0 ? (a) : -(a) - 1
```

which is incorrect when a is nonnegative (the –1 is lost).

It is also dangerous to use expressions with side effects as macro arguments. For example, the macro call abs(i++) expands to

```
((i++) >= 0 ? (i++) : (-(i++)))
```

No matter what the value of i happens to be, it gets incremented twice, not once, which probably isn't what you had in mind.

Function-like macros are *almost* unnecessary in C++. You can replace most function-like macros with inline functions. For example, replace the max macro above with

```
inline int max(int x, int y)
{
    return x >= y ? x : y;
}
```

You don't have to worry about parenthesizing to avoid precedence surprises, because this is a real function with scope and type checking. You also don't have to worry about side effects like you do with macros, such as in the call

```
max(x++,y++)
```

But the macro version has the advantage of being able to accept arguments of any type, you say? No problem. Define max as a template instead:

```
template<class T>
inline int max(const T& x, const T& y)
{
    return x > y ? x : y;
}
```

This function template and many others appear in the standard header <algorithm>.

Do keep in mind that inline is only a *hint* to the compiler. Not all functions are amenable to inlining, especially those with loops and complicated control structures. Your compiler may tell you when it can't inline a function. In most cases, it is still better to define a function out of line than it is to define it as a macro and lose the type safety that a real function affords.

Predefined Macros

Conforming implementations supply the built-in object-like macros in Table 3.2. The last three remain constant during the compilation of a source file. Any other predefined macros that a compiler provides must begin with a leading underscore, followed by either an uppercase letter or another underscore. C translators also define __STDC__, which is nonzero when compiling in standard mode. Most compilers provide multiple modes of compilation, some of which are not standard conforming. You may not redefine any of these macros with the #define directive, nor remove them with the #undef directive. Listing 3.1 illustrates these macros on a sample platform.

Conforming compilers also provide a function-like macro, assert, which you can use to put diagnostics in programs. If its argument evaluates to zero, assert prints the argument along with the source file and line (using __FILE__ and __LINE__) to standard error and aborts the program (see Listing 3.2).

A C compiler is allowed to provide macro versions for any functions in the standard C library (e.g., getc and putc usually come as macros for efficiency). Except for a handful of required function-like macros (viz., assert, setjmp, va_arg, va_end, and va_start), an

Table 3.2　Predefined macros

Macro	Value
__LINE__	The number of the current source line (equal to the number of newline characters read so far)
__FILE__	The name of the source file
__DATE__	The date of translation in the form "Mmm dd yyyy"
__TIME__	The time of translation in the form "hh:mm:ss"
__cplusplus	A long containing the date of the official C++ standard

Listing 3.1　Prints the predefined macros

```
// sysmac.cpp:  Print system macros
#include <iostream>
using namespace std;

main()
{
    cout << "__DATE__ == " << __DATE__ << endl;
    cout << "__FILE__ == " << __FILE__ << endl;
    cout << "__LINE__ == " << __LINE__ << endl;
    cout << "__TIME__ == " << __TIME__ << endl;
}


// Output:
__DATE__ == Nov 28 1996
__FILE__ == sysmac.cpp
__LINE__ == 7
__TIME__ == 09:37:38
```

implementation must supply true function versions for all functions in the standard C library. A macro version of a library function in effect hides its prototype from the compiler, so its arguments are not type checked during translation. To force the true function to be called, remove the macro definition with the #undef directive, for example

```
#undef getc
```

Alternatively, you can surround the function name in parentheses when you call it:

```
c = (getc)(stdin);
```

Listing 3.2   Illustrates an assertion failure

```
// fail.cpp
#include <iostream>
#include <cassert>
using namespace std;

main()
{
    int i = 0;
    assert(i > 0);
}

// Output:
C:>fail
Assertion failed: i > 0, file fail.cpp, line 8

Abnormal program termination
```

This cannot match the macro definition because a left parenthesis does not immediately follow the function name. Whether global functions in the standard C++ library are defined as `inline` or not is implementation defined.

Conditional Compilation

You can selectively include or exclude segments of code with conditional directives. The `#if` directive is handy when you want to comment-out long passages of code. You can't just wrap such sections in a single, enclosing comment, because they may contain C-style comments in the code itself, causing the outer comment to end prematurely. It is better to make the code in question the subject of an `#if` directive that always evaluates to 0:

```
#if 0
<put code to be ignored here>
#endif
```

The target of an `#if` directive must evaluate to an integer constant, and it obeys the usual C rule that nonzero means true, zero false. You cannot use casts or the `sizeof` operator in such expressions.

If you code in a mixed C/C++ environment, you know that you can link new C++ code with old C code. All you need to do is tell the C++ translator, via the `extern "C"` linkage specification, not to "mangle" the external names that match those in the C modules; for example,

```
extern "C" void f();       // f() was compiled under C conventions
```

The C portion of the standard C++ library needs to know whether to mangle names or not (explained in Chap. 1), depending on which mode you're compiling in (C or C++). If you peruse your standard C header files, you will notice that your vendor uses the __cplusplus macro to conditionally wrap standard C declarations with an extern "C" block according to the following pattern:

```
#if defined(__cplusplus)
extern "C"
{
#endif

<C declarations go here>

#if defined(__cplusplus)
}
endif
```

Preprocessing Operators

Sometimes you just want to know if a macro is defined, without using its value. For example, if you only support two compilers, you might have something like the following in your code:

```
#if defined(_MSCVER)
<put Microsoft-specific statements here>
#elif defined(__BCPLUSPLUS__)
<put Borland-specific statements here>
#else
#error Compiler not supported.
#endif
```

The defined operator evaluates to one if its target is present in the symbol table, which means that it was either the subject of a previous #define directive or the compiler provided it as a built-in macro. The #error directive prints its message to stderr and halts the translation process. It isn't necessary to assign a macro a value. For example, to insert debug trace output into your program, you can do the following:

```
#if defined(DEBUG)
fprintf(stderr,"x = %d\n",x);
#endif
```

To define the DEBUG macro, just insert the following statement before the first use of the macro:

```
#define DEBUG
```

The following equivalences exist:

```
#if defined(X)      <==>      #ifdef X
#if !defined(X)     <==>      #ifndef X
```

Table 3.3 Preprocessing operators

Operator	Usage
#	Stringizing
##	Token pasting
defined	Symbol table query

The defined operator is more flexible than the equivalent directives on the right because you can combine multiple tests as a single expression:

```
#if defined(__cplusplus) && !defined(DEBUG)
```

The defined operator is one of three preprocessor operators (see Table 3.3).

The operator #, the *stringizing* operator, encloses a macro argument in quotes. As the program in Listing 3.3 illustrates, this can be useful for debugging. The trace macro encloses its arguments in quotes so they become part of a printf format statement. For example, the expression trace(i,d) becomes

```
printf("i" " = %" "d" "\n",i);
```

Listing 3.3 Illustrates the stringizing operator

```
/* trace.c: Illustrate a trace macro for debugging */

#include <stdio.h>

#define trace(x,format) \
    printf(#x " = %" #format "\n",x)

main()
{
    int i = 1;
    float x = 2.0;
    char *s = "three";

    trace(i,d);
    trace(x,f);
    trace(s,s);
}

/* Output:
i = 1
x = 2.000000
s = three
*/
```

and, after the compiler concatenates adjacent string literals, it sees this:

```
printf("i = %d\n",i);
```

There is no way to build quoted strings like this without the stringizing operator, because the preprocessor ignores macros inside quoted strings. The *token-pasting* operator ## concatenates two tokens together to form a single token. The call trace2(1) in Listing 3.4 is translated into

```
trace(x1,d)
```

Any space surrounding these two operators is ignored.

Implementing `assert`

Implementing assert reveals an important fact about macros. Since the action of assert depends on the result of a test, you might first try an if statement:

```
#define assert(cond) \
if (!(cond)) __assert(#cond,__FILE__,__LINE__)
```

Listing 3.4   Illustrates the token-pasting operator

```
/* trace2.cpp: Illustrate a trace macro for debugging */
#include <stdio.h>

#define trace(x,format) \
    printf(#x " = %" #format "\n",x)
#define trace2(i) trace(x ## i,d)

main()
{
    int x1 = 1, x2 = 2, x3 = 3;
    trace2(1);
    trace2(2);
    trace2(3);
}

/* Output:
x1 = 1
x2 = 2
x3 = 3
*/
```

where the function __assert prints the message and halts the program. This causes a problem, however, when assert finds itself within an if statement:

```
if (x > 0)
    assert(x != y);
else
    /* whatever */
```

because it expands into

```
if (x > 0)
    if (!(x != y)) __assert("x != y","file.c",7);
else
    /* whatever */
```

The indentation is misleading because the second if intercepts the else:

```
if (x > 0)
    if (!(x != y))
        __assert("x != y","file.c",7);
    else        /* OOPS! New control flow! */
        /* whatever */
```

The usual fix for nested if problems like this is to use braces:

```
#define assert(cond) \
    {if (!(cond)) __assert(#cond,__FILE__,__LINE__)}
```

but this expands into

```
if (x > 0)
    {if (!(x != y)) __assert("x != y","file.c",7)};
else
    /* whatever */
```

and the combination }; in the second line creates a null statement that completes the outer if, leaving a dangling else, which is a syntax error. The correct way to define assert is in Listings 3.5 and 3.6. In general, when a macro must make a choice, it is good practice to write it as an expression and not as a statement.

Macro Magic

If you don't understand precisely what steps the preprocessor follows to expand macros, you can be in for some mysterious surprises. For example, if you insert the following line near the beginning of Listing 3.4

```
#define x1 SURPRISE!
```

then `trace2(1)` is expanded into

`trace(x ## 1,d)`

which in turn becomes

`trace(x1,d)`

But the preprocessor doesn't stop there. It *rescans* the line to see if any other macros need expanding. The final state of the program text that the compiler sees is in Listing 3.7.

To further illustrate, consider the text in Listing 3.8. It is not a complete program, by the way, but is for preprocessing only—don't try to compile it all the way. (If you have Borland C++ you can use the CPP command.) The output from the preprocessor appears in Listing 3.9. The `str` macro just puts quotes around its argument. It might appear that `xstr` is redundant,

Listing 3.5   An implementation of the `assert` macro (no NDEBUG stuff)

```
/* assert.h */
#ifndef ASSERT_H
#define ASSERT_H

extern void __assert(char *, char *, long);

#define assert(cond) \
    ((cond)        \
       ? (void) 0  \
       : __assert(#cond,__FILE__,__LINE__))

#endif
```

Listing 3.6   The `__assert` support function

```
/* xassert.c */
#include <stdio.h>
#include <stdlib.h>

void __assert(char *cond, char *fname, long lineno)
{
    fprintf(stderr,
            "Assertion failed: %s, file %s, line %ld\n",
            cond,fname,lineno);
    abort();
}
```

Listing 3.7 Preprocessed source with a surprise

```
main()
{
int SURPRISE! = 1, x2 = 2, x3 = 3;
printf("x1" " = %" "d" "\n",SURPRISE!);
printf("x2" " = %" "d" "\n",x2);
printf("x3" " = %" "d" "\n",x3);
return 0;
}
```

Listing 3.8 Illustrates macro rescanning

```
/* preproc.c: Test # and ## preprocessing operators
 *
 * NOTE:   DO NOT COMPILE! Preprocess only!
 */

/* Handy stringizing macros */
#define str(s) #s
#define xstr(s) str(s)

/* Handy token-pasting macros */
#define glue(a,b) a##b
#define xglue(a,b) glue(a,b)

/* Some definitions */
#define ID(x) "This is version " ## xstr(x)
#define INCFILE(x) xstr(glue(version,x)) ".h"
#define VERSION 2
#define ION ATILE

/* Expand some macros */
str(VERSION)
xstr(VERSION)
glue(VERSION,3)
xglue(VERSION,3)
glue(VERS,ION)
xglue(VERS,ION)

/* Expand some more */
ID(VERSION)
INCFILE(VERSION)
str(INCFILE(VERSION))
xstr(INCFILE(VERSION))
```

Listing 3.9 Preprocessed results from Listing 3.8

```
"VERSION"
"2"
VERSION3
23
2
VERSATILE

"This is version ""2"
"version2" ".h"
"INCFILE(VERSION)"
"\"version2\" \".h\""
```

but there is an important difference between it and `str`. The output of the statement `str(VERSION)` is, of course,

```
"VERSION"
```

but `xstr(VERSION)` expands to

```
str(2)
```

because arguments not connected with a # or ## are *fully expanded* before they replace their respective parameters. Then the statement is rescanned, giving "2". So in effect, `xstr` is a version of `str` that expands its argument before quoting it.

The same relationship exists between `glue` and `xglue`. The statement `glue(VERSION,3)` concatenates its arguments into the token `VERSION3`, but `xglue(VERSION,3)` first expands `VERSION`, giving

```
glue(2,3)
```

which in turn rescans into the token 23. The next two statements are a little trickier:

```
     glue(VERS,ION)
==   VERS ## ION
==   VERSION
==   2
```

and

```
     xglue(VERS,ION)
==   glue(VERS,ATILE)
==   VERS ## ATILE
==   VERSATILE
```

Of course, if VERSATILE were a defined macro it would expand further. The last four statements in Listing 3.8 expand as follows:

```
      ID(VERSION)
==    "This is version "xstr(2)
==    "This is version "str(2)
==    "This is version ""2"

      INCFILE(VERSION)
==    xstr(glue(version,2)) ".h"
==    xstr(version2) ".h"
==    "version2" ".h"

      str(INCFILE(VERSION))
==    #INCFILE(VERSION)
==    "INCFILE(VERSION)"

      xstr(INCFILE(VERSION))
==    str("version2" ".h")
==    #"version2" ".h"
==    "\"version2\" \".h\""
```

For obvious reasons, the # operator inserts escape characters before all embedded quotes and backslashes.

The macro replacement facilities of the preprocessor clearly offer you an incredible amount of flexibility (too much, some would say). There are two limitations to keep in mind:

1. If at any time the preprocessor encounters the current macro in its own replacement text, no matter how deeply nested in the process, it does not expand it but leaves it as is (otherwise the process would never terminate!). For example, given the definitions

```
#define F(f)  f(args)
#define args  a,b
```

   F(g) expands to g(a,b), but what does F(F) expand to? (Answer: F(a,b)).
2. If a fully expanded statement resembles a preprocessing directive (e.g., if after expansion the result is an #include directive), it is *not* invoked, but left verbatim in the program text. (Thank goodness!)

Character Sets, Trigraphs, and Digraphs

The character set you use to compose your program doesn't have to be the same as the one in which the program runs. This is certainly true of non-English applications. A C translator only understands English alphanumerics, the graphics characters used for operators and punctuators (there are 29 of them), and a few control characters (newline, horizontal tab, vertical tab, and form-feed). This is the *basic source character set*. The *execution character set* is implementation-defined, but must contain characters representing alert ('\a'), backspace ('\b'), carriage return ('\r'), and newline ('\n').

A C++ translator must also accept *universal character names*, which appear in source text as one of the following:

```
\uNNNN
\UNNNNNNNN
```

where the Ns represent a hexadecimal digit. The first form corresponds to the ISO 10646 encoding 0000NNNN (i.e., Unicode with leading zeros), and the second to NNNNNNNN.

Many non-U.S. keyboards do not support some of the elements of the basic source character set, making it difficult to write C programs. To overcome this obstacle, standard C defined a number of *trigraphs*, which are triplets of characters from the Invariant Code Set (ISO 646-1983) found in virtually every environment in the western world. Each trigraph corresponds to a

Table 3.4   Trigraph sequences

Trigraph	C source character
??	#
??(	[
??/	\
??)	]
??'	^
??<	{
??!	|
??>	}
??-	~

Listing 3.10   A "Hello, world!" program

```c
/* hello.c: Greet either the user or the world */
#include <stdio.h>

main(int argc, char *argv[])
{
    if (argc > 1 && argv[1] != NULL)
        printf("Hello, %s!\n",argv[1]);
    else
        printf("Hello, world!\n");
    return 0;
}
```

Listing 3.11   "Hello, World!" using trigraphs

```c
/* hello2.c:  Greeting program using trigraphs */
#include <stdio.h>

main(int argc, char *argv??(??))
??<
    if (argc > 1 && argv??(1??) != NULL)
        printf("Hello, %s!??/n",argv??(1??));
    else
        printf("Hello, world!??/n");
    return 0;
??>
```

character in the source character set which is not in ISO 646 (see Table 3.4). For example, whenever the preprocessor encounters the token ??= anywhere in your source text (even in strings), it replaces it with the encoding for the # character. The program in Listing 3.11 shows how to write the "Hello, world!" program from Listing 3.10 using trigraphs.

In an effort to enable more readable programs worldwide, C++ defines a set of *digraphs* and new reserved words for non-ASCII developers (see Table 3.5). Listing 3.12 shows what "Hello, world" looks like using these new tokens. Perhaps you agree that the symmetrical look of the bracketing operators is easier on the eye than trigraphs.

Table 3.5   New C++ digraphs and reserved words

Token	Translation
<%	{
%>	}
<:	[
:>	]
%%	#
bitand	&
and	&&
bitor	|
or	||
xor	^
compl	~
and_eq	&=
or_eq	|=
xor_eq	^=
not	!
not_eq	!=

Listing 3.12 "Hello, World!" with the new C++ digraphs and tokens

```
// hello3.cpp:  Greeting program using C++ digraphs
#include <cstdio>
using namespace std;

main(int argc, char *argv<::>)
<%
    if (argc > 1 and argv<:1:> != NULL)
        printf("Hello, %s!??/n",argv<:1:>);
    else
        printf("Hello, world!??/n");
    return 0;
%>
```

Phases of Translation

Standard C and C++ define nine distinct phases of translation. An implementation doesn't necessarily make nine separate passes through the code, of course, but the result of translation must
behave as if it had. The nine phases are:

1. Physical source characters are mapped into the source character set. This includes trigraph replacement and things like mapping a carriage return/linefeed to a single newline
   character in MSDOS environments. In C++ programs, any character not in the basic
   source character set is replaced by its universal character name.
2. All lines that end in a backslash are merged with their continuation line, and the backslash is deleted.
3. The source is parsed into preprocessing tokens, and comments are replaced with a single
   space character. The C++ digraphs are recognized as tokens.
4. Preprocessing directives are invoked and macros are expanded. Steps 1 through 4 are
   repeated for any included files recursively.
5. Source characters, escape sequences in character constants, and universal character
   names are mapped to members of the execution character set (e.g., '\a' would be converted to a byte value of 7 in an ASCII environment).
6. Adjacent string literals are concatenated.
7. Traditional compilation: lexical and semantic analysis, and translation to assembly or
   machine code.
8. (C++ only) Any pending template instantiations are performed.
9. Linking: external references are resolved and a program image is made ready for
   execution.

The preprocessor consists of Steps 1 through 4.

Summary

- The preprocessor doesn't understand the programming language
- Headers don't have to be files
- Remember to thoroughly parenthesize macros
- Prefer inline functions over function-like macros (except for stringizing and token pasting)
- Prefer `const` values over object-like macros
- Use the `assert` macro to catch conceptual errors that shouldn't happen
- Conditionally compile headers with a special macro (to avoid recursive inclusion)
- C and C++ support trigraphs for international keyboards. C++ supports more readable digraphs and other reserved words.

The Standard C Library, Part I

For the Adequate Programmer

Although it may not seem like it, C is a very small language. In fact, it was first implemented on a platform very small by today's standards. My first C compiler ran on a Commodore 64! C's simplicity and compactness make it ideal for systems programming and for developing programs that run in *embedded* systems, such as in automobiles or cameras.

A key difference between C in such freestanding environments and in a *hosted* environment, such as a desktop or midrange computer, is the presence of the standard C library. In a freestanding environment, a conforming compiler need only provide the types and macros specified in <float.h>, <limits.h>, <stdarg.h>, and <stddef.h>. Programmers who work on typical data processing projects take the library for granted; in fact, they think of it as part of the language. A large portion of everyday C code consists of library calls. Even I/O facilities like printf and scanf are part of the library, not the language.

The standard C library consists of functions, type definitions, and macros declared in fifteen header files. Each header more or less represents a domain of programming functionality, such as I/O or string-processing operations. Some macros and type definitions, such as NULL and size_t, appear in more than one header file for convenience. An unsigned integer type, size_t can hold the result of the sizeof operator and is suitable for array indices.

I like to divide the standard library into three groups (see Tables 4.1–4.3). Group I represents library components you should know thoroughly if you want to consider yourself a C programmer. Too often I have seen programs that "reinvent" basic library facilities, such as memcpy or strchr. To receive your paycheck in good conscience, though, you should really master Group II as well. And although you may need the functions in Group III only once in a blue moon, you should be familiar enough with them that you know how to use them when the need arises.

Table 4.1 Standard C headers: Group I (required knowledge for every C programmer)

`<ctype.h>`	Character handling
`<stdio.h>`	Input/Output
`<stdlib.h>`	Miscellaneous utilities
`<string.h>`	Text processing

Table 4.2 Standard C headers: Group II (tools for the professional)

`<assert.h>`	Assertion support for defensive programming
`<limits.h>`	System parameters for integer arithmetic
`<stddef.h>`	Universal types and constants
`<time.h>`	Time processing

Table 4.3 Standard C headers: Group III (power at your fingertips when you need it)

`<errno.h>`	Error detection
`<float.h>`	System parameters for real arithmetic
`<locale.h>`	Cultural adaptation
`<math.h>`	Mathematical functions
`<setjmp.h>`	Nonlocal branching
`<signal.h>`	Interrupt handling (sort of)
`<stdarg.h>`	Variable-length argument lists

I amply illustrate the standard C library throughout this book. Chapters 4 through 6 give an overview of the C library, bring to light some of the functions you may have overlooked, and reveal some behavior you may not be aware of. When a more detailed treatment suggests itself, I refer you to other chapters instead of repeating the material here. For a comprehensive reference of the standard C library, there is nothing better than P. J. Plauger's *The Standard C Library* (Prentice-Hall, 1992).

`<ctype.h>`

The functions in `<ctype.h>` support typical operations for handling single characters (see Table 4.4). For example, to determine if a character c is uppercase, use the expression `isupper(c)`. Many oldtime C programs would be peppered with expressions such as

```
('A' <= c && c <= 'Z')
```

instead, which makes poor reading. Putting such an expression in a macro helps, as in

```
#define ISUPPER(c) ('A' <= c & c <= 'Z')
```

Table 4.4   `<ctype.h>` functions

Character testing functions

`isalnum`	alphanumeric (`isalpha` ‖ `isdigit`)
`isalpha`	alphabetic
`iscntrl`	control (beware!)
`isdigit`	'0' through '9'
`isgraph`	visible when printed
`islower`	lowercase alphabetic
`isprint`	`isgraph` ‖ ' '
`ispunct`	`isgraph` && `!isalnum`
`isspace`	whitespace
`isupper`	uppercase alphabetic
`isxdigit`	`isdigit` ‖ 'a' thru 'f' ‖ 'A' thru 'F'

Character mapping functions

`tolower`	convert to lowercase (if applicable)
`toupper`	convert to uppercase (if applicable)

---

but this makes expressions with side effects (such as `ISUPPER(c++)`) unreliable, because its argument gets incremented twice. And of course the test for being between 'A' and 'Z' only gives the desired results with a character set that encodes the alphabet contiguously, such as ASCII. The character classification functions in `<ctype.h>` are safe and portable across all platforms.

It is important to avoid the tendency to assume that ASCII is always the execution character set. For example, ASCII control characters comprise the code 127 and those less than 32, but only seven control characters behave uniformly across all environments: alert ('\a'), backspace ('\b'), carriage return ('\r'), form feed ('\f'), horizontal tab ('\t'), newline ('\n'), and vertical tab ('\v'). The only functions that do not change behavior when you change locale are `isdigit` and `isxdigit`. (See Chap. 6 for more on locales).

Although you can assume that the digits '0' through '9' have contiguous codes in all C execution character sets, the hexadecimal digits, being alphabetic characters, do not. The function `atox` in Listing 4.1 shows how to convert a hexadecimal string to an integer value. Unfortunately, it only works for ASCII-like character sets. The offending line is

```
digit = toupper(*s) - 'A' + 10;
```

There is no guarantee that the expression

```
toupper(*s) - 'A'
```

will give the correct result. The version in Listing 4.2 works on any platform because it stores all hexadecimal digits contiguously in its own array. It searches the array with `strchr` and then uses pointer arithmetic to compute the value of the digit.

Listing 4.1   Converts a hex-string to a number in ASCII environments

```
#include <ctype.h>

long atox(char *s)
{
    long sum;

    /* Skip whitespace */
    while (isspace(*s))
        ++s;

    /* Do the conversion */
    for (sum = 0L; isxdigit(*s); ++s)
    {
        int digit;
        if (isdigit(*s))
            digit = *s - '0';
        else
            digit = toupper(*s) - 'A' + 10;
        sum = sum*16L + digit;
    }
    return sum;
}
```

Listing 4.2   A portable version of Listing 4.1

```
#include <ctype.h>
#include <string.h>

long atox(char *s)
{
    char xdigs[] = "0123456789ABCDEF";
    long sum;

    /* Skip whitespace */
    while (isspace(*s))
        ++s;

    /* Do the conversion */
    for (sum = 0L; isxdigit(*s); ++s)
    {
        int digit = strchr(xdigs,toupper(*s)) - xdigs;
        sum = sum*16L + digit;
    }

    return sum;
}
```

Listing 4.3   Converts a hex-string to a number via `sscanf`

```
#include <stdio.h>

long atox(char *s)
{
    long n = 0L;
    sscanf(s,"%lx",&n);
    return n;
}
```

<stdio.h>

The author of Listings 4.1 and 4.2 could have avoided a lot of trouble if he had only understood scanf formatting a little better. As Listing 4.3 illustrates, the %x format specifier does all the work of reading hexadecimal numbers for you. Unlike the previous two versions, it even handles a leading plus or minus sign. Both scanf and printf are laden with features that so many programmers overlook. (For more detail on these two functions, see Chap. 17.)

The printf/scanf families of functions shown in Table 4.5 perform *formatted I/O*. Furthermore, they provide these facilities for three types of *streams*: standard streams, file streams, and string (i.e., in-memory) streams. Formatting operates identically on the different types of streams, but of necessity the function names and calling sequences are somewhat different.

There are two other classes of input/output facilities provided by the <stdio.h> component of the standard C library: *character I/O* and *block I/O* (see Tables 4.6 and 4.7). The functions in Listing 4.4 and Listing 4.5 copy one file to another using character I/O and block I/O functions, respectively. Note that since fread does not return an error code, I must make an explicit call to ferror to detect a read error.

Table 4.5   Functions for formatted I/O defined in <stdio.h>

Fixed-length argument lists	
scanf	standard input
fscanf	file input
sscanf	in-core input
printf	standard output
fprintf	file output
sprintf	in-core output
Variable-length argument lists	
vprintf	standard output
vfprintf	file output
vsprintf	in-core output

Table 4.6 Character I/O functions in `<stdio.h>`

Single-character processing functions

getchar	standard input
getc	file input
ungetc	affects file input
fgetc	file input
putchar	standard output
putc	file output
fputc	file output

String processing functions

gets	standard input
fgets	file input
puts	standard output
fputs	file output

Table 4.7 Other `<stdio.h>` functions

Block I/O	*File positioning*
fread	fgetpos
fwrite	fsetpos
	fseek
Operations via filename	ftell
remove	rewind
rename	
	Error handling
Temporary files	clearerr
tmpfile	feof
tmpnam	ferror
File access functions	
fopen	
freopen	
fclose	
fflush	
setbuf	
setvbuf	

As Table 4.7 illustrates, `<stdio.h>` provides functions for file positioning. The time-worn functions `fseek` and `ftell` only work reliably on files opened in binary mode and are limited to positions that can be represented by a long integer. To overcome these limitations, the ANSI committee invented `fgetpos` and `fsetpos`, which use the platform-dependent abstract type `fpos_t` as a file position indicator (see Table 4.8).

Listing 4.4   A function that copies a file via byte I/O. Returns EOF on error.

```
/* copy1.c */
#include <stdio.h>

int copy(FILE *dest, FILE *source)
{
    int c;

    while ((c = getc(source)) != EOF)
        if (putc(c,dest) == EOF)  /* output error */
            return EOF;
    return 0;
}
```

Listing 4.5   A function that copies a file via block I/O

```
/* copy2.c */
#include <stdio.h>

int copy(FILE *dest, FILE *source)
{
    size_t count;
    static char buf[BUFSIZ];

    while (!feof(source))
    {
        count = fread(buf,1,BUFSIZ,source);
        if (ferror(source))
            return EOF;
        if (fwrite(buf,1,count,dest) != count)
            return EOF;
    }
    return 0;
}
```

The program outlined in Listing 4.6 puts the file-positioning functions to good use in a simple four-way scrolling browser for large files. It only keeps one screen's worth of text in memory. If you want to scroll up or down through the file, it reads (or rereads) the adjacent text and displays it. When scrolling down (i.e., forward) through the file, the file position of the data on the screen is pushed on a stack, and the program reads the next screenful from the current file position. To scroll up, it retrieves the file position of the previous screen from the stack. Chapter 19 has a complete version of the program and illustrates file I/O in greater detail.

Table 4.8   Types and macros defined in `<stdio.h>`

Types

`FILE`	Encapsulates file access info
`fpos_t`	File Position (returned by `fgetpos`)

Macros

`NULL`	Zero pointer
`EOF`	Special value representing end-of-file
`BUFSIZ`	Preferred stream buffer size
`FOPEN_MAX`	Max # of files open simultaneously
`FILENAME_MAX`	Max # of characters in a file name minus 1
`L_tmpnam`	Max # of characters in a tempfile name minus 1
`TMP_MAX`	Max # of distinct filenames returned from `tmpnam`
`SEEK_CUR`	Signals `fseek` to seek relative to current position
`SEEK_END`	Signals `fseek` to seek from end-of-file
`SEEK_SET`	Signals `fseek` to seek from start-of-file

Listing 4.6   Outline of a file-viewing program that illustrates file positioning

```
/* view.c: A simple 4-way-scrolling file browser */

/* cls(), display(), read_a_screen() omitted... */

main(int argc, char *argv[])
{
    fpos_t top_pos, stk_[MAXSTACK];
    /* Details omitted... */

top:
    /* Display initial screen */
    rewind(f);
    fgetpos(f,&top_pos);
    /* Details omitted... */

    for (;;)
    {
        switch(c = toupper(getchar()))
        {
            case 'D':  /* Display the next screen */
                if (!feof(f))
                {
                    PUSH(top_pos);
                    fgetpos(f,&top_pos);
                    read_a_screen(f);
                    display(file);
                }
                break;
```
continued

Listing 4.6   (continued)

```
            case 'U':  /* Display the previous screen */
                if (stkptr_ > 0)
                {
                    top_pos = POP();
                    fsetpos(f,&top_pos);
                    read_a_screen(f);
                    display(file);
                }
                break;

            case 'T':  /* Display first screen */
                stkptr_ = 0;
                goto top;

            case 'B':  /* Display last screen */
                while (!feof(f))
                {
                    PUSH(top_pos);
                    fgetpos(f,&top_pos);
                    read_a_screen(f);
                }
                display(file);
                break;

            case 'Q':  /* Quit */
                cls();
                return EXIT_SUCCESS;
        }
        /* Details omitted... */
    }
}
```

<stdlib.h>

The header <stdlib.h> is a bit of a catchall. It defines types, macros, and functions for memory management, sorting and searching, integer arithmetic, string-to-number conversions, sequences of pseudorandom numbers, interfacing with the environment, and converting multibyte strings and characters to and from wide character representations (see Table 4.9). The program in Listing 4.7 uses all four memory management functions to sort a text file. Whenever its array of pointers to char fills up, it expands it with realloc, which preserves the original contents. (See Chap. 20 for an in-depth treatment of memory management.)

Table 4.9 `<stdlib.h>` declarations

Types

`div_t`	structure returned by `div`
`ldiv_t`	structure returned by `ldiv`

Constants

`NULL`	
`EXIT_FAILURE`	Portable error code for `exit`
`EXIT_SUCCESS`	Portable success code for `exit`
`RAND_MAX`	Max value returned by `rand`
`MB_CUR_MAX`	Max # of bytes in a multibyte character

String conversion functions

`atof`	`strtod`
`atoi`	`strtol`
`atol`	`strtoul`

Random number functions

`rand`	Returns the next pseudorandom number
`srand`	"Seeds" the sequence of pseudorandom numbers

Memory management

`calloc`	`realloc`
`malloc`	`free`

Interface to the environment

`abort`	`getenv`
`atexit`	`system`
`exit`	

Searching and sorting

`bsearch`
`qsort`

Integer arithmetic

`abs`	`labs`
`div`	`ldiv`

Multibyte character functions

`mblen`	`mbctowcs`
`mbtowc`	`wcstombs`
`wctomb`	

Listing 4.7   Sorts files as large as available memory

```
/* sort.c */
#include <stdio.h>
#include <assert.h>
#include <stdlib.h>
#include <string.h>

#define MAXLINES 512

int comp(const void *, const void *);

main()
{
    int i;
    size_t nlines, maxlines = MAXLINES;
    static char s[BUFSIZ];
    char **lines = calloc(maxlines, sizeof(char *));

    /* Read file */
    for (nlines = 0; fgets(s,BUFSIZ,stdin); ++nlines)
    {
        if (nlines == maxlines)
        {
            /* Grow array another MAXLINES */
            size_t tlines
            maxlines += MAXLINES;
            lines = realloc(lines,maxlines*sizeof(char *));
            assert(tlines);
            lines = tlines;
        }

        /* Store this line */
        lines[nlines] = malloc(strlen(s)+1);
        assert(lines[nlines]);
        strcpy(lines[nlines],s);
    }

    /* Sort */
    qsort(lines,nlines,sizeof lines[0],comp);

    /* Print; free memory */
    for (i = 0; i < nlines; ++i)
    {
        fputs(lines[i],stdout);
        fflush(stdout);
        assert(!ferror(stdout));
        free(lines[i]);
    }
```

Listing 4.7 (continued)

```
        free(lines);
        return 0;
}

/* Compare function for qsort(): */
int comp(const void *p1, const void *p2)
{
        return strcmp(* (const char **) p1, * (const char **) p2);
}
```

The qsort function can sort an array of any type, even user-defined structures. Through its four parameters you tell qsort:

1. Where to find the array
2. How many elements there are
3. How big each element is, and
4. How to compare them

The fourth parameter is a function that takes two pointers, and returns a number that is negative if the item the first pointer refers to precedes the second, a positive number if the opposite is true, and 0 otherwise. The following program sorts an array of integers:

```
/* qsort.c: Illustrates qsort */

#include <stdlib.h>
#include <stdio.h>

int comp(const void*, const void*);

main()
{
        int i;
        int a[] = {34,75,78,123,98};
        int n = sizeof a / sizeof a[0];
        qsort(a, n, sizeof a[0], comp);
        for (i = 0; i < n; ++i)
                printf("%d ",a[i]);
        putchar('\n');
        return 0;
}

/* Output:
34 75 78 98 123
*/
```

The compare function, comp, casts the pointers to the correct type and returns their difference:

```
int comp(const void* p1, const void* p2)
{
    const int* pi1 = (const int*) p1;
    const int* pi2 = (const int*) p2;
    return *pi1 - *pi2;
}
```

If you wanted to sort an array of C-style strings, comp might look like the following:

```
int comp(const void* p1, const void* p2)
{
    const char** ps1 = (const char**) p1;
    const char** ps2 = (const char**) p2;
    return strcmp(*ps1, *ps2);
}
```

The search function bsearch searches a sorted list for a key. As with qsort, you supply it with a compare function and it returns a pointer to the array element containing the key (see Listing 4.8).

The program in Listing 4.9 illustrates some of <stdlib.h>'s more obscure functions. It "shuffles" a deck of 52 cards by creating a randomized sequence of the numbers 0 through 51. The srand function "seeds" the pseudorandom generator with the encoding of the current time and date. To determine the suit and denomination that corresponds to a number, I divide the number by 13, the number of cards in each suit. The remainder of this division is the denomination (0 through 12, corresponding to ace through king), and the quotient represents the suit as follows:

```
0 = clubs
1 = diamonds
2 = hearts
3 = spades
```

Listing 4.8 Searches a sorted array of records with the bsearch function

```
/* search.c */
#include <stdio.h>
#include <stdlib.h>
#include <string.h>

struct person
{
    char last[16];
    char first[11];
    char phone[13];
    int age;
};
```

Listing 4.8   (continued)

```c
static int comp(const void *, const void *);

main()
{
    int i;
    struct person *p;
    static struct person key = {"","","555-1965",0};
    static struct person people[] =
        {{"Ford","Henry","555-1903",98},
         {"Lincoln","Abraham","555-1865",161},
         {"Ford","Edsel","555-1965",53},
         {"Trump","Donald","555-1988",49}};

    /* Sort */
    qsort(people, 4, sizeof people[0], comp);

    /* Search */
    p = bsearch(&key, people, 4, sizeof people[0], comp);
    if (p != NULL)
    {
        printf(
                "%s, %s, %s, %d\n",
                p->last,
                p->first,
                p->phone,
                p->age
                );
    }
    else
        puts("Not found");
    return 0;
}

/* Compare function: key is the phone field */
static int comp(const void *x, const void *y)
{
    struct person *p1 = (struct person *) x;
    struct person *p2 = (struct person *) y;

    return strcmp(p1->phone,p2->phone);
}

/* Output: */
Ford, Edsel, 555-1965, 53
```

Listing 4.9   A card-shuffling program that illustrates the random number and integer division
functions in `<stdlib.h>`

```c
/* deal.c: Deal a hand from a shuffled deck of cards */
#include <stdio.h>
#include <stdlib.h>
#include <string.h>
#include <time.h>

#define DECKSIZE 52
#define SUITSIZE 13

main(int argc, char *argv[])
{
    int ncards = DECKSIZE;   /* Deal full deck by default */
    char deck[DECKSIZE];     /* An array of small integers */
    size_t deckp;
    unsigned int seed;

    /* Get optional hand size */
    if (argc > 1)
        if ((ncards = abs(atoi(argv[1])) % DECKSIZE) == 0)
            ncards = DECKSIZE;

    /* Seed the random number generator with encoding of the
    current time */
    seed = (unsigned int) time(NULL);
    srand(seed);

    /* Shuffle */
    deckp = 0;
    while (deckp < ncards)
    {
        int num = rand() % DECKSIZE;
        if (memchr(deck, num, deckp) == NULL)
            deck[deckp++] = (char) num;
    }

    /* Deal */
    for (deckp = 0; deckp < ncards; ++deckp)
    {
        div_t card = div(deck[deckp], SUITSIZE);
        printf(
                "%c(%c)%c",
                "A23456789TJQK"[card.rem],
                "CDHS"[card.quot],
                (deckp+1) % SUITSIZE ? ' ' : '\n'
            );
    }

    return 0;
}
```

Listing 4.9 (continued)

```
/* Output: */
A(C)  6(S)  7(C)  9(C)  3(H)  6(C)  8(D)  3(C)  6(D)  5(D)  2(H)  A(S)  4(H)
8(C)  8(H)  6(H)  J(S)  7(S)  Q(C)  2(C)  Q(H)  K(H)  4(C)  5(S)  T(H)  Q(S)
9(H)  T(D)  T(S)  9(D)  K(C)  3(S)  J(C)  5(C)  T(C)  K(S)  7(D)  2(D)  4(S)
8(S)  5(H)  A(D)  7(H)  3(D)  Q(D)  A(H)  2(S)  J(D)  9(S)  K(D)  J(H)  4(D)
```

The div function computes the quotient and remainder all at once and stores the result in a structure of type div_t, which has integer members quot and rem.

In some implementations, the functions in the scanf family call strtol to convert character strings to integers. Using strtol directly, however, you can read numbers in any base from 2 to 35, as the program in Listing 4.10 illustrates. Through its second argument, strtol updates nextp so you can progress through the string, converting one number after another. The

Listing 4.10 Uses strtol to read numbers in different bases

```c
#include <stdio.h>
#include <stdlib.h>

main()
{
    char *input = "101 123 45678 90abc g";
    char *nextp = input;
    long bin, oct, dec, hex, beyond;

    bin = strtol(nextp,&nextp,2);
    oct = strtol(nextp,&nextp,8);
    dec = strtol(nextp,&nextp,10);
    hex = strtol(nextp,&nextp,16);
    beyond = strtol(nextp,&nextp,17);

    printf("bin = %ld\n",bin);
    printf("oct = %lo\n",oct);
    printf("dec = %ld\n",dec);
    printf("hex = %lx\n",hex);
    printf("beyond = %ld\n",beyond);
    return 0;
}

/* Output: */
bin = 5
oct = 123
dec = 45678
hex = 90abc
beyond = 16
```

Listing 4.11   An even better version of `atox` using `strtol`

```
#include <stdlib.h>

long atox(char *s)
{
    return strtol(s,NULL,16);
}
```

functions `strtol` and `strtod` behave similarly for `unsigned long` and `double`, respectively. With `strtol` I can write a superior version of the `atox` conversion function, as shown in Listing 4.11.

The familiar functions `exit` and `abort` provide two ways of terminating a program. The function `abort` abruptly halts program execution with no guarantees of any cleanup, such as closing open files. Whenever you call `exit`, program execution also halts, but any open files are closed and all temporary files are deleted, and the integer argument you passed to `exit` is returned to the operating system. In addition `exit` is called if you let execution fall past the end of `main`. The very first thing `exit` does, however, is invoke any *exit handlers* you may have registered with `atexit`, which you do like this:

```
void my_handler();   /* This is your exit handler */
atexit(my_handler);
```

An exit handler must take no arguments and return `void`. Upon normal exit (i.e., return from `main` or a call to `exit`), all of your handlers are called in the reverse order they were registered in. You can register up to 32 exit handlers.

The `getenv` function allows you to query strings in your host environment. For example, to find the current setting of the PATH variable, which is common to many environments, you can do the following:

```
char *path = getenv("PATH");
```

The pointer refers to memory outside of your program, so if you want to keep the current value, you'll have to copy it to a program variable before your next call to `getenv`.

`<string.h>`

The functions defined in `<string.h>` are shown in Table 4.10. All the functions with the `str-` prefix expect null-terminated string arguments, and the `mem`-functions process raw memory. You've already seen `strchr` in Listing 4.2, and its companion `memchr` in Listing 4.9. To transfer raw bytes from one location to another, use `memcpy`—or `memmove`, if the source and destination buffers overlap. Judging by the number of times I've seen `memcpy` "reinvented" in others' code, I believe that it is the most overlooked function in the standard library.

Table 4.10   Functions defined in `<string.h>`

Copying

`memcpy`	`strcpy`
`memmove`	`strncpy`

Concatenation

`strcat`
`strncat`

Comparison

`memcmp`	`strncmp`
`strcmp`	`strxfrm`
`strcoll`	

Search functions

`memchr`	`strrchr`
`strchr`	`strspn`
`strcspn`	`strstr`
`strpbrk`	`strtok`

Miscellaneous

`memset`
`strerror`
`strlen`

The string search functions also too often go unused. The program in Listing 4.12 uses `strstr` to extract all lines from a text file that contain a given string. Due to their cryptic names, the following three `<string.h>` functions are probably the least used:

1. `size_t strspn(const char *s1, const char *s2)`
   "Spans" the characters from `s2` occurring in `s1`. In plain English, it returns the *index* of the first character in `s1` which is not in `s2`. The standard C++ string class calls this operation find_first_not_of.
2. `size_t strcspn(const char *s1, const char *s2)`
   "Spans" the characters not in `s2` occurring in `s1`. In other words, it returns the index of the first character in s1 which is in `s2`. The standard C++ string class calls this operation find_first_of.
3. `char *strpbrk(char *s1, const char *s2)`
   Like `strcspn`, but returns a *pointer* instead of an index.

The program in Listing 4.13 illustrates these functions. See Chapter 17 for more string examples.

Listing 4.12   Uses `strstr` to find substrings

```
/* find.c:   Extract lines from a file */

#include <stdio.h>
#include <stdlib.h>
#include <string.h>

main(int argc, char *argv[])
{
    char line[BUFSIZ];              /* See Table 4.7 for BUFSIZ */
    char *search_str;
    int lineno = 0;

    if (argc == 1)
        return EXIT_FAILURE;    /* Search string required! */
    else
        search_str = argv[1];

    while (gets(line))
    {
        ++lineno;
        if (strstr(line,search_str))
            printf("%d: %s\n",lineno,line);
    }

    return EXIT_SUCCESS;
}

/* Results from the command "find str <find.c": */
4: #include <string.h>
11:     char *search_str;
15:         return 1;    /* Search string required */
17:         search_str = argv[1];
22:         if (strstr(line,search_str))
```

Listing 4.13 Illustrates selected string search functions

```c
#include <stdio.h>
#include <string.h>

void display_span(char *, int);

main()
{
    char *s = "Eeek! A mouse device!";
    char *vowels = "AEIOUaeiou";
    char *punct = "`~!@#$%^&*()-_=+\\|[{]};:'\",<.>/?";
    char *ptr;

    display_span(s,strspn(s,vowels));
    display_span(s,strspn(s,punct));
    display_span(s,strcspn(s,vowels));
    display_span(s,strcspn(s,punct));

    ptr = strpbrk(s,vowels);
    puts(ptr);

    ptr = strpbrk(s,punct);
    puts(ptr);

    return 0;
}

void display_span(char *s, size_t index)
{
    printf("%d characters spanned: %.*s\n",
            index,index,s);
}

/* Output: */
3 characters spanned: Eee
0 characters spanned:
0 characters spanned:
4 characters spanned: Eeek
Eeek! A mouse device!
! A mouse device!
```

The Standard C Library, Part II

For the Polished Programmer

In the previous chapter I divided the 15 headers of the Standard C Library into three groups, each representing different levels of mastery (see Chap. 4, Tables 4.1–4.3). This chapter explores Group II, which if used will give a certain polish to your programming.

<assert.h>

In well-organized programs there are key points where you can make assertions, such as "the index points to the next open array element." It is important to test these assertions during development, and to document them for the maintenance programmer (which, of course, is often yourself). The standard C library provides the `assert` macro for this purpose. You could represent the assertion above, for example, as

```
#include <assert.h>
...
assert(nitems < MAXITEMS && i == nitems);
...
```

If the condition holds, all is well and execution continues. Otherwise, `assert` prints a message indicating the condition, the file name, and the line number, and then calls `abort` to terminate the program.

You should use `assert` to validate the internal logic of your program. If a certain thread of execution is supposed to be impossible, then say so with the call `assert(0)`, as in:

```
switch(color)
{
    case RED:
        ...
    case BLUE:
        ...
    case GREEN:
        ...
    default:
        assert(0);
}
```

The macro `assert` is also handy for validating parameters. A function that takes a string argument, for example, could do the following:

```
char * f(char *s)
{
    assert(s);
    ...
}
```

Assertions are meant to catch *logic* errors, of course, not *runtime* errors. For example, no runtime condition created by the user or the environment should ever create a NULL pointer; that's clearly your problem, so you might want to use `assert` in such cases (and catch them during debugging, of course!). A runtime condition such as a memory failure requires more bulletproof exception handling and is not a fit candidate for `assert`.

When your code is ready for production, you should turn off assertion processing (since you've caught all the bugs). To do so, you can either include the statement

```
#define NDEBUG
```

near the beginning of each translation unit, or you can define the macro on the command line if your compiler allows it (most use the -D switch). With NDEBUG defined, all assertions expand to a null macro, but the text remains in the code for documentation. Make sure you don't put necessary program operations in an `assert` macro.

`<limits.h>`

Ideally, portable programs do not depend directly on the particulars of any one environment. Even assuming that all bytes consist of eight bits is not safe. The header `<limits.h>` defines the upper and lower bounds for all integer types (see Table 5.1). The program in Listing 5.1 toggles each bit in an integer on and off. It uses the value CHAR_BIT, defined in `<limits.h>` as the number of bits in a byte, to determine the number of bits in an integer. As Listing 5.2 illustrates, you can also use `<limits.h>` to determine the most efficient data type to use for signed numeric values that must span a certain range.

Table 5.1   Toggles each bit in an integer

CHAR_BIT	8
SCHAR_MIN	−127
SCHAR_MAX	127
UCHAR_MAX	255
[if char == signed char]	
CHAR_MIN	SCHAR_MIN
CHAR_MAX	SCHAR_MAX
[else]	
CHAR_MIN	0
CHAR_MAX	UCHAR_MAX
[end if]	
MB_LEN_MAX	1
SHRT_MIN	−32767
SHRT_MAX	32767
USHRT_MAX	65535
INT_MIN	−32767
INT_MAX	32767
UINT_MAX	65535
LONG_MIN	−2147483647
LONG_MAX	2147483647
ULONG_MAX	4294967295

Listing 5.1   Uses the value CHAR_BIT defined in <limits.h>

```
/* bit3.c:    Toggle bits in a word */
#include <stdio.h>
#include <limits.h>

#define WORD      unsigned int
#define NBYTES    sizeof(WORD)
#define NBITS    (NBYTES * CHAR_BIT)
#define NXDIGITS (NBYTES * 2)

main()
{
    WORD n = 0;
    int i, j;
```

Listing 5.1 (continued)

```
    for (j = 0; j < 2; ++j)
        for (i = 0;  i < NBITS; ++i)
        {
            n ^= (1 << i);
            printf("%0*X\n",NXDIGITS,n);
        }

    return 0;
}

/* Output: */
0001
0003
0007
000F
001F
003F
007F
00FF
01FF
03FF
07FF
0FFF
1FFF
3FFF
7FFF
FFFF
FFFE
FFFC
FFF8
FFF0
FFE0
FFC0
FF80
FF00
FE00
FC00
F800
F000
E000
C000
8000
0000
```

Listing 5.2.   Uses `<limits.h>` to choose a suitable numeric type

```
/* range.c */
#include <stdio.h>
#include <limits.h>

#define LOWER_BOUND   <your min here>
#define UPPER_BOUND   <your max here>

/* Determine minimal numeric type for range */
#if LOWER_BOUND < LONG_MIN || LONG_MAX < UPPER_BOUND
    typedef double Num_t;
#elif LOWER_BOUND < INT_MIN || INT_MAX < UPPER_BOUND
    typedef long Num_t;
#elif LOWER_BOUND < SCHAR_MIN || SCHAR_MAX < UPPER_BOUND
    typedef int Num_t;
#else
    typedef signed char Num_t;
#endif

main()
{
    Num_t x;

    printf("sizeof(Num_t) == %d\n",sizeof x);
    return 0;
}
```

`<stddef.h>`

The header `<stddef.h>` defines three type synonyms and two macros (see Table 5.2). When you subtract two pointers that refer to elements of the same array (including one position past the end of the array), you get back the difference of the two corresponding subscripts, the magnitude of which will be the number of elements between the pointers. The type of the result is either an `int` or a `long`, whichever is appropriate for your environment. The header `<stddef.h>` defines the appropriate type for operations such as `ptrdiff_t`.

The `sizeof` operator returns a value of type `size_t`, which is the unsigned integer type that can represent the size of the largest data object you can declare in your environment (usually `unsigned int` or `unsigned long`). It is always the unsigned counterpart of the type used for `ptrdiff_t`. If you look through the headers in the Standard C Library, you'll find extensive use of type `size_t`. It is good idea to use `size_t` for all array indices and for pointer arithmetic (i.e., adding an offset to a pointer) unless for some reason you need the ability to count down past zero, which unsigned integers can't do.

Table 5.2 Definitions in `<stddef.h>`

Type synonym	
`ptrdiff_t`	type for pointer subtraction
`size_t`	type for `sizeof`
`wchar_t`	wide character type
Macros	
`NULL`	zero-pointer
`offsetof`	offset in bytes of structure members

The type `wchar_t` holds a *wide character*, an implementation-defined integral type for representing characters beyond standard ASCII. You define wide character constants with a pre-pended L, as in:

```
#include <stddef.h>
wchar_t  c = L'a';
wchar_t *s = L"abcde";
```

As Listing 5.3 illustrates, my environment defines a wide character as a two-byte integer, which is nicely compatible with the 16-bit Unicode standard for international characters (see Appendix 5.1, "Character Sets"). The `<stdlib.h>` functions listed in Table 5.3 use type `wchar_t`. The *Normative Addendum*, an official addendum to standard C accepted in 1993, defines many additional functions for handling wide and multibyte characters. For more detailed information, see P. J. Plauger's editorials in the April 1993 and May 1993 issues of the *C/C++ Users Journal*.

Listing 5.3 Illustrates wide character strings

```
/* wide.c */
#include <stddef.h>
#include <stdio.h>

main()
{
    char str[] = "hello";
    wchar_t wcs[] = L"hello";

    printf("sizeof str = %d\n",sizeof str);
    printf("sizeof wcs = %d\n",sizeof wcs);
    return 0;
}

/* Output: */
sizeof str = 6
sizeof wcs = 12
```

Table 5.3   `<stdlib.h>` functions that use `wchar_t`

mbtowc	translate multibyte character to wide character
wctomb	translate wide character to multibyte character
mbstowcs	translate multibyte string to wide string
wcstombs	translate wide string to multibyte string

The NULL macro is the universal zero-pointer constant. You should include a header that defines NULL (viz., stddef.h, stdio.h, stdlib.h, string.h, locale.h) to let the system be responsible for defining it. The header `<stddef.h>` is handy when you need NULL defined in a compilation unit and nothing else.

The offsetof macro returns the offset in bytes from the beginning of a structure to one of its members. Due to address alignment constraints, some implementations insert unused bytes between members in a structure, so you can't assume that the offset of a member is just the sum of the sizes of the members that precede it. For example, the program in Listing 5.4 exposes a one-byte gap in the Person structure after the name member, allowing the age member to start on a word boundary (a word is two bytes here). Use offsetof if you need an explicit pointer to a structure member, as in:

```
struct Person p;
int *age_p;
age_p = (int *) ((char *)&p + offsetof(struct Person, age));
```

Listing 5.4   offsetof exposes alignment within a structure

```
/* offset.c */
#include <stddef.h>
#include <stdio.h>

struct Person
{
    char name[15];
    int age;
};

main()
{
    printf("%d\n",offsetof(struct Person, age));
    return 0;
}

/* Output: */
16              /* not 15 as expected */
```

<time.h>

Most environments provide some mechanism for keeping time. Standard C provides the type clock_t, a numeric type that tracks *processor time*. The clock function returns an implementation-defined value of type clock_t that represents the current processor time. Unfortunately, what is meant by "processor time" varies across platforms, so clock by itself isn't very useful. You can, however, compare processor times and then divide by the constant CLOCKS_PER_SEC, thus rendering the number of seconds elapsed between two points in time. The program in Listings 5.5, 5.6, and 5.7 uses clock to implement simple stopwatch functions.

Listing 5.5   Stopwatch function declarations

```
/* timer.h */
void timer_reset(void);
void timer_wait(double nsecs);
double timer_elapsed(void);
```

Listing 5.6   Stopwatch function implementations

```
/* timer.c */
#include <time.h>
#include "timer.h"

static clock_t start = (clock_t) 0;

/* Reset the timer */
void timer_reset(void)
{
    start = clock();
}

/* Wait a number of seconds */
void timer_wait(double secs)
{
    clock_t stop = clock() +
                    (clock_t) (secs * CLOCKS_PER_SEC);
    while (clock() < stop);
        ;
}

/* Compute elapsed time in seconds */
double timer_elapsed(void)
{
    return (double)(clock() - start) / CLOCKS_PER_SEC;
}
```

Listing 5.7   Illustrates the stopwatch functions

```
/* t_timer.c:      Tests the stopwatch functions */
#include <stdio.h>
#include <limits.h>
#include "timer.h"

main()
{
    long i;

    timer_reset();

    /* Delay */
    for (i = 0; i < LONG_MAX; ++i)
            ;

    /* Get elapsed time */
    printf("elapsed time: %lf secs\n",timer_elapsed());
    return 0;
}

/* Output: */
elapsed time: 565.070000 secs
```

Listing 5.8   The definition of `struct tm` from `<time.h>`

```
struct tm
{
  int    tm_sec;      /* seconds (0 - 60) */
  int    tm_min;      /* minutes (0 - 59) */
  int    tm_hour;     /* hours (0 - 23) */
  int    tm_mday;     /* day of month (1 - 31) */
  int    tm_mon;      /* month (0 - 11) */
  int    tm_year;     /* years since 1900 */
  int    tm_wday;     /* day of week (0 - 6) */
  int    tm_yday;     /* day of year (0 - 365) */
  int    tm_isdst;    /* daylight savings flag */
};
```

The rest of the functions in `<time.h>` deal with *calendar time*. The `time` function returns a system-dependent encoding of the current date and time as type `time_t` (usually a `long`). The function `localtime` decodes a `time_t` into a `struct tm` (see Listing 5.8). The `asctime` function returns a text representation of a decoded time in a standard format, namely

```
Mon Nov 28 14:59:03 1994
```

Table 5.4 Definitions in `<time.h>`

Macros

NULL
CLOCKS_PER_SEC

Types

`size_t`	
`clock_t`	system clock type
`time_t`	encoded time/date value
`struct tm`	decoded time/date components

Functions

`difftime`	duration between two times
`mktime`	normalizes a `struct tm`
`time`	retrieves current time encoding
`asctime`	text representation of a time value
`ctime`	text representation of current time
`gmtime`	decodes into UTC time
`localtime`	decodes a time value
`strftime`	formats a decoded time

Table 5.4 provides a list of definitions in `<time.h>`. For more detail on time and date processing, see Chapter 19.

Appendix 5.1: Character Sets

A *script* is a set of symbols used to convey information in written text. There are over 30 major scripts in the world. Some scripts, such as Roman and Cyrillic, serve many languages. World scripts can be categorized according to the hierarchy in Table 5.5.

Most scripts are *alphabetic*. The Han script used by Chinese, Japanese, and Koreans, however, is an *ideographic* (or more accurately *logographic*) script. Each Han character represents an object or concept (what we call a word, although most Chinese words require two logograms); there is no notion of words composed from letters in an alphabet in these languages.

A *character set* is a collection of text symbols with an associated numerical encoding. The ASCII character set with which most of us are familiar maps the letters and numerals used in our culture to integers in the range [32,126], with special control codes filling out the 7-bit range [0,127]. As the 'A' in the acronym suggests, this is strictly an American standard. Moreover, it only specifies half of the 256 code points available in a single 8-bit byte. There are a number of extended ASCII character sets that fill the upper range [128,255] with graphic characters, accented letters, or non-Roman characters. Since 256 code points are not enough to cover even the Roman alphabets in use today, there are five separate, single-byte standards for applications

Table 5.5   World scripts

European
Armenian, Cyrillic, Georgian, Greek, Roman

Indic
Northern
   Bengali, Devanagari, Gujarati, Gurmukhi, Oriya
Southern
   Kannada (Kanarese), Malayalam, Sinhalese, Tamil, Telugu
Southeast
   Burmese, Khmer, Lao, Thai
Central Asian
   Tibetan

Middle Eastern
Arabic, Hebrew

East Asian (Oriental)
Han, Bopomofo, Kana (Hiragana + Katakana), Hangul

Other Asian
Lanna Thai, Mangyan, Mongolian, Naxi, Pollard, Pahawh Hmong, Tai Lü, Tai Nüa, Yi

African
Ethiopian, Osmanya, Tifinagh, Vai

Native American
Cree

Miscellaneous
Chemistry, Mathematics, Publishing Symbols, IPA (International Phonetic Alphabet)

that use Roman characters (see Table 5.6). The obvious disadvantage of single-byte character sets is the difficulty of simultaneously processing data from distinct regions in a single application, such as Greek and Hebrew, because the same code points are shared by the different encodings. A single-byte encoding is wholly unfit for Chinese, Japanese, and Korean, since there are thousands of Han characters.

One way to increase the number of characters in a single encoding is to map characters to more than one byte. A *multibyte* character set encoding maps a character to a variable-length sequence of one or more byte values. In one popular encoding, if the most significant bit of a byte is zero, the character is standard ASCII; if not, that byte and the next form a 16-bit code for a local character. Multibyte encodings are storage efficient because they have no unused bytes,

Table 5.6 Eight-bit character set standards

ISO 8859-1 (Latin-1)	Western European
ISO 8859-2 (Latin-2)	Eastern European
ISO 8859-3 (Latin-3)	Southeastern European
ISO 8859-4 (Latin-4)	Northern European
ISO 8859-5	Cyrillic
ISO 8859-6	Arabic
ISO 8859-7	Greek
ISO 8859-8	Hebrew
ISO 8859-9 (Latin-5)	Western European + Turkish

but they have the disadvantage of requiring special algorithms to compute indexes into a string, or to find string length, since characters are represented as a variable number of bytes. To overcome string-indexing problems, Standard C defines functions that process multibyte characters and that convert multibyte strings into *wide-character* strings (i.e., strings of wchar_t, usually 2-byte characters). These multibyte and wide character functions are commonly available only on XPG4-compliant UNIX platforms and Japanese platforms, however. The Normative Addendum to the C standard approved in 1993 defines many additional functions for processing sequences of multibyte and wide characters, and should entice U.S. vendors to step out of their cultural comfort zone.

Code Pages

Since standard ASCII consists of only 128 code points, there are 128 more waiting to be used in an 8-bit character encoding. It has been common practice to populate the upper 128 codes with characters suitable for local use. Such an encoding of the values 128–255, together with ASCII, is called a *code page* under MS-DOS and Microsoft Windows. The default code page for the IBM PC in the United States and much of Europe (#437) includes some box drawing and other graphic characters, as well as Roman characters with diacritical marks. Other MS-DOS code pages include

863	Canadian-French
850	Multilingual (Latin-1)
865	Nordic
860	Portuguese
852	Slavic (Latin-2)

Since code pages use code points in the range [128,255], it is important not to depend on or modify the high-bit value in any byte of your program's data (an all-too-common practice in the traditional UNIX world). A program that follows this discipline is called *8-bit clean*.

Character Set Standards

The world's most widely used character set is 7-bit ASCII. ISO 646 is essentially ASCII with a few codes left subject to localization. For example, the currency symbol—code point 0x24—is $ only in the United States and is allowed to "float" in order to adhere to local conventions. ISO 646 is sometimes called the *portable character set* (PCS) and is the standard alphabet for programming languages.

In order to take advantage of all 256 code points possible in a single-byte encoding, ISO 8859 defines nine 8-bit mappings to accommodate the alphabetic languages listed in Table 5.6. Each of these mappings retains ISO 646 as a subset; hence they differ mainly in the upper 128 code points. Some of these code points are the basis for MS-DOS code pages.

There is no official ISO standard for multibyte character sets in the Far East. There are local national standards, however, for each region of the Far East. There are also informal, PC-industry standards in common use based on national standards, including E-Ten, Big Five and Shift JIS.

ISO 10646

To simplify the development of internationalized applications, ISO developed the *Universal Multiple-Octet Coded Character Set* (ISO 10646) to accommodate all characters from all significant modern languages in a single encoding. An *octet* is a contiguous, ordered collection of eight bits, which is a *byte* on most systems. ISO 10646 allows for 2,147,483,648 characters, although only 34,168 have been defined. It is organized into 128 groups, each group containing 256 planes of 65,536 characters each (256 rows × 256 columns—see Figure 5.1).

Any one of the 2^{31} characters can be addressed by four octets representing—respectively—the group, plane, row, and column of its location in the four-dimensional space. Consequently, ISO 10646 is a 32-bit character encoding. ASCII code points are a subset of ISO 10646: You just add leading zeroes to fill out 32 bits. For example, the encoding in hexadecimal for the letter 'a' is 00000061 (i.e., Group 0, Plane 0, Row 0, Column 0x61). Plane 0 of Group 0, the only one of the 32,768 planes to date that has been populated, is called the *Basic Multilingual Plane* (BMP). ISO 10646 allows conforming implementations to be BMP-based, that is, only two octets, representing the row and column within the BMP, are required. The full four-octet form of encoding is called UCS-4, and the two-octet form UCS-2. Under UCS-2, therefore, the hexadecimal encoding for the letter 'a' is 0061 (Row 0, Column 0x61). Row 0 of the BMP is essentially ISO 8859-1 (Latin-1) with the U.S. dollar sign as the currency symbol.

ISO 10646 also defines *combining* characters, such as nonspacing diacritics. In conforming applications, combining characters always follow the base character that they modify. The UCS-2 encoding for 'á', then, consists of two 16-bit integers: 0061 0301 (0301 is the *non-spacing acute*). For compatibility with existing character sets, there is also a single UCS-2 code point for 'á' (00e1). In general, only Roman characters have such dual representations. Some non-

Figure 5.1 The topology of a typical ISO 10646 group.

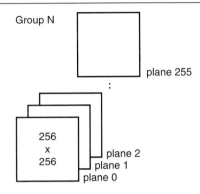

Roman languages, such as Arabic, Hindi, and Thai, require the use of combining characters. There are three levels of conformance for tools and applications:

Level 1   combining characters not allowed
Level 2   combining characters allowed for Arabic, Hebrew, and Indic scripts only
Level 3   combining characters allowed with no restrictions

Unicode

Unicode is a 16-bit encoding that supports most modern, written languages. It began independently of ISO 10646, but starting with Unicode version 1.1, it is now a subset of ISO 10646 (to be precise, it is UCS-2, Level 3). Vendors are now beginning to support Unicode, and tools are fast becoming available. Tools supporting the 32-bit encodings of ISO 10646 are not expected for many years, especially since no planes beyond the BMP have been populated. Unicode also defines mapping tables to translate Unicode characters to and from most national and international character set standards.

Some applications should readily convert to Unicode. Since ASCII is a subset, it is only necessary to change narrow (8-bit) characters to wide characters. In C and C++, this means replacing char declarations with wchar_t. Some other character sets, such as Thai and Hangul, appear in the same relative order within Unicode, so you just need to add or subtract a fixed offset. Converting Han characters requires a lookup table.

The Standard C Library, Part III

For the Complete Programmer

This chapter illustrates the functionality of the standard C headers not covered in the previous two chapters. See Chapter 4, Tables 4.1–4.3, for a categorization of all the headers in the standard C library.

`<float.h>`

Perhaps nothing varies so widely across different computer environments as floating-number systems. Some platforms require special hardware to make native floating-point instructions available, while others provide floating-point capability through software.

A floating-point number system is a collection of numbers that can be expressed in scientific notation with a fixed number of digits. To be precise, it is the finite set of numbers of the form: $\pm 0.d_1 d_2 \ldots d_\rho \times \beta^e$, where $m \leq e \leq M$. The parameters β, ρ, m, and M represent the *radix*, *precision*, *minimum exponent*, and *maximum exponent*, respectively. The header <float.h> provides manifest constants for these and other important floating-point parameters (see Table 6.1; also see Appendix 6.1, "Floating-point Number Systems"). As Table 6.1 illustrates, there are three potentially separate number systems for each implementation, one each for float, double, and long double.

`<math.h>`

Although C is not widely used in scientific programming, it provides a full-featured set of mathematical functions (see Table 6.2). Most of these functions have the standard names used in mathematics, so if you know what they are, you know how to use them. A few deserve special mention, however. As the program in Listing 6.1 illustrates, the fmod function computes the remainder of dividing is first argument by the second. The answer is 62.9558 because

$$1234.56 - 13 * 90.1234 == 62.9558$$

Table 6.1 Definitions in `<float.h>`

Parameter	Meaning	*"Minimum"* Value
FLT_RADIX	exponent base	2
FLT_ROUNDS	rounding mode	(*)
FLT_MANT_DIG	precision for float	
DBL_MANT_DIG	precision for double	
LDBL_MANT_DIG	precision for long double	
FLT_DIG	base-10 precision for float	6
DBL_DIG	same for double	10
LDBL_DIG	same for long double	10
FLT_MIN_EXP	min. exponent for float	
DBL_MIN_EXP	same for double	
LDBL_MIN_EXP	same for long double	
FLT_MIN_10_EXP	min. base-10 float exponent	-37
DBL_MIN_10_EXP	same for double	-37
LDBL_MIN_10_EXP	same for long double	-37
FLT_MIN	smallest float	1E-37
DBL_MIN	smallest double	1E-37
LDBL_MIN	smallest long double	1E-37
FLT_MAX_EXP	max. exponent for float	
DBL_MAX_EXP	same for double	
LDBL_MAX_EXP	same for long double	
FLT_MAX_10_EXP	max. base-10 float exponent	+37
DBL_MAX_10_EXP	same for double	+37
LDBL_MAX_10_EXP	same for long double	+37
FLT_MAX	largest float	1E+37
DBL_MAX	largest double	1E+37
LDBL_MAX	largest long double	1E+37
FLT_EPSILON	machine epsilon for float	1E-5
DBL_EPSILON	same for double	1E-9
LDBL_EPSILON	same for long double	1E-9

*Values for FLT_ROUNDS:

−1   indeterminable
0   toward zero
1   to nearest
2   toward positive infinity
3   toward negative infinity

Table 6.2 Functions defined in `<math.h>`

acos	arc-cosine
asin	arc-sine
atan	arc-tangent (principal value)
atan2	arc-tangent (full circle)
ceil	ceiling
cos	cosine
cosh	hyperbolic cosine
exp	power of *e*
fabs	absolute value
floor	floor (greatest-integer-in function)
fmod	modulus (remainder)
frexp	normalized fraction/exponent parts
ldexp	inverse of frexp
log	natural logarithm
log10	logarithm base 10
modf	integer/fractional parts
pow	raise a number to a power
sin	sine
sinh	hyperbolic sine
sqrt	square root
tan	tangent
tanh	hyperbolic tangent

The function `modf` puts the integer part of its argument in the location pointed to by its second argument, and returns the fractional part. The function `frexp` computes a normalized fraction x and an integer p such that its argument is equivalent to:

$$x \cdot 2^p$$

Its inverse, `ldexp`, calculates a floating-point number given x and p.

The floor of a number is itself, if it is an integer; otherwise it is the adjacent to the "left" on the number line, so the following relationships are valid:

```
floor(90.1234) == 90
floor(-90.1234) == -91
```

The ceiling of a number is the number to the right, so:

```
ceil(90.1234) == 91
ceil(-90.1234) == -90
```

The calculator program in Listing 6.2 also illustrates a number of `<math.h>` functions.

Listing 6.1   Illustrates several `<math.h>` functions

```c
#include <stdio.h>
#include <math.h>

main()
{
    double x = 1234.56, y = 90.1234, z, w;
    int p;

    printf("x == %g, y == %g\n",x,y);
    printf("fmod(x,y) == %g\n",fmod(x,y));
    printf("floor(y) == %g\n",floor(y));
    printf("ceil(y) == %g\n",ceil(y));
    w = modf(y,&z);
    printf("after modf(y,&z): w == %g, z == %g\n",w,z);
    w = frexp(y,&p);
    printf("after frexp(y,&p): w == %g, p == %d\n",w,p);
    printf("ldexp(w,p) == %g\n",ldexp(w,p));
    return 0;
}

/* Output */
x == 1234.56, y == 90.1234
fmod(x,y) == 62.9558
floor(y) == 90
ceil(y) == 91
after modf(y,&z): w == 0.1234, z == 90
after frexp(y,&p): w == 0.704089, p == 7
ldexp(w,p) == 90.1234
```

Listing 6.2   A simple calculator that illustrates some `<math.h>` functions

```c
/* calc.c:  Lame-brained Calculator */
#include <stdio.h>
#include <stdlib.h>
#include <math.h>
#include <string.h>
#include <ctype.h>

#define LINSIZ 40

char *getline(char *);
```

continued

Listing 6.2   (continued)

```
main()
{
    double  reg = 0.0;
    char    line[LINSIZ];

    while (getline(line) != NULL)
    {
        char *op;
        double val;

        /* Parse command string */
        val = strtod(line,&op);
        while (isspace(*op))
            ++op;
        strupr(op);

        /* Perform operation */
        if (*op == '+')
            reg += val;
        else if (*op == '-')
            reg -= val;
        else if (*op == '*')
            reg *= val;
        else if (*op == '/')
        {
            if (val != 0)
                reg /= val;
            else
            {
                puts("ERROR> invalid divisor <");
                continue;
            }
        }
        else if (*op == '=')
            reg = val;
        else if (*op == '^')
        {
            if (val < 0.0)
            {
                puts("ERROR> invalid exponent <");
                continue;
            }
            else if (val == 0.0)
                reg = 1.0;
            else if (val == 0.5)
                reg = sqrt(reg);
```

Listing 6.2   (continued)

```
                else
                    reg = pow(reg,val);
            }
            else if (strncmp(op,"NEGATE",1) == 0)
                reg = -reg;
            else if (strncmp(op,"MOD",1) == 0)
            {
                if (val == 0.0)
                {
                    puts("ERROR> invalid modulus <");
                    continue;
                }
                else
                    reg = fmod(reg,val);
            }
            else if (strncmp(op,"CEIL",1) == 0)
                reg = ceil(reg);
            else if (strncmp(op,"FLOOR",1) == 0)
                reg = floor(reg);
            else if (strncmp(op,"ROUND",1) == 0)
                reg = (reg < 0.0) ? ceil(reg - 0.5)
                                  : floor(reg + 0.5);
            else if (strncmp(op,"SQRT",1) == 0)
                reg = sqrt(reg);
            else if (strncmp(op,"QUIT",1) == 0)
                exit(0);
            else if (*op != '\0')
            {
                puts("ERROR> invalid operation <");
                continue;
            }

            printf("\t%s = %g\n",line,reg);
        }
        return 0;
    }

    char *getline(char *buf)
    {
        fputs("Calc> ",stdout);
        fflush(stdout);
        return gets(buf);
    }
```

Table 6.3   Definitions in `<errno.h>`

errno	Global integer indicating an error
EDOM	Domain error code
ERANGE	Range error code

`<errno.h>`

The header `<errno.h>` implements a simple error reporting facility. It defines a global integer `errno` to hold certain error codes generated by a number of library functions. The C standard requires vendors to provide only two codes, EDOM and ERANGE (see Table 6.3). The code EDOM indicates a *domain error*, which usually means that you passed bad arguments to function. For example, the `sqrt` function in `<math.h>` complains if you ask for the square root of a negative number. Some math functions set `errno` to ERANGE to indicate a *range error*, which means that a calculation on valid arguments would result in an arithmetic overflow or underflow. Most of the mathematical functions in the standard library use `errno` to report such errors. As the calculator in Listing 6.2 illustrates, you should set `errno` to zero before invoking any function that uses this facility, and then check it immediately after the function returns. The function `perror` prints its string argument followed by a colon, followed by a string representation of the last error recorded in `errno`. The expression `perror(s)` is equivalent to the expression:

```
printf("%s: %s\n",s,strerror(errno));
```

Defined in `<string.h>`, the function `strerror` returns the text that corresponds to `errno`.

The following functions from other standard library headers also set `errno` upon failure: `strtod`, `strtol`, `strtoul`, `fgetpos`, `fsetpos`, and `signal`. An implementation is free to provide other error codes beyond EDOM and ERANGE, and to use the `errno` facility with other functions, but such use is of course nonportable.

`<locale.h>`

A locale in standard C is a collection of preferences for the processing and display of information that is sensitive to culture, language, or national origin, such as date and monetary formats. There are five categories of information, named by macros defined in `<locale.h>`, on which locales have an effect (see Table 6.4). Each of these categories can be set to a different locale (e,g,. "american", "italian", etc.). For want of a better term, I call the collection of settings for all categories the *locale profile*.

Standard C specifies two functions that deal with locales directly:

```
struct lconv *localeconv(void);
char *setlocale(int category, char *locale);
```

The members of the `lconv` structure appear in Table 6.5. The function `localeconv` returns a static `lconv` object containing settings for the LC_MONETARY and LC_NUMERIC categories, and

Table 6.4 Locale categories

Category	Functionality
LC_COLLATE	Adapts `strcoll`, `strxfrm`, `wcscoll`, and `wcsxfrm` to the language/culture of the locale.
LC_CTYPE	Adapts the is*xxx*/isw*xxx* functions in `ctype.h` to the character set associated with the locale, and affects multibyte/wide character mapping.
LC_MONETARY	Sets parameters pertaining to the display of monetary values such as decimal point, grouping (e.g., thousands), group separator, etc. This category is purely advisory and affects no standard library functions.
LC_NUMERIC	Like LC_MONETARY, but for nonmonetary values (e.g., the decimal point may be different than for nonmonetary values).
LC_TIME	Adapts `strftime` and `wcsftime` to cultural specifications.

Table 6.5 The members of `struct lconv`

```
struct lconv
{
    char *decimal_point;
    char *thousands_sep;
    char *grouping;
    char *int_curr_symbol;
    char *currency_symbol;
    char *mon_decimal_point;
    char *mon_thousands_sep;
    char *mon_grouping;
    char *positive_sign;
    char *negative_sign;
    char int_frac_digits;
    char frac_digits;
    char p_cs_precedes;
    char p_sep_by_space;
    char n_cs_precedes;
    char n_sep_by_space;
    char p_sign_posn;
    char n_sign_posn;
};
```

`setlocale` changes the locale for the given category to that specified in locale. You can set all categories to the given locale by specifying a category of LC_ALL (see Listing 6.3). If locale is NULL, the current locale string for the category is returned. All implementations must support the minimalist "C" locale, and a native locale named by the empty string (which may be the same as the "C" locale).

`<setjmp.h>`

When you encounter an exceptional condition deep within a set of nested function calls, you need a "super goto" that branches to a safe point higher up in the function call stack. That's what the `setjmp`/`longjmp` mechanism is for. You record a point to return to with `setjmp`, and branch to it with `longjmp`. Here's the syntax:

```
#include <setjmp.h>

jmp_buf recover;

main()
{
    volatile int i = 0;
    for(;;)
    {
        if (setjmp(recover) != 0)
        {
            /* Recover from error in f() */
        }

        /* Get deeply nested... */
    }
    return 0;
}

...

void f()
{
    /* Do some risky stuff */

    if (<things go crazy>)
        longjmp(recover,1);

    /* else carry on */
}
```

A `jmp_buf` is an array that holds the system information necessary to restore execution at the `setjmp` point. For obvious reasons, a jump buffer must global. When you call `setjmp`, the system stores the *calling environment* parameters, such as the contents of the stack and instruction

Listing 6.3 Shows the effect of locale settings on the decimal point character and time formatting

```
/* tlocale.c:    Illustrates setlocale() -
 *
 *      NOTE:
 *      Compiled in Visual C++ under Windows NT
 */

#include <locale.h>
#include <stdio.h>
#include <time.h>

void print_stuff(void);

main()
{
    /* First in the C locale */
    puts("In the C locale:");
    print_stuff();

    /* Now try German */
    puts("\nIn the German locale:");
    setlocale(LC_ALL,"german");
    print_stuff();
    return 0;
}

void print_stuff(void)
{
    char text[81];
    time_t timer = time(NULL);

    printf("%.2f\n",1.2);
    strftime(text,sizeof text,"%A, %B %d, %Y (%x)\n",
            localtime(&timer));
    puts(text);
}

/* Output */
In the C locale:
1.20
Monday, March 17, 1997 (03/17/97)


In the German locale:
1,20
Montag, März 17, 1997 (17.03.97)
```

pointer registers, in `recover`. When called directly, `setjmp` always returns a zero. A call to `longjmp` restores the calling environment, so execution continues back at the `setjmp` call, with one difference: It appears as if `setjmp` has returned the second argument from the `longjmp` call (in this case a one). If you give `longjmp` a second argument of zero, it returns a one anyway. Since a `longjmp` performs an alternate return from a function, it interrupts the normal flow of a program, so you should use it only to handle unusual conditions. For a more thorough treatment of the `setjmp`/`longjmp` mechanism, see Chapter 12.

`<signal.h>`

A *signal* occurs when an unusual event interrupts the normal execution of a program, such as a divide-by-zero error or when the user presses the attention key (e.g., Control-C or Del). The header `<signal.h>` defines six "standard signals", shown in Table 6.6. These signals originated on the PDP architecture under UNIX, and may not all apply to your environment. An implementation may also define other signals, or it may ignore signals altogether, so signal handling is by nature nonportable. Chapter 12 explores signal handling in detail.

`<stdarg.h>`

This header provides a facility for you to define functions that have variable-length argument lists, like `printf` does. The `printf` function prototype in your compiler's `<stdio.h>` should look something like the following:

```
int printf(const char *, ...);
```

The ellipsis tells the compiler to allow zero or more arguments of any type to follow the first argument in a call to `printf`. For `printf` to behave correctly, the arguments that follow the format string must match the types of the corresponding edit descriptors in the format string. If there are fewer arguments than the format string expects, the results are undefined. If there are more arguments, they are ignored. The bottom line is that when you use the ellipsis in a function prototype you are telling the compiler not to type check your optional arguments because you think you know what you're doing—so be sure that you do. (See Table 6.7 for a list of definitions in `<starg.h>`.)

Table 6.6   Standard signals

SIGABRT	abnormal termination (raised by `abort()`)
SIGFPE	computational exception (e.g., overflow)
SIGILL	invalid function image (e.g., illegal instruction)
SIGINT	interactive attention (e.g., Control-C)
SIGSEGV	attempt to access protected memory
SIGTERM	termination request

Table 6.7 Definitions in `<stdarg.h>`

Type	Description
`va_list`	A variable-length argument list

Macros	Description
`va_start`	Initializes a `va_list`
`va_arg`	Gets next `arg` in a `va_list`
`va_end`	Closes a `va_list`

The program in Listing 6.4 shows how to use the `va_list` mechanism to find the largest integer in a variable-length argument list. As you can see, using variable-length argument lists requires two things on your part:

1. At least one fixed argument (always the last before the ellipsis) to initialize the `va_list`, and
2. Some mechanism that communicates the number and/or type of arguments to the function.

It follows, therefore, that the following function prototype is useless:

```
void f(...);      /* Location of args unknown */
```

There are a number of ways to satisfy the second requirement. The program in Listing 6.5 concatenates a variable number of strings into its fixed string argument. It processes one string after another until it finds a `NULL` pointer in the `va_list`. A call such as

```
concat(s,NULL);
```

initializes `s` to the empty string.

`va_list`'s as Arguments

Listing 6.6 has a useful function `fatal`, which prints a formatted message to `stderr` and exits gracefully. You call it as you would `printf`, with a format string and a list of parameters, such as

```
fatal("Error %d on device %d\n",err,dev);
```

What you would like to do is just pass the format string and print arguments to some function that implements the `printf` machinery. The C library function `vfprintf` makes this very easy. All you have to do is initialize a `va_list` with the print arguments and pass it as the third argument. As you would expect, the C library also has the companion functions `vprintf` and `vsprintf`.

Listing 6.4   Uses the <stdarg.h> macros to search a variable-length list of integers

```
/* max.c */
#include <stdio.h>
#include <stdarg.h>

int maxn(size_t count, ...)
{
    int n, big;
    va_list numbers;

    va_start(numbers,count);

    big = va_arg(numbers,int);
    while (count--)
    {
        n = va_arg(numbers,int);
        if (n > big)
            big = n;
    }

    va_end(numbers);
    return big;
}

main()
{
    printf("max = %d\n",maxn(3,1,3,2));
    return 0;
}

/* Output */
max = 3
```

Programmers coming from any other language may wonder why you need all of this machinery. For example, the Fortran programmer is quite accustomed to print statements that give no explicit information as to number or type in its argument list:

```
*    Output two numbers:
     PRINT *, x, y
```

To find the maximum of a list of numbers, only the numbers appear:

```
     PRINT *, MAX(1,3,2)
```

Listing 6.5   Concatenates a variable number of strings

```
/* concat.c */
#include <stdarg.h>
#include <stdio.h>
#include <string.h>

char * concat(char *s,...)
{
    va_list strings;
    char *p;

    /* Copy first string */
    va_start(strings,s);
    if ((p = va_arg(strings,char *)) == NULL)
    {
        *s = '\0';
        return s;
    }
    else
        strcpy(s,p);

    /* Append others */
    while ((p = va_arg(strings,char *)) != NULL)
        strcat(s,p);
    return s;
}

main()
{
    char buf[128];
    concat(buf,"Sweet","Talker","Betty","Crocker",NULL);
    printf("\"%s\"\n",buf);
    return 0;
}

/* Output */
"SweetTalkerBettyCrocker"
```

The reason you can do this in Fortran is that statements such as PRINT and MAX are *part of the language* (Fortran calls them *intrinsic functions*). The compiler knows their requirements and therefore can supply the appropriate information. In C, on the other hand, there is no input, output, or any other functionality built into the language except what the operators provide. The C philosophy is to keep the language small and to supply needed functionality with libraries.

Listing 6.6   Builds a variable format string by passing a `va_list` to `vfprintf`

```
/* fatal.c:   Exit program with an error message */
#include <stdio.h>
#include <stdlib.h>
#include <stdarg.h>
#include <string.h>

void fatal(char *fmt, ...)
{
    va_list args;

    if (strlen(fmt) > 0)
    {
        va_start(args,fmt);
        vfprintf(stderr,fmt,args);
        va_end(args);
    }
    exit(1);
}
```

Since the only communication between libraries and the compiler is the function call mechanism, you must provide a function all the needed information when you call it.

An Application

In financial and other numerical applications you often want to express integers separated by commas, such as monetary amounts:

$11,235,852

One approach converts the number to a string with `sprintf` and then traverses the string backwards, copying to another string and inserting commas as you go. Another approach, which I present here, solves the more general problem of creating strings backwards.

Listing 6.7 uses the function `prepend` to build a string backwards. You pass it the output buffer, an offset that points to the first character of the portion of the string already populated, and the string to `prepend`. The new offset is returned.

The following diagrams show the state of `s[]` after each call to `prepend`:

| ? | ? | ? | ? | ? | ? | t | h | r | e | e | \0 | offset = 6

| ? | ? | ? | t | w | o | t | h | r | e | e | \0 | offset = 3

| o | n | e | t | w | o | t | h | r | e | e | \0 | offset = 0

Listing 6.7   Illustrates the use of prepend

```
#include <stdio.h>
#include <assert.h>

#define WIDTH 11

extern int prepend(char *, unsigned, char *);

main()
{
    char s[WIDTH+1];
    int offset = WIDTH;

    s[offset] = '\0';
    offset = prepend(s,offset,"three");
    assert(offset >= 0);
    puts(s+offset);

    offset = prepend(s,offset,"two");
    assert(offset >= 0);
    puts(s+offset);

    offset = prepend(s,offset,"one");
    assert(offset >= 0);
    puts(s+offset);
    return 0;
}

/* Output */
three
twothree
onetwothree
```

Listing 6.8 has the implementation of prepend along with another function, preprintf, which allows you to prepend strings with formatting. The function preprintf uses vsprintf to create the formatted string, and then calls prepend to tack it onto the front of the existing string.

I can now implement a function commas, in terms of prepend and preprintf (see Listing 6.9). As I extract each digit in turn right to left by the usual remainder and quotient calculations, I push that digit onto a static character buffer, inserting commas where necessary. The function commas returns a pointer to the beginning of the completed string, which may or may not coincide with the beginning of the buffer. Note that the numeric base and the size of the groups are parameterized.

Listing 6.8   Functions to build strings backwards

```
/* preprint.c:  Functions to prepend strings */
#include <stdio.h>
#include <string.h>
#include <stdarg.h>
#include <stdlib.h>

int prepend(char *buf, unsigned offset, char *new_str)
{
    int new_len = strlen(new_str);
    int new_start = offset - new_len;

    /* Push a string onto the front of another */
    if (new_start >= 0)
        memcpy(buf+new_start,new_str,new_len);

    /* Return new start position (negative if underflowed) */
    return new_start;
}

int preprintf(char *buf, unsigned offset, char *format, ...)
{
    int pos = offset;
    char *temp = malloc(BUFSIZ);

    /* Format, then push */
    if (temp)
    {
        va_list args;

        va_start(args,format);
        vsprintf(temp,format,args);
        pos = prepend(buf,offset,temp);
        va_end(args);
        free(temp);
    }
    return pos;
}
```

Listing 6.9 Uses `prepend` and `preprintf` to format numbers with comma separators

```c
/* commas.c:    Converts a number into a string with commas */
#include <stdio.h>

#define BASE 10
#define GROUP 3

/* Need space to hold the digits of an unsigned long,
 * intervening commas and a null byte. It depends on
 * BASE and GROUP above (but logarithmically, not
 * as a constant, so we must define it manually here)
 */
#define MAXTEXT 14        /* For BASE = 10 */

int prepend(char *, unsigned, char *);
int preprintf(char *, unsigned, char *, ...);

char *commas(unsigned long amount)
{
    short offset = MAXTEXT-1,   /* where the string "starts" */
          place;                /* the power of BASE for current digit */
    static char text[MAXTEXT];

    text[offset] = '\0';

    /* Push digits right-to-left with commas */
    for (place = 0; amount > 0; ++place)
    {
        if (place % GROUP == 0 && place > 0)
            offset = prepend(text,offset,",");
        offset = preprintf(text,offset,"%x",amount % BASE);
        amount /= BASE;
    }

    return (offset >= 0) ? text + offset : NULL;
}
```

continued

Listing 6.9   (continued)

```
main()
{
    puts(commas(1));
    puts(commas(12));
    puts(commas(123));
    puts(commas(1234));
    puts(commas(12345));
    puts(commas(123456));
    puts(commas(1234567));
    puts(commas(12345678));
    puts(commas(123456789));
    puts(commas(1234567890));
    return 0;
}

/* Output */
1
12
123
1,234
12,345
123,456
1,234,567
12,345,678
123,456,789
1,234,567,890
```

Conclusion

In Chapters 4, 5, and 6 I have attempted to give the flavor of the functionality of the Standard C library. It is foolish to reinvent this functionality. Although I have surveyed the library in three groups of "decreasing" priority, my priority may not match yours. You'd be wise to master the entire library.

Appendix 6.1: Floating-point Number Systems

Mathematical manipulation of real numbers by computers has long been a source of frustration and confusion for students and practitioners alike. The program in Listing 6.10 shows how a simple sequence of sums can go awry. It calculates the expression e^x by the formula:

$$e^x = 1 + x + \frac{x^2}{2!} + \frac{x^3}{3!} + \cdots = \sum_{n=0}^{\infty} \frac{x^n}{n!}$$

Listing 6.10   Shows roundoff error in computing powers of e

```
/* round.c */
#include <stdio.h>
#include <math.h>

double e(double x);

main()
{
    printf("e(55.5) == %g, exp(55.5) == %g\n",
            e(55.5), exp(55.5));
    printf("e(-55.5) == %g, exp(-55.5) == %g\n",
            e(-55.5), exp(-55.5));
    printf("1/e(55.5) == %g\n",1.0 / e(55.5));
    return 0;
}

double e(double x)
{
    double sum1 = 1.0;
    double sum2 = 1.0 + x;
    double term = x;
    int i = 1;

    /* Calculate exp(x) via Taylor Series */
    while (sum1 != sum2)
    {
        sum1 = sum2;
        term = term * x / ++i;
        sum2 += term;
    }
    return sum2;
}

/* Output */
e(55.5) == 1.26866e+24, exp(55.5) == 1.26866e+24
e(-55.5) == -6.76351e+06, exp(-55.5) == 7.88236e-25
1/e(55.5) == 7.88236e-25
```

Things work correctly for positive arguments, but the result for negative arguments isn't even close! The problem, of course, is that computers, with their finite capabilities, can only represent a minuscule subset of the set of real numbers. A good chunk of numerical analysis deals with *roundoff error*, the chief hazard of finite-precision arithmetic.

In days gone by, many computers used *fixed-point* number systems, in which numbers are derived from a given radix (b), precision (p), and fraction size (f). For example, the values $b = 10$, $p = 4$, and $f = 1$ define the following set of 19,999 numbers:

$$F = \{-999.9, -999.8, \ldots, 999.8, 999.9\}$$

Since these numbers are evenly spaced, the maximum absolute error in representing any real number x in this system is bounded by .05, or, in other words,

$$|x - fix(x)| \leq .05$$

The set of machine integers form a fixed-point system with $f = 0$, and a maximum absolute error of 0.5 for systems that round, and no greater than 1.0 for systems that truncate.

Absolute error is not generally useful in mathematical computations, however. As is often the case, you are more often interested in percentages, or how one number differs relative to another. You compute the *relative error* of y with respect to x by the following formula:

$$\frac{|x - y|}{|x|}$$

Consider how the numbers 865.54 and .86554 are represented in F:

$$fix(865.54) = 865.5$$
$$fix(.86554) = .9$$

Because the number of decimals is fixed, the second is a much poorer fit than the first, which the relative errors illustrate:

$$\text{rel}(865.54) = \frac{|865.54 - 865.5|}{865.54} = .0000462$$

$$\text{rel}(.86554) = \frac{|.86554 - .9|}{.86554} = .0398$$

The second is 1000 times worse than the first!

Nowadays computers provide *floating-point* number systems, which represent numbers in the form

$$\pm 0.d_1 d_2 \ldots d_p \times \beta^e$$

where

$$m \leq e \leq M, 0 \leq d_i < \beta$$

This is like the scientific notation that you learned in school, except that the base (β) can be other than 10, and there is an upper limit on the precision (ρ). Most floating-point systems use a *normalized* representation, which means that d_1 cannot be zero. These number systems are called floating point for the obvious reason—the radix point "floats" and the exponent e adjusts accordingly to preserve the correct value. Now consider a floating-point system G defined by $\beta = 10$, $\rho = 4$, $m = -2$, and $M = 3$. The numbers used above are represented as:

$$fl(.86554) = .8655 \times 10^0$$
$$fl(865.54) = .8655 \times 10^3$$

Now look what happens when calculating the relative errors of the two representations:

$$\text{rel}(865.54) = \frac{|865.54 - 865.5|}{865.54} = .0000462$$

$$\text{rel}(.86554) = \frac{|.86554 - .8655|}{.86554} = .0000462$$

In a floating-point system, the relative error is the same whenever the digits and exponents are. It can be shown that the relative error of representing any real number within the range of a floating-point system is no greater than $\beta^{1-\rho}$, which is 0.001 in G.

Floating-point numbers are not evenly spaced. In G, for example, the next number greater than 1 is 1.001, a spacing of .001, but the next number after 10 is 10.01, which is 0.01 to the right. In general, the spacing among all numbers between powers of β, say between β^e and β^{e+1} is $\beta^{e+1-\rho}$. A trivial combinatorial analysis shows that each interval $[\beta^e, \beta^{e+1})$ has the same number of floating-point numbers, $(\beta-1)\beta^{\rho-1}$, and the total number of floating-point numbers is $2(M-m+1)(\beta-1)^{\rho-1}+1$ (so increasing ρ increases the *density* of the number system). And as shown above, although smaller numbers are closer together and larger numbers are farther apart, the relative spacing between consecutive floating-point numbers is essentially the same throughout the system. In particular, the relative spacing between two adjacent numbers within an interval $[\beta^e, \beta^{e+1})$ is $\beta^{1-\rho}$, and between β^{e+1} and its immediate predecessor is $\beta^{-\rho}$.

The quantity $\beta^{1-\rho}$, which also happens to be the spacing between 1.0 and its immediate successor, is called the *machine epsilon* (ε), and is a good measure of the granularity of a floating number system. The smallest floating-point magnitude other than zero is of course β^{m-1}, usually denoted as σ, and the largest magnitude, λ, is $\beta^M(1-\beta^{-\rho})$.

The standard C header `<float.h>` provides manifest constants for all of these parameters as follows:

```
β  ==  FLT_RADIX
ρ  ==  DBL_MANT_DIG
m  ==  DBL_MIN_EXP
M  ==  DBL_MAX_EXP
ε  ==  DBL_EPSILON
σ  ==  DBL_MIN
λ  ==  DBL_MAX
```

Listing 6.11   Illustrates use of machine epsilon in a root-finding algorithm

```c
/* root.c */
#include <stdio.h>
#include <float.h>
#include <math.h>
#include <assert.h>

#define sign(x) ((x < 0.0) ? -1 : (x > 0.0) ? 1 : 0)

#define PREC DBL_DIG
#define EPS   DBL_EPSILON

typedef double ftype;

ftype root(ftype a, ftype b, ftype (*f)(ftype))
{
    ftype fofa = f(a);
    ftype fofb = f(b);
    assert(a < b);
    assert(fofa * fofb < 0.0);

    /* Close-in on root via bisection */
    while (fabs(b - a) > EPS*fabs(a))
    {
        ftype x = a + (b-a)/2.0;
        ftype fofx = f(x);
        if (x <= a || x >= b || fofx == 0.0)
            return x;
        if (sign(fofx) == sign(fofa))
        {
            a = x;
            fofa = fofx;
        }
        else
        {
            b = x;
            fofb = fofx;
        }
    }
    return a;
}
```

Listing 6.11 (continued)

```
main()
{
    extern ftype f(ftype);
    printf("root == %.*f\n",PREC,root(-1.0,1.0,f));
    return 0;
}

ftype f(ftype x)
{
    return x*x + x - 1.0;
}

/* Output */
root == 0.618033988749895
```

The header <float.h> also provides the float and long double equivalents of the last five parameters, representing the three (not necessarily distinct) floating-point number systems in standard C (see Table 6.1).

The program in Listing 6.11 calculates a root of $x^2 + x + 1$ in the interval $[-1,1]$ by the method of bisection. The algorithm halves the interval (which must contain a sign change for the function f) until the relative spacing between the endpoints is less than or equal to machine epsilon. Such a loop may never terminate if you expect greater precision than this.

Should you find yourself in an environment that does not provide the parameters in <float.h>, you can compute β, ρ, and ε directly. To see how this is possible, remember that the spacing between consecutive floating-point numbers increases with the magnitude of the numbers. Eventually there is a point where the spacing between adjacent numbers is greater than one. In fact the first interval where this holds true is $[\beta^\rho, \beta^{\rho+1})$, because the integers therein require $\rho+1$ digits in their representation. The positive integers in a floating-point system are precisely these:

$$1, 2, \ldots, \beta^\rho - 1, \beta^\rho, \beta^\rho + \beta, \beta^\rho + 2\beta, \ldots, \beta^{\rho+1}, \beta^{\rho+1} + \beta^2, \ldots$$

To find the radix, the program in Listing 6.12 keeps doubling a until it reaches a point where the spacing exceeds 1. It then finds the next larger floating-point number and subtracts a to get β (b in Listing 6.12). The program then computes the smallest of b to get to that point again where the spacing between adjacent numbers exceeds 1, which power is the precision ρ. To find ε, the program finds the neighboring number to the right of 1, and subtracts 1.

Listing 6.12   Computes machine floating-point parameters

```c
/* machine.c */
#include <stdio.h>
#include <math.h>
#include <float.h>

main()
{
    int beta, p;
    double a, b, eps, epsp1, sigma, nums;

    /* Discover radix */
    a = 1.0;
    do
    {
        a = 2.0 * a;
        b = a + 1.0;
    } while ((b - a) == 1.0);

    b = 1.0;
    do
        b = 2.0 * b;
    while ((a + b) == a);
    beta = (int) ((a + b) - a);
    printf("radix:\n");
    printf("\talgorithm: %d\n",beta);
    printf("\tprovided: %d\n",FLT_RADIX);

    /* Compute precision in bits */
    p = 0;
    a = 1.0;
    do
    {
        ++p;
        a *= (double) beta;
        b = a + 1.0;
    } while ((b - a) == 1.0);
    printf("precision:\n");
    printf("\talgorithm: %d\n",p);
    printf("\tprovided: %d\n",DBL_MANT_DIG);

    /* Compute machine epsilon */
    eps = 1.0;
    do
    {
        eps = 0.5 * eps;
        epsp1 = eps + 1.0;
    } while (epsp1 > 1.0);
```

Listing 6.12   (continued)

```
    epsp1 = 2.0 * eps + 1.0;
    eps = epsp1 - 1.0;
    printf("machine epsilon:\n");
    printf("\talgorithm: %g\n",eps);
    printf("\tformula: %g\n",pow(FLT_RADIX,1.0-DBL_MANT_DIG));
    printf("\tprovided: %g\n",DBL_EPSILON);

    /* Compute smallest normalized magnitude */
    printf("smallest nonzero magnitude:\n");
    printf("\tformula: %g\n",pow(FLT_RADIX,DBL_MIN_EXP-1));
    printf("\tprovided: %g\n",DBL_MIN);

    /* Compute larget normalized magnitude */
    printf("largest nonzero magnitude:\n");
    printf("\tformula: %g\n",
            pow(FLT_RADIX,DBL_MAX_EXP-1) * FLT_RADIX *
            (1.0 - pow(FLT_RADIX,-DBL_MANT_DIG)));
    printf("\tprovided: %g\n",DBL_MAX);

    printf("smallest exponent: %d\n",DBL_MIN_EXP);
    printf("largest exponent: %d\n",DBL_MAX_EXP);

    nums = 2 * (FLT_RADIX - 1)
         * pow(FLT_RADIX,DBL_MANT_DIG-1)
         * (DBL_MAX_EXP - DBL_MIN_EXP + 1);
    printf("This system has %g numbers\n",nums);
    return 0;
}

/* Output (MS Visual C++ 4.2) */
radix:
    algorithm: 2
    provided: 2
precision:
    algorithm: 53
    provided: 53
machine epsilon:
    algorithm: 2.22045e-016
    formula: 2.22045e-016
    provided: 2.22045e-016
smallest nonzero magnitude:
    formula: 2.22507e-308
    provided: 2.22507e-308
largest nonzero magnitude:
    formula: 1.79769e+308
    provided: 1.79769e+308
smallest exponent: -1021
largest exponent: 1024
This system has 1.84287e+019 numbers
```

Key Concepts

Abstraction

Unlike a machine, the human mind has severe limitations on the amount of complexity it can handle. Life is inherently complex, and so are software systems that model reality. To master a complex system, it is necessary to focus only on the few things that matter most in a given context, and ignore the rest. This process, called *abstraction*, enables system designers to solve complex problems in an organized, manageable way. According to Grady Booch, "An abstraction denotes the essential characteristics of an object that distinguish it from all other kinds of objects and thus provide crisply-defined conceptual boundaries, relative to the perspective of the viewer" (*Object-Oriented Analysis and Design with Applications*, 2nd ed. (Benjamin-Cummings, 1994), p. 41).

Data Abstraction

Abstraction often manifests itself in software through *user-defined data types*, new classes of objects composed from built-in or other user-defined types. This concept is not new, of course, but languages that support it well, such as Ada, C++, CLOS, Java, Eiffel, and SmallTalk, have only recently seen widespread use.

If you've been programming in C for any length of time, you've probably used the `struct` mechanism. You've also had to provide functions to process those structures. Whether you knew it or not, you were simulating a user-defined type. Chances are, for example, you've needed to handle dates in a program. Listing 7.1 defines a `struct Date` and two functions for processing dates, one to format a date as month, day, year, and a function to compare dates. (See Listing 7.2 for the implementation and Listing 7.3 for a test program).

To use this abstract data type, you only need to know the protocol for its two functions, or in other words, its *interface*. You don't need to know how the functions were implemented, nor do you even need to know the structure layout. A well-defined abstraction allows you to concentrate on the outside view while ignoring implementation details. This concept of placing a barrier between interface and implementation is called *encapsulation*. There is a hole in the

Listing 7.1 A Date type in C

```c
/* date.h */
#ifndef DATE_H
#define DATE_H

struct Date
{
    int month;
    int day;
    int year;
};
typedef struct Date Date;   /* Not needed in C++ */

char *date_format(const Date*, char*);
int date_compare(const Date*, const Date*);

#endif
```

Listing 7.2 Implementation for the Date type

```c
/* date.c */
#include <stdio.h>
#include "date.h"

static const char *month_text[] =
    {"Bad month",   "January",   "February",   "March",    "April",
     "May",         "June",      "July",       "August",   "September",
     "October",     "November",  "December"};

char* date_format(const Date*dp, char* buf)
{
    sprintf(buf,"%s %d, %d",
            month_text[dp->month],dp->day,dp->year);
    return buf;
}

int date_compare(const Date* dp1, const Date* dp2)
{
    int result = dp1->year - dp2->year;
    if (result == 0)
        result = dp1->month - dp2->month;
    if (result == 0)
        result = dp1->day - dp2->day;
    return result;
}
```

Listing 7.3 Tests the `Date` type

```
/* tdate.c */
#include <stdio.h>
#include "date.h"

#define DATELEN 19

main()
{
    Date d1 = {10,1,1951}, d2 = {3,7,1995};
    char buf[DATELEN+1];
    int cmp;

    printf("d1 == %s\n",date_format(&d1,buf));
    printf("d2 == %s\n",date_format(&d2,buf));
    cmp = date_compare(&d1,&d2);
    printf("d1 %s d2\n", cmp < 0 ? "precedes"
                                 : (cmp > 0) ? "follows"
                                             : "equals");

    return 0;
}

/* Output:
d1 == October 1, 1951
d2 == March 7, 1995
d1 precedes d2
*/
```

encapsulation barrier for type `Date`, of course, because you can bypass the interface and directly manipulate one of the structure members, as in

```
dp->month = 7;
```

To close up that hole, you can take advantage of the fact that the interface itself doesn't need to know anything about a `Date`, it just needs a pointer to it. In Listing 7.4, I define `Date` as an *incomplete type*—I just state that it exists and nothing more. As a client you see only `date2.h`, and therefore know nothing about a `Date`'s layout or implementation. I complete the type in the implementation in Listing 7.5 (the test program is in Listing 7.6). This extra measure of protection costs you something, however. You now need to call explicit create and destroy functions, and you must access all `Date` objects through pointers only.

C++ improves support for user-defined data types in at least three ways: (1) it allows you to define the interface functions within the scope of the `struct`, (2) it has direct language support for prohibiting client access to implementation details, and (3) its constructors and

Listing 7.4   A safer Date type (sort of)

```
/* date2.h */
#ifndef DATE2_H
#define DATE2_H

/* Declare the incomplete Date type */
typedef struct Date Date;

Date* date_create(int, int, int);
char* date_format(const Date*, char*);
int date_compare(const Date*, const Date*);
void date_destroy(Date*);

#endif
```

Listing 7.5   Implementation for Listing 7.4

```
/* date2.c */
#include <stdio.h>
#include <stdlib.h>
#include "date2.h"

struct Date
{
    int month;
    int day;
    int year;
};

static const char *month_text[] =
    {"Bad month",    "January",    "February",    "March",    "April",
     "May",          "June",       "July",        "August",   "September",
     "October",      "November",  "December"};

Date* date_create(int m, int d, int y)
{
    Date* dp = malloc(sizeof(Date));
    if (dp == NULL)
        return NULL;

    dp->month = m;
    dp->day = d;
    dp->year = y;
    return dp;
}
```

Listing 7.5   (continued)

```
char* date_format(const Date* dp, char* buf)
{
    sprintf(buf,"%s %d, %d",
            month_text[dp->month],dp->day,dp->year);
    return buf;
}

int date_compare(const Date* dp1, const Date* dp2)
{
    int result = dp1->year - dp2->year;
    if (result == 0)
        result = dp1->month - dp2->month;
    if (result == 0)
        result = dp1->day - dp2->day;
    return result;
}

void date_destroy(Date* dp)
{
    free(dp);
}
```

destructors automate the task of initialization and cleanup. The Date class in Listings 7.7 and 7.8 differs from that in Listings 7.1 and 7.2 in the following ways:

1. The data members are private, so you can't access them directly in a client program (only the implementation of a member function can).
2. The interface functions are public member functions, so you can only apply them to Date objects, and the function names do not pollute the global namespace. The date_ prefix is no longer necessary, since the operations belong to the class. Note that format and compare are const member functions, because they do not alter a Date's data members.
3. A constructor replaces C's structure initialization syntax, and a destructor provides automatic cleanup when the associated object goes out of scope.
4. The text representations for the month names are now in the scope of struct Date (being static members).

The sample program in Listing 7.9 shows that you invoke member functions with the usual dot-operator for structure members.

Listing 7.6   Tests the new `Date` type

```
/* tdate2.c */
#include <stdio.h>
#include "date2.h"

#define DATELEN 19

main()
{
    Date *d1 = date_create(10,1,1951),
         *d2 = date_create(3,7,1995);
    char buf[DATELEN+1];
    int cmp;

    printf("d1 == %s\n",date_format(d1,buf));
    printf("d2 == %s\n",date_format(d2,buf));
    cmp = date_compare(d1,d2);
    printf("d1 %s d2\n", cmp < 0 ? "precedes"
                                : (cmp > 0) ? "follows"
                                            : "equals");
    date_destroy(d1);
    date_destroy(d2);
    return 0;
}

/* Output:
d1 == October 1, 1951
d2 == March 7, 1995
d1 precedes d2
*/
```

Listing 7.7   The `Date` type in C++

```
// date3.h
#ifndef DATE3_H
#define DATE3_H

struct Date
{
    Date(int, int, int);
    char* format(char*) const;
    int compare(const Date&) const;
```

Listing 7.7 (continued)

```
private:
    int month;
    int day;
    int year;

    static const char* month_text[13];
};

#endif
```

Listing 7.8 Implementation for the Date class

```
// date3.cpp
#include <stdio.h>
#include "date3.h"

const char* Date::month_text[13] =
    {"Bad month",   "January",   "February", "March",    "April",
     "May",         "June",      "July",     "August",   "September",
     "October",     "November", "December"};

Date::Date(int m, int d, int y)
    : month(m),
      day(d),
      year(y)
{}

char* Date::format(char* buf) const
{
    sprintf(buf,"%s %d, %d",month_text[month],day,year);
    return buf;
}

int Date::compare(const Date & dp2) const
{
    int result = year - dp2.year;
    if (result == 0)
        result = month - dp2.month;
    if (result == 0)
        result = day - dp2.day;
    return result;
}
```

Listing 7.9   Illustrates the `Date` class

```
// tdate3.cpp
#include <iostream>
#include "date3.h"

main()
{
    const size_t DATELEN = 19;
    char buf[DATELEN+1];

    Date d1(10,1,1951), d2(3,7,1995);
    cout << "d1 == " << d1.format(buf) << endl;
    cout << "d2 == " << d2.format(buf) << endl;
    int cmp = d1.compare(d2);
    cout << "d1 " << (cmp < 0 ? "precedes"
                                : (cmp > 0) ? "follows"
                                            : "equals")
         << " d2\n";
}

// Output:
d1 == October 1, 1951
d2 == March 7, 1995
d1 precedes d2
```

If it still bothers you that a client can see the layout of your data members, even though she cannot access them, you can hide the data member declarations in a new incomplete type, but this time with absolutely no impact on the `Date` interface (see Listings 7.10–7.11). To do this, I had to define the `DateRep` helper class, and for efficiency and simplicity, I gave the `Date` class direct access to the its data members by making it a *friend* to `DateRep`. The `Date` constructor now needs to create its associated `DateRep` object on the heap, so a destructor is needed to free the heap memory later. Only the include directive has to change in the test program in Listing 7.9 (from `date3.h` to `date4.h`). With a well-defined abstraction, you can change an implementation without inflicting much change on client code.

Operator Overloading

You can make user-defined types nearly as convenient to use as built-in types by adding operator functions to your class definition. In Listings 7.12–7.14, I've added the usual six relational operations and a stream inserter for easy output. For efficiency, I've also made the smaller functions inline (see the header file). Note also the inclusion of the header `<iosfwd>`, which

Listing 7.10 Hides the `Date`'s data in an incomplete type

```
// date4.h
#ifndef DATE4_H
#define DATE4_H

struct DateRep;

struct Date
{
    Date(int, int, int);
    ~Date();
    char* format(char*) const;
    int compare(const Date&) const;

private:
    struct DateRep* drep;

    static const char* month_text[13];
};

#endif
```

Listing 7.11 Implementation for Listing 7.10

```
// date4.cpp
#include <stdio.h>
#include "date4.h"

struct DateRep
{
    DateRep(int, int, int);

private:
    friend struct Date;

    int month;
    int day;
    int year;
};

const char* Date::month_text[13] =
    {"Bad month",    "January",   "February", "March",    "April",
     "May",          "June",      "July",     "August",   "September",
     "October",      "November",  "December"};
```

continued

Listing 7.11   (continued)

```
DateRep::DateRep(int m, int d, int y)
        : month(m),
          day(d),
          year(y)
{}

Date::Date(int m, int d, int y)
{
    drep = new DateRep(m,d,y);
}

Date::~Date()
{
    delete drep;
}

char* Date::format(char* buf) const
{
    sprintf(buf,"%s %d, %d",
            month_text[drep->month],
            drep->day,drep->year);
    return buf;
}

int Date::compare(const Date& dp2) const
{
    int result = drep->year - dp2.drep->year;
    if (result == 0)
        result = drep->month - dp2.drep->month;
    if (result == 0)
        result = drep->day - dp2.drep->day;
    return result;
}
```

provides forward declarations for the standard stream classes. Since an ostream object appears here only by reference, there is no need to include the iostream header, which is one of the largest in the standard C++ library. The implementation of operator<< shows that defining a stream inserter usually reduces to just inserting an object's members into the stream. Notice also that I'm using the class keyword in place of struct. The only difference between the two is that members of a struct are *public* by default, while for a class they default to *private*.

As the definition of the Person class in Listing 7.15 shows, you can compose a new type from other user-defined types, as well as built-in types. Each Person has a birth date, which is a Date object wholly contained within a Person object. The Person constructor passes the Date

Listing 7.12   Adds operators to the Date class

```cpp
// date5.h
#ifndef DATE5_H
#define DATE5_H

#include <iosfwd>
using std::ostream;

class Date
{
public:
    Date(int, int, int);
    int compare(const Date&) const;
    bool operator==(const Date&) const;
    bool operator!=(const Date&) const;
    bool operator<=(const Date&) const;
    bool operator>=(const Date&) const;
    bool operator<(const Date&) const;
    bool operator>(const Date&) const;
    friend ostream& operator<<(ostream&, const Date&);

private:
    int month;
    int day;
    int year;

    static const char* month_text[13];
};

inline bool Date::operator==(const Date& d2) const
{
    return compare(d2) == 0;
}

inline bool Date::operator!=(const Date& d2) const
{
    return compare(d2) != 0;
}

inline bool Date::operator<=(const Date& d2) const
{
    return compare(d2) <= 0;
}

inline bool Date::operator>=(const Date& d2) const
{
    return compare(d2) >= 0;
}
```

continued

Listing 7.12   (continued)

```cpp
inline bool Date::operator<(const Date& d2) const
{
    return compare(d2) < 0;
}

inline bool Date::operator>(const Date& d2) const
{
    return compare(d2) > 0;
}


#endif
```

Listing 7.13   Adds a stream inserter to the Date class implementation

```cpp
// date5.cpp
#include <iostream>
#include "date5.h"

const char* Date::month_text[13] =
    {"Bad month",    "January",   "February", "March",     "April",
     "May",          "June",      "July",     "August",    "September",
     "October",      "November",  "December"};

Date::Date(int m, int d, int y)
    : month(m),
      day(d),
      year(y)
{}

ostream& operator<<(ostream& os, const Date& d)
{
    os << Date::month_text[d.month]
       << ' ' << d.day
       << ", " << d.year;
    return os;
}

int Date::compare(const Date& dp2) const
{
    int result = year - dp2.year;
    if (result == 0)
        result = month - dp2.month;
    if (result == 0)
        result = day - dp2.day;
    return result;
}
```

Listing 7.14 Uses some `Date` comparison operators

```cpp
// tdate5.cpp
#include <iostream>
#include "date5.h"

main()
{
    Date d1(10,1,1951), d2(3,7,1995);

    cout << "d1 == " << d1 << endl;
    cout << "d2 == " << d2 << endl;

    cout << "d1 "
        << (d1 < d2 ? "precedes"
                    : (d1 > d2) ? "follows"
                                : "equals")
        << " d2" << endl;
}

// Output:
d1 == October 1, 1951
d2 == March 7, 1995
d1 precedes d2
```

information on to its `Date` subobject via the *initializer list*, which follows the colon in its function header in the implementation file (Listing 7.16). Notice how the overloaded `operator<<` implicitly uses `Date::operator<<`. Class `Person` also uses the C++ standard string class for its text data members.

Concrete Data Types

C++'s support for abstraction, and operator overloading in particular, can make using your own data types as convenient as using built-in types. What do you typically do with built-in types? You initialize them, assign them to other objects of compatible type, and pass them to or receive them back from functions. You can perform these actions in C++ with types that you define, as long as either you or the compiler provide certain special member functions. The presence of these member functions constitutes what is sometimes called a *concrete data type*, one that behaves much like a built-in type does. These functions include the

> copy constructor
> default constructor (and other constructors as needed)
> assignment operator
> destructor

Listing 7.15   Defines a `Person` data type

```cpp
// person.h
#ifndef PERSON_H
#define PERSON_H

#include <string>
#include "date5.h"

using namespace std; // For string

class ostream;

class Person
{
public:
    Person(const string& = "", const string& = "",
           const Date& = Date(0,0,0), const string& = "");
    bool operator==(const Person&) const;
    friend ostream & operator<<(ostream&, const Person&);

private:
    string last;
    string first;
    Date birth;
    string ssn;
};

#endif
```

Whenever an object is created, a constructor is called to initialize it. The initializer arguments must match a constructor's parameters in number and type. The *default constructor* is the one that takes no arguments. Another special constructor, called the *copy constructor* initializes a new object from an existing object of the same type, and has the signature `T(const T&)`, or `T(T&)`, for some type `T`. This constructor executes whenever you pass or return an object by value, or explicitly initialize a new object from an old one, as with `y` in the following example:

```cpp
T x;
...
T y = x;                // same as "T y(x)"
```

Listing 7.16 The `Person` class implementation

```cpp
// person.cpp
#include <iostream>
#include "person.h"

Person::Person(const string& l, const string& f,
               const Date& b, const string& s)
       : last(l),
         first(f),
         birth(b),
         ssn(s)
{}

ostream& operator<<(ostream& os, const Person& p)
{
    os << '{'
       << p.last << ','
       << p.first << ','
       << '[' << p.birth << ']' << ','
       << p.ssn
       << '}';
    return os;
}

bool Person::operator==(const Person& p) const
{
    return last == p.last &&
           first == p.first &&
           birth == p.birth &&
           ssn == p.ssn;
}
```

The assignment operator executes whenever you assign the value of an object to another existing object. It has the signature

```cpp
T& operator=(const T&)
```

and must always be a member function (not a global function). You can also define assignment from other types, such as from a C-style string to a date:

```cpp
Date& operator=(const char *);      // a possible Date member function
```

Note the assignment statement in Line 18, Listing 7.17 (p3 = p2;). I did not explicitly define Person::operator=, but it seems to have worked anyway. This is because the compiler generated it for me. The absence of operator= in the class definition caused the compiler to generate one that does *memberwise assignment*, like this:

```
Person& Person::operator=(const Person& p)
{
    last = p.last;
    first = p.first;
    birth = p.birth;
    ssn = p.ssn;
    return *this;
}
```

Listing 7.17   Illustrates the Person class

```
// tperson.cpp
#include <iostream>
#include "person.h"      // includes date5.h

main()
{
    Date d1(12,16,1947);
    Person p1("Richardson","Alice",d1,"123-45-6789");
    Person p2("Doe","John");

    cout << "p1 == " << p1 << endl;
    cout << "p2 == " << p2 << endl;
    cout << "p1 " << (p1 == p2 ? "does"
                                : "does not")
        << " equal p2" << endl;

    Person p3;
    p3 = p2;                    // line 18
    cout << "p3 " << (p3 == p2 ? "does"
                                : "does not")
        << " equal p2" << endl;
}

// Output:
p1 == {Richardson,Alice,[December 16, 1947],123-45-6789}
p2 == {Doe,John,[Bad month 0, 0],}
p1 does not equal p2
p3 does equal p2
```

Similarly, if you do not supply a copy constructor, the compiler generates this one:

```
Person::Person(const Person& p)
      : last(p.last),
        first(p.first),
        birth(p.birth),
        ssn(p.ssn)
{}
```

which, as you can see, calls the copy constructor for each member object.

If you define any constructor, other than a copy constructor (which is considered separately), the compiler will not generate a default constructor for you. The compiler-generated default constructor invokes the corresponding default constructor for all user-defined member objects. A compiler-generated destructor calls the destructors associated with any user-defined member objects.

The compiler-generated assignment operator and copy constructor for `Person` worked because the standard string class provides its own version of these two functions, and because the data members of the `Date` class are built in. In general, whenever the state of an object is contained entirely within the object itself, you do not need to override the compiler-generated member functions.

The `Person` class in Listings 7.18 and 7.19, for example, stores its text data on the heap via pointers to `char`. The compiler-generated assignment operator or copy constructor will only copy *pointers* to the receiving object, when what it really needs to do is allocate space on the heap to copy the text to. When I execute the test program on this class, Metaware's C++ compiler gives the following output:

```
p1 == {Richardson,Alice,[December 16, 1947],123-45-6789}
p2 == {Doe,John,[Bad month 0, 0],}
p1 does not equal p2
p3 does equal p2
***free(0x4c105c): Pointer already free
Aborting...
```

At program exit, the compiler calls the `Person` destructor to destroy p3, which frees the text memory on the heap. Since p2 points to the same memory, the destructor attempts to delete it a second time when p2 is destroyed. Listings 7.20 and 7.21 fix the problem by adding the missing member functions.

Listing 7.18   A flawed `Person` class that stores text on the heap

```
// person2.h
#ifndef PERSON2_H
#define PERSON2_H

#include "date5.h"

class ostream;

class Person
{
public:
    Person();
    Person(const char*, const char*, const Date&, const char*);
    ~Person();
    bool operator==(const Person&) const;
    friend ostream & operator<<(ostream&, const Person&);

private:
    char* last;
    char* first;
    Date birth;
    char* ssn;
};

#endif
```

Listing 7.19   The implementation for Listing 7.18, which is missing an assignment operator and copy constructor

```
// person2.cpp
#include <iostream.h>
#include <string.h>
#include <new.h>
#include "person2.h"

static char* clone(const char* s)
{
    // return a copy of a string on the heap
    char* p = new char[strlen(s) + 1];
    return strcpy(p,s);
}
```

Listing 7.19   (continued)

```
Person::Person()
      : birth(Date(0,0,0))
{
    last = clone("");
    first = clone("");
    ssn = clone("");
}

Person::Person(const char* l, const char* f,
               const Date& b, const char* s)
      : birth(b)
{
    last = clone(l);
    first = clone(f);
    ssn = clone(s);
}

Person::~Person()
{
    delete [] last;
    delete [] first;
    delete [] ssn;
}

ostream& operator<<(ostream& os, const Person& p)
{
    os << '{'
       << p.last << ','
       << p.first << ','
       << '[' << p.birth << ']' << ','
       << p.ssn
       << '}';
    return os;
}

bool Person::operator==(const Person& p) const
{
    return strcmp(last,p.last) == 0 &&
           strcmp(first,p.first) == 0 &&
           birth == p.birth &&
           strcmp(ssn,p.ssn) == 0;
}
```

Listing 7.20   A well-behaved version of Listing 7.18

```
// person3.h
#ifndef PERSON3_H
#define PERSON3_H

#include "date5.h"

class ostream;

class Person
{
public:
    Person();
    Person(const char* ,const char* ,const Date& ,const char*);
    Person(const Person&);              // NEW
    ~Person();
    Person& operator=(const Person&);   // NEW
    bool operator==(const Person&) const;
    bool operator<(const Person&) const;
    friend ostream& operator<<(ostream&, const Person&);

private:
    char* last;
    char* first;
    Date birth;
    char* ssn;
};

#endif
```

Type Abstraction

It is often useful to have abstractions that are independent of data type. Such is the case with *containers*. Containers are objects that hold other objects. A *set*, for example, is a container that provides operations to insert, remove, and test elements for membership. Listings 7.22–7.24 illustrate a class that implements a set type for integers. It uses a fixed-size array as the underlying data structure (although bit vectors implement sets of ordinal values more efficiently). If you were to define SetOfLong, or SetOfString, or a set for any other type supporting the equality operator, you would find that the only thing that changed would be the type of objects contained in the set. If you think about it, a set really shouldn't have to care about the type of objects it holds.

C++'s template mechanism allows you to define a generic `set` type that essentially ignores the type of the objects it contains by specifying that type as a parameter. With such a `set` template, you can ask for sets of `int`s and `string`s like this:

```
set<int> s1;
set<string> s2;
```

Chapter 8 covers templates in more detail.

Function Abstraction

Perhaps the most powerful contribution of the object-oriented programming paradigm is *function abstraction*, or, as it is more commonly known, *polymorphism*. Polymorphism occurs when

Listing 7.21   Adds the assignment operator and copy constructor to the `Person` class (compare Listing 7.19)

```
//person3.cpp
#include <iostream>
#include <string>
#include <new>           // for placement new
#include "person3.h"

static char* clone(const char*);

Person::Person(const Person& p)
      : birth(p.birth)
{
    last = clone(p.last);
    first = clone(p.first);
    ssn = clone(p.ssn);
}

Person& Person::operator=(const Person& p)
{
    if (this != &p)
    {
        last = clone(p.last);
        first = clone(p.first);
        ssn = clone(p.ssn);
    }
    return *this;
}

// The rest is as in Listing 7.19
```

Listing 7.22   A set type for integers, using a fixed-size array data structure

```
// set.h
#ifndef SET_H
#define SET_H

#include <stddef.h>  // For size_t

class ostream;

class SetOfInt
{
public:
    SetOfInt();
    bool contains(int) const;
    void insert(int);
    void remove(int);
    void print(ostream&) const;
    friend ostream& operator<<(ostream& os, const SetOfInt& s)
    {
        s.print(os);
        return os;
    }

private:
    enum {LIMIT = 64};
    int elems[LIMIT];
    size_t nelems;
};

#endif
```

you provide the user a function interface whose behavior automatically varies depending on the type of objects it interacts with, without any intervention from the user. This actually happens at the machine level, although no one ever notices. For example, the addition operators in the following code call different underlying algorithms in your processor's microcode:

```
int i = 2, j = 3;
double x = 4.0, y = 5.0;
int k = i + j;                // integer addition
int z = x + y;                // floating-point addition
```

Likewise, the expression p->f can call any number of functions related in an inheritance hierarchy, depending on the type of object the base class pointer p actually refers to at runtime, and if f is a *virtual function*. See Chapter 14 for more on polymorphism.

Listing 7.23   The `SetOfInt` implementation

```cpp
// set.cpp
#include <iostream>
#include <algorithm>     // for std::find, std::remove (see Chapter 17)
#include "set.h"

using namespace std;

SetOfInt::SetOfInt()
{
    nelems = 0;
}

bool SetOfInt::contains(int x) const
{
    const int* eof = elems + nelems;
    return std::find(elems,eof,x) != eof;
}

void SetOfInt::insert(int x)
{
    if (nelems < LIMIT && !contains(x))
        elems[nelems++] = x;
}

void SetOfInt::remove(int x)
{
    int* eof = elems + nelems;
    if (std::remove(elems,eof,x) != eof)
        --nelems;
}

void SetOfInt::print(ostream& os) const
{
    os << '{';
    for (int i = 0; i < nelems; ++i)
    {
        if (i > 0)
            os << ',';
        os << elems[i];
    }
    os << '}';
}
```

Listing 7.24   Tests the `SetOfInt` class

```
// tset.cpp
#include <iostream>
#include "set.h"

main()
{
    SetOfInt s;

    s.insert(77);
    s.insert(33);
    s.insert(500);
    cout << s << endl;

    s.remove(77);
    cout << s << endl;
    cout << "s "
         << (s.contains(77) ? "does" : "does not")
         << " contain 77" << endl;
}

// Output:
{77,33,500}
{33,500}
s does not contain 77
```

Summary

- Complexity is an unavoidable fact of life
- Abstraction is a tool to manage complexity
- Well-defined abstract data types separate interface from implementation
- C++ classes support data abstraction
- Member access control qualifers (`private` and `protected`) support encapsulation
- Concrete types should have well-defined constructors, a copy constructor, an assignment operator, and a destructor
- Operator overloading can help concrete types behave like built-in types
- Templates support type abstraction
- Virtual functions support function abstraction

Templates

Chapter 1 introduced reference parameters with a function to swap integers:

```cpp
#include <iostream>
using namespace std;

void swap(int& x, int& y)
{
    int temp = x;
    x = y;
    y = temp;
}

main()
{
    int a = 1, b = 2;
    swap(a,b);
    cout << "a == " << a << ", b == " << b << endl;
}

// Output:
a == 2, b == 1
```

What if you need to swap objects of other types? You can take advantage of function overloading, of course, and provide a different version of swap for each data type you might need, as in

```cpp
void swap(int& x, int& y)
{
    int temp = x;
    x = y;
    y = temp;
}
```

```
void swap(float& x, float& y)
{
    float temp = x;
    x = y;
    y = temp;
}

void swap(char*& x, char*& y)
{
    char* temp = x;
    x = y;
    y = temp;
}
```

Now you can call swap the same way for each different pair:

```
#include <iostream>
using namespace std;

main()
{
    int a = 1, b = 2;
    float c = 100.0, d = 200.0;
    char *s = "hello", *t = "goodbye";

    swap(a,b);
    cout << "a == " << a << ", b == " << b << endl;
    swap(c,d);
    cout << "c == " << c << ", d == " << d << endl;
    swap(s,t);
    cout << "s == " << s << ", t == " << t << endl;
}

// Output:
a == 2, b == 1
c == 200, d = 100
s == goodbye, t == hello
```

Two observations immediately surface:

1. When you need to process a new type, you need to create a new overload of swap and
   rebuild your software.
2. The *logic* for each overload is identical. Only the data types change.

Wouldn't it be nice if you could capture the swap process just once and substitute different types
of parameters transparently?

Generic Programming

What we need here is support for *type abstraction*, a mechanism that allows us to use data types as parameters. For you reckless developers who live by the philosophy, "When in doubt, use the preprocessor," you might think of making the type a macro parameter. The following macro will generate the code for an arbitrary version of swap:

```
// swap1.h:
#define genswap(T)          \
void swap(T& x, T& y) \
{                           \
    T temp = x;             \
    x = y;                  \
    y = temp;               \
}
```

The test program now becomes

```
#include <iostream>
#include "swap1.h"
using namespace std;

// Generate the needed code:
genswap(int)
genswap(float)
genswap(char*)

main()
{
    // (same as before)
}
```

Although this program works, it certainly looks strange with those macro invocation statements that end without a semicolon. And there is still the chance that you will forget to instantiate all the overloads you need, requiring another turn around the edit-and-compile cycle. Besides, aren't function-like macros supposed to be near extinct in C++? Why can't you just tell the compiler to do all this work for you?

Function Templates

You can, of course. A *function template* is a formal language mechanism that automatically generates code for a function with the appropriate data types inferred from the context of an actual function call. A template for the swap function would look like this:

```
// swap2.h (Template version)
template<class T>
void swap(T& x, T& y)
{
    T t = x;
    x = y;
    y = t;
}
```

The prefix `template<class T>` tells the compiler that the function definition that follows uses T as a type parameter. When the compiler encounters an actual invocation of `swap`, such as

```
swap(a,b);
```

it deduces T from the type of the arguments a and b, and then generates the code for

```
void swap(int& x, int& y).
```

You can now remove the references to the `genswap` macro, and run the test program like this:

```
#include <iostream>
#include "swap2.h"

using std::cout;
using std::endl;
main()
{
    // (same as before)
}
```

It turns out that a `swap` function template is already defined in the standard library, so I had to replace

```
using namespace std;
```

with the statements

```
using std::cout;
using std::endl;
```

to avoid having `std::swap` conflict with my `swap` template. See Chapter 11 for more about namespaces and the `using` keyword. You could also just rename `swap` to something else, of course.

Note that the body of the `swap` template is totally contained in a single include file. Normally you don't define non-inline functions there, but remember that `swap` is *not* a function—it is a *template*, a pattern as it were, that the compiler uses to generate functions on demand. It is common practice to include all of the code of a template in a single include file. (As this book goes to press, this *inclusion model* of template compilation is the only one supported in the Microsoft Windows world, while most UNIX compilers support the *separation model*, wherein function bodies can reside in a separate implementation file. I use only the inclusion model in this book).

It is possible to define a function template with a parameter that is not used in the function argument list; for example,

```
template<class To, class From>
To convert(const From& f)
{
    return To(f);
}
```

Since functions are distinguished by the arguments in a function call, there is no way to infer the type of the parameter `To` in a call to `convert`. In this case you explicitly qualify the function call to specify which instantiation you require:

```
string s = convert<string>("foo");
string s = convert<string,char*>("bar"); // char* optional
```

The first call to `convert` deduces the second template parameter (`From`) as `char*` from the argument "foo". You can also qualify both types explicitly, as the second call illustrates.

Class Templates

C++ also allows *class templates*, where the types used within a class can appear as template parameters. The `SetOfInt` class in Chapter 7, for example, operates independently of the type of objects it holds. You can define a `Set` template by replacing all instances of `int` (when used as the type of the contained objects in `SetOfInt`) with a formal template parameter (see Listing 8.1). To instantiate a template class, you specify the type(s) you want within brackets, as in

```
Set<int> s1;
Set<float> s2;
Set<string> s3;
```

The member functions defined in a class template become in effect function templates, as Listing 8.1 illustrates. Note the token `Set<T>` wherever a class name is required. That's because `Set` is a template, not a class. (`Set<T>` represents a class.) The test programs in Listings 8.2 and 8.3 use sets of `int` and `string`, respectively.

Listing 8.1   A Set class template

```cpp
// set.h
#ifndef SET_H
#define SET_H
#include <iostream>
#include <algorithm>
#include <stddef.h>

template<class T>
class Set
{
public:
    Set();
    bool contains(const T&) const;
    void insert(const T&);
    void remove(const T&);
    void print(std::ostream&) const;
private:
    enum {LIMIT = 64};
    T elems[LIMIT];
    size_t nelems;
};

template<class T>
Set<T>::Set()
{
    nelems = 0;
}

template<class T>
bool Set<T>::contains(const T& x) const
{
    const T* eof = elems + nelems;
    return std::find(elems,eof,x) != eof;
}

template<class T>
void Set<T>::insert(const T& x)
{
    if (nelems < LIMIT && !contains(x))
        elems[nelems++] = x;
}
```

Listing 8.1   (continued)

```
template<class T>
void Set<T>::remove(const T& x)
{
    T* eof = elems + nelems;
    if (std::remove(elems,eof,x) != eof)
        --nelems;
}

template<class T>
void Set<T>::print(std::ostream& os) const
{
    os << '{';
    for (int i = 0; i < nelems; ++i)
    {
        if (i > 0)
            os << ',';
        os << elems[i];
    }
    os << '}';
}

// A Global function:
template<class T>
std::ostream& operator<<(std::ostream& os, const Set<T>& s)
{
    s.print(os);
    return os;
}

#endif
```

Listing 8.2   Tests a set of integers

```
// tset.cpp
#include <iostream>
#include "set.h"
using namespace std;

main()
{
    Set<int> s;

    s.insert(77);
    s.insert(33);
    s.insert(500);
    cout << s << endl;
```

continued

Listing 8.2   (continued)

```
        s.remove(77);
        cout << s << endl;
        cout << "s "
            << (s.contains(77) ? "does" : "does not")
            << " contain 77" << endl;
}

// Output:
{77,33,500}
{33,500}
s does not contain 77
```

Listing 8.3   Tests a set of strings

```
// tsets.cpp
#include <iostream>
#include <string>
#include "set.h"
using namespace std;

main()
{
    Set<string> s;

    s.insert("one");
    s.insert("two");
    s.insert("three");
    cout << s << endl;

    s.remove("three");
    cout << s << endl;
    cout << "s "
        << (s.contains("three") ? "does" : "does not")
        << " contain \"three\"" << endl;
}

// Output:
{one,two,three}
{one,two}
s does not contain "three"
```

On rare occasion you may need to define a member function that is itself an independent template. The *member template* facility allows you to do this:

```
#include <iostream>
using namespace std;

template<class T>
class A
{
public:
    A()
    {
        cout << "default ctor\n";
    }
    template<class B> A(const B& b)
    {
        cout << "converting from " << b << "\n";
    }
    template<class C> void f(C c)
    {
        cout << c << endl;
    }
};
```

In the following test program, the declaration of a invokes the default constructor `A<int>::A()`. The call `a.f("hello")` instantiates `void A<int>::f(char*)`, and the next call instantiates `void A<int>::f(int)`. Defining a2 requires the constructor `A<float>::A(const int&)`, and the last function call creates code for `void A<float>::f(char)`. Arguments for the template parameter C must be compatible with `std::ostream::operator<<`, or the compiler will issue a diagnostic.

```
main()
{
    A<int> a;
    a.f("hello");
    a.f(1);

    A<float> a2(120);
    a2.f('c');
}

// Output:
default ctor
hello1
converting from 120
c
```

For convenience, I fully defined the members of A above *in situ*, meaning that the function bodies appear in the class template definition itself. To define f outside of A's definition requires the following syntax:

```
template<class T> template<class C>
void A<T>::f(C c) {...}
```

Template Parameters

In addition to member data and functions, classes can also contain types, defined as either nested classes or as typedefs. Consider the following class declarations:

```
#include <iostream>
using namespace std;

class Foo
{
public:
    typedef int U;
};

class Bar
{
public:
    typedef char* U;
};

template<class T>
class Baz
{
    typename T::U x;
public:
    Baz(const typename T::U& t) : x(t){};
    void f() {cout << x << endl;}
};

main()
{
    Baz<Foo> b1(1);
    b1.f();

    Baz<Bar> b2("hello!");
    b2.f();
}

// Output:
1
hello!
```

Compilers can easily get confused with declarations like Baz<T>::x. Whenever you use something like T::U, where T is a template type parameter and U is a type, use the keyword `type-name` to tell the compiler that T::U is a type. You can also use `typename` in place of `class` in formal template parameter declarations.

Templates can also have *nontype* parameters, the most common of which is an integral value used as a dimension for a container. Listing 8.4 defines a fixed-size `Set` template, where the second template parameter (`LIMIT`) becomes the dimension of the underlying array. You declare such a `Set` like this:

```
Set<int, 10> s;
```

Nontype template arguments must be compile-time constant expressions yielding either an integral value (including enumerated constants), a pointer, or a reference. Floating-point values are not allowed.

Listing 8.4   A `Set` template with a nontype template parameter

```
// set2.h

#ifndef SET_H
#define SET_H
#include <iostream>
#include <algorithm>
#include <stddef.h>

template<typename T, size_t LIMIT>
class Set
{
public:
    Set();
    bool contains(const T&) const;
    void insert(const T&);
    void remove(const T&);
    void print(std::ostream&) const;

private:
    T elems[LIMIT];
    size_t nelems;
};

template<typename T, size_t LIMIT>
Set<T,LIMIT>::Set()
{
    nelems = 0;
}

// etc.
```

You can also use a *default template parameter*, so your users can choose either to specify the size of the container or to rely on your published default value. In this case, you would define Set as follows:

```
template<typename T, size_t LIMIT = 10>
class Set
{
    // etc.
```

and the declaration

```
Set<int> s;
```

would set LIMIT to 10.

Default template parameters can also be type parameters. For example, the definition of actual set template in the standard C++ library begins like this:

```
template<class Key, class Compare = less<Key>,
        class Allocator = allocator<Key> >
    class set {...
```

Unless the user specifies a Compare function object and an allocator, the default ones will be instantiated. (See Chapter 16 for more about standard containers).

Template Specialization

It is conceivable that you may want to override the code generated by a template on occasion. Consider, for example, the following function template for comparing two objects:

```
template<class T>
int comp(const T& t1, const T& t2)
{
    return (t1 < t2) ? -1 : (t1 == t2) ? 0 : 1;
}
```

A char* instantiation of comp (or any pointer type, for that matter) will not behave correctly, of course. To customize comp for C-style strings, you can provide an *explicit specialization*, as follows:

```
template<>
int comp<const char*>(const char*& t1, const char*& t2)
{
    return strcmp(t1,t2);
}
```

As long as this specialization is declared before you call comp with C-style string arguments, it will override the default instantiation from the primary template. The program in Listing 8.5 shows that you can specialize a template in a number of syntactically different ways, including

Listing 8.5   Illustrates function template specialization

```cpp
// spec.cpp
#include <iostream>
#include <string.h>          // Standard C
#include <string>

using namespace std;

template<class T>
size_t bytes(T& t)
{
    cout << "(using primary template)\n";
    return sizeof t;
}

size_t bytes(char*& s)
{
    cout << "(using char* overload)\n";
    return strlen(s) + 1;
}

size_t bytes<wchar_t*>(wchar_t*& w)
{
    cout << "(using wchar_t* specialization)\n";
    return 2*(wcslen(w) + 1);
}

template<>
size_t bytes<>(string& s)
{
    cout << "(using string explicit specialization)\n";
    return sizeof s;
}

template<>
size_t bytes<float>(float& x)
{
    cout << "(using float explicit specialization)\n";
    return sizeof x;
}
```

continued

Listing 8.5   (continued)

```
main()
{
    int i;
    cout << "bytes in i: " << bytes(i) << endl;
    char *s = "hello";
    cout << "bytes in s: " << bytes(s) << endl;
    wchar_t *w = L"goodbye";
    cout << "bytes in w: " << bytes(w) << endl;
    string t;
    cout << "bytes in t: " << bytes(t) << endl;
    float x;
    cout << "bytes in x: " << bytes(x) << endl;
    double y;
    cout << "bytes in y: " << bytes(y) << endl;
    return 0;
}

// Output:
(using primary template)
bytes in i: 4
(using char* overload)
bytes in s: 6
(using wchar_t* specialization)
bytes in w: 16
(using string explicit specialization)
bytes in t: 16
(using float explicit specialization)
bytes in x: 4
(using primary template)
bytes in y: 8
```

simple function overloading, but the explicit specialization above is recommended for consistency of style. You can also specialize classes (see Listing 8.6).

It is even possible to specialize only *some* of a class template's parameters. In Listing 8.7 the *partial specialization* A<T*,U> will be used to instantiate A objects whenever the first template argument is a pointer to any type, and A<T,T> will be invoked whenever the argument types are identical. Whenever you see angle brackets with types immediately following a class template name, you know you're looking at a template specialization. As you saw above, some full specializations do not need them, but partial specializations always need them. Partial specialization of function templates is not supported in C++.

Listing 8.6   Illustrates a class template specialization

```cpp
// spec2.cpp
#include <iostream>
using namespace std;

template<typename T>
class A
{
public:
    A() {cout << "primary\n";}
};

class A<char>
{
public:
    A() {cout << "char specialization\n";}
};

template<>
class A<float>
{
public:
    A() {cout << "float specialization\n";}
};

main()
{
    A<int> a1;
    A<char> a2;
    A<float> a3;
}

// Output:
primary
char specialization
float specialization
```

Summary

- Templates implement *type abstraction*. You can think of the template facility as a compile-time mechanism that takes types as parameters.
- The compiler instantiates a function from a function template when it encounters a related function invocation in your code, inferring its type parameter(s) from the arguments of the function call (unless you explicitly provide them).

Listing 8.7   Illustrates partial specialization of class templates

```cpp
// partial.cpp
#include <iostream>
using namespace std;

template<class T, class U>
class A
{
public:
    A() {cout << "primary template\n";}
};

template<class T, class U>
class A<T*, U>
{
public:
    A() {cout << "<T*,U> partial specialization\n";}
};

template<class T>
class A<T, T>
{
public:
    A() {cout << "<T,T> partial specialization\n";}
};

template<class T, U>
class A<int, U>
{
public:
    A() {cout << "<int, U> partial specialization\n";}
};

main()
{
    A<char, int> a1;
    A<char*, int> a2;
    A<float, float> a3;
    A<int, float> a4;
}

// Output:
primary template
<T*,U> specialization
<T,T> specialization
<int,U> specialization
```

- Classes are instantiated from a class template when you declare them with explicit type arguments.
- You can provide both type and nontype parameters in template declarations. Nontype parameters must be compile-time, constant expressions.
- Default template arguments are allowed. Like default function arguments, they must only appear as trailing arguments in a template declaration.
- You can override the template instantiation mechanism for specific sets of template arguments via template specialization. Partial specialization, where only some of the template parameters are specialized, is also allowed and is recognized in code by angle brackets following the template name.

CHAPTER 9

Bit Manipulation

T he ability to manipulate the individual bits of an integer is essential in systems programming. In the MSDOS and UNIX file systems, for example, each disk file has an associated attribute byte. You can delete-protect a file or even omit it from directory listings, depending on which attribute bits you set. Before the days of C, most programmers had to resort to assembly language to manipulate bits. Nowadays, with bitwise operators and the host system interface that most compilers provide, there is almost nothing that you cannot do with your operating system from within a C program. In this chapter I review common bit-twiddling techniques and introduce the `bitset<N>` and `vector<bool>` class templates from the standard C++ library.

Bitwise Operators

There are six bitwise operators (see Table 9.1). As the program in Listing 9.1 illustrates, *the bitwise-or* operator sets a bit in the result if either one of the corresponding bits in the operands is set ("set" means "has the value one"). For example,

```
     01010101    (== 0x55)
|    11110000    (== 0xf0)
-------------
=    11110101    (== 0xf5)
```

The *bitwise-and* operator sets only those bits whose corresponding operands are both set:

```
     01010101
&    11110000
-------------
=    01010000    (== 0x50)
```

Listing 9.1 Illustrates bitwise operators

```
// bit1.cpp
#include <iostream>
#include <iomanip>
using namespace std;

main()
{
    typedef unsigned int word;
    typedef unsigned char byte;
    byte a = 0x55;
    byte b = 0xf0;

    cout.setf(ios::hex, ios::basefield);
    cout.setf(ios::uppercase);
    cout.fill('0');

    cout << "a | b == " << setw(2) << word(a | b) << endl;
    cout << "a & b == " << setw(2) <<  word(a & b) << endl;
    cout << "a ^ b == " << setw(2) <<  word(a ^ b) << endl;
    cout << "~a == " << setw(2) <<  word(byte(~a)) << endl;
    cout << "a << 1 == " << setw(2) <<  word(a << 1) << endl;
    cout << "b >> 6 == " << setw(2) <<  word(a >> 6) << endl;
}

// Output:
a | b == F5
a & b == 50
a ^ b == A5
~a == AA
a << 1 == AA
b >> 6 == 03
```

Table 9.1 Bitwise operators

Operator	Meaning
&	bitwise and
|	bitwise or
^	bitwise exclusive–or
~	bitwise complement
<<	shift left
>>	shift right

The *bitwise-exclusive-or* operator sets those bits when one or the other (but not both) of the original operands is set:

```
    01010101
^   11110000
    ------------
=   10100000     (== 0xa0)
```

The *bitwise-not* operator "flips" each bit by making each one a zero and vice versa. The cast to int in Listing 9.1 (i.e., word) is needed because cout tries to print chars as characters instead of numbers. The cast to unsigned char (i.e., byte) is necessary because standard-conforming compilers always promote chars to ints before applying bitwise operations. Without the cast the output would be

```
~a == FFFFFFAA
```

since standard output mechanisms never truncate significant values in numbers, and ints on my platform are four bytes wide.

The *shift operators* shift all bits left or right the number of positions specified in the right operand. Bits that "fall off the end" are lost. The left-shift operator resets all vacated bits. When shifting signed integers to the right, some machines zero-fill while others replicate the sign bit. Consequently, it is common practice for bit manipulation to declare integers unsigned, which always zero-fill when you shift them to the right.

Accessing Individual Bits

Quite often you need to set, reset, or test individual bits. If not too many bits are involved, you might consider using bitfield structures. For example, suppose you are only interested in bits 4 and 5 of an integer. Logically, bits are numbered right to left, starting from zero (i.e., the bit number is the power of two represented by each place in the binary representation of a number). On a little-endian machine (see Chapter 2 for an explanation of "endian"), the following structure would be suitable:

```
struct bits4_5
{
    unsigned : 4;              /* Skip bits 0 up thru 3 */
    unsigned bit4 : 1;
    unsigned bit5 : 1;
};
```

A big-endian architecture calls for

```
struct bits4_5
{
    unsigned int : 10;        /* Skip bits 15 down thru 6 */
    unsigned int bit5 : 1;
    unsigned int bit4 : 1;
};
```

You can then process the bits via the named variables:

```
unsigned int x;
struct bits4_5 *xp = (struct bits4_5 *) &x;
xp->bit4 = 0;          /* reset bit4 */
xp->bit5 = 1;          /* set bit5 */
f(xp);                 /* Perhaps f might modify the bits */
if (xp->bit4)          /* Is bit4 still set? */
    ...
```

This technique is somewhat unattractive, however: It lacks portability and makes processing a large number of bits cumbersome. The preferred method to manipulate arbitrary, individual bits is via the bitwise operators. For example, to set the ith bit of an integer, form a mask with a one in the ith bit position and zeroes elsewhere (I'll call it the *one-mask)*, then bitwise-or it into the number:

```
x |= (1u << i);
```

To turn a bit off, form the complement of the above mask (the *zero-mask*) and bitwise-and it in:

```
x &= ~(1u << i);
```

The program in Listing 9.2 sets all the bits of an integer in turn, logically right to left, and resets them in the same order. The quantity CHAR_BIT, from <limits.h>, is the number of bits in a byte.

To toggle a bit, exclusive-or the one-mask into the number:

```
x ^= (1u << i);
```

To see if a bit is set or not, bitwise-and the integer with the same mask:

```
x & (1u << i);
```

This expression returns zero if the bit is not set, or nonzero (two to the ith power, actually) if it is set. The following useful idiom returns a zero or one only, in case you want to use the result as an index into an array:

```
!!(x & (1u << i));
```

The header file in Listing 9.3 defines macros for nondestructive versions of these operations, and declares some useful functions. The function implementations in Listing 9.4 use the nbits macro to compute the size of an unsigned int in bits. The function fputb prints an unsigned integer in binary form with bit-zero rightmost and with leading zeroes if necessary. The function fgetb reads a string of bit characters and converts it into an unsigned. The curious statement

```
sprintf(format," %%%d[01]",nb);
```

Listing 9.2   Sets and resets individual bits

```cpp
// bit2.cpp:  Set and reset individual bits
#include <iostream>
#include <iomanip>
#include <climits>        // <limits.h>
using namespace std;

main()
{
    typedef unsigned short word;
    const size_t NBYTES = sizeof(word);
    const size_t NBITS = NBYTES * CHAR_BIT;
    const size_t NXDIGITS = NBYTES * 2;
    word n = 0;

    cout.setf(ios::hex, ios::basefield);
    cout.setf(ios::uppercase);
    cout.fill('0');

    // Set each bit in turn:
    for (int i = 0; i < NBITS; ++i)
    {
        n |= (1u << i);
        cout << setw(NXDIGITS) << n << endl;
    }
    cout << endl;

    // Now turn them off:
    for (int i = 0; i < NBITS; ++i)
    {
        n &= ~(1u << i);
        cout << setw(NXDIGITS) << n << endl;
    }
}

// Output:
0001
0003
0007
000F
001F
003F
007F
00FF
01FF
03FF
07FF
```

Listing 9.2   (continued)

```
0FFF
1FFF
3FFF
7FFF
FFFF

FFFE
FFFC
FFF8
FFF0
FFE0
FFC0
FF80
FF00
FE00
FC00
F800
F000
E000
C000
8000
0000
```

Listing 9.3   Declarations for bit access functions

```
/* bit.h:    Bitwise functions for unsigned ints */
#ifndef BIT_H
#define BIT_H

#include <stdio.h>
#include <limits.h>

#define mask1(i)    (1u << i)
#define mask0(i)   ~(1u << i)

#define set(n,i)      ((n) | mask1(i))
#define reset(n,i)    ((n) & mask0(i))
#define toggle(n,i)   ((n) ^ mask1(i))
#define test(n,i)    !!((n) & mask1(i))

#define nbits(x) (sizeof(x) * CHAR_BIT)
```

continued

Listing 9.3   (continued)

```
unsigned fputb(unsigned, FILE *);
unsigned fgetb(FILE *);
unsigned count(unsigned);

#endif
```

Listing 9.4 Implementation file for `bit.h`

```
/* bit.c:     Bit operations for unsigned ints */
#include <stdio.h>
#include <limits.h>
#include <stdlib.h>
#include <string.h>
#include "bit.h"

unsigned fputb(unsigned n, FILE *f)
{
    int i;
    size_t nb = nbits(n);

    /* Print the binary form of a number */
    for (i = 0; i < nb; ++i)
        fprintf(f,"%d",test(n,nb-1-i));
    return n;
}

unsigned fgetb(FILE *f)
{
    unsigned n = 0;
    size_t nb = nbits(n);
    size_t slen;
    char *buf = malloc(nb+1);
    char format[9];
    int i;

    if (buf == NULL)
        return 0;

    /* Build read-format (e.g., " %16[01]") */
    sprintf(format," %%%d[01]",nb);
    if (fscanf(f,format,buf) != 1)
        return 0;
```

Listing 9.4 (continued)

```
    /* Set corresponding bits in n */
    slen = strlen(buf);
    for (i = 0; i < slen; ++i)
        if (buf[slen-1-i] == '1')
            n = set(n,i);

    free(buf);
    return n;
}

unsigned count(unsigned n)
{
    unsigned sum = 0;

    while (n)
    {
        if (n & 1u)
            ++sum;
        n >>= 1;
    }
    return sum;
}
```

builds a scan format string that skips whitespace and then reads up to nb ones and zeroes or until it scans a nonbit character. You might think that you could avoid the sprintf by using a variable-width format descriptor in the scan:

```
fscanf(f," %*[01]",nb,buf);
```

Unfortunately, variable-width substitution doesn't work with scan sets. (For more on scan sets and related text processing, see Chapter 17.)

The count function computes the number of one-bits in a number by right-shifting one bit at a time and testing bit-zero. The test program in Listing 9.5 illustrates these functions.

Large Bitsets

Since standard C/C++ guarantees that a long holds at least 32 bits, an unsigned long is often large enough to hold all the flags you'll need in an application. Listings 9.6 and 9.7 illustrate Bitmask, an efficient, low-overhead C++ class that gives you easy access to the bits in a long. But what if you need more bits than an integer holds? For example, suppose that you must create a "picklist" user interface object. A picklist is a scrollable, pop-up listbox that allows the user to choose multiple entries. The number of entries can easily exceed the number of bits in a long

Listing 9.5 Illustrates the bit access functions from `bit.h`

```c
/* tbit.c:  Use bit operations from bit.h */
#include <stdio.h>
#include "bit.h"

main()
{
    int i;
    unsigned int n = 0;
    size_t nb = nbits(n);

    /* Set the even bits */
    for (i = 0; i < nb; i += 2)
        n = set(n,i);
    printf("n == %08X (",n);
    fputb(n,stdout);
    printf("), count == %d\n",count(n));

    /* Toggle the upper half */
    for (i = nb/2; i < nb; ++i)
        n = toggle(n,i);
    printf("n == %08X (",n);
    fputb(n,stdout);
    printf("), count == %d\n",count(n));

    /* Reset the lower half */
    for (i = 0; i < nb/2; ++i)
        n = reset(n,i);
    printf("n == %08X (",n);
    fputb(n,stdout);
    printf("), count == %d\n",count(n));

    /* Read a bit string */
    fputs("Enter a bit string: ",stderr);
    n = fgetb(stdin);
    printf("n == %08X (",n);
    fputb(n,stdout);
    printf("), count == %d\n",count(n));

    return 0;
}

/* Sample Execution:
n == 55555555 (01010101010101010101010101010101), count == 16
n == AAAA5555 (10101010101010100101010101010101), count == 16
n == AAAA0000 (10101010101010100000000000000000), count == 8
Enter a bit string: 10100100010000100000010000001
n == 0A442081 (00001010010001000010000010000001), count == 7
*/
```

Listing 9.6 A 32-bit `Bitmask` class

```
// bitmask.h:        Access bits in an unsigned long
#include <stddef.h>
#include <assert.h>
#include <limits.h>

#if !defined(BITMASK_H)
#define BITMASK_H

class Bitmask
{
    typedef unsigned long _Block;

public:
    explicit Bitmask(_Block n = 0ul);
    bool test(size_t pos) const;
    void set(size_t pos);
    void set1(size_t pos, bool val);
    void reset(size_t pos);
    void reset();

    Bitmask& operator|=(const Bitmask&);
    Bitmask& operator&=(const Bitmask&);
    friend Bitmask operator|(const Bitmask&, const Bitmask&);
    friend Bitmask operator&(const Bitmask&, const Bitmask&);
    Bitmask operator~() const;

    operator _Block() const;
    size_t size() const;

private:
    Block m_Bits;
};


inline Bitmask::Bitmask(_Block n)
{
    m_Bits = n;
}

inline bool Bitmask::test(size_t pos) const
{
    assert(0 <= pos && pos < size());
    return m_Bits & (1ul << pos);
}
```

continued

Listing 9.6   (continued)

```
inline void Bitmask::set(size_t pos)
{
    assert(0 <= pos && pos < size());
    m_Bits |= (1ul << pos);
}

inline void Bitmask::set1(size_t pos, bool val)
{
    val ? set(pos) : reset(pos);
}

inline void Bitmask::reset(size_t pos)
{
    assert(0 <= pos && pos < size());
    m_Bits &= ~(1ul << pos);
}

inline void Bitmask::reset()
{
    m_Bits = 0ul;
}

inline Bitmask& Bitmask::operator|=(const Bitmask& b)
{
    m_Bits |= b.m_Bits;
    return *this;
}

inline Bitmask& Bitmask::operator&=(const Bitmask& b)
{
    m_Bits &= b.m_Bits;
    return *this;
}

inline Bitmask operator|(const Bitmask& b1, const Bitmask& b2)
{
    return Bitmask(b1.m_Bits | b2.m_Bits);
}

inline Bitmask operator&(const Bitmask& b1, const Bitmask& b2)
{
    return Bitmask(b1.m_Bits & b2.m_Bits);
}
```

Listing 9.6   (continued)

```
inline Bitmask Bitmask::operator~() const
{
    return Bitmask(~m_Bits);
}

inline Bitmask::operator Bitmask::_Block() const
{
    return m_Bits;
}

inline size_t Bitmask::size() const
{
    return sizeof(_Block) * CHAR_BIT;
}

#endif
```

Listing 9.7   Tests the `Bitmask` class

```
// tbitmask.cpp:    Tests the Bitmask class
#include "bitmask.h"
#include <iostream>
using namespace std;

main()
{
    Bitmask b;

    cout.setf(ios::boolalpha);
    cout.setf(ios::hex, ios::basefield);

    b.set(1);
    b.set(3);
    cout << b << endl;

    b.reset(1);
    cout << b << endl;
    cout << b.test(1) << endl;
    cout << b.test(2) << endl;
    cout << b.test(3) << endl;

    b |= Bitmask(0xabcdef00);
    cout << b << endl;
```

continued

Listing 9.7 (continued)

```cpp
    // Print entire bitmask as a binary string:
    for (int i = b.size()-1; i >= 0; --i)
        cout << (b.test(i) ? '1' : '0');
    cout << endl;
}

// Output:
a
8
false
false
true
abcdef08
10101011110011011110111100001000
```

integer. The most efficient way to track the state of each entry is to associate a *bitset* with the picklist: If the user highlights the ith entry, then you set the ith bit.

You can of course use an array of unsigned integers to hold the bits you need:

```
array index:      0   1   . . .     N-2    N-1
              ┌────┬────┬────────┬────────┬────┐
              │XX  │    │        │        │    │
              └────┴────┴────────┴────────┴────┘
bit position: n-1                      . . . 210
```

If you need n bits, then you need N = ceil(n / BLKSIZ) array elements, where BLKSIZ is the number of bits in an unsigned (or whatever integral type you derive the array from). If n is not a multiple of BLKSIZ, then there will be unused bits in the zeroth block (represented by XX above). Accessing a particular bit now reduces to finding the particular block it resides in and computing the offset for the mask to apply to that block. To find the right block, notice the following pattern:

Bits in this range	are in this block,	and b/BLKSIZ ==
[0 , BLKSIZ-1]	N-1	0
[BLKSIZ , 2*BLKSIZ-1]	N-2	1
. . .	. . .	. . .
[(N-1)*BLKSIZ , n-1]	0	N-1

If b is the bit number in question, then

B + b/BLKSIZ == N-1

where B is the number of the block we are after. Therefore,

```
B = N-1 - b/BLKSIZ
```

The offset of bit b within block B is simply

```
offset = b % BLKSIZ
```

If `bits` is the array name, then, you can process the bth bit with these expressions:

```
bits[B] |=  (1u << offset);     /* set */
bits[B] &= ~(1u << offset);     /* reset */
bits[B] ^=  (1u << offset);     /* toggle */
!!(bits[B] & (1u << offset));   /* test */
```

   The header file in Listing 9.8 presents an interface for processing arbitrarily large bitsets. In addition to the functions already discussed, it adds conversions to and from unsigned in case

Listing 9.8 Bits object interface

```
/* bits.h:    Large bit sets */
#ifndef BITS_H
#define BITS_H

#include <stdio.h>

typedef struct bits Bits;

Bits* bits_create(size_t nbits);
unsigned bits_to_uint(const Bits *);
Bits* bits_from_uint(Bits *, unsigned);
Bits* bits_set(Bits* , size_t bit);
Bits* bits_set_all(Bits* );
Bits* bits_reset(Bits*, size_t bit);
Bits* bits_reset_all(Bits*);
Bits* bits_toggle(Bits*, size_t bit);
Bits* bits_toggle_all(Bits *);
int bits_test(const Bits*, size_t bit);
int bits_any(const Bits*);
size_t bits_count(const Bits*);
Bits* bits_put(Bits*, FILE *);
Bits* bits_get(Bits*, FILE *);
void bits_destroy(Bits*);

#endif
```

you are working with only word-sized bitsets and want to interface with your host environment. The statement

```
typedef struct bits Bits;
```

declares `struct bits` as an incomplete type with synonym `Bits`. The definition of the structure is in the implementation file (see Listing 9.9; for a discussion on incomplete types, see Chapter 2). If you want to use another integral type for the base array, just substitute it for `unsigned int` in Line 10 of `bits.c` (Listing 9.9).

A `Bits` object consists of the number of bits allowed, the array of integers, the number of elements in the array, and a mask to reset the unused bits to zero after certain operations that set them. The test program in Listing 9.10 shows how you might use a `Bits` object in an application.

Listing 9.9   `Bits` object implementation

```
/* bits.c */
#include <stdio.h>
#include <stdlib.h>
#include <limits.h>
#include <string.h>
#include <assert.h>
#include "bits.h"

/* Pick the base integral type */
typedef unsigned int Block;          /* line 10 */

/* Some implementation specifics */
#define BLKSIZ            (CHAR_BIT * sizeof(Block))
#define offset(b)         (b % BLKSIZ)
#define mask1(b)          ((Block)1 << offset(b))
#define mask0(b)          (~mask1(b))

/* Data Structure */
typedef struct bits
{
    size_t nbits_;      /* The # of bits */
    Block *bits_;       /* The base array */
    size_t nblks_;      /* The # of blocks in base array */
    Block clean_mask_;  /* To mask off unused bits */
} Bits;
```

Listing 9.9   (continued)

```c
/* Private functions */
static size_t word_(const Bits* bp, size_t bit)
{
    return bp->nblks_ - 1 - bit/BLKSIZ;
}

static void set_(Bits* bp, size_t b)
{
    bp->bits_[word_(bp,b)] |= mask1(b);
}

static void reset_(Bits* bp, size_t b)
{
    bp->bits_[word_(bp,b)] &= mask0(b);
}

static void toggle_(Bits* bp, size_t b)
{
    bp->bits_[word_(bp,b)] ^= mask1(b);
}

static int test_(const Bits* bp,size_t b)
{
    return !!(bp->bits_[word_(bp,b)] & mask1(b));
}

static size_t count_block_(Block n)
{
    size_t sum = 0;

    while (n)
    {
        if (n & (Block)1)
            ++sum;
        n >>= 1;
    }
    return sum;
}

static void cleanup_(Bits* bp)
{
    if (bp->nbits_ % BLKSIZ)
        bp->bits_[0] &= bp->clean_mask_;
}
```

continued

Listing 9.9   (continued)

```c
/* Implementation of public interface starts here */
Bits* bits_create(size_t nbits)
{
    Bits *bp = malloc(sizeof(Bits));
    size_t nbytes;

    if (bp == NULL)
        return NULL;

    /* Allocate base array */
    bp->nblks_ = (nbits + BLKSIZ - 1) / BLKSIZ;
    nbytes = bp->nblks_ * sizeof(Block);
    bp->bits_ = malloc(nbytes);
    if (bp->bits_ == NULL)
    {
        free(bp);
        return NULL;
    }

    memset(bp->bits_,'\0',nbytes);
    bp->nbits_ = nbits;
    bp->clean_mask_ = ~(Block)0 >> (bp->nblks_*BLKSIZ - nbits);
    return bp;
}

unsigned bits_to_uint(const Bits* bp)
{
    size_t nblks = sizeof(unsigned) / sizeof(Block);
    if (nblks > 1)
    {
        int i;
        unsigned n = bp->bits_[bp->nblks_ - nblks];

        /* Collect low-order subblocks into an unsigned */
        if (nblks > bp->nblks_)
            nblks = bp->nblks_;
        while (--nblks)
            n = (n << BLKSIZ) | bp->bits_[bp->nblks_ - nblks];
        return n;
    }
    else
        return (unsigned) bp->bits_[bp->nblks_ - 1];
}
```

Listing 9.9   (continued)

```c
Bits* bits_from_uint(Bits* bp, unsigned n)
{
    size_t nblks = sizeof(unsigned) / sizeof(Block);
    assert(bp);
    memset(bp->bits_, '\0', bp->nblks_ * sizeof(Block));
    if (nblks > 1)
    {
        int i;
        if (nblks > bp->nblks_)
            nblks = bp->nblks_;
        for (i = 1; i <= nblks; ++i)
        {
            bp->bits_[bp->nblks_ - i] = (Block) n;
            n >>= BLKSIZ;
        }
    }
    else
        bp->bits_[bp->nblks_ - 1] = n;

    return bp;
}

Bits* bits_set(Bits* bp, size_t bit)
{
    assert(bp && (bit < bp->nbits_));
    set_(bp,bit);
    return bp;
}

Bits* bits_set_all(Bits* bp)
{
    assert(bp);
    memset(bp->bits_,~0u,bp->nblks_*sizeof(Block));
    cleanup_(bp);
    return bp;
}

Bits* bits_reset(Bits* bp, size_t bit)
{
    assert(bp && (bit < bp->nbits_));
    reset_(bp,bit);
    return bp;
}
```

continued

Listing 9.9 (continued)

```
Bits* bits_reset_all(Bits* bp)
{
    assert(bp);
    memset(bp->bits_,'\0',bp->nblks_*sizeof(Block));
    return bp;
}

Bits* bits_toggle(Bits* bp, size_t bit)
{
    assert(bp && (bit < bp->nbits_));
    toggle_(bp,bit);
    return bp;
}

Bits* bits_toggle_all(Bits* bp)
{
    size_t nw;

    assert(bp);
    nw = bp->nblks_;
    while (nw--)
        bp->bits_[nw] = ~bp->bits_[nw];
    cleanup_(bp);
    return bp;
}

int bits_test(const Bits* bp,size_t bit)
{
    assert(bp && (bit < bp->nbits_));
    return test_(bp,bit);
}

int bits_any(const Bits* bp)
{
    int i;

    assert(bp);
    for (i = 0; i < bp->nblks_; ++i)
        if (bp->bits_[i])
            return 1;
    return 0;
}
```

Listing 9.9 (continued)

```c
size_t bits_count(const Bits* bp)
{
    int i;
    size_t sum;

    assert(bp);
    for (i = 0, sum = 0; i < bp->nblks_; ++i)
        sum += count_block_(bp->bits_[i]);
    return sum;
}

Bits* bits_put(Bits* bp, FILE *f)
{
    int i;

    assert(bp);
    for (i = 0; i < bp->nbits_; ++i)
        fprintf(f,"%d",bits_test(bp,bp->nbits_-1-i));
    return bp;
}

Bits* bits_get(Bits* bp, FILE *f)
{
    char *buf;
    char format[9];

    /* Reset all bits */
    assert(bp);
    bits_reset_all(bp);

    /* Allocate string buffer */
    buf = malloc(bp->nbits_+1);
    if (buf == NULL)
        return 0;

    /* Build read-format (e.g., " %16[01]") */
    sprintf(format," %%%d[01]",bp->nbits_);
    if (fscanf(f,format,buf) == 1)
    {
        int i;
        size_t slen = strlen(buf);
```

continued

Listing 9.9 (continued)

```
            /* Set corresponding bits in bitset */
        for (i = 0; i < slen; ++i)
            if (buf[slen-1-i] == '1')
                bits_set(bp,i);
    }
    free(buf);
    return bp;
}

void bits_destroy(Bits* bp)
{
    assert(bp);
    free(bp->bits_);
    free(bp);
}
```

Listing 9.10   Illustrates bits objects

```
/* tbits.c:   Test the Bits Interface */
#include <stdio.h>
#include <assert.h>
#include "bits.h"

#define NBITS 36

main()
{
    int i;
    unsigned int n;
    Bits* bp = bits_create(NBITS);

    assert(bp);

    /* Set the even bits */
    for (i = 0; i < NBITS; i += 2)
        bits_set(bp,i);
    bits_put(bp,stdout);
    printf(" (%d)\n",bits_count(bp));

    /* Toggle the upper half */
    for (i = NBITS/2; i < NBITS; ++i)
        bits_toggle(bp,i);
    bits_put(bp,stdout);
    printf(" (%d)\n",bits_count(bp));
```

Listing 9.10   (continued)

```
    /* Reset the lower half */
    for (i = 0; i < NBITS/2; ++i)
        bits_reset(bp,i);
    bits_put(bp,stdout);
    printf(" (%d)\n",bits_count(bp));

    /* Read a bit string */
    fputs("Enter a bit string: ",stderr);
    bits_put(bits_get(bp,stdin),stdout);
    printf(" (%d)\n",bits_count(bp));

    /* Convert to and from unsigned */
    n = bits_to_uint(bp);
    printf("n: %u\n",n);
    bp = bits_from_uint(bp,n);
    bits_put(bp,stdout);
    printf(" (%d)\n",bits_count(bp));

    /* Test any() and test() */
    printf("any? %d\n",bits_any(bp));
    printf("test(0)? %d\n",bits_test(bp,0));

    /* Toggle and reset */
    bits_put(bits_toggle_all(bp),stdout);
    printf(" (%d)\n",bits_count(bp));
    bits_put(bits_reset_all(bp),stdout);
    printf(" (%d)\n",bits_count(bp));
    bits_put(bits_set_all(bp),stdout);
    printf(" (%d)\n",bits_count(bp));

    bits_destroy(bp);
    return 0;
}

/* Sample execution:
010101010101010101010101010101010101 (18)
101010101010101010010101010101010101 (18)
101010101010101010000000000000000000 (9)
Enter a bit string: 101001000100001000001000000100000001
101001000100001000001000000100000001 (8)
n: 1142980865
000001000100001000001000000100000001 (6) /* The lower 32 bits remain */
```

continued

Listing 9.10   (continued)

```
any? 1
test(0)? 1
111110111011110111110111111011111110 (30)
000000000000000000000000000000000000 (0)
111111111111111111111111111111111111 (36)
*/
```

Bit Strings

The storage scheme in a bits object puts bit-zero last in the array, so bits are numbered right to left, just as they are in single integers. In situations where there is no numerical application of bitsets, like the picklist example above, it might seem more natural to number bits from left to right, like a string. It is trivial to modify `bits.c` to make this change in orientation.

```
array index:     0     1   . . .   N-2   N-1
                ┌─────┬─────┬─────┬─────┬─────┐
                │     │     │     │     │  XX │
                └─────┴─────┴─────┴─────┴─────┘
bit position: 012 . . .                    n-1
```

The block for the bth bit is now

```
B = b / BLKSIZ
```

and the offset is calculated from the left instead of the right of the block:

```
offset = BLKSIZ - b%BLKSIZ - 1
```

Wish List

There are a number of features we could and should add to these objects. It would be convenient to provide bitwise operations that apply to entire objects, for example

```
Bits *bp1, *bp2, *bp3;
/* ... */
bits_and(bp3,bp1,bp2);
bits_shift_left(bp3,4);
```

For bit strings, it would seem natural to allow them to grow and shrink, just like strings. Before we get too carried away, however, it's time to turn to the standard C++ library, which provides a `bitset` class template and accommodates left-to-right bit strings with `vector<bool>`, a specialization of the `vector` class template.

The `bitset` Template

The standard C++ library defines a class template `bitset`, which behaves much like `struct bits` above, but with the improved convenience you would expect from C++. It is also the only template in the library that has a *nontype* template parameter, which represents the fixed number of bits it manages. Its definition begins like this:

```
template<size_t N>
class bitset
{
    // etc.
};
```

Since the number of bits is available to the compiler at template-instantiation time, the underlying buffer can be allocated on the stack, so there is no need to use the free store like struct bits does. As Listing 9.11 shows, `bitset` supplies all the usual bitwise operators. It also provides `operator[]`, so you can access individual bits with array notation, as in

```
if (b[i])
    ...
```

or

```
b[j] = false;
```

Listing 9.11   Tests the `bitset` class template

```
// tbitset.cpp: Test the bitset class template
#include <iostream>
#include <bitset>
#include <string>
using namespace std;

const size_t NBITS = 36;
void print(const bitset<NBITS>&);

main()
{
    bitset<NBITS> b;
    cout.setf(ios::boolalpha);

    // Set the even bits:
    for (int i = 0; i < b.size(); i += 2)
        b.set(i);
    print(b);

    // Toggle the upper half:
    for (int i = b.size()/2; i < b.size(); ++i)
        b.flip(i);
    print(b);
```

continued

Listing 9.11   (continued)

```
    // Reset the lower half:
    for (int i = 0; i < b.size()/2; ++i)
        b.reset(i);
    print(b);

    // Read a bit string:
    cout << "Enter a bit string: ";
    string s;
    cin >> s;
    bitset<NBITS> b2(s);
    print(b2);

    // Test any() and test():
    cout << "any? " << b2.any() << endl;
    cout << "test(0)? " << b2.test(0) << endl;

    // Toggle, reset, and set:
    b2.flip();
    print(b2);
    b2.reset();
    print(b2);
    b2.set();
    print(b2);
}

void print(const bitset<NBITS>& b)
{
    cout << b.to_string() << " (" << b.count() << ")\n";
}

// Output:
01010101010101010101010101010101010101 (18)
10101010101010101001010101010101010101 (18)
10101010101010101000000000000000000000 (9)
Enter a bit string: 10100100010000100001000000100000001
10100100010000100001000000100000001 (8)
any? true
test(0)? true
01011011101111011111011111011111110 (28)
00000000000000000000000000000000000000 (0)
11111111111111111111111111111111111111 (36)
```

The `vector<bool>` Template Specialization

The library also provides a special version of the `vector` container that is optimized for storing bits. As you would expect, it has a left-to-right orientation and can therefore be thought of as a dynamically sized bit string. In addition to the usual `vector` operations, it provides the `flip` member function, which either toggles all bits (`b.flip`) or an individual bit (`b[i].flip`). The other bitwise operations are not available with `vector<bool>`. See Listing 9.12 for a sample program.

Listing 9.12

```
// tbitvec.cpp:     Test vector<bool>
#include <iostream>
#include <string>
#include <vector>
#include <algorithm>
using namespace std;

void print_alpha(const vector<bool>&);
void print_digits(const vector<bool>&);

main()
{
    vector<bool> b;

    // Populate:
    b.resize(4);        // "0000"
    b[0] = 1;           // "1000"
    b[3] = true;        // "1001"

    // Print as boolean:
    print_alpha(b);

    // Print numerically:
    print_digits(b);

    // Insert some more at front (LIFO order):
    for (int i = 0; i < 5; ++i)
        b.insert(b.begin(), bool(i % 2));
    print_digits(b);

    // Toggle bits:
    b.flip();
    print_digits(b);
```

continued

Listing 9.12   (continued)

```
    // Individual bit access:
    b[1] = false;
    b[2] = 0;
    b[3].flip();
    print_digits(b);

    // Resize:
    b.resize(5);
    print_digits(b);
}

void print_alpha(const vector<bool>& b)
{
    cout.setf(ios::boolalpha);
    copy(b.begin(), b.end(), ostream_iterator<bool>(cout," "));
    cout << endl;
}

void print_digits(const vector<bool>& b)
{
    cout.unsetf(ios::boolalpha);
    copy(b.begin(), b.end(), ostream_iterator<bool>(cout,""));
    cout << endl;
}

// Output:
true false false true
1001
010101001
101010110
100110110
10011
```

Summary

- Bit manipulation supports systems programming and can reduce memory requirements
- The bitwise operators allow access to subsets of the bits of an integer (but be careful of their operator precedence!)
- The bitset class template supports efficient manipulation of fixed-size bitsets
- The vector<bool> template specialization supports dynamically sized bit strings.

Conversions and Casts

$\mathbf{S}$ince C was invented mainly for systems programming, it has features that are "close to the machine." These include increment and decrement operators (which usually map to a single machine instruction), bitwise operations, pointers and addressing operators, and a rich set of low-level data types. What other language has eight flavors of integers? It is essential for a C/C++ programmer to know how objects of different types interact. A compiler implicitly converts an object from one type to another when different data types are intermixed, such as in arithmetic expressions, or when an object is assigned or passed as an argument to an object of a different type. In most cases the conversion consists of reinterpreting the underlying bit pattern rather than actually altering it, although a conversion may sometimes widen or narrow the object. (*Note:* Except where specified otherwise, all examples in this chapter use 32-bit integer arithmetic).

Integral Promotion

In an environment where short, int, and long are all distinct sizes, the eight integral types obey the following sequence of inequalities with respect to the maximum value each can represent:

```
signed char   <  unsigned char   <  signed short   <  unsigned short
              <  signed int       <  unsigned int   <  signed long
              <  unsigned long
```

In most environments, however, int is equivalent to either a short or a long. In any case, only objects of type int and long, or their unsigned varieties, are used in integral expressions. When an object of an integral type narrower than int is used in an expression, it is *promoted* to an int (or unsigned int, if needed) for the computation. Consider the following program, for example:

```
/* char1.c */
#include <stdio.h>
main()
{
    char c1 = 100;
    char c2 = 200;
    char c3 = c1 + c2;
```

```
    printf("c1 == %d\n",c1);
    printf("c2 == %d\n",c2);
    printf("c3 == %d\n",c3);
    return 0;
}
```

```
// Output:
c1 == 100
c2 == -56
c3 == 44
```

In an environment where a char is an 8-bit byte, this prints the value 44. The interesting feature of this program appears if you ask, what happens to c2? Why does c2 print as -56? The value 200 is out of range for a signed char, so c2 is interpreted as -56. But there is even more to consider here. Except for the char* format specification, printf doesn't type-check its arguments, therefore c2 is promoted to int before printf even sees it. A compiler is free to implement plain char as either a signed or unsigned char. As you can see, the compiler I used for these examples uses the former. A standard-conforming compiler promotes a signed char to an int by *sign extension*, which means that it populates the new high bits with the same value as the original char's sign bit. Here's what happens when you change the print statements to do hexadecimal output:

```
c1 == 0x64
c2 == 0xFFFFFFC8
c3 == 0x2C
```

A char holding the value 200 (0xC8) has the most significant bit set, so it promotes to an int with value 0xFFFFFFC8. The program then calculates the sum

```
    00000064
+   FFFFFFC8
    --------
=   (1)0000002C
```

which truncates to 0x2C or 44.

Declaring the variables as unsigned char gives the following:

```
// Decimal
c1 == 100
c2 == 200
c3 == 44
```

```
// Hexadecimal:
c1 == 0x64
c2 == 0xC8
c3 == 0x2C
```

The sum 300 overflows the maximum value a byte can hold. The result is the amount of the overflow, which can be expressed as a modulus operation:

```
44 == 300 % 256
```

where 256 == UCHAR_MAX + 1. (UCHAR_MAX is defined in <limits.h>.) As you can see, unsigned chars promote by filling the high bits with zeroes. In this case the program computes the sum

```
  00000064
+ 000000C8
  --------
= 0000012C
```

which truncates to 0x2C, which again is 44.

The difference in promoting signed versus unsigned quantities can be significant. For example, the "dump" program in Listing 10.1 prints each byte of its input file as two hexadecimal digits, 16 per row, followed by the corresponding ASCII representation (see the output in Listing 10.6). If the array buf hadn't been declared unsigned, any byte values greater than or equal to 128 would display with an extra, prepended FFFFFF, causing the output to be misaligned (recompile and see for yourself).

Listing 10.1 A hexadecimal/ASCII dump program

```
/* dump.c:  Display a file's bytes in hex and ASCII */
#include <stdio.h>
#include <ctype.h>

const int NBYTES = 16;
void dump(FILE *, char *);

main(int argc, char *argv[])
{
    /* Process files on command-line */
    for (int i = 1; i < argc; ++i)
    {
        FILE *f;

        if ((f = fopen(argv[i],"rb")) == 0)
            fprintf(stderr,"Can't open %s\n");
        else
        {
            dump(f,argv[i]);
            fclose(f);
            putchar('\f');
        }
    }
    return 0;
}
```

continued

Listing 10.1   (continued)

```c
void dump(FILE* f, char* s)
{
    unsigned char buf[NBYTES];
    int count;
    long size = 0L;

    printf("Dump of %s:\n\n",s);
    while ((count = fread(buf,1,NBYTES,f)) > 0)
    {
        /* Print byte counter */
        printf(" %06X ",size += count);

        /* Print Hex Bytes */
        for (int i = 0; i < NBYTES; ++i)
        {
            /* Print gutter space between columns */
            if (i == NBYTES / 2)
                putchar(' ');

            /* Display hex byte */
            if (i < count)
            {
                printf(" %02X",buf[i]);
                if (!isprint(buf[i]))
                    buf[i] = '.';
            }
            else
            {
                /* Spacing for partial last line */
                fputs("   ",stdout);
                buf[i] = ' ';
            }
        }

        /* Print Text Bytes */
        printf("  |%16.16s|\n",buf);
    }
}
```

Exercise

Examine the output of the program in Listing 10.3. The two sides of the assignment

```c
y = x + x;
```

print differently. Why?

Listing 10.2   Partial output from the command dump dump.exe

```
000010 4D 5A 50 00 02 00 00 00   04 00 0F 00 FF FF 00 00  |MZP............|
000020 B8 00 00 00 00 00 00 00   40 00 1A 00 00 00 00 00  |........@.......|
000030 00 00 00 00 00 00 00 00   00 00 00 00 00 00 00 00  |................|
000040 00 00 00 00 00 00 00 00   00 00 00 00 00 01 00 00  |................|
000050 BA 10 00 0E 1F B4 09 CD   21 B8 01 4C CD 21 90 90  |.........!..L.!..|
000060 54 68 69 73 20 70 72 6F   67 72 61 6D 20 6D 75 73  |This program mus|
000070 74 20 62 65 20 72 75 6E   20 75 6E 64 65 72 20 57  |t be run under W|
000080 69 6E 33 32 0D 0A 24 37   00 00 00 00 00 00 00 00  |in32..$7........|
```

//etc...

Demotions

The result of converting an integer to a narrower, unsigned type is the remainder on division by 2^n, where n is the size in bits of the unsigned type, which explains why converting 200 to unsigned char resulted in 44 on page 230. Such a conversion is called a *demotion*, or equivalently, a *narrowing conversion*. If the narrower type is signed, however, the result is implementation defined if the smaller type cannot represent the larger value. As Listing 10.4 shows, my 16-bit compiler just truncates high-order bits, if necessary, and interprets the value according to two's-complement arithmetic. For example, the bit pattern for 60000U is

```
1110 1010 0110 0000
```

Listing 10.3   Integral promotion exercise

```
// promote3.cpp
#include <stdio.h>

main()
{
    char x = 124;
    char y = x + x;

    printf("x == %02X\n",x);
    printf("x + x == %02X\n",x+x);
    printf("y == %02X\n\n",y);
}

// Output:
x == 7C
x + x == F8
y == FFFFFFF8
```

Listing 10.4   Illustrates narrowing conversions (16-bit version!)

```c
/* narrow.c */
#include <stdio.h>

void f(int);
void g(short);

main()
{
    unsigned n = 60000U;
    long m = 70000L;
    float x = 1.23e10;

    f(n);
    f(x);
    g(m);
    return 0;
}

void f(int i)
{
    printf("%d\n",i);
}

void g(short i)
{
    printf("%hd\n",i);
}

/* Output:
-5536
7168
4464
*/
```

To interpret this as a negative integer, the two's-complement rules say to flip the bits and add one to find the magnitude:

```
  0001 0101 1001 1111
+                   1
  -------------------
= 0001 0101 1010 0000
```

which is 5536, so `(int)60000U == -5536`.

The bit pattern for `70000L` is:

`0000 0000 0000 0001 0001 0001 0111 0000`

The conversion to `short` (which is the same as `int` in a 16-bit environment) simply truncates the top 16 bits, leaving the value 4464.

Converting a floating-point number to an integer discards the fractional part, but in an implementation-defined manner. When a floating-point value is too large to fit in an integer, the result is undefined.

Arithmetic Conversions

Working with floating-point numbers has been likened to moving piles of sand—every time you handle one you lose a little. Most real numbers and large integers are not representable in a finite floating-point number system; the closest one available is used in calculations instead. Listing 10.5 illustrates this fact. The roundoff error inherent in finite-precision arithmetic caused the product 100 * 23.4 to land closer to 2339 than 2340.

There are three levels of floating-point precision defined in standard C/C++: `float`, `double`, and `long double`. The values representable as `float` are a subset of those representable as `double`, which in turn are a subset of the `long double` numbers. Unadorned constants, such as 100.0, are of type `double`. To force a constant to be of another floating type, you can use a suitable suffix, as Table 10.1 illustrates.

Listing 10.5 Illustrates the inaccuracies of floating-point arithmetic

```
// float.cpp
#include <stdio.h>
main()
{
    int i = 100;

    i *= 23.4;
    printf("%d\n",i);
    printf("100 * 23.4 %s 2340.0\n",
           (100 * 23.4 == 2340.0) ? "==" : "!=");
}

// Output:
2339
100 * 23.4 != 2340.0
```

Table 10.1   Suffixes and `printf` format descriptors for floating-point types

Type	Suffix	Example	Format specifier
float	f or F	100.0f, 100.0F	%f
double	none	100.0	%f
long double	l or L	100.0l, 100.0L	%Lf

When demoting a floating-point number to another floating-point type of smaller precision, like `double` to `float`, there are three possible outcomes:

1. The source number being demoted is outside the range of the target type. In this case, the result is undefined.
2. The source number is within range of but not representable by the target type. The result is the nearest higher or lower value, depending on the rounding algorithm used (which is implementation defined).
3. The source number is exactly representable in the target precision, in which case there is no loss in precision.

The program in Listing 10.6 shows that `ULONG_MAX`, the largest `unsigned long` integer (4,294,967,295 on my platform), is not representable in my compiler's set of `float`s, but `ULONG_MAX+1` is (because it's a power of two and the floating-point number system is binary based). Both `double` and `long double` have sufficient precision to represent `ULONG_MAX`, however.

Listing 10.6   Illustrates the three floating-point types

```
// float2.cpp
#include <stdio.h>
#include <limits.h>

main()
{
    float x = ULONG_MAX;
    double y = ULONG_MAX;
    long double z = ULONG_MAX;

    printf("%f\n",x);
    printf("%f\n",y);
    printf("%Lf\n",z);
}

// Output:
4294967296.000000
4294967295.000000
4294967295.000000
```

When two numbers of different types appear as operands in a binary arithmetic operation, the expression is *balanced* either by converting one type to the other, or, in the case of small integers, by performing the usual integral promotions. If either operand is of floating-point type, then the narrower type object is converted to the largest floating-point type. If both arguments are integers, they undergo integral promotion so that the operands are temporarily either int or long (or their unsigned versions, as appropriate). Then the object of narrower type is converted to the wider type for the operation. In other words, the types used in a binary, numeric operation are promoted upward within one of the following prioritized lists, depending on the relationship between long and int:

if sizeof(long) > sizeof(int):

```
long double
double
float
unsigned long
long
unsigned int
int
```

if sizeof(long) == sizeof(int):

```
long double
double
float
unsigned long == unsigned int
long == int
```

Function Prototypes

Function prototypes do more than just type-check function arguments at compile time. They also provide information that the compiler uses to automatically convert arguments to the type of the corresponding parameter. For example, a common error that went undetected by old-style function definitions (i.e., without prototypes) was passing an integer argument to a double parameter:

```
    f(1);       /* Big trouble! f expects a double */
    ...

void f(x)
double x;
{
    ...
```

As Listing 10.7 illustrates, providing a fully prototyped declaration of such a function before you use it forces an implicit conversion from int to double. It also shows that a narrowing

Listing 10.7. Exposes the automatic conversions performed via prototypes

```
/* proto.c */
#include <stdio.h>

void f2(short,double);

main()
{
    f1(1,3);
    f1(1.0, 3.0);

    f2(1,3);
    f2(1.0,3.0);
    f2(1.0e6,3.0e6);
}

f1(x,y)              /* Old-style function declaration */
short x;
double y;
{
    printf("%d, %f\n",x,y);
}

void f2(short x, double y)
{
    printf("%d, %f\n",x,y);
}

/* Output:
1, 0.000000
0, 0.000000
1, 3.000000
1, 3.000000
16960, 3000000.000000
*/
```

conversion, in this case from `double` to `int`, can be dangerous (because the integer representation of `1.0e6` is not representable in a 16-bit `short`).

You are responsible for *unchecked arguments*. For example, in the following prototype for `printf`, the ellipsis specification indicates that any number of arguments of any type may follow the first parameter:

```
printf(const char *,...);
```

Since the compiler has no way of knowing what these should be, it has no way of catching the following error:

```
#include <stdio.h>

main()
{
    int x = 1;
    printf("%ld\n",x);        /* Mismatch ! */
}
```

```
// Output:
65537
```

The compiler can only perform *default promotions* on unchecked arguments, which consist of integral promotion and converting type float to a double.

Explicit Conversions

All of the conversions discussed so far are implicit conversions; they happen without any intervention on your part. You can explicitly request a conversion at any time with a cast operator. For example, in the following assignment, the fractional part of x has no effect.

```
int i;
double x;
/* ... */
i = i + x;
```

The sequence of events is, however,

1. Convert i to a double.
2. Add (double) i to x using double arithmetic.
3. Truncate the result to an integer and assign to i.

If you're counting nanoseconds, you can avoid the double arithmetic by casting x to an int:

```
i = i + int(x);
```

Casts can come in handy when dealing with pointers. If you have need to inspect the bytes of an integer, for example, you can do this:

```
int i;
char *cp = (char *) &i;
char hi_byte = *cp++;
char lo_byte = *cp;
/* etc. */
```

The cast is necessary to convince the compiler that you know what you're doing, since it normally doesn't allow mixing pointers to different types. It is not necessary to use casts when assigning to pointers to and from void* in C or to a void* in C++. It is an error to assign from a void pointer without a cast in C++.

Function-style Casts

Since a cast is an explicit conversion that you use to get around the C++ type system, you should use casts sparingly. Some have argued that C's casting syntax is ugly, so C++ also allows *function-style* casts. For example you can rewrite the statement

```
i = i + (int)x;
```

as

```
i = i + int(x);
```

Besides being easier on the eye, this notation is compatible with the use of constructors for creating temporaries and initializing objects, as in:

```
#include "foo.h"            // defines class Foo
Foo f = Foo(1) + Foo(2);
```

In this case, class Foo must have a constructor that takes a single-integer argument. See the section on user-defined conversions below for more detail. Old-style casts of the form (T)x are still available, but not recommended.

One drawback with function-style casts is that only single-token type names can be used. For example, the following statement is illegal:

```
const unsigned char *p = const unsigned char *(p);
```

The work-around for this problem is to use a typedef:

```
typedef unsigned char *const_ucharp;
const unsigned char *p = const_ucharp(p);
```

Since casts are potentially dangerous, maybe an ugly syntax is a blessing, since it stands out from normal code. The preferred technique nowadays is to use C++'s new-style casts, discussed below.

const Correctness

The const qualifier is a critical element of the C++ type system. Whenever you have a pointer or reference function parameter that is read-only, for example, you should declare it const. Consider the prototype for memcpy:

```
void *memcpy(void *to, const void *from, size_t n);
```

The pointer to the source buffer `from` is declared as a *pointer to `const`*, meaning that the function has no intention of altering what it points at. This not only guards against inadvertent assignment within the function, but allows you to pass a pointer to `const` as an argument. If the `const` qualifier were missing in the second parameter, then you could not pass `t` in the following:

```
char *s = ...;
const char *t = ...;
memcpy(s,t,10);
```

The compiler needs a guarantee that `memcpy` will not try to modify what `t` points at. With `const` in the prototype, pointers to both `const` and non-`const` can be passed to `t`.

All of the above applies to references as well as to pointers. A common idiom for passing objects by value in C++ is to pass a `const` reference:

```
void g(const Foo& f);
```

This guarantees that `g` will not modify `f` (without a cast, anyway).

You can also declare that a pointer itself cannot change by placing `const` after the asterisk:

```
char * const p;
*p = 'a';     // OK, only the pointer is const
++p;          // Error, can't modify pointer
```

To disallow modification of both the pointer and the contents referenced, use `const` in both places:

```
const char * const p;
char c;
c = *p;           // OK - can read contents
*p = 'a';         // Error
++p;              // Error
```

A `const` member function in a C++ class promises not to modify the object to which it applies. For example, a `Date` class might have separate functions to inspect and alter the number of the month:

```
class Date
{
    int month_;
    // rest of implementation omitted
public:
    int month() const;   // return month
    void month(int);     // change month
    // etc.
};
```

The observer function `month` is `const`, because it just returns the current value. Therefore, both of the following function invocations are valid:

```
const Date d1;
Date d2;
d1.month();
d2.month();
```

But you can't change d1's month, as in

```
d1.month(10);
```

because you can't call a non-const member function for a const object. The compiler detects the error via the type of the underlying this pointer for the associated object. When the object is non-const, the type of this is Date* const, meaning "this is a const pointer to Date". So you can't alter this (that would be weird, anyway), but you can alter what it points to; therefore you can change its private data within a non-const member function. On the other hand, if the underlying object is const, then this has the following declaration:

```
const Date* const this;
```

which disallows modifying any members. The const member functions expect such a this pointer, so if you invoke one with a non-const object, there is a mismatch and the compiler complains.

Nevertheless, sometimes you may want to alter a data member within a const member function. For example, a function may not alter anything that the user is aware of, but there may be some private state variable that is convenient to update (such as values cached for efficiency). You still want to enable the user to invoke the function for const members, since s/he doesn't need to know about your optimization secrets. This use of the const concept is sometimes called *semantic const-ness* (as opposed to *bitwise const-ness*). Consider the following class definition, for example:

```
class B
{
public:
    void f() const;
private:
    int state;
};
```

To allow B::f to alter state, and still be called for const objects, you have two options. First, you can "cast away const" from this in the implementation of f:

```
void B::f() const
{
    ((B*)this)->state = ...;        // Modification legal here
    ...
}
```

Remember that the type of `this` in `f` is `const B* const`. The expression `(B*)this` suspends the `const`-ness temporarily, allowing you to make the assignment. An even better way to cast away `const` is to use one of the *new-style* casts:

```
const_cast<B*>(this)->state = ...;     // Modification legal here
```

The second (and vastly superior) option is to declare `state` to be a *mutable* data member, like this:

```
class B
{
public:
    void f() const;
private:
    mutable int state;
};
```

This allows you to modify `state` without a cast, even if `this` is `const`.

User-Defined Conversions

A class with a constructor that takes a single argument defines an implicit conversion from the type of that argument to the type of the class. For example, the rational number class that appears in Listings 10.8–10.10 has the following constructor:

```
Rational(int n = 0, int d = 1);
```

which allows zero, one, or two arguments when initializing a rational number. Whenever an integer appears in an expression with a `Rational` object, the integer is implicitly converted to a `Rational` with a denominator of one. This allows such statements as the following to be meaningful:

```
Rational y(4);
cout << 2 / y << endl;
```

When the compiler sees the expression

```
2 / y
```

it looks for a global function with signature `operator/(int,Rational)`. Failing that, it notices the existence of the function `operator/(const Rational&,const Rational&)`, in addition to the built-in `operator/(int,int)`. It therefore looks for a conversion of either `int` to `Rational`, or `Rational` to `int`. If both conversions existed (which they don't here), the compiler would complain, since it wouldn't know which one to pick. Because class `Rational` allows a constructor with a single integer argument, the compiler uses that to convert 2 to `Rational(2)`, and then invokes `operator/(Rational(2),y)`.

Listing 10.8   Interface and inline functions for fractional arithmetic class

```
// rational.h

#include <iosfwd>        // Contains key iostream declarations
                         // (Less overhead than <iostream>)
using namespace std;

class Rational
{
public:
    Rational(int n = 0, int d = 1);

    // Operations for rationals
    friend Rational operator+(const Rational&, const Rational&);
    friend Rational operator-(const Rational&, const Rational&);
    friend Rational operator*(const Rational&, const Rational&);
    friend Rational operator/(const Rational&, const Rational&);
    Rational operator-() const;

    // I/O operations
    friend ostream& operator<<(ostream&, const Rational&);
    friend istream& operator>>(istream&, Rational&);

private:
    int num;
    int den;
    void reduce();
    static int gcd(int, int);
};

inline Rational::Rational(int n, int d)
{
    num = n;
    den = d;
    reduce();
}

inline Rational operator+(const Rational& a, const Rational& b)
{
    Rational r(a.num*b.den + b.num*a.den, a.den*b.den);
    r.reduce();
    return r;
}

inline Rational operator-(const Rational& a, const Rational& b)
{
    Rational r(a.num*b.den - b.num*a.den, a.den*b.den);
    r.reduce();
    return r;
}
```

Listing 10.8   (continued)

```
inline Rational operator*(const Rational& a, const Rational& b)
{
    Rational r(a.num*b.num, a.den*b.den);
    r.reduce();
    return r;
}

inline Rational operator/(const Rational& a, const Rational& b)
{
    Rational r(a.num*b.den, a.den*b.num);
    r.reduce();
    return r;
}

inline Rational Rational::operator-() const
{
    return Rational(-num,den);
}
```

Listing 10.9   Tests class `Rational`

```
// trat.cpp
#include <iostream>
#include "rational.h"
using namespace std;

main()
{
    Rational x, y(4), z(5,7);

    x = 3;
    cout << "x == " << x << endl;
    cout << "y == " << y << endl;
    cout << "z == " << z << endl;

    cout << "x + y == " << x + y << endl;
    cout << "y - z == " << y - z << endl;
    cout << "x * 2 == " << x * 2 << endl;
    cout << "2 / y == " << 2 / y << endl;
}

// Output:
x == 3 / 1
y == 4 / 1
z == 5 / 7
x + y == 7 / 1
y - z == 23 / 7
x * 2 == 6 / 1
2 / y == 1 / 2
```

Listing 10.10   Implementation of the `Rational` class

```cpp
// rational.cpp
#include <iostream>
#include "rational.h"
using namespace std;

// Find greatest common divisor of 2 ints (Euclid's algorithm)
int Rational::gcd(int x, int y)
{
    while (y != 0)
    {
        int rem = x % y;
        x = y;
        y = rem;
    }
    return x;
}

// Reduce fraction lowest terms
void Rational::reduce()
{
    int g = gcd(num,den);

    if (g > 1)
    {
        num /= g;
        den /= g;
    }
}

istream& operator>>(istream& is, Rational& r)
{
    char c;

    is >> r.num >> c;
    if (c == '/')
        is >> r.den;
    else
    {
        r.den = 1;
        is.putback(c);
    }
    r.reduce();
    return is;
}

ostream& operator<<(ostream& os, const Rational& r)
{
    os << r.num << " / " << r.den;
    return os;
}
```

It is significant that `operator/(const Rational&, const Rational&)` is a global function. If I had defined `operator/` as a member function instead, as in

```
Rational Rational::operator/(const Rational&)
```

then the compiler would be able to evaluate the expression `y/2`, but not `2/y`, because member operator functions require the left operand to be an object of their class. You could provide functions to service all possible combinations of operands, however, for example,

```
// These handle r/r, r/i, and i/r, resp.
Rational Rational::operator/(const Rational&)
Rational Rational::operator/(int);
Rational operator/(int, const Rational&);
```

This strategy doesn't require any conversions at all from `int` to `Rational`, but it can make creating classes with a large number of operators quite tedious. Defining global operator functions in conjunction with appropriate constructors allows symmetrical, mixed-mode binary operations with minimum fuss.

Although you don't want to in this case (because of the ambiguity mentioned above), how would you define an implicit conversion from `Rational` to `int`? There is no `int` class definition available to which you can add single-argument constructors whenever you need a conversion from a new type to `int`. There needs to be some way within a class definition itself to provide a conversion from the class type to other types, even built-in ones. You do this with a *conversion operator*. To convert objects of a class to type `T`, say, just define the following function as a member of the class:

```
operator T() const;
```

For an implicit `Rational`-to-`int` conversion, you would add the following to class `Rational`:

```
// Return integer part:
operator int() const {return num/den;}
```

If you feel you must have a conversion from `Rational` to `int`, you can make it an explicit conversion with a member function like the following:

```
int to_int() const {return num/den;}
```

and call it when you need it, as in

```
int i = r.to_int();
```

Some implementations provide a string class that includes a `char*` conversion operator to allow use of a string object as an argument to the ANSI-C string functions that require a `char*` argument; for example,

```
string s;
strcpy(s, "hello");
```

The program in Listing 10.11 shows that you still need to be careful about using such conversions with functions with unchecked arguments. The expression

```
(char*) s
```

invokes `string::operator char*` and returns a pointer to `data`, as expected. But since the second and subsequent arguments to `printf` are unchecked, no implicit conversion takes place in the second invocation of `printf`.

If you have a class with a single-argument constructor, but you don't want implicit conversions enabled, you can disable them with the `explicit` qualifier. The standard C++ containers declare all of their single-argument constructors `explicit`. For example, the constructor

```
explicit vector<T>::vector(size_t n, const T& = T())
```

allows you to initialize a vector with n default values, as in

```
vector<string> v(5);      // Start with 5 empty strings
```

Listing 10.11   Shows that unchecked arguments do not get converted

```
// uncheck.cpp
#include <stdio.h>
#include <string.h>

class string
{
public:
    string(char *s)
        {strcpy(data = new char[strlen(s)+1], s);}
    operator char*()
        {return data;}
private:
    int dummy;
    char *data;
};


main()
{
    string s = "hello";
    printf("%s\n",(char*) s);
    printf("%s\n",s);
}

// Output:
hello
(null)
```

Without the `explicit` qualifier, the statement

```
v = 10;
```

would create a temporary vector with 10 default elements and assign it to v, which is very strange behavior. The `explicit` keyword can only modify constructor declarations.

Beefing up `operator[]`

A typical `string` class implementation includes member functions with the following signatures:

```
char& operator[](size_t);
char operator[](size_t) const;
```

The implementation of the first method usually goes something like this:

```
char& string::operator[](size_t pos)
{
    return data[pos];
}
```

where `data` is the underlying array of characters. This member function provides the typical subscripting action that no programmer can live without:

```
string s;
char c = s[0];
```

Because `string::operator[]` returns a reference, it can be used as an lvalue, as in the assignment

```
s[0] = 'a';
```

What about the situation where different actions need to be taken, depending on whether the subscript is on the left-hand rather than the right-hand side of the assignment? Such is the case with the `bitset` class template in the standard C++ library. For example, the expression

```
bitset<16> b;
b[0] = 1;
```

wants to *set* bit zero, but the following expression *tests* bit zero:

```
int x = b[0];
```

Since the two operations are quite different in any reasonable implementation, we need some way of distinguishing when the subscripting occurs on the left versus the right side of an assignment. The solution is to introduce a new class—called `reference`, say—with only two public member functions: an assignment operator and an implicit integer conversion (see Listing 10.12). Class

reference, which I have nested within a sample class Foo, privately maintains a reference to the
Foo object it will index, along the index position itself. The constructor is private so only a Foo
object can create a temporary reference object (Foo is a friend to reference).

The function Foo::operator[] just returns a temporary reference object—nothing
more. Therefore, the assignment

```
int x = f[i];
```

Listing 10.12   Distinguishes lvalues from rvalues with operator[]

```
// brackets.cpp
#include <iostream>
using namespace std;

class Foo
{
public:
    class reference
    {
        friend class Foo;

        Foo& foo;
        int index;
        reference(Foo& f, int idx) : foo(f), index(idx)
        {}

    public:
        int operator=(int val)
        {
            cout << "assigning " << val << " to position "
                << index << endl;

            // Normally do lvalue case here...

            return val;
        }
        operator int() const
        {
            cout << "assigning from position " << index << endl;

            // Normally do rvalue case here...

            return 1;
        }
    };
```

Listing 10.12   (continued)

```
      reference operator[](int idx)
      {
          return reference(*this, idx);
      }
};

main()
{
    Foo f;
    int x = f[0];
    cout << "x == " << x << endl;
    f[0] = 1;
    return 0;
}

// Output:
assigning from position 0
x == 1
assigning 1 to position 0
```

which is equivalent to

```
int n = f.operator[](i);
```

becomes

```
int n = reference(f,i);
```

The compiler naturally looks for a conversion from `reference` to `int`, which it finds in `Foo::reference::operator int`, which in this case returns 1, but you can substitute the right thing for your `Foo` rvalue.

For the `lvalue` case, the statement

```
f[i] = 1;
```

becomes

```
reference(f,i) = 1;
```

which in turn invokes

```
reference(f,i).operator=(1);
```

for the lvalue case.

New-Style Casts

A cast is your way of telling the compiler to allow you to do something potentially dangerous, because you think you know what you're doing. Too often, though, you don't know what you're doing (no offense!), and you spend days tracking down an insidious pointer conversion error or similar bug. It is interesting that programmers use a single cast notation for so many different purposes:

- to reinterpret the bit pattern of an object
- to widen or narrow a value
- to traverse a class hierarchy
- to cast away const or volatile
- to do some implementation-dependent magic.

The new-style casts in C++ attempt to minimize the chances for error by categorizing the different types of operations you typically use casts for. If you cast incorrectly, they tell you—either at compiletime or runtime, depending on the situation.

The new cast mechanisms are:

```
dynamic_cast

static_cast

reinterpret_cast

const_cast
```

The dynamic_cast operator provides safe *downcasts*. You can always assign a pointer to derived class to a pointer to a base class, for example:

```
class B {...};
class D : public B {...} ;
D d;
B* bp = &d;
```

This is safe because a D *is a* B. Assigning from a B* to a D* only makes sense if the referenced object is in fact a D. This type of pointer conversion is called a downcast because it travels "down" the class hierarchy (most people draw base classes at the top of a class diagram). To determine whether such a cast is safe requires *runtime type information* (RTTI). A C++ compiler keeps runtime information for objects of all built-in and *polymorphic* types (types that have at least one virtual function). The dynamic_cast operator returns a null pointer if the downcast is unsafe, otherwise it returns the original pointer cast to the new type, like this:

```
D* dp = dynamic_cast<B*> bp;
if (dp)
{
    // okay to use dp for stuff
    // specific to a D object.
}
```

The other three new-style cast operators are compile-time mechanisms. All of the new-style casts use template-like angle bracket notation for the target type.

You use `static_cast` when you really *do* know that a B* points to a D*, so runtime checking isn't necessary. You also use it for invoking standard and user-defined conversions explicitly, which probably makes `static_cast` the most widely used category of casts for code that you are migrating from C.

To do everything but navigate a class hierarchy or cast away `const` or `volatile`, use `reinterpret_cast`. If you need to cast integers to and from pointer types, including zero to a null pointer, this is the cast to use. It is just about as unsafe as traditional cast notation, except that you're not likely to use it much, due to the presence of the other three new-style casts and because it sticks out like a sore thumb:

```
int j;
int *ip = &j
char *cp = reinterpret_cast<char *>(ip); // trust me!
```

As you may have surmised, `const_cast` makes abundantly clear your intentions to cast away const:

```
void B::f() const
{
    // Modify data member of a const object:
    const_cast<B*>(this)->state = ...;
    ...
}
```

The type of the argument must be the same as the target type in brackets, except for the presence of `const` and/or `volatile` qualifiers ("cv-qualifiers"). No other new-style cast can alter the state of cv-qualifiers.

Summary

- C and C++ provide implicit type conversions to facilitate mixed-mode operations
- Integral types are promoted as needed in operations
- Floating-point operations are "balanced" by standard conversions
- Function prototypes help the compiler provide implicit conversions

• Implicit conversion of user-defined types can sometimes be undesirable
• Make single-argument constructors `explicit` when you want to avoid implicit conversions
• Casts make conversions explicit
• Prefer function-style casts (i.e., constructor syntax) over C-style casts
• Use new-style casts when they apply (i.e., always, except when using constructor calls)
• Always use `const` when it applies
• Prefer semantic `const`-ness over bitwise `const`-ness
• The `mutable` storage class makes casting away `const` unnecessary in most cases
• RTTI allows safe downcasts.

Answer to Exercise

Since the value of x is 0x7C(124), in the expression

```
x + x
```

both occurrences of x are promoted to 0x0000007C, which added together are 0x000000F8. No further conversion takes place. The y value 0xF8, however, promotes to 0xFFFFFFF8 because the high bit is set.

Visibility

What's in a Name?

Every token in a C or C++ program that begins with a letter or an underscore, other than keywords and macros, names one of the following entities:

- data object
- function
- type definition (typedef)
- tag for a class/structure, union or enumeration
- member of a class/structure, union
- enumeration constant
- label
- template

These entities are active at certain times and places in your program, depending on how and where their declarations appear. Whether you are aware of it or not, when you declare an identifier you determine its *scope*, *lifetime*, *linkage*, and *namespace*. In this chapter I will illustrate these interrelated concepts as Standard C++ defines them.

Scope

The scope of an identifier is the region of your program's text where you can use that identifier or, in other words, where it is *visible*. Declarations introduce identifiers into a scope determined at compile time. There are five types of scope in Standard C++:

Local—a contiguous region within a pair of matching braces { } that begins where the declarator first appears and ends with the first subsequent closing brace

Function Prototype—the region from where an identifier occurs in a function prototype to the end of the prototype

Function—the entire body of a function (only labels have function scope)

Class—the region including a class's declaration, as well as all member function bodies, default arguments, and constructor initializer lists for that class

Namespace—the region whence an identifier first appears within a named or unnamed namespace body; *global scope*, which extends to the end of the translation unit, is a special case of namespace scope.

Formal parameters have the same scope as if they were declared in the outermost block of their function. Identifier names are optional in function prototypes, and serve only for documentation if they appear.

In Listing 11.1, the optional identifier `val` serves only as documentation, and is not visible outside of `f`'s prototype. The formal parameter `i` in the definition of `f` is visible immediately after the opening brace. Since each block introduces a new scope, the `i` initialized by `j` in the innermost block temporarily hides the `i` in the outer block. The value of `j` is available to initialize `i` in the inner block because `j` was declared first. If `j` had been declared like this:

```
{
    int j = i;      // outer i
```

Listing 11.1   Illustrates local scope

```
/* scope1.c:   Illustrates local scope and prototype scope: */
#include <stdio.h>

void f(int val);

main()
{
    f(1);
}

void f(int i)
{
    printf("i == %d\n",i);

    {
        int j = 10;
        int i = j;
        printf("i == %d\n",i);
    }
}

/* Output:
i == 1
i == 10
*/
```

then j would have received the value one. There is no conflict because the inner i isn't visible until the next statement. An identifier is visible as soon as its declarator is complete. This means that the following declaration is ill-formed (if not downright silly):

```
{
    int i = i;
```

Since int i is sufficient to declare an integer named i, the i on the right is the same as on the left, and i is left uninitialized.

Only labels have function scope. The difference between function scope and the scope of the outermost block of a function is that labels are visible throughout the outermost block, even before they are "declared," but identifiers with block scope are visible only after their point of declaration.

In C, an identifier declared outside of any block or function parameter list has *file scope*. Such identifiers are sometimes referred to as *global* and are visible from their point of declaration until the end of the translation unit, unless hidden by an identifier of the same name with block scope. The C program in Listing 11.2 illustrates function and file scope. Since the identifier i with file scope (the one initialized to 13) is visible only after its declaration, it would be an

Listing 11.2 Illustrates function and file scope

```
/* scope2.c:  Illustrate function and file scope */
#include <stdio.h>

main()
{
    void f1(int);
    void f2(void);

    f1(23);
    f2();
    return 0;
}

int i = 13;

void f1(int i)
{
    for (;;)
    {
        float i = 33.0;

        printf("%f\n",i);
        goto exit;
    }
```

continued

Listing 11.2   (continued)

```
exit:
    printf("%d\n",i);
}

void f2(void)
{
    printf("%d\n",i);
}

/* Output:
33.000000
23
13
*/
```

error to try to use it in the main program. The global i is not available anywhere in f1 since f1 has its own parameter named i. The innermost block of f1, in turn, hides that parameter with its own i (the types don't have to be the same). Since f2 declares no identifiers named i, it has access to the global i. The declarations of f1 and f2 in main inject those names into the body of main only. It would be an error, for example, to call f2 from f1.

Minimal Scoping

Thoughtful placement of declarations can greatly enhance the readability of a program. Most programmers still seem to follow the convention, required by languages such as Fortran and Cobol, of placing all declarations together in a single section of the source code. This gives you the advantage of always knowing where to look for variable definitions. But when a program gets large, you spend a good deal of time flipping back and forth between the declaration of an identifier and where it is used. Those of you who program in Microsoft Windows know that Hungarian notation, a convention of encoding the type of an identifier into its name, evolved as a means of compensating for the distance between the declaration and use of names, and from the lack of prototypes and type checking in pre-ANSI C. I prefer instead a simple technique known to C++ programmers that, when coupled with modular design, renders strange-looking Hungarian names unnecessary in most cases. I call it *minimal scoping,* a technique recommended from the beginning of C++ by its designer, Bjarne Stroustrup. Simply put, it means to declare an identifier as near as possible to its first use.

For example, what do you infer from the following program segment?

```
void f()
{
    int i, j;
    ...
}
```

Even though you might only use i and j in a small portion of f, the declaration says that they are available *everywhere* within the function. Therefore, i and j probably have more scope than they deserve. If, for example, i and j only apply under certain conditions, you can easily limit their scope by declaring them within an appropriate inner block:

```
void f()
{
    ...
    if (<some condition>)
    {
        int i = 7;
        int j = 2 * i;
        // only use i and j here
    }
    ...
}
```

Notice also that I don't declare them until I can initialize them. C++ encourages minimal scoping by allowing declarations to appear anywhere a statement can, such as,

```
for (int i = 0; i < n; ++i)
    ...
```

The index i is visible from its point of declaration to the end of the body of the loop. Minimal scoping aids readability because you don't even see identifiers until you need to—when they add meaning to the program.

Class Scope

Because member names are local to their class, every class creates a new scope. The scope of a class includes its declaration, all member function bodies, and constructor initializers. You can only access members of a class in one of the following ways:

1. as the target of the . operator (e.g., x.foo, where x is an object of the class or of a derived class)
2. as the target of the -> operator (e.g., xp->foo, where xp points to either an object of the class or an object of a derived class)
3. as the target of the *scope resolution operator* used with the name of its class or a base class (e.g., ios::binary—this applies only to static members)
4. from within the body of a member function of the class or of a derived class.

These rules are themselves subject to the rules of the access, indicated by the *access specifiers* public, protected, and private. Private members are only accessible to member functions of the class and friends of the class. Protected members are also accessible to members and friends of derived classes. Public members are available universally.

Listing 11.3 has a definition of our familiar Date class, Listing 11.4 contains the implementation, and a test program is in Listing 11.5. If you want to know the month of a certain date, you do not attempt to access the data member directly, for example,

```
Date d;                         // today's date
cout << d.month_;               // access denied
```

You use the appropriate member function instead:

```
Date d;                         // today's date
cout << d.month();              // OK
```

Listing 11.3   Definition of Date class

```
// date.h
#if !defined(DATE_H)
#define DATE_H

#include <string>
#include <cassert>
using namespace std;

class Date
{
public:
    Date();
    Date(int y, int m, int d);

    // Accessors:
    void year(int);
    void month(int);
    void day(int);

    // Mutators:
    int year() const;
    int month() const;
    int day() const;

    // Other:
    int compare(const Date&);
    operator string() const;
    static bool isleap(int);
    static int endOfMonth(int, int);
```

Listing 11.3 (continued)

```
private:
    int year_;
    int month_;
    int day_;

    static int dtab[2][13];
};

inline Date::Date(int y, int m, int d)
{
    assert(1 <= m && m <= 12);
    assert(1 <= d && d <= endOfMonth(y,m));
    year_ = y;
    month_ = m;
    day_ = d;
}

inline int Date::year() const
{
    return year_;
}

inline int Date::month() const
{
    return month_;
}

inline int Date::day() const
{
    return day_;
}

inline void Date::year(int y)
{
    year_ = y;
}

inline void Date::month(int m)
{
    assert(1 <= m && m <= 12);
    month_ = m;
}
```

continued

Listing 11.3   (continued)

```
inline void Date::day(int d)
{
    day_ = d;
}

inline bool Date::isleap(int y)
{
    return y%4 == 0 && y%100 != 0 || y%400 == 0;
}

inline int Date::compare(const Date& r)
{
    int ydiff = year_ - r.year_;
    int mdiff = month_ - r.month_;
    return ydiff ? ydiff
                 : (mdiff ? mdiff
                          : day_ - r.day_);
}

inline int Date::endOfMonth(int y, int m)
{
    assert(1 <= m && m <= 12);
    return dtab[int(isleap(y))][m];
}

#endif
```

Most of the members of the Date class are *nonstatic*. Each Date object has its own copy of each nonstatic data member (i.e., month_, day_, and year_), and each nonstatic member function must be called in connection with a Date object (e.g., d.month). A *static* member belongs to the entire class instead of an individual object. (Some object-oriented languages call static data members *class variables* and static member functions *class methods*, while they call the nonstatic equivalents *instance variables* and *instance methods*). Using the scope resolution operator in connection with a class name allows you to access a static class member directly. Since the isleap member function is public, you can use it to determine the "leapness" of any year like this:

```
int y = 1994;
if (Date::isleap(y))
    // It's a leap year...
else
    // It's not...
```

You must explicitly define static data members at file scope (see the definition of dtab in Listing 11.4).

As `Date::day(int)` in Listing 11.3 shows, other class members are in scope within the body of a member function, so you can access them directly without explicit scope resolution. Every nonstatic member function has a hidden parameter that points to the object it is called with and that is available to you through the keyword `this`. Inside of `Date::day(int)`, the compiler interprets the usage of `day_`, `isleap`, and `dtab` as if you had written `this->day_`, `Date::dtab`, and `Date::isleap` instead. There is no `this` pointer for static member functions since there is no associated object. Hence using the identifier `day_` unadorned in a static member function such as `isleap` makes no sense (what object does it belong to?), and would refer to an identifier of the same name from an enclosing scope, if there was one. Static member functions can refer directly only to enumerations, nested class names, and other static members.

Listing 11.4   Implementation of `Date` class

```cpp
// date.cpp
#include <iostream>
#include <cassert>
#include <ctime>
#include <cstdio>
#include "date.h"
using namespace std;

// Must initialize static members outside the class definition:
int Date::dtab[2][13] =
{
  {0, 31, 28, 31, 30, 31, 30, 31, 31, 30, 31, 30, 31},
  {0, 31, 29, 31, 30, 31, 30, 31, 31, 30, 31, 30, 31}
};

Date::Date()
{
    // Get today's date
    time_t tval = ::time(0);
    struct tm *tmp = ::localtime(&tval);

    month_ = tmp->tm_mon+1;
    day_ = tmp->tm_mday;
    year_ = tmp->tm_year + 1900;
}

Date::operator string() const
{
    char buf[9];
    sprintf(buf,"%04d%02d%02d",year_,month_,day_);
    return string(buf);
}
```

Listing 11.5   Tests the `Date` class

```
// tdate.cpp
#include <iostream>
#include "date.h"
using namespace std;

main()
{
    Date d1, d2(1951, 10, 1);
    cout << "d1 == " << d1 << endl;
    cout << "d2 == " << d2 << endl;
    cout << "d1.compare(d2): " << d1.compare(d2) << endl;
    cout << "d2.compare(d1): " << d2.compare(d1) << endl;
}

// Output:
d1 == 19970104
d2 == 19511001
d1.compare(d2): 46
d2.compare(d1): -46
```

Since the code for `Date::day_(int)` is part of a scope, any local or member identifier with the same name as a global identifier hides a like-named identifier in an enclosing scope. For example, in the unlikely case that I had a global identifier named `day_`, it would be hidden by the data member `day_` inside all nonstatic member functions of `Date`. You can still access a global identifier, however, by using the scope resolution operator without a prefix:

```
day_ = ::day_;            // assign global day_ to member
```

In effect, C++ allows you to "unhide" global identifiers. Here's another example:

```
int i = 10;

main()
{
    int i = 20;
    cout << "local i: " << i << endl;
    cout << "global i: " << ::i << endl;
    return 0;
}

// Output:
local i: 20
global i: 10
```

You can "unhide" any identifier that occurs in a namespace by using the name of the namespace as a scope qualifier (see section on "Namespace Scope"). It is good practice to explicitly qualify global functions with the scope resolution operator for documentation purposes, and to avoid name conflicts with member names (see the implementation of the constructor `Date::Date` in Listing 11.3).

When trying to bind a name to a unique declaration, a C++ compiler first searches enclosing scopes for that name. Once found, it then checks for access permission and then applies overload resolution. Consider, for example, the following classes:

```
class B
{
public:
    void f();
};

class D : public B
{
    void f();            // private!
};

main()
{
    D d;
    d.f();
}
```

There is a function in the scope of class D named f, so the compiler stops looking. Since D::f is private, the compiler issues a diagnostic. Suppose for a moment that the signature of D::f was void f(int) instead. There still is no attempt to bind the expression d.f to B::f, because the name in D hides the name in B. In other words, the scope of a derived class is enclosed by the scope of its base class. If you want to execute B::f on a D object, you must do so explicitly:

```
d.B::f();
```

Nested Classes

In addition to data members, member functions, and enumerated constants, you can define other classes within a class definition. For example, a common string-class implementation technique called *copy-on-write* allows several string objects to point to the same underlying text (see Listing 11.6). It only makes a separate copy when one of the strings changes its contents (this saves time when strings are passed as parameters—local read-only processing uses a "shared" copy). A separate class (Srep) handles the details of connecting and disconnecting references to the underlying text. There is no reason for the Srep class to be globally accessible, so I define it inside the String class. The implementation in Listing 11.7 shows how to use the scope resolution operator to reach the members of Srep. For example, to inform the compiler that I want to define the constructor Srep, I use the identifier String::Srep::Srep.

Listing 11.6   A copy-on-write string class design

```
// str.h:  String class with reference counting
class String
{
public:
    // Constructors / Destructor
    String(const char *s);
    String(const String& s);
    ~String();
    // other members omitted...

private:
    class Srep
    {
    public:
        Srep(const char*);
        ~Srep();
        char *rep;
        size_t count;
    };

    Srep *rep;
};
```

      In the unusual case that a name in a nested class hides a name in an enclosing class, you can reach the outer instance with the scope resolution operator (only if it's public, of course; the usual access rules apply to and from nested classes). For example, in the following situation:

```
class A
{
    static int i;

    class B
    {
        int i;
        void f() { cout << i + A::i; }
    };
};
```

you can still reach the i in class A by the expression A::i.

Local Classes

A class defined within a function definition is called a *local class* (see Listing 11.8). Its name is local to the function body, like any other identifier declared therein. You must define all member

Listing 11.7 Implementation for Listing 11.6

```cpp
// str.cpp
#include <iostream.h>
#include <cstring>
#include "str.h"
using namespace std;

String::String(const char *buf)
{
    if (!buf)
        rep = new Srep("");
    else
        rep = new Srep(buf);
}

String::String(const String& s)
{
    rep = s.rep;
    rep->count++;
}

String::~String()
{
    if (--rep->count <= 0)
        delete rep;
}

String::Srep::Srep(const char* s)
{
    strcpy(rep = new char[strlen(s)+1], s);
    count = 1;
}

String::Srep::~Srep()
{
    delete [] rep;
}
```

functions within the class definition. You can't define them at file scope, because the class is not visible there. This also rules out static data members of Local, since you must define them at file scope. You can't define function bodies elsewhere within f, either, because function definitions cannot nest in C or C++. For the same reason, a member function of Local can't refer to an automatic variable of f. As always, member access rules apply, so k is not visible in f outside of Local.

Listing 11.8 Defines a Local class

```cpp
// local.cpp
#include <iostream>
using namespace std;

int i = 10;

main()
{
    void f();
    f();
}

void f()
{
    static int j = 20;

    class Local
    {
        int k;

    public:
        Local(int i) : k(i) {}
        void a() {cout << k+i << endl;}
        void b() {cout << k+j << endl;}
    };

    Local l(30);
    l.a();
    l.b();
}

// Output:
40
50
```

Classic Namespaces

An identifier can play various roles in a program. For example, in the following excerpt, pair is both a function name and a structure tag:

```cpp
struct pair {int x; int y;};

void pair(struct pair p)
{
    printf("(%d,%d)\n",p.x,p.y);
}
```

The compiler keeps separate lists of identifiers used in different roles, so there is no danger of ambiguity. These lists are called *namespaces*. There are four different kinds of namespaces in standard C:

1. labels
2. tags for structures, unions, and enumerations
3. members of structures and unions
4. ordinary identifiers (i.e., all others: data objects, functions, types, and enumeration constants).

Because of the preeminence of types in C++, you can use structure tags (which are really class names) without the `struct` keyword, for example:

```
void f(pair p);    // struct keyword optional
```

In other words, all `struct` names act as type names, as if you had also defined a `typedef` with the same name as the tag, like this:

```
typedef struct pair pair;
```

This means that you cannot use a name as both a structure tag and a `typedef` for a different type in the same scope. Since `typedef`s belong to the space of ordinary identifiers, C++ has merged that namespace with the tag namespace (Numbers 2 and 4 above). As a compatibility gesture, you are still allowed to define functions with the same name as a tag, mainly because of the following common C practice:

```
struct stat{...};
extern int stat();
```

Problems can now arise, however, when you use the same name for `struct` tags and ordinary identifiers. In the program in Listing 11.9, the local integer `pair` hides the global `struct` identifier, causing the compiler to flag the line

```
pair p = {pair,pair};
```

as an error. You can get around this problem by using the `struct` or `class` keyword explicitly:

```
struct pair p = {pair,pair};
```

Namespace Scope

In C++, file scope is just a special case of *namespace scope*. A C++ namespace is an optionally named declarative region, allowing you to group declarations together for your own purpose; for example,

```
namespace MyNamespace
{
    void f();
}
```

Listing 11.9   Shows that tags and variables share the same namespace

```
// pair.cpp:
#include <iostream>
using namespace std;

struct pair {int x; int y;};

main()
{
    int pair = 0;
    pair p = {pair,pair};     // error

    cout << pair << endl;
    cout << p.x << ',' << p.y << endl;
}
```

Since f belongs to MyNamespace, it is not visible anywhere else by default. To use f, you have three options:

1. Use a fully qualified name, as in

   ```
   #include "mystuff.h"          // Defines MyNamespace
   ...
   MyNamespace::f();
   ```

2. Tell the compiler that *any use* of f refers to MyNamespace::f, like this:

   ```
   #include "mystuff.h"          // Defines MyNamespace
   using MyNamespace::f;         // A using declaration
   ...                           // imports all overloads of f!
   f();                          // calls MyNamespace::f
   ```

3. Instruct the compiler to search MyNamespace for any names it tries to find:

   ```
   #include "mystuff.h"          // Defines MyNamespace
   using namespace MyNamespace;  // A using directive
   ...
   f();                          // calls MyNamespace::f if there
                                 // are no other conflicting f's
   ```

A *using declaration* like that in Option 2 above injects the selected name into the current scope, thus hiding any other declaration of the same name that might have already been in scope. A *using directive* opens the entire selected namespace for name resolution. If there are multiple declarations of the same name in scope, the compiler will issue the usual diagnostic.

Namespaces were originally conceived to solve difficulties in using libraries. Before namespaces, vendors had to attach prefixes to names in the libraries they distributed, so that you could avoid name conflicts when using their functionality concurrently with that of other vendors. Now you can pick and choose what features you want without worrying about inconvenient compile and link errors:

```
#include "vendorA.h"      // contains f() and g()
#include "vendorB.h"      // contains f() and g()

using vendorA::f;
using vendorB::g;
```

Namespace are unique in that their declarative regions can span multiple files. For example, you can declare and implement MyNamespace in two files, like this:

File 1
```
// myname.h
namespace MyNamespace
{
    void f();
} // NOTE: No semi-colon!
```

File 2
```
// myname.cpp
void MyNamespace::f()
{
    // implementation goes here...
}
```

If the name of a namespace is too long for your tastes, you can declare an *alias* more to your liking:

```
namespace notSoLong = ReallyReallyLongNamespaceName;
using notSoLong::f;
using notSoLong::g;
```

The declarations in a namespace do not all have to appear contiguously in the same translation unit. The set of names that belongs to a namespace is the union of all the names declared within like-named namespace blocks in all translation units.

The *global namespace* is the declarative region outside of any namespace block. It behaves as if it were declared with some unique name, such as

```
namespace unique
{
    ...
}
```

The same name is used in all translation units so that identifiers with external linkage can be resolved (see "Linkage" below). If you want global identifiers to be private to a translation unit, you can qualify them with the static keyword (a la C), as in

```
static int private_integer;
static void private_function();
```

or you can declare them in the *unnamed namespace*, which is unique to each translation unit:

```
namespace
{
    int private_integer;
    void private_function();
}
```

The latter is the preferred method in C++ programs.

Lifetime

The lifetime or *storage duration* of an object is the duration between the time the object is created and the time it is destroyed. Objects that have *static* duration are created and initialized once, prior to their *first use*, and are destroyed when the program terminates normally. Objects with global scope, as well as objects declared with the static specifier at block scope, have static duration. Listing 11.10 has an example of the latter. The variable n is initialized once at program startup and retains its most recently assigned value throughout the program. (Its scope, however, is just the body of the function count.)

Function parameters and objects declared within a block without the extern or static specifier have *automatic* duration. Such objects are created anew every time execution enters their block. Every time execution enters a block normally, then any initialization you may have specified is also performed. It is an error in C++ to jump into any block in such a way that you bypass any declarations that require initialization. When execution falls through or jumps past the end of a block, or returns from a function, all automatic variables in that scope are destroyed.

The program in Listing 11.11 illustrates both static and automatic duration with the familiar factorial function. The token n!, pronounced "n-factorial" (without yelling), denotes the product of all positive integers from n down to 1. For example,

$3! = 3 \times 2 \times 1$
$4! = 4 \times 3 \times 2 \times 1$
(etc.)

Most math textbooks give the following equivalent recursive definition instead:

$n! = \{$if $n <= 1$ then 1, otherwise $n * (n - 1)!\}$

Listing 11.10   Illustrates static storage

```cpp
// lifetime.cpp:   Illustrate static storage duration
#include <iostream>
using namespace std;

main()
{
    int count(void);
    int i;

    for (i = 0; i < 5; ++i)
        cout << count() << endl;
}

int count(void)
{
    static int n = 0;

    return ++n;
}

// Output:
1
2
3
4
5
```

You can render this concisely in C++ with the following recursive function:

```cpp
long fac(long n)
{
    return (n <= 1) ? 1 : n * fac(n-1);
}
```

When n is greater than one, fac calls itself recursively with an argument one less than it started with. This action temporarily suspends the current scope and creates a new one, with its own copy of n. This continues until the most deeply nested copy of n is equal to one. This scope terminates and returns the value 1 to the scope that called it, and so on up to the original invocation. For example, consider the execution of the expression fac(3):

```cpp
fac(3):   return (3 <= 1) ? 1 : 3 * fac(2);
```

Listing 11.11 Illustrates recursion and static storage

```
/* recurse.c:   Illustrate recursion and storage duration */
#include <stdio.h>

main()
{
    long n;
    long fac(long);

    fputs("Enter a small integer: ",stderr);
    scanf("%ld%*c",&n);
    printf("\n%ld! = %ld\n",n,fac(n));
    return 0;
}

long fac(long n)
{
    static int depth = 0;
    auto long result;
    void print_current(int,long);

    print_current(++depth,n);
    result = (n <= 1) ? 1 : n * fac(n-1);
    print_current(depth--,result);

    return result;
}

void print_current(int depth, long n)
{
    int i;

    // Indent to show depth
    for (i = 0; i < depth; ++i)
        fputs("    ",stdout);

    printf("%ld\n",n);
}

/* Output:
Enter a small integer: 3
    3
        2
            1
            1
        2
    6

3! = 6
*/
```

This calls `fac(2)`:

```
fac(2):  return (2 <= 1) ? 1 : 2 * fac(1);
```

which in turn calls `fac(1)`:

```
fac(1):  return (1 <= 1) ? 1 : fac(0);
```

which returns the value 1:

```
fac(1):    return 1;
```

`fac(2)` now resumes and returns the following to `fac(3)`:

```
fac(2):    return 2 * 1;
```

which returns the value 6 to the original caller.

The program in Listing 11.11 traces this recursive computation by wrapping the factorial formula with statements to print the value coming into the function and the computed value going out. It keeps track, with the static variable `depth`, of how deeply the recursion has nested. Since `depth` has static duration, it is allocated and initialized once, prior to the first invocation of `fac`, and retains its value across function calls (including recursive ones). Only automatic variables, such as n in the `fac` function, are replicated with each recursive call. The `auto` keyword is purely documentary, since all variables with block scope are automatic by default.

Objects that reside on the free store as returned by the new operator have *dynamic storage duration*, which is a topic interesting enough to merit a chapter of its own (see Chap. 20).

Lifetime of Temporaries

Compilers sometimes generate temporary objects when evaluating expressions at runtime. The expression $x = a + b + c$, for example, may require a temporary. Perhaps statements like the following would execute:

```
temp = b + c;
x = a + temp;
// destroy temp here
```

In order to conserve resources, it is important for the compiler to destroy temporaries early, but not too early. Consider the class declaration:

```
class string
{
public:
    string(const char*);
    operator const char*();
    string operator+(const string&);    //concatenation
    // other members omitted
};
```

The `const char*` operator lets you use string arguments with standard C library functions, for example,

```
// Well-formed example:
string s, t;
...
printf("%s\n",(const char*)(s+t));
```

You would certainly want the temporary from the expression `s+t` to persist long enough for `printf` to process it. It you try breaking it into two statements, you'll be disappointed:

```
// Ill-formed example:
string s, t;
...
const char *p = s + t;
printf("%s\n",p);
```

In standard C++, the temporary assigned to `p` will *not* persist until the `printf` statement, rendering the above code ill-formed. The rule is that temporaries remain until the end of the *full expression* in which they appear. In most cases, this just means until the end of the enclosing statement, so that temporaries do not persist from one statement to the next. A full expression is one that is not part of another expression, such as an initializer; the controlling expression of an `if`, `while`, or `switch`; the expressions in a `for` statement; and an expression returned from a function.

The only exception to this rule is for references bound to a temporary. For example, consider the following statements:

```
class T {/* whatever ... */};
T f();
const T &r = f();
```

The temporary object returned by `f` persists as long as `r` is in scope, as you would expect.

Linkage

An identifier in one scope can refer to an object of the same name in another scope according to the rules of *linkage*. Each name declared in a legal C++ program will fall into exactly one of the following linkage attributes:

External Linkage—links names across translation units in a program

Internal Linkage—links names throughout a single translation unit

No Linkage—certain names are unique, hence, they have no linkage.

Functions and other global identifiers declared without the `static` keyword have external linkage. There must be only one *definition* of each such object, but there may be many declarations that refer to that definition. If the following declaration occurs at global scope in a file:

```
// file1.cpp
int x;
```

then it can used in another file at any scope where the following declaration is in scope:

```
// file2.cpp
extern int x;
```

The extern specifier in essence says, "Find a global object named x in some translation unit," which can be an object with external linkage in another translation unit, or one with internal linkage in the same translation unit. When declaring (but not defining) a function, the *extern* qualifier is implicit:

```
// file1.c
int f(void)
{
    return 1;
}
```

```
// file2.cpp
int f(void);        // extern specifier for functions is implicit -
                    // links to f in file1.cpp
```

Functions and objects declared within a namespace (including the global namespace) with the static specifier have internal linkage. Declarations within the unnamed namespace also have internal linkage. Identifiers with internal linkage are visible only within their translation unit. This use of the keyword static has little to do with the static storage duration specifier discussed previously. It's a good idea to commit the following pseudo-formulas to memory:

```
static + block scope == static storage duration
static + global scope == internal linkage
```

The first use of static affects lifetime; the second, linkage.

Certain program entities, which are always unique, are said to have no linkage. These include objects with block scope without an extern specifier, function parameters, and anything other than a function or object, such as labels, tag names, member names, typedef names, and enumeration constants.

The source files in Listings 11.12 and 11.13 constitute a single executable program that illustrates the different types of linkage. The integer i at file scope in Listing 11.12 has external linkage because it does not have the static specifier. A variable of the same name in another file can refer to it if declared with the extern specifier, as Listing 11.13 does. (It is an error to have two *definitions* of the same object with external linkage, e.g., two i's qualified by neither static nor extern.)

Listing 11.12   Illustrates external linkage

```
// linkage1.cpp:  Links with linkage2.cpp
#include <iostream>
using namespace std;

namespace
{
    void f1(int);          // Internal
    void f2(void);         // Internal
    int k = 7;             // Internal
}

main()
{
    extern void f1(int);   // Internal
    extern void f2(void);  // Internal
    extern void f3(void);  // External

    f1(23);
    f2();
    f3();
    return 0;
}

int i = 13;                // External

void f1(int i)             // Internal
{
    for (;;)
    {
        float i = 33.0;    // No Linkage
        cout << i << endl;

        extern int k;      // External!!!
        cout << k << endl;
        goto exit;
    }

exit:                      // No linkage
    cout << i << endl;
}

void f2(void)              // Internal Linkage
{
    cout << i << endl;
}
```

Listing 11.12   (continued)

```
// Output:
33
8
23
13
16
```

Listing 11.13   Links with Listing 11.12

```
// linkage2.cpp:   Links with linkage1.cpp
#include <iostream>
using namespace std;

extern int i;                 // External
int k = 8;                    // External

namespace
{
    int j = 3;                // Internal (unnamed namespace)
}

void f3(void)                 // External
{
    cout << i+j << endl;
}
```

The functions f1 and f2 have internal linkage because they use the static specifier. The float object named i in f1 has no linkage because it is declared at block scope without the extern specifier. The integer j in Listing 11.13 has internal linkage because it is in the unnamed namespace, and the function f3 has external linkage because of the absence of the static specifier.

The following three lines from Listing 11.12 require particular explanation:

```
extern void f1(int);          // Internal
extern void f2(void);         // Internal
extern void f3(void);         // External
```

Since the extern specifier means "link with something with global scope," the declarations f1 and f2 in main link, respectively, with the functions of the same name in the same file, which happen to have internal linkage. It is important that you declare f1 and f2 static at file scope before the `extern` references in `main`, else the compiler will assume that they have external linkage (like it does `f3`), which conflicts with the actual function definitions later in the file.

Unlike C, `const` objects in C++ at file scope have internal linkage, unless declared with the `extern` specifier. This allows the common practice of placing `const` in include files without the linker complaining about multiple references. If you want `const` objects with external linkage, qualify each with `extern` and initialize only one, as in

File 1
```
extern const int x = 10;
```

File 2
```
extern const int x;        // refers to x in File 1
```

A class name declared at namespace scope (i.e., a nonlocal class, which means probably every class name you'll ever see!) has external linkage and, therefore, so do its member functions, static data members, enumeration, and nested classes. Static members have external linkage, which explains why you must explicitly define them at file scope. They are essentially global identifiers that also obey scope resolution and member access rules. Non-inline class member functions have external linkage, which allows them to be defined in a separate file from the class declaration. Nonmember inline functions have internal linkage.

Because the `inline` keyword is merely a hint to the translator, it is difficult to classify the linkage of inline member functions. If such a function is inlined, you can think of it as having internal linkage (it is common practice to put them in the class header file, anyway). If the compiler is unable to insert the code inline, it must create an out-of-line function. Some implementations like to have only one out-of-line definition to save code space, but this implies external linkage. The standard merely states that an inline member function must have only one definition in a program.

Type-safe Linkage

As Chapter 1 explains, in standard C there is no guarantee that a function defined in one translation unit will be used correctly in another. For example, consider the source files:

File 1
```
void f(double x)
{
    ...
}
```

File 2
```
extern void f(int);
...
    f(1);
```

The function defined in File 1 is expecting a double argument, but someone misinformed the user in File 2, and the program is broken. Traditional C discipline calls for both files to include a common header file that has the correct prototype for f. C++ takes this responsibility from the programmer and gives it to the development environment through the concept of *type-safe linkage*, which guarantees that the two versions of f above do not link. Most implementations achieve this by encoding information about the formal parameters into a hidden name that the linker sees (this is usually called *name mangling*). For example, a compiler might encode the name in File 1 as

```
f__Fd       // "f is a function taking a double"
```

and the one in File 2 as

```
f__Fi       // "f is a function taking an int"
```

Since the linker sees two distinct names, the reference to f from File 2 to File 1 is not resolved, causing a linker error. Hence, you can't even produce an executable program unless you call your functions correctly!

"Language" Linkage

C++ appeals to C programmers for a number of reasons. Most of what they know applies unchanged in C++. They can ease their way into object-oriented programming by first using C++ as a "better C" until they get used to its syntax and idiosyncrasies. But production programmers need something even more important: to be able to use existing C code without even *recompiling*. It might seem that the name encoding that supports overloading makes this impossible. How do you call a C function, f(double) say, from a C++ program when the C name is f (or more commonly, _f), and the C++ name is f__Fd? You can instruct the compiler to link with a C function via *linkage specification*:

In the C++ file:
```
extern "C" f();
```

The extern "C" specification tells the compiler to generate the link name according to C rules so the linker can find it in the existing C object code. An implementation may support other language linkage specifications in addition to "C". The language quoted is part of the function's type, but not its *signature* (the sequence of argument types used in function overload resolution). Linkage specifications may only appear in namespace scope.

Summary

- The *scope* of an identifier is the region of program text where it is visible.
- A *local scope* is a contiguous region of program text delimited by braces {}.

- The declaration of class members must appear in a lexically contiguous region of program text. The actual definitions of member functions and static data member can (and usually should) be in other translation units.
- Namespace scopes can span multiple translation units. A namespace consists of the union of all its declarations in all translation units.
- Declarations at file scope are in the *global namespace*. There is only one global namespace in an entire program.
- A declaration in a nested scope *hides* a declaration of the *same name* in an enclosing scope, regardless of other considerations such as type, signature, and access permissions.
- A compiler resolves name binding by first considering scope, then access specification, then overload resolution.
- The lifetime of an object is the duration between the time it is created and the time it is destroyed. There are three types of storage duration: *automatic*, *static*, and *dynamic*.
- Static objects are initialized once, prior to their first use. Automatic objects are initialized each time execution enters their scope.
- Identifiers can have *external linkage* (visible in multiple translation units), *internal linkage* (visible throughout a single translation unit), or *no linkage*.
- Objects with external linkage must be *defined* in a named namespace (including the secretly named global namespace).
- Identifiers in the unnamed namespace have internal linkage.
- Implementations may support linkage to entities in other programming languages; extern "C" is required of all implementations.

Control Structures

Over a quarter-century ago Edsgar Dijkstra wrote his now famous letter entitled "GOTO Statement Considered Harmful," which, as the title suggests, made a strong case for never using a branching construct in a program.[1] In another letter he wrote, ". . . for some time I knew that, as a programmer, I could live quite happily without any form of the goto statement, but . . . in the mean time my considered opinion is that I cannot live happily with the goto statement."[2] There followed a notorious movement to eliminate the goto construct altogether. Professors refused to accept students' programming assignments if they contained a goto. Languages were designed without a goto construct. The upside of all this was that as an industry we learned to think "structured," that is, to organize our software in a more logical and maintainable fashion. The downside is that sometimes a goto is just what the doctor ordered. Almost all current programming languages in widespread use support some form of goto, Java being a notable exception with its labeled breaks taking goto's place.

In this chapter I will discuss the mechanisms available to structure the logic of your C/C++ programs. These include not only the goto-less constructs of structured programming, but also branching techniques that range from the simplistic to the sophisticated: break, goto, nonlocal jumps with setjmp/longjmp, and signals.

Structured Programming

In 1966 Bohm and Jacopini proved mathematically that it is possible to express any algorithm in terms of only three constructs, along with an arbitrary number of boolean flags.[3] The three constructs are

1. sequences of statements
2. alternation (e.g., if-else, switch)
3. repetition (e.g., while, for, do).

We usually call programs that use only these mechanisms *structured* programs. Unfortunately, when structured design gurus began their hard-sell to the industry, most programming professionals were making a living with Cobol, Fortran IV, and assembler language, while Basic was gaining popularity in educational settings. Of these languages, only Cobol had the `else` construct. Telling a Fortran programmer that he shouldn't use a `goto` usually resulted in him telling *you* where to go to. Besides, we were proud of our expert ability to cram complex logic into as few lines as possible—who cares if the lame-brains couldn't decipher such "elegance"? We couldn't have done this great work without the `goto`. Speaking of the structured programming revolution, P. J. Plauger once said, "Us converts waved this interesting bit of news under the noses of the unreconstructed assembly-language programmers who kept trotting forth twisty bits of logic and saying, 'I betcha can't structure *this*.' Neither the proof by Bohm and Jacopini nor our repeated successes at writing structured code brought them around one day sooner than they were ready to convince themselves."[4]

Listing 12.1 has a vintage Basic program that plays the game of "Hi-lo." You think of a number between 1 and 100, and just tell the computer whether its guesses are high, low, or right on. As long as you give honest responses, the binary search algorithm will find your number in seven guesses or less (because `ceil(`$\log_2 10$`))` `==` 7). Compare this program to the C++ version in Listing 12.2. The Basic version is just under half the size of the C++ version, but is it more readable? Is it as maintainable? Is the structure of the logic evident from the shape of the program? No, no, no!

As a consequence of Bohm and Jacopini's work, it became natural to use alternation and repetition as the basic tools of thought when designing a logical process. It was soon quite

Listing 12.1   A Basic program to play Hi-Lo

```
100 rem A very old Basic program to play Hi-Lo
110 print "Think of a number between 1 and 100"
120 print "If you don't cheat, I'll figure it out"
130 print "in seven guesses or less!"
140 lo = 1
150 hi = 100
160 if lo > hi then print "You cheated!" : goto 240
170 g = int((lo + hi) / 2)
180 print "Is it";g;" (L/H/Y)?"
190 input r$
200 if r$ = "L" then lo = g+1 : goto 160
210 if r$ = "H" then hi = g-1 : goto 160
220 if r$ <> "Y" then print "What? Try again..." : goto 190
230 print "What fun!"
240 print "Wanna play again?"
250 input r$
260 if r$ = "Y" then 140
```

Listing 12.2   A C++ Hi-Lo program

```cpp
// hi-lo.cpp
#include <iostream>
#include <cctype>
using namespace std;

main()
{
    cout << "Think of a number between 1 and 100.\n"
         << "If you don't cheat, I'll figure it out\n"
         << "in seven guesses or less!"
         << endl;

    bool done = false;      // Loop control variable

    while (!done)
    {
        char response;
        int guess;

        // Play the Game:
        bool found = false;    // Loop control variable
        int lo = 1, hi = 100;
        while (!found && lo <= hi)
        {
            // Get guess:
            guess = (lo + hi) / 2;
            cout << "Is it " << guess << " (L/H/Y): " << endl;
            cin >> response;
            response = toupper(response);

            // Narrow the search range:
            if (response == 'L')
                lo = guess + 1;
            else if (response == 'H')
                hi = guess - 1;
            else if (response != 'Y')
                cout << "What? Try again..." << endl;
            else
                found = true;
        }

        // Print results:
        if (lo > hi)
            cout << "You cheated!" << endl;
        else
            cout << "Your number was " << guess << endl;
```

continued

Listing 12.2   (continued)

```
            cout << "Wanna play again? " << endl;
            cin >> response;
            done = toupper(response) != 'Y';
      }
}


// Sample Execution (numbers are 37 and 99):
c:>hi-lo
Think of a number between 1 and 100.
If you don't cheat, I'll figure it out
in seven guesses or less!

Is it 50 (L/H/Y): h
Is it 25 (L/H/Y): l
Is it 37 (L/H/Y): y
Your number was 37
What fun!
Wanna play again? y
Is it 50 (L/H/Y): l
Is it 75 (L/H/Y): l
Is it 88 (L/H/Y): l
Is it 94 (L/H/Y): l
Is it 97 (L/H/Y): l
Is it 99 (L/H/Y): l
Is it 100 (L/H/Y): h
You cheated!
Wanna play again? n
```

popular to describe procedures in structured prose, or *pseudocode*—a terse, verbal description governed by loops and conditions. You describe conditionals much the same as in any of the languages that support the `if-else` construct:

```
if <condition>
    do this...
else
    do that
```

To choose from a group of related values, there is the `case` statement:

```
case x of
    1: do this...
    2: do that...
otherwise: do the other thing...
```

There are separate controls for the various flavors of loops. Most of the time you need a control that tests its condition before entering the loop body:

```
while <condition>
    do this...
```

A `for` loop is good for processes that must execute a specific number of times, as in

```
for i = 1 to n
    do something dependent on i
```

or for processing a sequence of items:

```
for each student on the roster
    calculate something...
```

On rare occasion you might need a loop that tests its controlling condition after executing the loop body:

```
repeat
    get user input
until input is in the range [1..5]
```

Listing 12.3 has a *pseudocode* description of a process to merge two sorted text files. It reads a line from each file and prints the one that lexicographically precedes the other. The process repeats until it empties one of the files, at which point it just outputs the rest of the other file.

It is important that loop conditions relate to your design in a direct and understandable way. To ensure this, you might insert a comment at the beginning of the loop body that states, in terms of the problem space, what the condition of the loop means. If it clearly expresses the solution you had in mind, you've crafted an effective loop. You can also do the same thing at the end of the loop. See the implementation of the merge procedure in Listing 12.5 for an example. (The input data is in Listing 12.4).

Listing 12.3   Pseudocode for a procedure to merge two text files

```
open and read first line from each file
while (neither file has been exhausted)
{
    determine which line comes next
    print that line
    get a fresh line from the corresponding file
}

empty the remaining active file, if any
close files
```

Listing 12.4   Input files for Listings 12.5 and 12.7

FILE1.DAT

brown
fox
quick
the

FILE2.DAT

dog
jumped
lazy
over
the

FILE3.DAT

and
cow
jumped
moon
over
the
the

Listing 12.5   C implementation of Listing 12.3

```cpp
// merge1.cpp: Merge two sorted files to standard output
#include <iostream>
#include <fstream>
#include <cstring>     // For strcmp()
#include <cstdlib>     // For EXIT codes
#include <cassert>
using namespace std;

main(int argc, char *argv[])
{
    const int BUFSIZ = 128;
    char buf1[BUFSIZ], buf2[BUFSIZ];

    // Open files:
    if (argc != 3)
        return EXIT_FAILURE;
    ifstream f1(argv[1]);
    ifstream f2(argv[2]);

    // Do the merge:
    f1.getline(buf1,BUFSIZ);
    f2.getline(buf2,BUFSIZ);
```

Listing 12.5 (continued)

```
    while (f1 && f2)
    {
        // (INVARIANT: both buffers have fresh lines)

        // Print and refresh the appropriate line:
        if (strcmp(buf1,buf2) <= 0)
        {
            cout << buf1 << endl;
            f1.getline(buf1,BUFSIZ);
        }
        else
        {
            cout << buf2 << endl;
            f2.getline(buf2,BUFSIZ);
        }
    }
    // (INVARIANT: At least one file has been exhausted)

    // Empty the remaining file:
    while (f1)
    {
        // (INVARIANT: buf1 has a fresh line)
        cout << buf1 << endl;
        f1.getline(buf1,BUFSIZ);
    }
    assert(f1.eof());    // (INVARIANT: file1 has been exhausted)

    while (f2)
    {
        // (INVARIANT: buf2 has a fresh line)
        cout << buf2 << endl;
        f2.getline(buf2,BUFSIZ);
    }
    assert(f2.eof());    // (INVARIANT: file2 has been exhausted)

    return EXIT_SUCCESS;
}
// Sample execution:
c:>merge1 file1.dat file2.dat
brown
dog
fox
jumped
lazy
over
quick
the
the
```

You can easily extend the merge algorithm to process a larger number of files. At first glance you might think that the loop control statement

```
while (neither file has been exhausted)
```

should become

```
while (no file has been exhausted)
```

But if you have n files, say, then when that loop finishes you will still have n-1 active files to continue merging. You need to stay inside the merge loop until only one file is still active:

```
while (number of active files > 1)
    (etc.)
```

This requires that you keep a list of active files from which you will delete an entry when its file runs out of input lines. The design now looks like this:

```
while (number of active files > 1)
{
    determine which line comes next
    print that line
    if (the corresponding file is now empty)
        delete it from the list of active files
    else
        get a fresh line from the file
}

empty the remaining file
```

Since you have introduced a mechanism to track the active files, you might as well stay in the loop until the last file is empty and there is nothing else to do. The pseudocode in Listing 12.6 reflects this change, as do the invariants in the implementation in Listing 12.7. The program in Listing 12.7 keeps track of the state of the files in a list of pointers to `FileInfo` objects, which hold the current line of text and a pointer to its file stream. The `FileInfo` constructor and the function `getNextLine` work together to enforce the invariant that each file in the list holds a fresh line.

Branching

Even if it is possible to program without gotos, it is often convenient to branch out of the middle of a loop (a special case of a goto). Using C++'s break statement can keep you from littering your code with extraneous loop control variables. For example, the variables done and found in Listing 12.2 exist only to terminate their loops. Most C++ programmers do without them (see Listing 12.8, where I use break statements instead).

Listing 12.6   Pseudocode for a procedure to merge an arbitrary number of files

```
open and read first line from each file
while (a file with a fresh line remains)
{
    determine which lines comes next lexicographically
    print that line
    if (the corresponding file is now at end-of-file)
        delete it from the list of active files
    else
        get a fresh line from the file
}
```

Listing 12.7   C++ implementation of Listing 12.6

```cpp
// merge2.cpp: Merge files to standard output
#include <iostream>
#include <fstream>
#include <cstdlib>
#include <string>
#include <list>
using namespace std;

const int BUFSIZ = 128;

struct FileInfo
{
    ifstream* f;
    char line[BUFSIZ];
    FileInfo(char* fname)
    {
        f = new ifstream(fname);
        f->getline(line,BUFSIZ);
    }
    ~FileInfo()
    {
        f->close();
        delete f;
    }
};

main(int argc, char *argv[])
{
    string getNextLine(list<FileInfo*>&);
```

continued

Listing 12.7   (continued)

```cpp
    if (argc == 1)
        return EXIT_FAILURE;

    // Open files—read first line:
    list<FileInfo*> flist;
    for (int i = 0; i < argc-1; ++i)
        flist.push_back(new FileInfo(argv[i+1]));

    // Do the merge:
    while (flist.size() > 0)
        cout << getNextLine(flist) << endl;

    return EXIT_SUCCESS;
}

string getNextLine(list<FileInfo*>& flist)
{
    // Find next line in sort order:
    char* next = "\xff";
    list<FileInfo*>::iterator small;
    list<FileInfo*>::iterator p = flist.begin();
    while (p != flist.end())
    {
        FileInfo* fp = *p;
        if (strcmp(next,fp->line) > 0)
        {
            small = p;
            next = fp->line;
        }
        ++p;
    }

    // Advance corresponding file stream to a fresh line:
    FileInfo* fp = *small;
    ifstream* f = fp->f;
    char* line = fp->line;
    string minLine(line);
    f->getline(line,BUFSIZ);
    if (f->eof())
    {
        // Close and remove this entry:
        delete fp;
        flist.erase(small);
    }

    // (INVARIANT: each flist entry still has a fresh line)
    return minLine;
}
```

Listing 12.7 (continued)

```
// Sample execution:
c:>merge2 file1.dat file2.dat file3.dat
and
brown
cow
dog
fox
jumped
jumped
lazy
moon
over
over
quick
the
the
the
the
```

Listing 12.8 Removes extraneous loop controls from Listing 12.2

```
// hi-lo2.cpp:  Removes extraneous boolean flags
#include <iostream>
#include <cctype>
using namespace std;

main()
{
    cout << "Think of a number between 1 and 100.\n"
         << "If you don't cheat, I'll figure it out\n"
         << "in seven guesses or less!"
         << endl;

    for (;;)             // An idiom for REPEAT FOREVER
    {
        int lo = 1, hi = 100;
        char response;
        int guess;

        // Play the Game:
        while (lo <= hi)
        {
            // Get guess:
            guess = (lo + hi) / 2;
            cout << "Is it " << guess << " (L/H/Y): " << endl;
            cin >> response;
            response = toupper(response);
```
continued

Listing 12.8   (continued)

```
            // Narrow the search range:
            if (response == 'L')
                lo = guess + 1;
            else if (response == 'H')
                hi = guess - 1;
            else if (response != 'Y')
                cout << "What? Try again..." << endl;
            else
                break;
        }

        // Print results:
        if (lo > hi)
            cout << "You cheated!" << endl;
        else
            cout << "Your number was " << guess << endl;

        cout << "Wanna play again? " << endl;
        cin >> response;
        if (toupper(response) != 'Y')
            break;
    }
}
```

Suppose you decide to rewrite the `if-else` statements under the comment `// Narrow the search range` in Listing 12.8 as a `switch` statement:

```
// Narrow the search range:
switch(response)
{
    case 'L':
        lo = guess + 1;
        break;
    case 'H':
        hi = guess - 1;
        break;
    case 'Y':
        puts("What? Try again...");
        break;
    default:
        break;            // This doesn't work!
}
```

Unfortunately the `break` under the default case exits the `switch`, not the loop. In this case you can use a `goto` or use the `if-else` construct as before.

Exiting deeply nested loops with a `goto` can be much clearer than the boolean flag approach the purists advocate. Consider this excerpt that searches a three-dimensional array for a certain value:

```
for (i = 0; i < n; ++i)
    for (j = 0; j < m; ++j)
        for (k = 0; k < s; ++k)
            if (a[i][j][k] == x)
                goto found;

found:
    /* use i, j, and k here */
```

A naive attempt at a nonbranching version gives:

```
for (done = 0, i = 0; !done && i < n; ++i)
    for (j = 0; !done && j < m; ++j)
        for (k = 0; !done && k < s; ++k)
            if (a[i][j][k] == x)
                done = 1;

/* Fix indexes (yuck!) */
--i, --j, --k;
```

Even if you don't mind the way this looks, it passes control to the enclosing loops all the way to the top level instead of exiting immediately, which increments the loop variables beyond their current values.

Using the `goto` as a multilevel loop exit can help restore things to a stable state after a serious error, as in

```
main()
{
    // Some one-time initialization here

    for (;;)
    {
        // Some more initialization here

        // Things get deeply nested...

                if (<things go crazy>)
                    goto recover;
    }
recover:;
}
```

Note the semicolon following the label. Labels can't stand alone, but must always occur as part of a *labeled statement*.

Nonlocal Branching

What if you encounter an exceptional condition deep within a set of nested function calls and your recover point is back in a function higher up in the call chain (like main)? What you need is a super goto that branches across functions. That's what the setjmp/longjmp mechanism is for. You record a point to return to with setjmp, and branch to it with longjmp. Here's the syntax:

```
#include <setjmp.h>

jmp_buf recover;

main()
{
    volatile int i = 0;
    for(;;)
    {
        if (setjmp(recover) != 0)
        {
            /* Recover from error in f() */
        }

        /* Get deeply nested... */
    }
    return 0;
}

...

void f()
{
    /* Do some risky stuff */

    if (<things go crazy>)
        longjmp(recover,1);

    /* else carry on */
}
```

A jmp_buf is an array that holds the system information necessary to restore execution at the setjmp point. (Obviously, a jump buffer must global). When you call setjmp, the system stores the *calling environment* (such as the contents of the stack and instruction pointer registers, etc.) in recover. The setjmp always returns a zero when called directly. A call to longjmp restores the calling environment, so execution continues back at the setjmp call, with one difference: It appears as if setjmp has returned the second argument from the longjmp call (in this case a one). If you give longjmp a second argument of zero, it returns a one anyway. Since a `longjmp` performs an alternate return from a function, it interrupts the normal flow of a program, so you should use it only to handle unusual conditions.

The function containing the `setjmp` target must still be active (i.e., must not yet have returned to its caller), otherwise the calling environment will no longer be valid. And of course, it is a bad idea to have more than one `setjmp` target with the same `jmp_buf` variable. (Now that would be confusing!) Since calling environments typically involve registers and since a compiler is free to store automatic variables in registers, you have no idea if an automatic object will have the correct value when you return from a `longjmp`. You should declare automatics in any function containing a `setjmp` with the `volatile` qualifier, which guarantees that the inner workings of `longjmp` will leave them undisturbed.

There is another consequence of not being able to trust automatic storage during a `longjmp`: the `setjmp` call itself must not appear in an expression that may generate a temporary object, such as an intermediate computation. For this reason a call to `setjmp` may appear as the sole controlling expression only in an `if` or `switch` statement, or as an operand in an equality expression. You cannot reliably assign the result of `setjmp` to another variable. The program in Listing 12.9, which deletes subdirectory trees, calls `setjmp` from within a `switch` statement. (See Chap. 19 for details on the directory I/O functions.) The command-line variables `argc` and `agrv` are declared `volatile`, since they reside on the stack in a function that contains a `setjmp`. The two casts to `char*` in the second half of `main` cast away `volatile` before calling their respective functions. The loop in function `rd` illustrates the `continue` statement, which skips to the next loop iteration. The response file in Listing 12.7 is needed to compensate for the strange behavior of the MS-DOS `del` command, which requires a keyboard response to delete all the files in a directory.

Listing 12.9 Recursive directory delete program that illustrates nonlocal branching

```
/* ddir.c: Remove subdirectory tree */
#include <stdio.h>
#include <stdlib.h>
#include <io.h>
#include <string.h>
#include <sys/stat.h>
#include <setjmp.h>
#include <dirent.h>
#include <dir.h>

/* longjmp return codes */
#define BAD_DIR 1
#define DIR_OPEN_ERR 2
#define FILE_DEL_ERR 3
#define DIR_DEL_ERR 4
```

continued

Listing 12.9   (continued)

```
/* DOS-specific macros—change for other OS */
#define CMD_FORMAT "del *.* <%s > nul"
#define CMD_LEN 17

char Response_file[L_tmpnam+1] = "/";

/* Calling environment buffer */
jmp_buf env;


main(volatile int argc, volatile char **argv)
{
    FILE *f;
    volatile char *old_path = getcwd(NULL,64);
    void rd(char *);

    /* Create response file for DOS del command */
    tmpnam(Response_file+1);
    if ((f = fopen(Response_file,"w")) == NULL)
        abort();
    fputs("Y\n",f);
    fclose(f);

    switch(setjmp(env))
    {
        case BAD_DIR:
            fputs("Invalid directory\n",stderr);
            break;
        case DIR_OPEN_ERR:
            fputs("Error opening directory\n",stderr);
            break;
        case FILE_DEL_ERR:
            fputs("Error deleting file\n",stderr);
            break;
        case DIR_DEL_ERR:
            fputs("Error deleting directory\n",stderr);
            break;
    }

    /* Delete the directories */
    while (--argc)
        rd((char *) *++argv);

    /* Cleanup */
    remove(Response_file);
    chdir((char *) old_path);
    return 0;
}
```

Listing 12.9   (continued)

```
void rd(char* dir)
{
    char sh_cmd[L_tmpnam+CMD_LEN];
    DIR *dirp;
    struct dirent *entry;
    struct stat finfo;

    /* Log onto the directory that is to be deleted */
    if (chdir(dir) != 0)
        longjmp(env,BAD_DIR);
    printf("%s:\n",strlwr(dir));

    /* Delete all normal files via OS shell */
    sprintf(sh_cmd,CMD_FORMAT,Response_file);
    system(sh_cmd);

    /* Delete any remaining directory entries */
    if ((dirp = opendir(".")) == NULL)
        longjmp(env,DIR_OPEN_ERR);
    while ((entry = readdir(dirp)) != NULL)
    {
        if (entry->d_name[0] == '.')
            continue;
        stat(entry->d_name,&finfo);
        if (finfo.st_mode & S_IFDIR)
            rd(entry->d_name);    /* Subdirectory */
        else
        {
            /* Enable delete of file, then do it */
            chmod(entry->d_name,S_IWRITE);
            if (unlink(entry->d_name) != 0)
                longjmp(env,FILE_DEL_ERR);
        }
    }
    closedir(dirp);

    /* Remove the directory from its parent */
    chdir("..");
    if (rmdir(dir) != 0)
        longjmp(env,DIR_DEL_ERR);
}
```

Signals

A *signal* can occur when an unusual event interrupts the normal execution of a program, such as a divide-by-zero error or when the user presses the attention key (e.g., Control-C or Del). The header `<signal.h>` defines the following "standard signals":

SIGABRT	abnormal termination (raised by `abort`)
SIGFPE	computational exception (e.g., overflow)
SIGILL	invalid function image (e.g., illegal instruction)
SIGINT	interactive attention (e.g., Control-C)
SIGSEGV	attempt to access protected memory
SIGTERM	termination request

These signals originated on the PDP architecture under UNIX, and may not all apply to your environment. An implementation may also define other signals or may ignore signals altogether, so signal handling is by nature nonportable.

Signals come in two flavors: *synchronous* and *asynchronous*. A synchronous signal is one that your program raises, such as dividing by zero, overflowing a floating-point operation, or issuing a call to the `abort` function. You can raise a signal explicitly with a call to `raise`, for example:

```
raise(SIGABRT);
```

An asynchronous signal occurs due to forces that your program can't foresee, such as a user pressing the attention key.

The default response to most signals is usually to abort the program, but you can either arrange for signals to be ignored or provide your own custom *signal handlers*. The following statement from Listing 12.10

```
signal(SIGINT,SIG_IGN);
```

tells the environment to ignore any keyboard interrupt requests (Control-C on my machine). The keyboard input process still echoes the ^C token on the display, but it does not pass control to the default signal-handling logic that terminates the program. The statement

```
signal(SIGINT,SIG_DFL)
```

restores the default behavior, so you can halt the program from the keyboard.

The program in Listing 12.11 invokes the library function `signal` to install a function (abort_handler) to respond to SIGABRT. A signal handler must take an integer argument and return void. The first call to `abort` transfers control to abort_handler, passes SIGABRT as the integer argument (which I don't happen to use in this case), and prints the message

```
Abort signal intercepted
```

Listing 12.10 Turns off keyboard interrupt requests

```
/* ignore.c: Ignores interactive attention key */
#include <stdio.h>
#include <signal.h>

main()
{
    char buf[BUFSIZ];
    int i;

    /* Ignore keyboard interruptions */
    signal(SIGINT,SIG_IGN);

    while (gets(buf))
        puts(buf);

    /* Restore default attention key handling
       so the user can abort from the keyboard */
    signal(SIGINT,SIG_DFL);
    for (i = 1; ; ++i)
        printf("%d%c",i,(i%15 ? ' ' : '\n'));
}

/* Sample Execution
c:>ignore
hello
hello
^C
there
there
^C
^Z
1 2 3 4 5 6 7 8 9 10 11 12 13 14 15
16 17 18 19 20 21 22 23 24 25 26 27 28 29 30
31 32 33 34 35 36 37 38 39 40 41 42 43 44 45
46 47 48 49 50 51 52 53 54 55 56 57 58 59 60
61 62 63 64 65 66 67 ^C
*/
```

When execution enters a signal handler, the environment considers the associated signal "handled" before the very first statement executes. This breaks any subsequent association between your handler and the signal, and it restores the default handling. This means that if your handler returns, it will not get control back the next time that signal is raised. That is why, when control resumes where it was interrupted in main and it calls abort the second time, the program actu-

Listing 12.11   Intercepts the SIGABRT (abort) signal

```
/* abort.c:  Handle SIGABRT */

#include <stdio.h>
#include <signal.h>
#include <stdlib.h>


void abort_handler(int sig);

main()
{
    /* Install signal handler */
    if (signal(SIGABRT,abort_handler) == SIG_ERR)
        fputs("Error installing abort handler\n",stderr);

    abort();
    abort();
    return 0;
}

void abort_handler(int sig)
{
    fputs("Abort signal intercepted\n",stderr);
}

/* Output:
Abort signal intercepted
Abnormal program termination
*/
```

ally terminates. In practice, an abort handler should not return but should terminate the program with a call to exit instead. Likewise, if you return from a SIGFPE handler, the results are undefined.

If you want to handle a signal every time it occurs, your handler should reinstall itself every time it executes. As the SIGINT handler (ctrlc) in Listing 12.12 illustrates, you should do this at the beginning of an asynchronous signal handler. If you put it off until later in the function, the same signal can occur before you've reinstalled it, causing you to lose the signal to the system default handler. In fact, there is very little an asynchronous signal can do safely. The signal you're processing could have occurred during the execution of a library function. Since the standard C library is not guaranteed to be reentrant on all platforms, it would be a bad idea to call that library function from your handler. The rule of thumb is: Don't call library functions from within a function that handles an asynchronous signal. Nor should you call any function

Listing 12.12 A safe `SIGINT` handler that counts keyboard interrupts

```c
/* ctrlc.c:  A safe SIGINT handler */
#include <stdio.h>
#include <signal.h>

void ctrlc_handler(int sig);

volatile sig_atomic_t ccount = 0;

main()
{
    char buf[BUFSIZ];

    /* Install SIGINT handler */
    if (signal(SIGINT,ctrlc_handler) == SIG_ERR)
        fputs("Error installing ctrlc handler\n",stderr);

    /* Do some I/O */
    while (gets(buf))
        puts(buf);

    /* Restore default handler */
    signal(SIGINT,SIG_DFL);
    printf("You pressed ctrlc %d times\n",ccount);
    return 0;
}

void ctrlc_handler(int sig)
{
    /* Reinstall handler immediately */
    signal(sig,ctrlc_handler);

    ++ccount;
    return;
}

/* Sample Execution
c:>ctrlc
hello
hello
^C
there
there
^C
^Z
You pressed ctrlc 2 times
*/
```

Listing 12.13   A skeleton for a command interpreter—illustrates branching out of a signal handler

```
/* shell.c: A skeleton for a command interpreter */
#include <stdio.h>
#include <signal.h>
#include <setjmp.h>
/* etc. */

jmp_buf restart;

void ctrlc(int sig);

main()
{
    /* Install signal handler */
    signal(SIGINT,ctrlc);

    /* Return here on keyboard interrupt */
    setjmp(restart);

    /* Do any other initialization here... */

    for (;;)
    {
        int command_code;
        /* etc... */

        /* Read and parse command here... */

        /* Execute internal command here */
        switch(command_code)
        {
            case 'Q':
                return 0;   /* quit */

            /* Lots of cases may follow... */
        }
    }
}

void ctrlc(int sig)
{
    /* Reinstall handler */
    signal(sig,ctrlc);

    /* Jump back to command line */
    longjmp(restart,1);
    return;
}
```

that might raise another signal. As the `ctrlc` function shows, there are only two safe things you can do before returning from an asynchronous handler:

1. Call `signal` to reinstall the handler, and
2. Assign a value to a static object of type `volatile sig_atomic_t`.

The type `sig_atomic_t` is an integral type that is guaranteed not to be interrupted by a signal while it is being accessed. You can use such a value as a flag or counter when normal execution resumes. Although redundant, it is a good practice to place an explicit `return` statement at the end of a handler that returns, to distinguish it from one that halts the program.

In spite of what the preceding paragraph says, it is nevertheless routine practice in many environments to `longjmp` out of an asynchronous signal handler. (It works fine under DOS and most of the time under UNIX.) As a common example, Listing 12.13 has the outline of a command-line interpreter, a program that reads a sequence of text commands and performs the indicated functions (similar to `sh` in UNIX or DOS's `COMMAND.COM`). If you press the attention key from deep within the logic of an internal command, you want to return to the command loop, not terminate the program.

Summary

- Any algorithm can be expressed with sequences of statements, alternation, and repetition, along with an arbitrary number of boolean variables.
- Use `if-else`, or `switch-case` for alternation.
- Use `while`, `for`, or `do-while` for repetition.
- Indicate invariant conditions with assertions and/or comments.
- `break` exits the closest-enclosing loop or switch.
- `continue` skips to the next iteration of the closest-enclosing loop.
- Only use `goto` to break out of nested loops.
- Use the `setjmp`/`longjmp` mechanism for alternate returns under exceptional conditions.
- Trap synchronous and asynchronous signals with a signal handler.

References

[1] Edsgar Dijkstra, "GOTO Statement Considered Harmful," *CACM* 11:3 (March 1968), 147.

[2] Edsgar Dijkstra, "Stepwise Program Construction," printed in *Selected Writings on Computing: A Personal Perspective* (Springer-Verlag, 1982), p. 2.

[3] C. Bohm and G. Jacopini, "Flow Diagrams, Turing Machines, and Languages with Only Two Formation Rules," *CACM* 9:5 (May 1966), p. 266.

[4] P. J. Plauger, *Programming on Purpose, Essays on Software Design* (Englewood Cliffs, NJ: Prentice-Hall, 1993), p. 25.

Exceptions

Error Handling Alternatives

With the traditional programming languages of yore, a developer's alternatives for handling errors consisted mainly of the following:

1. Ignore them
2. Check return codes (fastidiously).

The first alternative should find its way only into toy programs, such as school assignments or magazine articles, that aren't discussing exceptions. Such a nonstrategy just won't do for anything you plan to execute. Consider the program in Listing 13.1, for example, which deletes an entire directory tree using standard POSIX directory-handling functions. (For an explanation of these functions, see Chap. 18.) What could possibly go wrong? Well, I see the following potentialities:

a. The chosen directory doesn't exist
b. The directory is read-protected
c. Files in the directory are deleteprotected
d. The directory itself is delete protected.

For this reason, most C library functions return a status code, which you can test to detect if an error occurred. As Listing 13.2 illustrates, this requires a lot of checking throughout a

Listing 13.1   A program that deletes an entire directory subtree

```
/* ddir.c:  Remove subdirectory tree */
#include <stdio.h>
#include <stdlib.h>
#include <io.h>
#include <string.h>
#include <sys/stat.h>
#include <dirent.h>
#include <dir.h>

main(int argc, char **argv)
{
    char *old_path = getcwd(NULL,64);
    void rd(char *);

    /* Delete the directories */
    while (--argc)
        rd(*++argv);

    /* Restore directory */
    chdir(old_path);
    return 0;
}

void rd(char* dir)
{
    void erase_dir(void);

    /* Log onto the directory to be deleted */
    chdir(dir);

    /* Delete all normal files via OS shell (DOS version) */
    system("del /q *.* > nul");

    /* Delete any remaining directory entries */
    erase_dir();

    /* Remove the directory from its parent */
    chdir("..");
    rmdir(dir);
}

void erase_dir()
{
    DIR *dirp;
    struct dirent *entry;
    struct stat finfo;
```

continued

Listing 13.1   (continued)

```
/* Erase the current directory */
dirp = opendir(".");
while ((entry = readdir(dirp)) != NULL)
{
    if (entry->d_name[0] == '.')
        continue;
    stat(entry->d_name,&finfo);
    if (finfo.st_mode & S_IFDIR)
        rd(entry->d_name);          /* Subdirectory */
    else
    {
        /* Enable delete of file, then do it */
        chmod(entry->d_name,S_IWRITE);
        unlink(entry->d_name);
    }
}
closedir(dirp);
}
```

deeply nested call chain—the deeper it gets, the more tired you get. Since the goal in such cases is to return to some safe state, it would be nice if there were some way to yank the thread of execution "out of the deep" and place it higher up in the call chain. Well, there is such a mechanism, which brings us to a third error handling alternative:

3. Use *nonlocal jumps* to reroute the thread of execution.

This is what C's setjmp/longjmp mechanism is all about, as Chapter 12 illustrated (see Listing 12.9). The setjmp function uses a *jump buffer* (jmp_buf), which is a compiler-defined structure that records information sufficient to restore control to a previous point in the program. When setjmp first executes, it initializes the buffer and returns zero. If a longjmp call further down in the call chain refers to the same jmp_buf, then control transfers immediately back to the setjmp call, this time as if it returned the second argument from the longjmp call. It would really confuse things if you could return a zero via a longjmp call (which *you* would never do, I realize), so if some other foolish programmer makes the attempt, setjmp will return a one anyway.

It would seem that all problems are solved, and I can bid you adieu. It turns out, however, that jumping out of a function into another higher up in the call chain can be risky in C++. The main problem, as Listing 13.3 illustrates, is that automatic variables created in the

Listing 13.2   Same as Listing 13.1 but with return codes

```
/* ddir2.c:   Remove subdirectory tree */
#include <stdio.h>
#include <stdlib.h>
#include <io.h>
#include <string.h>
#include <sys/stat.h>
#include <dirent.h>
#include <dir.h>

/* Return codes */
#define BAD_DIR 1
#define DIR_OPEN_ERR 2
#define FILE_DEL_ERR 3
#define DIR_DEL_ERR 4

main(int argc, char **argv)
{
    char *old_path = getcwd(NULL,64);
    int rd(char *);

    while (--argc)
    {
        int code = rd(*++argv);
        switch(code)
        {
            case BAD_DIR:
                puts("Invalid directory");
                break;
            case DIR_OPEN_ERR:
                puts("Error opening directory");
                break;
            case FILE_DEL_ERR:
                puts("Error deleting file");
                break;
            case DIR_DEL_ERR:
                puts("Error deleting directory");
                break;
        }
    }

    chdir(old_path);
    return 0;
}
```

continued

Listing 13.2 (continued)

```c
int rd(char* dir)
{
    int erase_dir(void);
    int code;

    if (chdir(dir))
        return BAD_DIR;
    system("del /q *.* > nul");

    code = erase_dir();
    if (code)
        return code;

    chdir("..");
    if (rmdir(dir))
        return DIR_DEL_ERR;
    return 0;
}

int erase_dir()
{
    DIR *dirp;
    struct dirent *entry;
    struct stat finfo;

    if ((dirp = opendir(".")) == NULL)
        return DIR_OPEN_ERR;

    while ((entry = readdir(dirp)) != NULL)
    {
        if (entry->d_name[0] == '.')
            continue;
        stat(entry->d_name,&finfo);

        if (finfo.st_mode & S_IFDIR)
            rd(entry->d_name);
        else
        {
            chmod(entry->d_name,S_IWRITE);
            if (unlink(entry->d_name))
            {
                closedir(dirp);
                return FILE_DEL_ERR;
            }
        }
    }
    closedir(dirp);
    return 0;
}
```

Listing 13.3   Illustrates objects left undestroyed by `longjmp`

```cpp
// destroy1.cpp
#include <iostream>
#include <csetjmp>
using namespace std;

class Foo
{
public:
    Foo() {cout << "Foo constructor\n";}
    ~Foo() {cout << "Foo destructor\n";}
};

jmp_buf env;

main()
{
    void f();
    if (setjmp(env) == 0)
        f();
    else
        cout << "Returned via longjmp" << endl;
    return 0;
}

void f()
{
    void g();
    Foo x;
    g();
}

void g()
{
    Foo x;
    longjmp(env,1);
}

// Output:
Foo constructor
Foo constructor
Returned via longjmp
```

execution thread between the `setjmp` and `longjmp` may not get properly destroyed. Fortunately, C++ provides for such alternate returns that *know* about destructors, via the exception handling mechanism. So, if you program in C++, you might consider this final error-handling alternative:

4. Use exceptions.

Stack Unwinding

The program in Listing 13.4 is a rewrite of Listing 13.3 using exceptions. You turn on exception catching in a region of code by surrounding it with a `try` block. You place *exception handlers* immediately after the `try` block. An exception handler is like a definition for a function named by the keyword `catch`. You raise an exception with a `throw` expression. The statement

```
throw 1;
```

causes the compiler to search back up the chain of nested function calls for a handler that can catch an integer, so control passes to that handler in `main`. The runtime environment invokes destructors for all automatic objects constructed after execution entered the `try` block. This process of destroying automatic variables on the way to an exception handler is called *stack unwinding*.

As you can see, executing a `throw` expression is semantically similar to calling `longjmp`, and a handler is like a `setjmp`. Just as you cannot `longjmp` into a function that has already returned, you can only jump to a handler associated with an "active" `try` block, that is, one that execution control has not yet exited. After a handler executes, control passes to the first statement after all the handlers associated with the `try` block (in this case `return 0`).

The notable differences between exceptions and the `setjmp`/`longjmp` facility are

1. Exception handling is a *language mechanism,* not a library feature. The overhead of transferring control to a handler is invisible to the programmer.
2. The compiler tracks all automatic variables that have destructors and executes those destructors when necessary (i.e, it unwinds the stack).
3. Local variables in the function that contains the `try` block are "safe"—you don't need to declare them `volatile` to keep them from being corrupted, as you do with `setjmp`.
4. Handlers are found by matching the *type* of the exception object that you throw. This allows you to handle categories of exceptions with a single handler and to classify them via inheritance.
5. Exception handling is a *runtime mechanism.* You can't always tell which handler will catch a specific exception by examining the source code.

Listing 13.4   Illustrates stack unwinding

```cpp
// destroy2.cpp
#include <iostream>
using namespace std;

class Foo
{
public:
    Foo() {cout << "Foo constructor" << endl;}
    ~Foo() {cout << "Foo destructor" << endl;}
};

main()
{
    void f();
    try          // Turn on exception handling
    {
        f();
    }
    catch(int)
    {
        cout << "Caught exception" << endl;
    }
    return 0;
}

void f()
{
    void g();
    Foo x;
    g();
}

void g()
{
    Foo x;
    throw 1;
}

// Output:
Foo constructor
Foo constructor
Foo destructor
Foo destructor
Caught exception
```

The last point is significant. C++ exception handling allows a clean separation between error *detection* and *error handling*. A library developer may be able to detect when an error occurs, such as an argument out of range, but he doesn't know what to do about it. You, the user, can't always detect an exceptional condition, but you know how your application needs to handle it. Hence exceptions constitute a protocol for runtime error communication between components of an application.

It is also significant to realize that C++ exception handling is designed around the *termination model*; that is, when an exception is thrown, there is no direct way to get back to the throw point and resume execution where you left off, like you can in languages like Ada that follow the *resumption model*. C++ exceptions are for rare, synchronous events.

Catching Exceptions

Since exceptions are a runtime and not a compiletime feature, standard C++ specifies the rules for matching exceptions to catch-parameters a little differently than those for finding an overloaded function to match a function call. You can define a handler for an object of type T in one of the following ways (the variable t is optional, just as it is for ordinary functions in C++):

```
catch(T t)
catch(const T t)
catch(T& t)
catch(const T& t)
```

Such handlers can catch exception objects of type E if

1. T and E are the same type, or
2. T is an *accessible base class* of E at the throw point, or
3. T and E are pointer types and there exists a standard pointer conversion from E to T at the throw point.

T is an accessible base class of E if there is an inheritance path from E to T with all derivations public. To understand Item 3, let E be a type pointing to type F, and T a type that points to type U. Then there exists a standard pointer conversion from E to T if

1. T is the same type as E, except it may have added any or both of the qualifiers const and volatile, or

2. T is a void*, or

3. U is an unambiguous, accessible base class of F, which means that F's members can refer to members of U without ambiguity (this is usually only a concern with multiple inheritance).

The bottom line of all these rules is that exceptions and catch parameters must either match exactly, or the exception caught by pointer or reference must be derived from the type of the catch parameter. For example, the following exception is *not* caught:

```cpp
#include <iostream>
using namespace std;

void f();

main()
{
    try
    {
        f();
    }
    catch(long)
    {
        cerr << "caught a long" << endl;
    }
}

void f()
{
    throw 1;  // not a long!
}
```

When the system can't find a handler for an exception, it calls the standard library function terminate, which by default aborts the program. You can substitute your own termination function by passing it as a parameter to the set_terminate, as the following program illustrates:

```cpp
// terminat.cpp
#include <iostream>
#include <exception>
#include <cstdlib>
using namespace std;
```

```
void handler()
{
    cout << "Renegade exception!\n";
    exit(EXIT_FAILURE);
}

void f();

main()
{
    set_terminate(handler);

    try
    {
        f();
    }
    catch(long)
    {
        cerr << "caught a long" << endl;
    }
}

void f()
{
    throw 1;
}

// Output:
Renegade exception!
```

The following exception *is* caught, since there is a handler for an accessible base class:

```
#include <iostream>

class B {};
class D : public B {};

void f();

main()
{
    try
    {
        f();
    }
```

```
    catch(const B&)
    {
        cerr << "caught a B" << endl;
    }
}

void f()
{
    throw D();
}
```

An exception caught by a pointer can also be caught by a `void*` handler.

> **Question:** Since the context of a `throw` statement is lost when control transfers to a handler, how can the exception object still be available in the handler?

> **Answer:** Good question! Here is another area where exception handling differs from function calls. The runtime mechanism creates a temporary copy of the thrown object for use by the handler. This suggests that it is never really a good idea to define catch parameters with value semantics, since a second copy will be made. Also, it can be dangerous to define a catch parameter as a pointer, because you may not know if it came from the heap or not (in which case you must `delete` it). The best strategy is always to *catch by reference*. And even though the exception is a temporary, you can catch it as a non-`const` reference if you want (yet another departure from the normal function-processing rules to accommodate exception handling).

Standard Exceptions

The standard C++ library throws exception objects of types found in the following class hierarchy:

```
exception
        logic_error
                domain_error
                invalid_argument
                length_error
                out_of_range
        runtime_error
                range_error
                overflow_error
                underflow_error
        bad_alloc
        bad_cast
        bad_exception
        bad_typeid
```

A logic error indicates an inconsistency in the internal logic of a program, or a violation of pre-conditions on the part of client software. For example, the substr member function of the standard string class throws an out_of_range exception if you ask for a substring beginning past the end of the string. Runtime errors are those that you cannot easily predict in advance and are usually due to forces external to a program. A range error, for example, violates a postcondition of a function, such as arithmetic overflow from processing legal arguments.

A bad_alloc exception occurs when heap memory is exhausted (see "Memory Management" below). C++ will generate a bad_cast exception when a dynamic_cast to a reference type fails. If you rethrow an exception from within an unexpected handler, it gets converted into a bad_exception (see "Exception Specifications" below). If you attempt to apply the typeid operator to a null expression, you get a bad_typeid exception.

The program in Listing 13.5 derives the dir_error exception class from runtime_error, since the associated errors are detected by the return status of system services. The exception base class has a member function called what that returns the string argument that created the exception. I use this to pass information about the error to the exception handler. The handler with the ellipsis specification (catch(...)) will catch any exception, so the order of handlers in program text is significant: You should always order them according to their respective types from the most specific to the most general.

Resource Management

While stack unwinding takes care of destroying automatic variables, there may still be some cleanup left to do. For example, consider the following function that processes a file:

```
void f(const char* fname)
{
    FILE* fp = fopen(fname,"r");
    if (fp)
    {
        // Process file; we just throw an exception for illustration:
        throw 1;        // force an exception
        fclose(fp);     // This won't happen
    }
}
```

The file will not get closed if an exception occurs in the middle of f. One way to guarantee that a resource will be deallocated is to catch all exceptions in the function where the deallocation takes place. The handler in f in Listing 13.6 closes the file and then passes whatever exception occurred on up the line by *rethrowing* it (that's what throw without an argument does). This technique could be tedious, however, if you use the same resource in many places.

Listing 13.5   Illustrates an Exception class

```cpp
// ddir3.cpp:  Remove subdirectory tree
#include <cstdio>
#include <cstdlib>
#include <io.h>
#include <cstring>
#include <sys/stat.h>
#include <csetjmp>
#include <dirent.h>
#include <dir.h>

#include <stdexcept>
#include <string>
using namespace std;

// Exception class
struct dir_error : public runtime_error
{
    dir_error(const string& msg) : runtime_error(msg){}
};

main(int argc, char** argv)
{
    char* old_path = getcwd(NULL,64);
    void rd(const char*);

    while (--argc)
    {
        try
        {
            rd((const char*) *++argv);
        }
        catch (const dir_error& x)
        {
            printf("Directory error: %s\n",x.what());
        }
        catch (const exception& x)
        {
            printf("Error: %s\n",x.what());
        }
        catch (...)
        {
            puts("Unknown error");
        }
    }
```

continued

Listing 13.5 (continued)

```
    // Cleanup :
    chdir(old_path);
}

void rd(const char* dir)
{
    if (chdir(dir) != 0)
        throw dir_error("Invalid directory");
    system("del /q *.* > nul");

    erase_dir();

    chdir("..");
    if (rmdir(dir) != 0)
        throw dir_error("Error deleting directory");
}

void erase_dir()
{
    if ((dirp = opendir(".")) == NULL)
        throw dir_error("Error opening directory");
    struct dirent* entry;

    while ((entry = readdir(dirp)) != NULL)
    {
        if (entry->d_name[0] == '.')
            continue;
        struct stat finfo;
        stat(entry->d_name,&finfo);
        if (finfo.st_mode & S_IFDIR)
            rd(entry->d_name);
        else
        {
            chmod(entry->d_name,S_IWRITE);
            if (unlink(entry->d_name))
            {
                closedir(dirp);
                throw dir_error("Error deleting file");
            }
        }
    }
    closedir(dirp);
}
```

Listing 13.6   Deallocates a resource in the midst of handling an exception

```cpp
// destroy4.cpp
#include <cstdioh>
using namespace std;

main()
{
    void f(const char*);
    try
    {
        f("file1.dat");
    }
    catch(int)
    {
        puts("Caught exception");
    }
}

void f(const char* fname)
{
    FILE* fp = fopen(fname,"r");
    if (fp)
    {
        try
        {
            throw 1;
        }
        catch(int)
        {
            fclose(fp);
            puts("File closed");
            throw;  // Rethrow
        }

        fclose(fp); // The normal close
    }
}

// Output:
File closed
Caught exception
```

A better method arranges things so that stack unwinding will deallocate the resource auto-matically. In Listing 13.7, I create a local class `File` whose constructor opens the file and whose destructor closes it. Since the `File` object x is automatic, its destructor is guaranteed to execute as the stack unwinds. You can use this technique to handle any number of resources safely.

Listing 13.7   Illustrates the principle that "resource allocation is initialization"

```cpp
// destroy5.cpp
#include <cstdio>
using namespace std;

main()
{
    void f(const char*);
    try
    {
        f("file1.dat");
    }
    catch(int)
    {
        puts("Caught exception");
    }
}

void f(const char* fname)
{
    class File
    {
        FILE* f;

    public:
        File(const char* fname, const char* mode)
        {
            f = fopen(fname, mode);
        }
        ~File()
        {
            fclose(f);
            puts("File closed");
        }
    };
```

Listing 13.7 (continued)

```
    File x(fname,"r");
    throw 1;
}

// Output:
File closed
Caught exception
```

Constructors and Exceptions

One of the motivations for adding exceptions to the language was to compensate for the fact that constructors have no return value. Before exceptions, it was very awkward to handle a resource error in a constructor. For example, what happens if the call to `fopen` fails in Listing 13.8? One solution uses an internal state variable that you test before using the resource. The program in Listing 13.9 uses the file pointer returned from `fopen` to determine whether the resource is available. The `void*` conversion operator returns a nonzero pointer value if all is well, so you can test the state like this:

```
if (x)
    // All is well
else
    // Resource unstable
```

Listing 13.8 Uses internal state to track a resource

```
// destroy6.cpp
#include <cstdio>
using namespace std;

main()
{
    void f(const char*);
    try
    {
        f("file1.dat");
    }
```

continued

Listing 13.8   (continued)

```
    catch(int)
    {
        puts("Caught exception");
    }
}

void f(const char *fname)
{
    class File
    {
        FILE* f;
    public:
        File(const char* fname, const char* mode)
        {
            f = fopen(fname, mode);
        }
        ~File()
        {
            if (f)
            {
                fclose(f);
                puts("File closed");
            }
        }
        operator void*() const
        {
            return f ? (void *) this : 0;
        }
    };

    File x(fname,"r");
    if (x)
    {
        // Use file here
        puts("Processing file...");
    }
    throw 1;
}

// Output:
Processing file...
File closed
Caught exception
```

Listing 13.9 Throws an exception in a constructor

```cpp
// destroy7.cpp
#include <cstdio>
using namespace std;

class File
{
    FILE* f;

public:
    File(const char* fname, const char* mode)
    {
        f = fopen(fname, mode);
        if (!f)
            throw 1;
    }
    ~File()
    {
        if (f)
        {
            fclose(f);
            puts("File closed");
        }
    }
};

main()
{
    void f(const char*);
    try
    {
        f("file1.dat");
    }
    catch(int x)
    {
        printf("Caught exception: %d\n",x);
    }
}
```

continued

Listing 13.9   (continued)

```
void f(const char* fname)
{
    File x(fname,"r");
    puts("Processing file...");
    throw 2;
}

// Output:
Processing file...
File closed
Caught exception: 2
```

Having to test an object before each use can be quite tedious, however. As Listing 13.9 illustrates, it may be more convenient to throw an exception directly from the constructor.

Everything is fine as long as all your File objects are automatic, but what if you allocate one from the free store? As the program in Listing 13.10 illustrates, since a File* is just a

Listing 13.10   Reveals memory leak problems when using the new operator with exceptions

```
// destroy8.cpp
#include <cstdio>
using namespace std;

class File
{
    FILE* f;

public:
    File(const char* fname, const char* mode)
    {
        f = fopen(fname, mode);
        if (!f)
            throw 1;
    }
    ~File()
    {
        if (f)
        {
            fclose(f);
            puts("File closed");
        }
    }
};
```

Listing 13.10   (continued)

```
main()
{
    void f(const char*);
    try
    {
        f("file1.dat");
    }
    catch(int x)
    {
        printf("Caught exception: %d\n",x);
    }
}

void f(const char* fname)
{
    File* xp = new File(fname,"r");
    puts("Processing file...");
    throw 2;
    delete xp;        // Won't happen
}

// Output:
Processing file...
Caught exception: 2
```

pointer, no destructor is called. Since allocating dynamic objects is so common in C++, the standard library provides auto_ptr, a class template with the following interface:

```
template<class T> class auto_ptr
{
  public:
    explicit auto_ptr (T* = 0);
    auto_ptr(auto_ptr<T>&);
    void operator=(auto_ptr<T>& r);
    ~auto_ptr();                 // calls delete on underlying pointer
    T& operator*();              // calls T::operator*
    T* operator->();             // calls T::operator->
    T* get() const;              // returns the underlying pointer
    T* release();                // loses pointer
    T* reset(T* = 0);            // releases old owner first
};
```

As you can see in Listing 13.11 you can "wrap" the result of a new expression in an auto_ptr object. The auto_ptr's operator* and operator-> members forward the respective operations on to the underlying pointer, so you can use it normally. Since the auto_ptr object itself resides on the stack, its destructor is called, which in turn calls delete for the T* it owns.

Recall that when you create an object on the free store, as in

```
T* p = new T;
```

the system calls operator new to allocate the memory for the new object before initializing it. If T throws an exception, you don't need to be concerned about a memory leak—the runtime system calls operator delete to free the memory that the call to operator new allocated. C++ always cleans up partially created objects when an exception occurs.

Listing 13.11   Fixes the memory leak with auto_ptr

```cpp
// destroy9.cpp
#include <cstdio>
#include <memory>          // For auto_ptr
using namespace std;

class File
{
    FILE* f;

public:
    File(const char* fname, const char* mode)
    {
        f = fopen(fname, mode);
        if (!f)
            throw 1;
    }
    ~File()
    {
        if (f)
        {
            fclose(f);
            puts("File closed");
        }
    }
};
```

Listing 13.11   (continued)

```
main()
{
    void f(const char*);
    try
    {
        f("file1.dat");
    }
    catch(int x)
    {
        printf("Caught exception: %d\n",x);
    }
}

void f(const char* fname)
{
    auto_ptr<File> xp = new File(fname,"r");
    puts("Processing file...");
    throw 2;
}

// Output:
Processing file...
File closed
Caught exception: 2
```

Memory Management

Before exceptions, if a new operation failed to allocate an object, it returned a null pointer, just like malloc does in C:

```
T *tp = new T;
if (tp)
    // Use new object
```

C++ now stipulates that a memory allocation failure results in a bad_alloc exception. The standard library as well as third-party libraries may make generous use of the free store. Since a memory allocation request can occur when you least expect it, almost any program you write should be prepared to handle a bad_alloc exception. The obvious way is to supply a handler:

```
#include <new>
catch(const bad_alloc& x)
{
    cerr << "Out of memory: " << x.what() << endl;
    abort();
}
```

Depending on your application, you may be able to do something more interesting than this handler does, such as recover some memory and return to some stable state to try again.

If you prefer the classic behavior of returning a null pointer, you can use a special version of the new operator:

```
#include <new>
// ...
    T* tp = new (nothrow) T;
    if (tp)
        // use tp...
```

Yet another way of handling out-of-memory conditions is to replace parts of the memory allocation machinery itself. When a memory allocation fails, C++ calls the default new handler, which in turn throws a bad_alloc exception. You can provide your own handler by passing its address to set_new_handler, much like I did with set_terminate above.

Exception Specifications

You can enumerate the exceptions that a function will throw with an *exception specification*:

```
class A;
class B;

void f() throw(A,B)
{
    // Whatever
}
```

This definition states that only exceptions of type A or B will escape f. Besides being good documentation, the runtime system verifies that only the allowable types of exceptions occur, whether directly in f or indirectly from deeper down the call chain. In the presence of any other

exception, control passes to the standard library function unexpected, which by default terminates the program. The definition of f above is therefore equivalent to

```
void f()
{
    try
    {
        // Whatever
    }
    catch(const A&)
    {
        throw;                  // rethrow
    }
    catch(const B&)
    {
        throw;                  // rethrow
    }
    catch(...)
    {
        unexpected();
    }
}
```

You can provide your own unexpected handler by passing it to the standard library function
set_unexpected, as follows:

```
// unexpect.cpp
#include <iostream>
#include <exception>
#include <cstdlib>
using namespace std;

main()
{
    void f() throw();
    void handler();

    set_unexpected(handler);
    f();
}

void f() throw()
{
    throw 1;
}
```

```
void handler()
{
    cout << "Detected unexpected exception\n";
    exit(EXIT_FAILURE);
}

// Output:
Detected unexpected exception
```

The definition void f() throw() {...} disallows any exceptions from escaping from f; that is, it is equivalent to

```
void f()
{
    try
    {
        // Whatever ...
    }
    catch(...)
    {
        unexpected();
    }
}
```

A function without an exception specification can throw any exception.

The challenge with exception specifications is that f may call other functions that throw other exceptions. You must know what exceptions are possible and either include them in the specification for f, or handle them explicitly within f itself. This can be a problem if a future version of the services f uses adds new exceptions. If those new exceptions are derived from A or B, you don't have a problem, but that is not likely to happen with commercial libraries. A good rule of thumb: If a function f calls another function that does not have an associated exception specification, then don't declare one for f. Also, since template parameters can usually be of almost any type, you may not be able to predict which exceptions might occur from that type's member functions. Bottom line: Templates and exception specifications don't mix.

An Error Handling Strategy

There is one category of errors I haven't yet discussed that I like to refer to as "my stupid mistakes." The first person possessive adjective is significant here. Whether you know it or not (but I hope you do), all developers make logical assumptions as they construct software. For example, there are many times when I can say, "This pointer can't be null here," and I know it will always be true *if* I have crafted things the way I intended. To make the assertion explicit and enforceable, I insert the following statement to say so:

```
assert(p);
```

The `assert` macro, defined in `<assert.h>`, will abort the program with an error message indicating the offending line number and file name if the expression in parentheses evaluates to zero. When *I* use the assert macro, it means that *I* have control over the conditions that govern the assert expression. Other developers like to use `assert` to check for user errors, or even for preconditions on a parameter, but I think this is a mistake. An assertion is just that, an *assertion*, and if I have no control over the assertion, I shouldn't make it.

A more involved example might help to illustrate. Consider the following function from an object-oriented persistence framework that writes an object's data record to a database:

```
bool Update::Write()
{
    CRecordset* pRS = m_pTableX->GetRecordset();
    assert(pRS);
    if (!pRS->CanUpdate())
        Throw2(PFX,UPDATE_ERROR,"Database not updatable");

    bool status;
    try
    {
        status = pRS->Update();
    }
    catch (CDBException *ep)
    {
        string msg = ep->m_strError + ep->m_strStateNativeOrigin;
        ep->Delete();
        Throw2(PFX,UPDATE_ERROR,msg);
    }

    return status;
}
```

The function `GetRecordset` returns a pointer to a *Recordset*, a Microsoft Foundation Class library abstraction for doing relational database I/O. I have designed this system so that `pRS` *can't* be null. If it is, then *my* software is broken. On the other hand, I have no control over whether the connection to the database that you have provided is updateable, so I throw an exception instead (I'll explain the `Throw2` macro shortly). This gives you, my client, an opportunity to fix things at *runtime*, if you plan ahead, instead of having to quit your program and have your user start over. I look upon input arguments to a function the same way. So, my first suggestions for error handling are

1. Make assertions liberally, but *only* for things you have first-hand control over
2. Throw exceptions for errors you can't handle locally, including invalid arguments.

Notice that in the example above I handle database errors by throwing my own brand of exception. That's because my clients don't need to know about the underlying mechanism I use to access the database. All they know is that they are using my component, and my component can throw exceptions. All they have to do, then, is to catch the exceptions I throw, or that the standard C++ library might (like memory failure, which I don't catch), like this:

```
try
{
    // call one of my functions here:
    p->Write();
}
catch (PFX_Exception& x)
{
    // Do whatever you have to; here I just print a message:
    cout << "PFX exception: " << x.what() << endl;
}
catch (exception& x)
{
    cout << "C++ exception: " << x.what() << endl;
}
catch (...)
{
    cout << "Unknown exception" << endl;
}
```

My persistence component has a number of classes, but it only has one exception class, which derives from exception (see Listings 13.12 and 13.13). Having more than one exception class per component just makes things complicated for clients. In addition, I have all my exceptions include in their what message the file name and line number where the exception was thrown from, since that important information is not otherwise available. To do this, I use the following preprocessor trick:

```
// xcept.h:    Useful throw macros

#include <exception>
#include <string>

// Macro trick to quote a number:
#define str_(x) #x
#define xstr_(x) str_(x)
```

Listing 13.12   The `PFX_Exception` class header

```
// pfxxcept.h
#include "xcept.h"            // See chapter text
using std::exception;
using std::string;

class PFX_Exception : public exception
{
public:
    PFX_Exception(int cod, const string& msg = "")
        : exception(s_ErrorStrings[cod] + ":" +  msg)
    {}
    enum {BAD_OBJ_ID, CONNECT_ERROR, RECORDSET_ERROR,
          REQUERY_ERROR, UPDATE_ERROR, LOCK_ERROR,
          VERSION_ERROR, TRANS_ERROR, READ_ONLY_ERROR,
          INIFILE_ERROR,
          NUM_ERRORS};

private:
    static string s_ErrorStrings[NUM_ERRORS];
};
```

Listing 13.13   `PFX_Exception` implementation

```
// pfxxcept.cpp
#include "pfxxcept.h"

string PFX_Exception::s_ErrorStrings[NUM_ERRORS] =
{
    "Bad Objid",
    "Connection open failed",
    "Recordset open failed",
    "Recordset requery failed",
    "Recordset update failed",
    "Record lock failed",
    "Object out of date with database",
    "Transaction error",
    "Attempt to Write a ReadOnly object",
    "INI File name missing"
};
```

```
// Macro for convenient exception throwing
// (includes standard message, file, line #)
#define Throw(Type, cod) \
throw Type ## _Exception(Type ## _Exception:: ## cod, \
                         std::string(__FILE__ ## ":Line "
                         ## xstr_(__LINE__)))

#define Throw2(Type, cod, txt) \
throw Type ## _Exception(Type ## _Exception:: ## cod, \
                         txt + std::string(":" ## \
                         __FILE__ ## ":Line " ## \
                         xstr_(__LINE__)))
```

The Throw macro above transforms a call, such as

```
Throw(PFX,LOCK_ERROR);
```

into the statement

```
throw PFX_Exception(???);
```

where ??? represents a string argument that includes the current file name and line number, using the predefined macros __FILE__ and __LINE__, respectively. The PFX_Exception derives from exception and supplies predefined strings corresponding to integer error codes (like LOCK_ERROR) to the exception constructor. The *stringizing* preprocessor operator (#) above puts quotes around its argument, and the *token-pasting* operator (##) combines its arguments into a single preprocessor token. (These operators were discussed in Chap. 2). The Throw2 allows you to add extra text at the throw point. For example, if you caught an exception thrown by the expression

```
Throw2(PFX,RECORDSET_ERROR,"Extra Text");
```

then the *what*-string for the exception might render:

```
Recordset Open Error:Extra Text:txcept.cpp:Line 18
```

Summary

Perhaps the most important thing to say about exceptions is that you should only use them in truly exceptional circumstances. Like setjmp and longjmp, they interrupt the normal control flow of a program. There should be relatively few exception handlers compared to the number of functions in a typical program. In addition, exceptions have been designed for synchronous events only, so beware—exceptions and signals don't mix. As far as efficiency is concerned, experience so far suggests that exceptions bloat your code size by five to fifteen percent for each try block and its associated nested functions. You only pay in speed, though, if exceptions get thrown.

- Don't use `setjmp` and `longjmp` in the presence of objects that have constructors and destructors. Use exceptions instead. When an exception is thrown, all automatic objects on the stack are destroyed up to the catch point.
- Exceptions allow separate program components to communicate about error conditions.
- You should provide a handler for any exception that may be thrown in a program.
- Handlers are chosen by matching the type of the object thrown.
- Arrange adjacent handlers from the most specific to the least specific type handled.
- If you use the standard library, be prepared to catch exceptions in the standard hierarchy (at the very least, of type `exception`).
- Wrap resource allocation in automatic objects to ensure that destructors get called as needed.
- Wrap the result of a `new` expression in an `auto_ptr` to guarantee that the destructor is called properly.
- You can use exception specifications to document and enforce the types of exceptions that your functions can throw.
- Use assertions to guard against your (the immediate developer) mistakes *only*.
- Define one exception class per component, derived from `exception` (or `runtime_error` or `logic_error`, if applicable).

Object-oriented Programming

What makes a language object oriented? There was a time when market hype made it difficult for the man on the street to find a straight answer to this question, but the answer is simple: object-oriented languages support three concepts:

1. Data abstraction via encapsulation (see Chapter 7)
2. Inheritance
3. Polymorphism.

Data abstraction, or the ability to define new types, enhances programs by allowing the developer to name program entities that correspond to the problem at hand. A personnel application, for example, might define an `Employee` class, perhaps as a superset of the following:

```
class Employee
{
public:
    Employee(const string& ename, double erate) : name(ename)
    {
        rate = erate;
    }

    // Accessors:
    string getName() const {return name;}
    double getRate() const {return rate;}
    double getTimeWorked() const {return timeWorked;}

    // Methods:
    void recordTime(double etime) {timeWorked = etime;}
    double computePay() const;
```

```
private:
    string name;
    double rate;
    double timeWorked;
};

double Employee::computePay() const
{
    const double& hours = timeWorked;
    if (hours > 40)
        return 40*rate + (hours - 40)*rate*1.5;
    else
        return rate * hours;
}
```

With this class definition in place you can instantiate `Employee` objects and invoke their member functions, for example:

```
main()
{
    Employee e("John Hourly",16.50);
    e.recordTime(52.0);
    cout << e.getName() << " gets "
        << e.computePay() << endl;
}

// Output:
John Hourly gets 957.00
```

But what if there are different kinds of employees? Many employers, for instance, distinguish between hourly and salaried employees. A definition for `SalariedEmployee` might look like this:

```
class SalariedEmployee
{
public:
    SalariedEmployee(const string& ename, double erate)
        : name(ename)
    {
        rate = erate;
    }

    // Accessors:
    string getName() const {return name;}
    double getRate() const {return rate;}
    double getTimeWorked() const {return timeWorked;}
```

```
    // Methods:
    void recordTime(double etime) {timeWorked = etime;}
    double computePay() const;

private:
    string name;
    double rate;
    double timeWorked;
};


double SalariedEmployee::computePay() const
{
    return rate * timeWorked;
}
```

The only difference between these two classes is the name of the class and the implementation of the `computePay` method. How can you factor out the commonality to save on keyboarding and code space? The experienced C developer would add a *type tag*, an integer code that identifies the flavor of `Employee`. That way you don't even need the `SalariedEmployee` class. Such a class definition might look like the following:

```
class Employee
{
public:
    Employee(const string& ename, double erate, int etype)
        : name(ename)
    {
        rate = erate;
        type = etype;
    }

    string getName() const {return name;}
    double getRate() const {return rate;}
    double getTimeWorked() const {return timeWorked;}

    void recordTime(double etime) {timeWorked = etime;}
    double computePay() const;
    enum {HOURLY, SALARIED};

private:
    int type;
    string name;
    double rate;
    double timeWorked;
};
```

```
double Employee::computePay() const
{
    switch(type)
    {
    case HOURLY:
        if (timeWorked > 40)
            return 40*rate + (timeWorked - 40)*rate*1.5;
        else
            return rate * timeWorked;

    case SALARIED:
        return rate * timeWorked;
    }
}
```

Such an arrangement requires computePay to test for the type of the object so it can do the right thing. Users now indicate the type of Employee object they want via a constructor argument, as in:

```
main()
{
    Employee e("John Hourly", 16.50, Employee::HOURLY);
    e.recordTime(52.0);
    cout << e.getName() << " gets "
         << e.computePay() << endl;

    Employee e2("Jane Salaried", 1125.00, Employee::SALARIED);
    e2.recordTime(1.0);
    cout << e2.getName() << " gets "
         << e2.computePay() << endl;
}
```

```
// Output:
John Hourly gets 957.00
Jane Salaried gets 1125.00
```

Now, what would happen if a new type of employee was needed, ExemptEmployee, say? You would need to:

1. Add a new type tag, Exempt, to the enumeration, and
2. Add a case to the switch statement in computePay.

That doesn't seem like a lot of work, but it quickly turns into a maintenance nightmare as the number of methods depending on the flavor of employee increases. And you have lost the benefit of class SalariedEmployee, which makes clear to both the compiler and the maintenance programmer that there are two distinct types in the solution space. What's a developer to do?

Inheritance

C++ allows you to declare SalariedEmployee in terms of the first version of Employee as follows:

```cpp
// Derive from Employee:
class SalariedEmployee : public Employee
{
public:
    SalariedEmployee(const string&, double);
    double computePay() const;
};

SalariedEmployee::SalariedEmployee(const string& ename,
                                   double erate)
                : Employee(ename, erate)
{}

double SalariedEmployee::computePay() const
{
    return getRate() * getTimeWorked();
}
```

The class SalariedEmployee *inherits*, or *is derived from.* from Employee. As a derived class, it has all that Employee does, as well as access to any nonprivate Employee member. The only thing you need to define in the derived class is what *differs* from the base class—in this case, the implementation of computePay. The SalariedEmployee constructor simply passes the attributes it was initialized with to its Employee part in an initializer list. You can now use both classes without having to test for tags yourself, and you don't have any duplicated code. Even more important, you can add the ExemptEmployee class simply by deriving it from Employee (or from SalariedEmployee, if applicable) but without having to change any code in the base class.

If it bothers you that you have to call the methods getRate and getTimeWoked in SalariedEmployee::computePay, you can replace the private keyword with protected in Employee:

```cpp
protected:
    string name;
    double rate;
    double timeWorked;
```

The protected members are available to all derived objects but nowhere else. You can then rewrite computePay as:

```cpp
double SalariedEmployee::computePay() const
{
    return rate * timeWorked;
}
```

Just as it is usually a bad idea to make data members public, making them protected can also be a liability, since derived clients might depend on them. The best solution might be to have protected member functions to control access to protected data.

The phrase

```
class SalariedEmployee : public Employee
```

says that `Employee` is a *public base class* for `SalariedEmployee`. This means that no inherited member will have more than `public` access (which admittedly isn't saying much). In other words, no *restrictions* are placed on base class members when used through a derived class object. This type of inheritance implements an "is-a" relationship between the derived and base classes, because everything accessible from the base part of a derived object is still accessible through the derived object to its clients. This is the most common type of inheritance encountered in C++ programs. With `protected` inheritance, any `public` base members are "demoted" to `protected` when accessed through a derived object, so no clients of the derived class can see any part of the base subobject (only derived objects can). No `private` base class members are in any way accessible through a derived object. Bottom line: The access specifier that qualifies class derivation is a *filter* that governs access rights for *clients* of derived objects. You can, however, override any demotion due to protected or private inheritance with an *access declaration*. For example, in the following class declarations, `B::f` is restored to public access for the clients of `D`:

```
class B
{
public:
    void f();
    void g();
};

class D : protected B
{
public:
    B::f;      // keep f public
};
```

You can't give a member more access than it originally had, of course.

Heterogeneous Collections

C++ allows a pointer to a base class to actually point to a derived class object; for example,

```
SalariedEmployee s("Another employee", 1000.00);
Employee* p = &s;
```

This is consistent with the fact that a `SalariedEmployee` *is* an `Employee`, and therefore can stand in for an `Employee` object in any `Employee` operations. This allows you to keep pointers to both kinds of objects in a single array, as in

```
main()
{
    Employee e("John Hourly",16.50);
    e.recordTime(52.0);
    SalariedEmployee e2("Jane Salaried",1125.00);
    e2.recordTime(1.0);
    Employee* elist[] = {&e, &e2};
    int nemp = sizeof elist / sizeof elist[0];

    for (int i = 0; i < nemp; ++i)
        cout << elist[i]->getName() << " gets "
             << elist[i]->computePay() << endl;
}
```

There is a subtle bug lurking in the code above, however, that appears after I add a trace statement to the `computePay` method in each class:

```
// Output:
Employee::computePay()
John Hourly gets 957.00
Employee::computePay()
Jane Salaried gets 1125.00
```

Jane Salaried's pay was computed with the wrong function! It's merely a coincidence that the answer came out correct (which is what makes this bug subtle). Since `elist` was declared as an array of pointers to `Employee`, the expression `elist[i]->computePay` always invokes `Employee::computePay`. In the absence of any other mechanism, C++ binds a function invocation to a particular function at compile time, a process known as *static binding*. Since there is no way to determine which type of object `elist[i]` is actually referring to, the compiler uses the only information that it has: the type of the pointer (`Employee*`). What you need is a way to tell the compiler to *dynamically bind* the function call to the correct class method, depending on the type of object `elist[i]` actually points to at the moment.

Virtual Functions and Polymorphism

All you need to make calls to `computePay` dynamically bound is to declare it `virtual` in the `Employee` class:

```
class Employee
{
    // ...
    virtual double computePay() const;
    // ...
};
```

Figure 14.1   Virtual function table for the `Employee` class

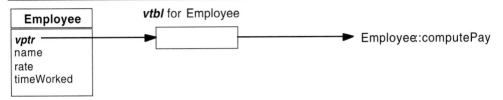

That's it! Now the output of the program above is:

```
// Output:
Employee::computePay()
John Hourly gets 957.00
SalariedEmployee::computePay()
Jane Salaried gets 1125.00
```

That was easy! The effect is as if a runtime query were made to determine what type of object was involved, but the process is more clever and efficient than that. When a class has one or more virtual functions, it has a hidden pointer data member, sometimes called a vptr (pronounced "vee-pointer") that points to a table of function pointers, the elements of which in turn point to the virtual functions declared for that class (see Fig. 14.1).

When the compiler sees the call to the virtual function computePay, it generates an indirect function call through the virtual function table that the current object's vptr points to, something like

```
vptr[0]()     // computePay is the 0th virtual function in Employee
```

Each class derived (directly or indirectly) from Employee will have its own virtual function table, and each derived object's vptr points to that vtbl. Therefore, if you have overridden any inherited virtual functions in a derived class, they will be invoked by virtue of the indirection through the current object type's virtual function table. For each function that you don't override in a derived class, the corresponding entry in the derived virtual function table will be the one inherited from the base class. It is not necessary to use the virtual keyword in the declaration of an override of an inherited virtual function in the derived class—once a function is declared virtual it remains virtual all the way down the inheritance hierarchy. If you add new virtual functions in a derived class, their addresses will be appended to the vtbl.

Exercise 14.1

Just to make sure you understand the virtual function mechanism, which functions will be invoked in the following program? Which function is not virtual? (Answer appears at the end of the chapter.)

```
#include <iostream>
using namespace std;

class A
{
public:
    virtual void f();
    virtual void g();

class B : public A
{
public:
    void g();
    virtual void h();
};

class C : public B
{
public:
    void g();
    void i();
};

main()
{
    C c;

    A* pA = &c;
    pA->f();
    pA->g();

    B* pB = &c;
    pB->f();
    pB->g();
    pB->h();

    C* pC = &c;
    pC->f();
    pC->g();
    pC->h();
    pC->i();
}
```

The word *polymorphism* is derived from the Greek and literally means "many forms." It is used in object-oriented parlance to associate multiple expressions of an idea with a single name, or in other words, to deliver variable behavior through a single interface. As sophisticated as that sounds, the notion of polymorphism is an everyday one, to be sure. For example, consider automobile-like vehicles (i.e., cars, trucks, etc.; see Fig. 14.2). The reason you can drive almost any truck once you've mastered driving a car is that the *interface* is the same—a steering wheel, accelerator, and brake pedal, all arranged in a standard way. When you step on a brake pedal, you are issuing the command to stop, but *how* your command is fulfilled may actually vary, depending on the type of vehicle you are driving at the moment (e.g., large trucks typically have air brakes, rather than disc brakes, drum brakes, etc.). Polymorphism is at work even with a simple mathematical expression, such as $x + y$. If these symbols appear in a computer program, the microcode that actually executes depends whether the objects are integers or floating-point numbers. Likewise, when you need the amount of an employee's pay to print a paycheck or a report, you don't want to worry about how to compute it—you just want results. The virtual function mechanism enables the developer to deliver a uniform interface to users, but with an implementation that automatically adjusts behavior as needed according to the *dynamic type* of an object, and at the mere runtime cost of dereferencing a function pointer.

Abstract Base Classes

Sometimes a class represents a concept, such as an entire inheritance hierarchy, and will never be instantiated, such as the Vehicle hierarchy in Figure 14.2.

In this case, Vehicle is just a grouping mechanism. Any members that pertain to all derived classes belong in Vehicle, but you would never instantiate any Vehicle objects. Such a class is called an *abstract class*. There are two ways to make a class abstract in C++:

1. Declare at least one *pure virtual function*
2. Declare at least one *protected constructor*, and no public constructors.

Figure 14.2 A Vehicle class hierarchy

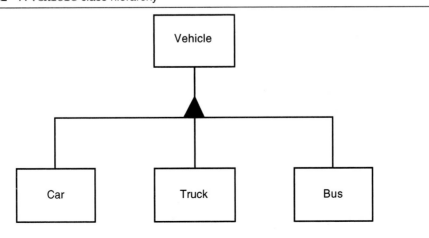

You declare a virtual function as pure by appending the characters =0, as in:

```
virtual void stop() = 0;     // Vehicle::stop()
```

Typically, a pure virtual function has no body, since you expect each derived class to implement its own version. The collection of pure virtual functions in a root class determines the *interface* that derived classes must implement. The compiler will prohibit the creation of an object of a class that has a pure virtual function.

The Employee class already discussed favors hourly employees by virtue of its computePay implementation. It might make more sense to have an abstract Employee class, which just defines those things that are common to all types of employee as follows:

```
class Employee
{
public:
    Employee(const string& ename, double erate) : name(ename)
    {
        rate = erate;
    }

    string getName() const {return name;}
    double getRate() const {return rate;}

    void recordTime(double etime) {timeWorkd\ed = etime;}
    virtual double computePay() const = 0;

protected:
    string name;
    double rate;
    double timeWorked;
};
```

You can then define HourlyEmployee similar to SalariedEmployee, like this:

```
class HourlyEmployee : public Employee
{
public:
    HourlyEmployee(const string& ename, double erate)
        : Employee(ename, erate)
    {}
    double computePay() const;
};

double HourlyEmployee::computePay() const
{
    cout << "HourlyEmployee::computePay()\n";
    const double& hours = timeWorked;
```

```
    if (hours > 40)
        return 40*rate + (hours - 40)*rate*1.5;
    else
        return rate * hours;
}
```

Another use for abstract base classes is to endow another class with some functionality not related to its primary purpose. For example, with multiuser situations, it is often critical to keep track of how many clients are sharing a particular resource, so you don't deallocate the resource prematurely. The following class implements reference counting:

```
class Counted
{
public:
    long Attach() {return ++m_RefCount;}
    long Detach()
    {
        return (--m_RefCount > 0) ? m_RefCount
                              : (delete this, 0);
    }
    long NumClients() const {return m_RefCount;}

protected:
    Counted() {m_RefCount = 0;}
    virtual ~Counted() {assert(m_RefCount == 0);}

private:
    long m_RefCount;
};
```

Since the only constructor is `protected`, you can't instantiate `Counted` objects directly, but members of a class derived from `Counted` can. The `Attach` method increments the count, while the `Detach` method decrements it. If the reference count reaches zero in `Detach`, the object destroys itself via the `delete` operator (so the resource must have been created on the heap via `new`). The typical idiom for using this kind of class is as follows:

1. Provide a static `Create` method in the derived resource class that allocates a new derived object on the heap and does an initial `Attach` to its `Counted` subobject (to increment the count to one). This guarantees that the resource will be available for all subsequent clients.
2. Pass a pointer to the resource as an argument to the client constructor, which will also `Attach` to the resource.
3. Client destructors `Detach` from the resource.
4. When you are ready to release the shared resource, do a final `Detach`.

The following program illustrates this technique.

```
class Resource : public Counted
{
public:
    static Resource* Create()
    {
        Resource* pR = new Resource;
        pR->Attach();
        return pR;
    }
};

class Client
{
public:
    Client(Resource* pR)
    {
        pRes = pR;
        pRes->Attach();
    }
    ~Client() {pRes->Detach();}

private:
    Resource* pRes;
};

main()
{
    // Create a Resource to be shared:
    Resource* pR = Resource::Create();    // count is 1

    // Use the Resource:
    Client b1(pR);                        // count is 2
    Client b2(pR);                        // count is 3

    // Undo the original Attach:
    pR->Detach();                         // count is 2

    // b2.Client:~Client() will reduce count to 1.
    // b1.Client:~Client() will reduce count to 0
    //    after which the Resource will self-destruct.
}
```

Case Study: A Framework for Object Persistence

The shift to the object-oriented paradigm has brought about a focus on business objects. User interfaces are seen as merely a way to present business object information, and databases just

Figure 14.3   The sales domain

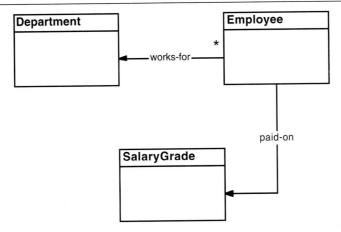

store an object's data attributes—more and more development efforts tend to emphasize the *business object model*. Business objects naturally fall into one or more business *domains*, such as sales or personnel (see Fig. 14.3).

Object-oriented programming languages provide mechanisms for encapsulation, inheritance, and polymorphism, but, like most other programming languages, do not directly support persistent storage of program data. Traditional solutions to this shortcoming have included direct file I/O, using embedded SQL calls, or relying on third-party file access libraries. But a key feature of the object-oriented paradigm is that objects should know how to take care of themselves; clients simply make a request through the class interface and don't concern themselves with implementation details. For example, if you wanted to give a certain employee a raise, you might want the ability to do something like the following in C++:

```
// Give employee #23437 a raise if he's in Sales:
Employee emp(23437);
Department* dept = emp.GetDept();
if (dept->GetType() == SALES)
{
    emp.SetSalary(emp.GetSalary() * 1.25);
    emp.Write();
}
```

There should be no need to worry about file names, field names, or any other artifacts of storage—an object just knows what to do.

Of course, you don't always know the numeric ID of an object, so you should be able to retrieve a list of objects according to some reasonable criteria and then pick all or some of those returned. The following example processes a list of employees:

```
// Give everyone in Sales a raise:
EmployeeQuery q;
q.AddSelect(OBJID, SALES);
q.Execute();
while (!q.IsEOF())
{
    // Instantiate object to invoke its methods:
    Employee emp(q.GetObjID());
    emp.SetSalary(emp.GetSalary() * 1.25);
    emp.Write();
    q.Next();     // Go to next record
}
```

While object-oriented databases exist that offer this convenient functionality, they are still somewhat immature and are not yet in widespread use in the corporate workplace. The rest of this chapter presents a framework, named PFX, which gives business object models persistence with relational databases. PFX (for "Persistence Framework") is an actual production component that serves as a fundamental component of the client-server infrastructure at a large western U.S. corporation.

A *framework* is a collection of tightly coupled classes that act as a unit in providing some service, such as a graphical user interface library. To use a framework, you customarily derive from key (usually abstract) framework classes to adapt their functionality to your needs. Customizing the framework usually consists of overriding the virtual functions the framework provides. PFX is a traditional framework consisting of four classes, three of which are abstract, and is packaged in a single library (see Fig. 14.4). Frameworks are the chief delivery mechanism for *reuse* in object-oriented systems: You reuse the design and the portion of the implementation provided, and then tune the functionality to your situation by adding or replacing part of the implementation. The other main reuse vehicle in C++, of course, is the template facility, which applies when you don't necessarily want to customize functionality, but rather when you want to apply existing services to new types.

Figure 14.4 PFX classes

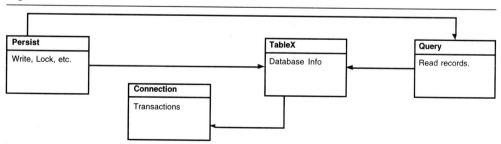

Database Access

The PFX framework needs some way to access the database where object attributes reside. One of the most widely used access standards in client-server environments today is the Open Database Connectivity specification (ODBC) from Microsoft Corporation. ODBC defines a standard application-programming interface (API) in the C language for performing database transactions and processing query result sets. ODBC drivers exist for most popular database management systems. The Microsoft Foundation Class library (MFC), which is supported by most Windows-based C++ compilers, has two classes, CDatabase and CRecordset, that translate your database requests into ODBC calls. The CRecordset is an abstract class that you derive from to read from and write to a database table. Suppose, for instance, that an Employee table has the following schema and data:

OBJID	ENAME	JOB	MGRID	HIREDATE	SALARY	DEPTID
7369	SMITH	CLERK	7902	17-DEC-80	800	20
7499	ALLEN	SALESMAN	7698	20-FEB-81	1600	30
7521	WARD	SALESMAN	7698	22-FEB-81	1250	30
7566	JONES	MANAGER	7839	02-APR-81	2975	20
7654	MARTIN	SALESMAN	7698	28-SEP-81	1250	30
7698	BLAKE	MANAGER	7839	01-MAY-81	2850	30
7782	CLARK	MANAGER	7839	09-JUN-81	2450	10
7788	SCOTT	ANALYST	7566	09-DEC-82	3000	20
7839	KING	PRESIDENT		17-NOV-81	5000	10
7844	TURNER	SALESMAN	7698	08-SEP-81	1500	30
7876	ADAMS	CLERK	7788	12-JAN-83	1100	20
7900	JAMES	CLERK	7698	03-DEC-81	950	30
7902	FORD	ANALYST	7566	03-DEC-81	3000	20
7934	MILLER	CLERK	7782	23-JAN-82	1300	10

The Class Wizard in the Microsoft Visual C++ Compiler will read this table through an ODBC connection, and generate a recordset class derived from CRecordset (see Listings 14.1 and 14.2). You can use this class (EmpRec) as follows:

```
#include "empr.h"

CDatabase db;
db.Open("ODBC;DSN=Personnel");        // ODBC connection string

EmpRec rec(&db);
rec.m_strFilter = "[Employee ID] = 5";   // WHERE clause
rec.Open();
while (!rec.IsEOF())
{
    // Process record, then ...
    rec.MoveNext();
}
```

Listing 14.1   The `EmpRec` `Recordset` interface

```
// EmpR.h : header file
#include <afxdb.h>      // Microsoft file

class EmpRec : public CRecordset
{
public:
    EmpRec(CDatabase* pDatabase = NULL);

// Field/Param Data
    //{{AFX_FIELD(EmpRec, CRecordset)
    double      m_ObjID;
    double      m_DeptID;
    CString     m_Name;
    CTime       m_HireDate;
    CString     m_Job;
    double      m_MgrID;
    double      m_Salary;
    //}}AFX_FIELD

// Overrides
    // ClassWizard generated virtual function overrides
    //{{AFX_VIRTUAL(EmpRec)
    virtual CString GetDefaultConnect();  // Default connection string
    virtual CString GetDefaultSQL();       // Default SQL for Recordset
    virtual void DoFieldExchange(CFieldExchange* pFX);  // RFX support
    //}}AFX_VIRTUAL
};
```

A recordset can process any table and can also be used for read-only operations on a database view.

Mapping Objects to Relational Schema

The primary rule for storing objects in relational databases is "a table for each class, a row for each object of its class." Since all objects must have a unique identity, it is customary to have a numeric field for this purpose, with no other role than to represent objects. (It is possible to use other than numeric fields for object identity in PFX, but it requires more work on the user's part.) Things get a little more complicated with object containment, however. If objects of class A each contain an object of type B, how should that be reflected in the database? PFX accommodates containment by *reference*, which means, if B is a first-class business object—that is, B has object identity, as opposed to a value-based object, such as a date or an address—then you

Listing 14.2 EmpRec implementation

```cpp
// EmpR.cpp : implementation file (FXW)
#include "EmpR.h"

EmpRec::EmpRec(CDatabase* pdb)
        : CRecordset(pdb)
{
    //{{AFX_FIELD_INIT(EmpRec)
    m_ObjID = 0.0;
    m_DeptID = 0.0;
    m_Name = _T("");
    m_Job = _T("");
    m_MgrID = 0.0;
    m_Salary = 0.0;
    m_nFields = 7;
    //}}AFX_FIELD_INIT
    m_nDefaultType = snapshot;
}

CString EmpRec::GetDefaultConnect()
{
    return _T("");
}

CString EmpRec::GetDefaultSQL()
{
    return _T("[EMPLOYEE]");
}

void EmpRec::DoFieldExchange(CFieldExchange* pFX)
{
    //{{AFX_FIELD_MAP(EmpRec)
    pFX->SetFieldType(CFieldExchange::outputColumn);
    RFX_Double(pFX, _T("[OBJID]"), m_ObjID);
    RFX_Double(pFX, _T("[DEPTID]"), m_DeptID);
    RFX_Text(pFX, _T("[ENAME]"), m_Name);
    RFX_Date(pFX, _T("[HIREDATE]"), m_HireDate);
    RFX_Text(pFX, _T("[JOB]"), m_Job);
    RFX_Double(pFX, _T("[MGRID]"), m_MgrID);
    RFX_Double(pFX, _T("[SALARY]"), m_Salary);
    //}}AFX_FIELD_MAP
}
```

should have a foreign key in the A table that represents a row in the B table. You then provide methods to process the B object associated with an A object, as in

```
class A
{
public:
    B* GetB() const {return new B(m_BobjID);}
    Date GetBirth() const {return m_BirthDate;}
    // etc.

private:
    // Attributes of A, including:
    double m_BobjID;        // Foreign key to associated B object
    Date m_BirthDate;       // Value-objects stored in place

    // NOTE: No B* member needed (methods handle all needs)
};
```

The GetB method provides the contained object only when called upon, which saves time instantiating an A object. The default Write method in PFX only stores the immediate object (e.g., just A's attributes, not those of the B it is associated with), but you can override this if you wish.

What about derived objects? PFX assumes the "one hierarchy, one table" approach. All objects in the same hierarchy share the same table and have a numeric field that identifies the type of each object. With variable-length storage schemes, such as in the Oracle DBMS, there is no worry about wasted space when storing high up in the hierarchy an object that doesn't use all the attributes. Besides, most of the variation in a well-defined class hierarchy tends to be in behavior anyway, not in attributes.

PFX Architecture

PFX consists of four major classes, three of which are abstract and must be specialized by the user (see Fig. 14.5). The three classes to be specialized are as follows:

1. **TableX** provides access to table information, as well as basic database operations such as lock a record, remove a record, check for existence of a record, and find the next available number to use as an object ID in the table associated with a business object. User-derived classes must provide the table name and names of all the fields in the table.
2. **Query** provides methods to formulate query criteria and navigate a query result set. User classes provide methods for accessing specific attributes.
3. **Persist** provides basic methods for creating objects and writing them to the database. Users provide methods to read and modify attributes, and also add business functions as needed.

Figure 14.5 Using PFX

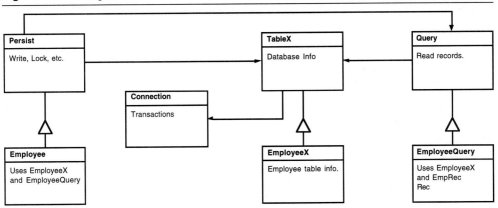

The fourth PFX class, `Connection`, is a concrete class that encapsulates the behavior of a database connection, including transaction processing. Since a connection is a shared resource, it inherits from `Counted`:

```
// connect.h: Connection Class Interface
class Connection : public CDatabase, public Counted
{
    typedef CDatabase Super;

public:
    static Connection* Create(const CString&, BOOL rOnly = FALSE);
    Connection* Copy(BOOL rOnly = FALSE) const;

    CString GetConnectionStr() const;
    void BeginTrans();
    void Commit();
    void Rollback();
    BOOL InTrans() const;

protected:
    Connection(const CString& conSpec, BOOL readOnly = FALSE);
    virtual ~Connection();

    BOOL m_InTransFlag;          // Currently in a transaction?
};
```

The `Connection` class does most of its work by invoking corresponding member functions in the `CDatabase` class. (See Listing 14.3). All PFX classes have protected constructors: `Connection`, because it must reside on the heap (and can only come into existence via its static `Create` function); the other three, because they are abstract classes that must be specialized.

Listing 14.3　The `Connection` implementation

```cpp
// connect.cpp
#include "connect.h"
#include "pfxxcept.h"

using namespace Persistence;

Connection* Connection::Create(const CString& conStr, BOOL rOnly)
{
    Connection* pCon = new Connection(conStr,rOnly);
    pCon->Attach();
    return pCon;
}

Connection* Connection::Copy(BOOL rOnly) const
{
    Connection* pNewCon = new Connection(GetConnectionStr(),rOnly);
    pNewCon->Attach();
    return pNewCon;
}

Connection::Connection(const CString& conSpec, BOOL rOnly)
{
    // Open the Connection
    try
    {
        int options = CDatabase::noOdbcDialog |
                      CDatabase::useCursorLib;
        if (rOnly)
            options |= CDatabase::openReadOnly;
        OpenEx(conSpec,options);

        // Set AUTOCOMMIT off:
        ASSERT(m_hdbc);
        RETCODE result = SQLSetConnectOption(m_hdbc,
                                             SQL_AUTOCOMMIT,
                                             SQL_AUTOCOMMIT_OFF);
        if (result == SQL_ERROR)
            Throw2(PFX,CONNECT_ERROR,
                   _T("Set AUTOCOMMIT off failed"));
    }
    catch (CDBException* ep)
    {
        CString msg = ep->m_strError + ep->m_strStateNativeOrigin;
        ep->Delete();
            Throw2(PFX,CONNECT_ERROR,msg);
    }
```

Listing 14.3 (continued)

```
    m_InTransFlag = FALSE;
}

void Connection::BeginTrans()
{
    if (!CanTransact())
            Throw(PFX,TRANS_ERROR);

    // Repeated calls are benign
    if (!m_InTransFlag)
    {
        Super::BeginTrans();
        m_InTransFlag = TRUE;
    }
}

void Connection::Commit()
{
    if (!CanTransact() || !m_InTransFlag)
            Throw(PFX,TRANS_ERROR);

    Super::CommitTrans();
    m_InTransFlag = FALSE;
}

void Connection::Rollback()
{
    if (!CanTransact() || !m_InTransFlag)
            Throw(PFX,TRANS_ERROR);

    Super::Rollback();
    m_InTransFlag = FALSE;
}
```

A Code Walkthrough

Since PFX uses MFC, it has to comply with MFC's conventions, which include

- using the MFC CString class instead of std::string
- using MFC'c BOOL type in place of bool, where FALSE/TRUE replace false/true
- all quoted strings are wrapped in the _T macro for character set portability.

Keep this in mind as we review the PFX code.

The process of inheriting from the PFX framework is quite mechanical and easily auto-mated. In fact, a proprietary tool that reads recordset class definitions generated all such files in this chapter (viz. Listings 14.4, 14.6, 14.8, 14.11, and 14.12).

Listing 14.4 contains the *data dictionary*, a text file with database information in a standard Windows initialization-file format. Listing 14.5 has the `TableX` class interface. The `TableX` class defines database-related functions as pure virtuals, since clients must provide the actual information in derived classes. It also implements functions to lock or remove a record, and to obtain the next available object ID number. The `EmployeeX` class in Listing 14.6 defines numeric codes for field names that are used in building queries.

The `Query` class defined in Listing 14.7 has query-building and -navigation functions. Its `Execute` method is `virtual` in case you want to do special processing before a query is sent to the database for execution. In Listing 14.8, `EmployeeQuery` provides accessor functions to obtain query results by attribute name. Since all `EmployeeQuery` members are small and amenable to inlining, there is no `EmpQ.cpp` file.

Listing 14.4 The data dictionary

```
// Test.ini: Contains Database info for this project

[Connection]
DEBUG=DSN=Oracle7-tables;UID=scott;PWD=tiger
RELEASE=DSN=Oracle7-tables;UID=scott;PWD=tiger

[Department]
Table=DEPARTMENT
SequenceStr=S_Department
NumFields=3
0=OBJID
1=LOCATION
2=NAME

[Employee]
Table=EMPLOYEE
SequenceStr=S_Employee
NumFields=7
0=OBJID
1=DEPTID
2=ENAME
3=HIREDATE
4=JOB
5=MGRID
6=SALARY
```

Listing 14.5 The `TableX` interface

```cpp
// tableX.h
class TableX
{
public:
    virtual ~TableX();
    virtual CString BusObjName() const = 0;
    virtual CString TableName() const = 0;
    virtual CString SequenceStr() const = 0;
    virtual int NumFields() const = 0;
    virtual CString GetIniFile() const;

    CString ConnectionStr() const;
    Connection* GetConnection() const;
    CString SQLName(int fldNum) const;
    double NextVal() const;
    BOOL Exists(double objID) const;
    void Lock(double id) const;
    void Remove(double id) const;
    CString GetProfileValue(const CString& category,
                            const CString& key) const;

    static CString NumericVal(double);
    static CString StringVal(const CString&);
    static CString StringVal(double);
    static CString DateVal(const FullDate& d);
    static void SetIniFile(const CString& fname);
    static double NextVal(const CString& seq, Connection* pCon);
    static CString& PrepareDBString(CString& s);
    static void Remove(Connection* pCon, const CString& table,
                       const CString& idName, double idVal);

    enum {NUMERIC_NULL = -1};

protected:
    TableX(Connection* pCon);
    Connection* m_pConnection;
    static CString s_IniFile;
};
```

Listing 14.6   EmployeeX interface

```
// EmpX.h - contains EmployeeX declaration
#include "tablex.h"

class EmployeeX : public TableX
{
    typedef TableX Super;

    public:
        // Field IDs:
        enum
        {
            OBJ_ID,
            DEPT_ID,
            NAME,
            HIRE_DATE,
            JOB,
            MGR_ID,
            SALARY,
            NUM_IDS
        };

        EmployeeX(Connection* pCon);

        // Overrides:
        CString TableName() const;
        CString BusObjName() const;
        CString SequenceStr() const;
        int NumFields() const;

         // Department Codes
        enum {ACCOUNTING = 10, RESEARCH = 20, SALES = 30,
              OPERATIONS = 40};

    private:
        static const CString s_BusObjName;
        static CString s_TableName;
        static CString s_SequenceStr;
        static CStringArray s_FieldNames;
        static int s_NumFields;
        static BOOL s_LoadedFlag;
```

Listing 14.6   (continued)

```
        // Function overrides for loading field names:
        CStringArray& FieldList();
        BOOL FieldsLoaded() const;
        void MarkFieldsLoaded();
};

inline EmployeeX::EmployeeX(Connection* pCon)
                : TableX(pCon)
{}
```

Listing 14.7   The Query interface

```
// query.h
class Query
{
public:
    ~Query();
    virtual BOOL Execute(UINT = CRecordset::snapshot);
    int NumFields() const;

    // Query navigation functions
    BOOL First();
    BOOL Last();
    BOOL Next();
    BOOL Prev();
    // (functions omitted to save space)

    // Query-building functions
    // (functions omitted to save space)

    // Sort Functions
    // (functions omitted to save space)

protected:
    Query(TableX*, CRecordset*);

    CRecordset* m_pRecordset;
    TableX* m_pTableX;
    CString m_Filter;
    CString m_Sort;
};
```

Listing 14.8   EmployeeQuery interface and implementation

```
// EmpQ.h - contains EmployeeQuery declaration
#include <afxdb.h>          // For CRecordset constants and CString
#include "query.h"
#include "fulldate.h"
#include "empx.h"
#include "empr.h"

class EmployeeQuery : public Query
{
    typedef Query Super;
    typedef EmpRec* RecPtr;     // Cast to correct Recordset type

    public:
        EmployeeQuery(Connection* pCon);

        // Additional accessors for Employee:
        double GetObjID() const;
        double GetDeptID() const;
        CString GetName() const;
        LDS_Date::FullDate GetHireDate() const;
        CString GetJob() const;
        double GetMgrID() const;
        double GetSalary() const;
};

inline EmployeeQuery::EmployeeQuery(Connection* pCon)
                    : Query(new EmployeeX(pCon), new EmpRec(pCon))
{}

inline double EmployeeQuery::GetObjID() const
{
    using TableX;
    return ID(CLIENT_REC->m_ObjID);     // special TableX macro for IDs
}

inline double EmployeeQuery::GetDeptID() const
{
    double temp = CLIENT_REC->m_DeptID;
    return (temp == AFX_RFX_DOUBLE_PSEUDO_NULL) ? TableX::NUMERIC_NULL
                                                : temp;
}

// (Other Get-functions omitted to save space)
```

Listing 14.9 The `Persist` interface

```
// persist.h
class  Persist
{
public:
    virtual ~Persist();

    // Operations on objects:
    virtual void Write();
    virtual void WriteAsNew();
    virtual void Remove();
    virtual void Lock();
    void Refresh();

    // Accessors, etc.
    double GetObjID() const;
    Connection* GetConnection() const;
    TableX* GetX() const;
    virtual BOOL IsDirty() const = 0;
    BOOL IsValid() const;
    operator void*() const;

protected:
    Persist(TableX* pX, double id = TableX::NUMERIC_NULL);
    virtual BOOL Read_(double objID) = 0;
    virtual CString InsertValuesStr() const = 0;
    virtual CString UpdateValuesStr() const = 0;
    virtual void ClearFieldFlags() = 0;
    virtual void MarkFieldFlags() = 0;
    double NextID() const;
    void AddRec();
    void UpdateRec();

    // Attributes common to all persistent objects:
    double m_ObjID;
    TableX* m_pTableX;
    BOOL m_ValidFlag;
};
```

The `Persist` class has methods to read and write a single record (see Listings 14.9 and 14.10). As much logic as possible has percolated up to `Persist`, leaving only the necessities for derived classes to complete. The `Employee` class (Listings 14.11 and 14.12) derives from `Persist` and provides the attributes and field names for `Persist` to use in inserting and updating a record. The last four functions in `Employee`—`WhoIWorkFor`, `WhoWorksForMe`, `GetBoss`, and `GetDept`—go beyond simple I/O, and consist of the only code not machine generated (in other words, the fun part!). The first two take advantage of the fact that this system uses an Oracle database, hence the specialized SQL code.

Listing 14.10 The `Persist` implementation

```cpp
// persist.cpp
#include "persist.h"
#include "pfxxcept.h"
#include "util.h"

using namespace Persistence;
using namespace Utility;

void Persist::Write()
{
    if (IsDirty())
    {
        Connection* pCon = GetConnection();

        // Force a transaction:
        if (pCon->CanTransact() && !pCon->InTrans())
            pCon->BeginTrans();

        if (m_ValidFlag)
            UpdateRec();
        else
            AddRec();

        ASSERT(IsValid());
        ClearFieldFlags();
    }
}

void Persist::Remove()
{
    if (m_ObjID == TableX::NUMERIC_NULL || !m_ValidFlag)
        Throw(PFX,BAD_OBJ_ID);

    // Delete this object's record:
    ASSERT(m_pTableX);
    m_pTableX->Remove(m_ObjID);
    m_ValidFlag = FALSE;
}

void Persist::Lock()
{
    if (m_ObjID <= 0 || !m_ValidFlag)
        Throw2(PFX,LOCK_ERROR,_T("No record in database"));

    m_pTableX->Lock(m_ObjID);
}
```

Listing 14.10   (continued)

```
void Persist::Refresh()
{
    if (m_ObjID == TableX::NUMERIC_NULL || !Read_(m_ObjID))
        Throw(PFX,READ_ERROR);
    ClearFieldFlags();
    ASSERT(m_ValidFlag);
}

void Persist::AddRec()
{
    ASSERT(m_ObjID == TableX::NUMERIC_NULL);    // Can I do this?

    Connection* pCon = GetConnection();
    if (!pCon->CanUpdate())
        Throw2(PFX,INSERT_ERROR,_T("Connection not updatable"));

    m_ObjID = NextID();
    ASSERT(m_ObjID);

    ASSERT(m_pTableX);
    CString sql = _T("insert into ") + m_pTableX->TableName()
                + _TCHAR(' ') + InsertValuesStr();

    try
    {
        pCon->ExecuteSQL(sql);
    }
    catch (CDBException* ep)
    {
        CString msg = ep->m_strError + ep->m_strStateNativeOrigin;
        ep->Delete();
        Throw2(PFX,INSERT_ERROR,msg);
    }

    m_ValidFlag = TRUE;
}

void Persist::UpdateRec()
{
    Connection* pCon = GetConnection();
    if (!pCon->CanUpdate())
        Throw2(PFX,UPDATE_ERROR,_T("Connection not updatable"));
```

continued

Listing 14.10   (continued)

```cpp
    // Do nothing if no fields are dirty:
    CString updateValues = UpdateValuesStr();
    if (updateValues.IsEmpty())
        return;

    ASSERT(m_ObjID > 0);

    ASSERT(m_pTableX);
    CString sql = _T("update ") + m_pTableX->TableName()
                + _T(" set ") + UpdateValuesStr()
                + _T(" where ") + m_pTableX->SQLName(0)
                + _T(" = ") + NumToStr(m_ObjID);

    try
    {
        pCon->ExecuteSQL(sql);
    }
    catch (CDBException* ep)
    {
        CString msg = ep->m_strError + ep->m_strStateNativeOrigin;
        ep->Delete();
        Throw2(PFX,UPDATE_ERROR,msg);
    }
}
```

Listing 14.11   Employee class interface

```cpp
// Emp.h - contains Employee declaration
#include <afx.h>
#include "persist.h"
#include "fulldate.h"
#include "empx.h"
#include "bits.h"

class EmployeeQuery;
class Department;             // added manually

class Employee : public Persist
{
    public:
        // Construction
        Employee(Connection* pClient,
                 double id = TableX::NUMERIC_NULL);
        Employee(const EmployeeQuery& q);
```

Listing 14.11   (continued)

```cpp
    // Accessors
    double GetDeptID() const;
    CString GetName() const;
    FullDate GetHireDate() const;
    CString GetJob() const;
    double GetMgrID() const;
    double GetSalary() const;
    BOOL IsDirty() const;

    // Assignment
    void SetDeptID(double deptID);
    void SetName(const CString& name);
    void SetHireDate(const FullDate& hireDate);
    void SetJob(const CString& job);
    void SetMgrID(double mgrID);
    void SetSalary(double salary);

     // Other operations (added manually):
    EmployeeQuery* Employee::WhoIWorkFor() const;
    EmployeeQuery* Employee::WhoWorksForMe() const;
    Employee* Employee::GetBoss() const;
    Department* Employee::GetDept() const;

    static BOOL Exists(Connection* pCon, double objid);

protected:
    BOOL Read_(double id);                  // override
    CString InsertValuesStr() const;        // override
    CString UpdateValuesStr() const;        // override
    void ClearFieldFlags();                 // override
    void MarkFieldFlags();                  // override
    TableX* MakeX() const;

private:
    // Private Data Members
    double m_DeptID;
    CString m_Name;
    FullDate m_HireDate;
    CString m_Job;
    double m_MgrID;
    double m_Salary;
    bits<EmployeeX::NUM_IDS> fieldFlags;
```

continued

Listing 14.11   (continued)

```
            // Disabled operations (not implemented)
            Employee(const Employee&);
            void operator=(const Employee&);
};

inline double Employee::GetDeptID() const
{
    return m_DeptID;
}

// (Remaining Get functions omitted to save space)

inline void Employee::SetDeptID(double deptID)
{
    m_DeptID = deptID;
    fieldFlags.set(EmployeeX::DEPT_ID);
}

// (Remaining Set functions omitted to save space)

inline BOOL Employee::Exists(    Connection* pCon, double objid)
{
    return EmployeeX(pCon).Exists(objid);
}

inline void Employee::ClearFieldFlags()
{
    fieldFlags.reset();
}

inline void Employee::MarkFieldFlags()
{
    fieldFlags.set();
}

inline BOOL Employee::IsDirty() const
{
    return fieldFlags.any();
}
```

Listing 14.12 Employee class implementation

```cpp
// Emp.cpp - class for handling Employees
#include "emp.h"
#include "empq.h"
#include "empx.h"
#include "connect.h"
#include "pfxxcept.h"
#include "dept.h"

Employee::Employee(Connection* pClient, double id)
        : Persist(new EmployeeX(pClient), id),
          m_Name(_T("")),
          m_HireDate(_T("")),
          m_Job(_T(""))
{
    if (!Read_(id))
    {
        m_DeptID = TableX::NUMERIC_NULL;
        m_MgrID = TableX::NUMERIC_NULL;
        m_Salary = TableX::NUMERIC_NULL;
    }
}

Employee::Employee(const EmployeeQuery& q)
        : Persist(new EmployeeX(q.GetConnection()), q.GetObjID())
{
    if (!q.IsEOF() && !q.IsBOF())
    {
        m_DeptID = q.GetDeptID();
        m_Name = q.GetName();
        m_HireDate = q.GetHireDate();
        m_Job = q.GetJob();
        m_MgrID = q.GetMgrID();
        m_Salary = q.GetSalary();
        m_ValidFlag = TRUE;
    }
}

BOOL Employee::Read_(double id)
{
    m_ValidFlag = FALSE;

    if (id > 0)
    {
        // Execute objid query:
        EmployeeQuery q(GetConnection());
        q.AddSelect(EmployeeX::OBJ_ID, id);
        q.Execute();
```

continued

Listing 14.12   (continued)

```
        // Initialize data members (m_pConnection and m_ObjID
        // already done)
        if (!q.IsEOF() && !q.IsBOF())
        {
            m_DeptID = q.GetDeptID();
            m_Name = q.GetName();
            m_HireDate = q.GetHireDate();
            m_Job = q.GetJob();
            m_MgrID = q.GetMgrID();
            m_Salary = q.GetSalary();
            m_ValidFlag = TRUE;
        }
    }

    return m_ValidFlag;
}

CString Employee::InsertValuesStr() const
{
    // Build components of INSERT statement:
    CString fields = _T("(") + m_pTableX->SQLName(0);
    int nFields = m_pTableX->NumFields();
    for (int i = 1; i < nFields; ++i)
        fields += _T(",") + m_pTableX->SQLName(i);
    fields += _T(") values ");

    // This order must match the Registry ColumnName order!!!
    // (This is generated by the Framework Wizard)
    CString values = _T("(") + TableX::NumericVal(m_ObjID);
    values += _T(",") + TableX::NumericVal(m_DeptID);
    values += _T(",") + TableX::StringVal(m_Name);
    values += _T(",") + TableX::DateVal(m_HireDate);
    values += _T(",") + TableX::StringVal(m_Job);
    values += _T(",") + TableX::NumericVal(m_MgrID);
    values += _T(",") + TableX::NumericVal(m_Salary);
    values += _T(")");

    return fields + values;
}

CString Employee::UpdateValuesStr() const
{
    // Assemble SET clauses for dirty fields:
    // (The loop starts at 1 because the objID
    //  is field 0, and must not be changed)
```

Listing 14.12   (continued)

```
    CString result;
    for (int i = 1; i < EmployeeX::NUM_IDS; ++i)
    {
        if (fieldFlags.test(i))
        {
            if (!result.IsEmpty())
                result += _TCHAR(',');
            result += m_pTableX->SQLName(i) + _T("=");

            switch (i)
            {
                case EmployeeX::DEPT_ID:
                    result += TableX::NumericVal(m_DeptID);
                    break;
                case EmployeeX::NAME:
                    result += TableX::StringVal(m_Name);
                    break;
                case EmployeeX::HIRE_DATE:
                    result += TableX::StringVal(m_HireDate.ToString());
                    break;
                case EmployeeX::JOB:
                    result += TableX::StringVal(m_Job);
                    break;
                case EmployeeX::MGR_ID:
                    result += TableX::NumericVal(m_MgrID);
                    break;
                case EmployeeX::SALARY:
                    result += TableX::NumericVal(m_Salary);
                    break;
            }
        }
    }

    return result;
}


// These four methods were hand coded:
EmployeeQuery* Employee::WhoIWorkFor() const
{
    EmployeeQuery* pQ = new EmployeeQuery(GetConnection());
    CString filter;
    filter.Format(_T("1 = 1 connect by objid = prior mgrid"
                    " start with objid = %.0f"), m_ObjID);
    pQ->SetFilter(filter);
    pQ->Execute();
    return pQ;
}
```

continued

Listing 14.12   (continued)

```cpp
EmployeeQuery* Employee::WhoWorksForMe() const
{
    EmployeeQuery* pQ = new EmployeeQuery(GetConnection());
    CString filter;
    filter.Format(_T("1 = 1 connect by prior objid = mgrid"
                    " start with objid = %.0f"), m_ObjID);
    pQ->SetFilter(filter);
    pQ->Execute();
    return pQ;
}

Employee* Employee::GetBoss() const
{
    return m_MgrID ? new Employee(GetConnection(), m_MgrID) : 0;
}

Department* Employee::GetDept() const
{
    return m_DeptID ? new Department(GetConnection(), m_DeptID) : 0;
}
```

Listing 14.13   A program illustrating Persistent Employee and Department objects

```cpp
// test.cpp: Illustrates Employee and Department Classes
#include <iostream.h>
#include "connect.h"
#include "dept.h"
#include "deptQ.h"
#include "emp.h"
#include "empQ.h"
#include "tablex.h"
#include "util.h"
#include "rcdxcept.h"

using namespace Persistence;
using namespace Utility;

main()
{
    CString iniFile = _T("/test.ini");
    TableX::SetIniFile(iniFile);
    CString conStr = GetProfileValue(iniFile,_T("Connection"),
                                     _T("Debug"));
```

Listing 14.13 (continued)

```cpp
Connection* pC;
try
{
    cerr << "Connecting..." << endl;
    pC = Connection::Create(conStr);
    ASSERT(pC);
}
catch (Exception& x)
{
    cerr << x.GetMessage() << endl;
    cin.get();
    return 1;
}
cout << endl;

cout << "Departments:" << endl;
cout << "===========" << endl;

DepartmentQuery q(pC);
q.Execute();
while (!q.IsEOF())
{
    cout << q.GetObjID() << ','
         << q.GetName() << ','
         << q.GetLocation() << endl;
    q.Next();
}
cout << endl;

cout << "Employees:" << endl;
cout << "=========" << endl;

EmployeeQuery q2(pC);
q2.Execute();
while (!q2.IsEOF())
{
    cout << q2.GetObjID() << ','
         << q2.GetName() << ','
         << q2.GetHireDate().ToString() << ','
         << q2.GetSalary() << ','
         << q2.GetJob() << endl;
    q2.Next();
}
cout << endl;
```

continued

Listing 14.13   (continued)

```cpp
// Inspect Sales Employee data:
cout << "Sales Dept:\n";
cout << "==========\n";
q2.ResetSelect();
q2.AddSelect(EmployeeX::DEPT_ID, EmployeeX::SALES);
q2.Execute();
double empID = 0;
while (!q2.IsEOF())
{
    CString name = q2.GetName();
    cout << name << endl;
    if (name == "TURNER")
        empID = q2.GetObjID(); // Save TURNER's ID
    q2.Next();
}
cout << endl;

if (empID)
{
    // Instantiate TURNER and his Boss:
    Employee e(pC, empID);
    Employee* pBoss = e.GetBoss();
    cout << "TURNER's Boss: ";
    cout << pBoss->GetName() << endl;

    // Instantiate his Department:
    Department* pDept = e.GetDept();
    cout << "TURNER's Department: "
         << pDept->GetName() << endl;
    delete pDept;
    cout << endl;

    // Print TURNER's fellow workers:
    EmployeeQuery* pQ = pBoss->WhoWorksForMe();
    cout << "Who works for TURNER's boss:\n";
    while (!pQ->IsEOF())
    {
        cout << pQ->GetName() << endl;
        pQ->Next();
    }
    delete pQ;
    delete pBoss;
    cout << endl;
```

Listing 14.13   (continued)

```cpp
        // Print TURNER's line of command upward:
        pQ = e.WhoIWorkFor();
        cout << "Who TURNER works for:\n";
        while (!pQ->IsEOF())
        {
            cout << pQ->GetName() << endl;
            pQ->Next();
        }
        delete pQ;
    }

    // Create a new department:
    Department d(pC);
    d.SetName("ICS");
    d.SetLocation("CHQ");
    d.Write();
    pC->Commit();
    double deptNo = d.GetObjID();

    // Add New Employees:
    Employee e(pC);
    e.SetName("Einstein");
    e.SetDeptID(deptNo);
    e.SetHireDate(CString(_T("19970512")));
    e.SetJob(_T("Genius"));
    e.SetSalary(10000);
    e.Write();
    double mgrID = e.GetObjID();

    e.SetName("Feynman");
    e.SetDeptID(deptNo);
    e.SetHireDate(CString(_T("19970513")));
    e.SetJob(_T("Asst."));
    e.SetSalary(5000);
    e.SetMgrID(mgrID);
    e.WriteAsNew();

    pC->Commit();
    pC->Detach();
    cin.get();
    return 0;
}
```

Listing 14.14   Output from Listing 14.13

```
Departments:
===========
10,ACCOUNTING,NEW YORK
20,RESEARCH,DALLAS
30,SALES,CHICAGO
40,OPERATIONS,BOSTON

Employees:
=========
7369,SMITH,19801217,800,CLERK
7499,ALLEN,19810220,1600,SALESMAN
7521,WARD,19810222,1250,SALESMAN
7566,JONES,19810402,2975,MANAGER
7654,MARTIN,19810928,1250,SALESMAN
7698,BLAKE,19810501,2850,MANAGER
7782,CLARK,19810609,2450,MANAGER
7788,SCOTT,19821209,3000,ANALYST
7839,KING,19811117,5000,PRESIDENT
7844,TURNER,19810908,1500,SALESMAN
7876,ADAMS,19830112,1100,CLERK
7900,JAMES,19811203,950,CLERK
7902,FORD,19811203,3000,ANALYST
7934,MILLER,19820123,1300,CLERK

Sales Dept:
==========
ALLEN
WARD
MARTIN
BLAKE
TURNER
JAMES

TURNER's Boss: BLAKE
TURNER's Department: SALES

Who works for TURNER's boss:
BLAKE
ALLEN
WARD
MARTIN
TURNER
JAMES

Who TURNER works for:
TURNER
BLAKE
KING
```

Figure 14.6 Interaction of PFX objects

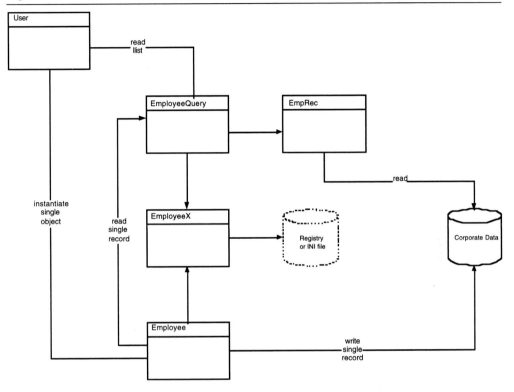

Figure 14.6 summarizes how PFX-based user objects interact to provide persistence and query capability. The complete source code is available at http://www.freshsources.com/.

Summary

- Object-oriented languages support *data abstraction*, *inheritance*, and *polymorphism*.
- Inheritance makes generalization-specialization relationships explicit in your code and saves work by factoring common code into a base class. Inheritance also allows you to add new derived classes without affecting existing code.
- Public inheritance represents an *is-a* relationship between a derived class and its base class.
- A pointer-to-base can also point to a derived object. Derived objects can always substitute for base objects.
- *Polymorphism* means having a single interface with an associated implementation that varies automatically as needed with the types of objects involved. C++ supports polymorphism via virtual functions.
- *Virtual functions* simulate dynamic binding via tables of function pointers.

• *Abstract classes* are classes that cannot be instantiated. They are used to specify an interface that derived classes must implement, or to endow a class with some particular functionality. An abstract class either has a pure virtual function, or it has no public constructors.

• A *framework* is a collection of tightly coupled classes that provide the majority of some domain of functionality. Clients complete or enhance functionality by inheriting from framework classes and overriding their virtual functions.

Answer to Exercise 14.1

The following functions are executed:

```
A::f
C::g

A::f
C::g
B::h

A::f
C::g
B::h
C::i
```

Note: `C::i` is not virtual.

PART III

Leveraging the Standard Library

Algorithms

No one initiated into the realm of computer programming would deny that algorithms are the "stuff of computer science."[1] Programs spend their machine cycles "doing things" to data. So many of those "things" are done time and time again, so we give an aggregation of operations a name and call it an algorithm. Webster's defines *algorithm* as:

> **al•go•rithm**: a rule of procedure for solving a mathematical problem (as of finding the greatest common divisor) that frequently involves repetition of an operation.

In his classic text, *Fundamental Algorithms,*[2] Knuth specifies Euclid's algorithm for finding the greatest common divisor of two integers, one of the oldest known algorithms, as follows:

> **Algorithm E** (Euclid's Algorithm). Given two positive integers m and n, find their greatest common divisor, that is, the largest positive integer that evenly divides both m and n.
>
> **E1**. [Find remainder.] Divide m by n and let r be the remainder.
>
> **E2**. [Is it zero?] If $r = 0$, the algorithm terminates; n is the answer.
>
> **E3**. [Interchange.] Set $m \leftarrow n$, $n \leftarrow r$, and go back to Step E1.

In C such a function might look like

```
/* Euclid's Algorithm */
#include <assert.h>

int gcd(int m, int n)
{
    int r;
    assert(m > 0 && n > 0);

    while ((r = m % n) != 0)
    {
        m = n;
        n = r;
    }
    return n;
}
```

This simple program is sufficient to illustrate the following aspects of algorithms:

1. **Finiteness**. In other words, an algorithm must *terminate*. The ability to interrupt processes on a computer is a testament to the fact that we sometimes fail to ensure this important feature! Given that m and n are positive, then r is in the range [0,n) (i.e., $0 = r <$ n). Since the value currently in r plays the role of n the next time around the loop, successive values of r form a strictly decreasing sequence, and therefore must eventually reach zero, guaranteeing that the algorithm will halt.

2. **Input**. An algorithm accepts zero or more parameters as initial data. Parameters are often accompanied by constraints, or *preconditions*, which must be met for the algorithm to function correctly. You can verify these conditions with an *assertion*, as I did above, or by setting an error condition via a return code or by throwing an exception. (See Chap. 13 for a discussion of these techniques).

3. **Output**. Given that the preconditions are met, an algorithm promises to deliver some data in return, or to cause some condition to occur as a side effect, or both. The side effects are often called *postconditions*. The preconditions, postconditions, and data returned constitute an algorithm's contract with the user.

Complexity

We are usually also very interested in an algorithm's *efficiency*. For example, the procedure that searches an array from beginning to end for a given value will always give the desired result, but it can be very wasteful if the sequence is already sorted (you should use a *binary search* instead). One way to compare algorithms is to measure their *complexity*, usually taken to mean the count of its key operations. Consider a linear search function, such as

```
// A linear search:
int search(int* data, int n, int x)
{
    for (int i = 0; i < n; ++i)
        if (data[i] == x)
            return i;
    return -1;
}
```

The key operation of this function compares each element to the search key, x. For n > 0, the search loop will execute somewhere between one and n times. If the elements are in no particular order, then on average we expect n/2 comparisons for any given key, and in the worst case there will be n comparisons. We call this an "order-n" algorithm, and we say that its complexity is "linear," because the number of operations is always proportional to n.

This categorization of algorithm complexity is essentially an application of the "big-oh" notation from mathematics. Given a function, $f(n)$, a sequence x_n is $O(f(n))$ (read "big-oh of f of n") if for large *n*,

$$|x_n| = m \, |f(n)|$$

where m is constant. The linear search function above is $O(n)$, because the number of comparisons is always bounded by n (i.e., $f(n) = n$, and $m = 1$).

    Now consider a binary search algorithm:

```
// Binary search (assumes data is sorted in ascending order)
int search(int* data, int n, int x)
{
    int begin = 0;
    int end = n;
    while (begin < end)
    {
        int mid = (begin + end) / 2;      // mid < end
        assert(mid < end);
        if (x == data[mid])
            return mid;
        else if (x < data[mid])
            end = mid - 1;
        else // x > data[mid]
            begin = mid + 1;
    }
    return -1;
}
```

How many times does this `while` loop iterate? Each trip around the loop reduces the amount of data left to search by half, so the loop executes no more than the number of times you can divide n by two (using integer arithmetic) until the result is one (i.e., until there is only one element left to check). The largest power of two that is less than or equal to n obeys:

$$2^p \leq n$$
$$\rightarrow \quad p \leq \log_2 n$$

so the least upper bound on the number of iterations will either be p or $p+1$, depending on whether n is a power of two or not. Using the mathematical concept of *ceiling* (the smallest integer greater than or equal to a given number), the number of iterations, i, obeys

$$i \leq \lceil \log_2 n \rceil \qquad \text{// notation for ceiling(log}_2\text{n)}$$

Binary search is therefore $O(\log_2 n)$. If you compare the graphs of $f(x) = x$ and $f(x) = \log_2 x$, the latter is much smaller than the former for large x, so an $O(\log_2 n)$ algorithm is preferable to a linear one.

    The best complexity we could hope for is *constant time* (i.e., $O(1)$). Finding the minimum in a sorted sequence, for example, is a constant time algorithm, because it is always the 0-th element, no matter the size of the list. Certain hashing algorithms also exhibit constant time behavior. (For more information on complexity and hashing, see a good book on the analysis of algorithms.[3])

The complexity measures most often found in common algorithms are, in ascending order:

Complexity	Representative Algorithms
O(1)	Hashing, special algorithms
O(logn)	Binary search, other tree searches
O(n)	Simple sequence traversals, such as linear search
O(nlogn)	Quicksort, Heapsort
O(n^2)	Simple sort algorithms (e.g., bubble, insertion), various matrix algorithms, std::search

To ensure adequate performance, the C++ standard specifies complexity constraints on the algorithms in the standard library. (See the listing of algorithms in Appendix A).

Generic Algorithms

The standard C++ library contains a linear search algorithm named find, which you could use like this:

```
// find1.cpp: Searches an array of integers
#include <algorithm>
#include <iostream>
using namespace std;
main()
{
    int a[] = {45,23,89,12,78};
    int n = sizeof a / sizeof a[0];
    int* past = a + n;

    int* p = find(a, past, 12);
    if (p != past)
        cout << "found " << *p << " in position "
            << p - a << endl;
    else
        cout << "item not found\n";
}

// Output:
found 12 in position 3
```

Like find, most of the algorithms in the standard C++ library operate on a *range*, such as the one delimited by the pointers a and past above. The second pointer always points to one position *past* the end of the sequence being processed, a convention borrowed from ANSI C, which allows a pointer to point to a position just past the end of an array as long as you don't dereference it. The algorithm find is a *generic* algorithm because it can process a sequence of almost any type. For example, you could search an array of strings like this:

```
// find2.cpp: Searches an array of strings
#include <algorithm>
#include <iostream>
#include <string>
using namespace std;
```

```
main()
{
    string a[] = {"Albert", "Charles", "Horatio"};
    int n = sizeof a / sizeof a[0];
    string* past = a + n;

    string* p = find(a, past, "Charles");
    if (p != past)
        cout << "found " << *p << " in position "
            << p - a << endl;
    else
        cout << "item not found\n";
}
```

```
// Output:
found Charles in position 1
```

As the program in Listing 15.1 illustrates, you can even use find on arrays of user-defined types as long as that type supports certain operations. How is find so smart? Because it is a *function template*. From what we have seen so far, you could implement find as follows:

```
// One possible implementation for find()
template<class T>
T* find(T* start, T* past, const T& v)
{
    while (start != past)
    {
        if (*start == v)
            break;
        ++start;
    }
    return start;
}
```

When the compiler sees the expression find(a, past, v) in Listing 15.1, it instantiates the function find(Person*, Person*, const Person&). You can see from the implementation that find should work on any type that allows you to compare two objects for equality (which is why I included operator==(const Person&, const Person&) in Listing 15.1). Chapter 16 discusses how standard C++ categorizes its algorithms' iteration mechanisms, and how they can be used with the various containers in the standard library. This chapter uses only array containers in its illustrations.

Sometimes searching on object equality isn't exactly what you want. You might want to find the first element that is less than a particular value, for example, or you may want find to consider only a subset of an object when making comparisons, such as a single data member. The program in Listing 15.2 uses a version of find, called find_if, that lets you provide a function that determines the success of a search. The function isCharles is an example of a *predicate*, which is just a function (or *function object*, see below) that returns a bool. The function

Listing 15.1   Searches an array of user-defined types

```cpp
// find3.cpp
#include <algorithm>
#include <iostream>
#include <string>
using namespace std;

struct Person
{
    string name;
    int year;
    int month;
    int day;
    Person() : name("")
    {
        year = month = day = 0;
    }
    Person(const string& nm, int y, int m, int d)
          : name(nm)
    {
        year = y;
        month = m;
        day = d;
    }
};

bool operator==(const Person& p1, const Person& p2)
{
    return p1.name  == p2.name && p1.year == p2.year &&
           p1.month == p2.month && p1.day == p2.day;
}

ostream& operator<<(ostream& os, const Person& p)
{
    os << '{' << p.name << ',' << p.month
       << '/' << p.day  << '/' << p.year << '}';
    return os;
}

main()
{
    Person a[3];
    a[0] = Person("Albert", 1901,1,20);
    a[1] = Person("Charles", 1897,3,11);
    a[2] = Person("Horatio", 1835,12,6);
```

Listing 15.1   (continued)

```
    int n = sizeof a / sizeof a[0];
    Person* past = a + n;
    Person v("Charles", 1897,3,11);

    Person* p = find(a, past, v);
    if (p != past)
        cout << "found " << *p << " in position "
            << p - a << endl;
    else
        cout << "item not found\n";
}


// Output:
found {Charles,3/11/1897} in position 1
```

Listing 15.2   Searches a sequence using a predicate

```
// find4.cpp: Uses a Predicate
#include <algorithm>
#include <iostream>
#include <string>
using namespace std;

struct Person
{
    // Same as in Listing 15.1
};

bool isCharles(const Person& p)
{
    return p.name == "Charles";
}

ostream& operator<<(ostream& os, const Person& p)
{
    os << '{' << p.name << ',' << p.month
        << '/' << p.day  << '/' << p.year << '}';
    return os;
}
```

continued

Listing 15.2   (continued)

```
main()
{
    Person a[3];
    a[0] = Person("Albert", 1901,1,20);
    a[1] = Person("Charles", 1897,3,11);
    a[2] = Person("Horatio", 1835,12,6);
    int n = sizeof a / sizeof a[0];
    Person* past = a + n;

    Person* p = find_if(a, past, isCharles);
    if (p != past)
        cout << "found " << *p << " in position "
            << p - a << endl;
    else
        cout << "item not found\n";
}
```

isCharles is a unary function that returns true if the name member of its Person argument is the string "Charles". The algorithm find_if traverses its range, applying isCharles to each object in turn until it evaluates to true. Many standard algorithms have such _if versions that take a predicate for custom match criteria.

Function Objects

The isCharles predicate isn't terribly useful, of course, since it only knows how to search for one specific key. Unless you can come up with a more flexible technique, you'll have to write isAlbert, isHoratio, and so on. You might think of adding a string parameter to isCharles (and renaming it, of course, to something like byName), thus customizing each call to find_if, but find_if expects its search predicate to be a unary function that takes a certain parameter type (Person, in this case). It would be nice if you could construct functions on the fly, but alas, C++ is not Lisp. The solution is to apply the *universal law of abstraction*: "When you need to implement a new concept, create a new class."[4] What you need is an object that you can initialize with a search key and that can act like a unary function. The requirement to act like a function is easily met by overloading the *function call* operator. If class X defines operator, and if x is an object of class X, then the expression x calls x.operator. In C++, an instance of such a class is called a *function object*. Here is the definition of a function object that compares the name member of a Person object with a given string:

```
struct byName
{
    string name;
    byName(const string& s) : name(s) {}
    bool operator()(const Person& p) {return p.name == name;}
};
```

The call to find_if must now change accordingly:

```
Person* p = find_if(a, past, byName("Charles"));
```

The expression byName("Charles") constructs a temporary byName object with its name member initialized to "Charles". The code for find_if might look something like the following:

```
template<class T, class Pred>
T* find_if(T* start, T* past, Pred p)
{
    while (start != past && !p(*start))
        ++start;
    return start;
}
```

where Pred represents any class that has a member with the signature bool operator(const T&). The expression !p(*start) then reduces to !byName("Charles").operator()(* start).

The standard C++ library predefines a number of useful function objects (see Appendix C). To illustrate, first consider the accumulate algorithm, which sums up the elements of a sequence:

```
#include <numeric>          // defines accumulate
...
int sum = accumulate(a, past, 0);
```

There is a more general version of accumulate, which takes a fourth argument that represents an arbitrary binary function. If you wanted to accumulate the product of the elements of a sequence instead of the sum, you would need a binary function that multiplies its arguments for accumulate to work with. You could always code it yourself, but you might consider letting the library create it for you with the multiplies function object, like this:

```
#include <numeric>
#include <functional>       // defines function objects
...
int prod = accumulate(a, past, 1, multiplies<long>());
```

Note the long template argument, since the product could conceivably overflow an int. Except for the unusual base class in the following code, the definition for multiplies is what you would expect:

```
template<class T>
struct multiplies : binary_function<T, T, T>   // explained below
{
    T operator()(const T& x, const T& y) const
    {
        return (x * y);
    }
};
```

By using function objects with function object *adapters*, which allow you to customize and combine function objects (see below), you can fine tune algorithm predicates to a great level of detail without ever having to write a function yourself.

Function Taxonomy

Since creating function objects is something you'll want to do often, the standard library has some features to make the job easier, but first it's helpful to understand that C++ classifies functions as follows:

1. *Generators*—functions that take no argument and return a single value.
2. *Unary Functions*—take one argument of any type and return a single value.
3. *Binary Functions*—take two arguments of any (possibly distinct) types and return a single value.

The standard random number function rand is a good example of a generator. Most of the time, however, you care about unary and binary functions. To take advantage of all of the function object machinery in the standard C++ library, you need to use *adaptable* unary and binary function objects, which are just function objects with nested typedefs describing the argument and return types. An adaptable version of the byName function object would look like this:

```
struct byName
{
    typedef bool return_type;
    typedef Person argument_type;
    string name;
    byName(const string& s) : name(s) {}
    bool operator()(const Person& p) {return p.name == name;}
};
```

There is a class template, however, named unary_function, that you can derive from that will record these types for you so you don't have to enter the typedef statements:

```
template<class ArgType, class RetType>
struct unary_function
{
    typedef ArgType argument_type;
    typedef RetType result_type;
};
```

As you saw in the definition of `multiplies` earlier, there is also a `binary_function` template, which records the types `first_argument_type`, `second_argument_type`, and `result_type`. The definition of an adaptable `byName` now looks like:

```
struct byName : unary_function<Person, bool>
{
    string name;
    byName(const string& s) : name(s) {}
    bool operator()(const Person& p) {return p.name == name;}
};
// argument_type == Person, result_type == bool
```

With adaptable function objects you can use function object adapters to create sophisticated function objects on demand.

Function Object Adapters

A function object adapter is a function template that takes one or more function objects and other optional values as parameters and that returns a new function object (see Appendix C for a complete listing). The adapter `not1`, for example, logically negates the sense of its unary predicate argument, so that the following statement will find the first `Person` object in the array with a name other than `"Charles"`:

```
Person* p = find_if(a, past, not1(byName("Charles")));
```

The adapter `not1` is essentially a wrapper that calls its argument and negates the result before returning it.

The adapter `bind2nd` transforms a binary function object into a unary one by saving a given value to use as the second argument. For example, to find a particular `Person` object, we can combine `bind2nd` with `equal_to` to form a suitable predicate:

```
Person v("Charles", 1897, 3, 11);
find_if(a, past, bind2nd(equal_to<Person>(), v));
```

The adaptable binary function object `equal_to<Person>` is instantiated from the predefined template `equal_to` and takes two `Person` objects as arguments. The `bind2nd` adapter creates a unary function object that stores the value of v. Whenever `find_if` calls that new unary function object's `operator(const Person&)` with a `Person` object from the array as an argument, that function object in turn calls `equal_to<Person>` with v as the second argument. Thus each `Person` object in a is compared to v until a match is found. There is also a `bind1st` adapter, which would work equally well in this case, since comparing for equality is commutative.

The example above requires a full `Person` object as a search key. To reduce the search to just a comparison of name strings as before, you could make `byName` a binary predicate and use `bind2nd`, as the following statements illustrate:

```
struct byName : binary_function<Person, string, bool>
{
    bool operator()(const Person& p, const string& s) const
    {
        return p.name == s;
    }
};
...
find_if(a, past, bind2nd(byName(), "Charles"));
```

Note that this version of byName doesn't have to store any data (because bind2nd does).

If this wasn't easy enough, there is yet another adapter, ptr_fun, that builds a function object from a function pointer, so all you really have to do is provide the compare function to begin with, as in

```
bool byName(const Person& p, const string& s)
{
    return p.name == s;
}
```

and then call find_if like this:

```
find_if(a, past, bind2nd(ptr_fun(byName), "Charles"));
```

The adapter ptr_fun deduces whether its argument is a unary or binary function, and returns a suitable adaptable function object.

Algorithm Taxonomy

As you saw in Appendix C, there are quite a number of generic algorithms in the standard C++ library, each falling into one of three groups:

1. *General sequence algorithms*, which perform common operations on sequences of objects (e.g., find, find_if, count, copy, transform, etc.).
2. *Sorting-related algorithms*, such as sort and partial_sort, which reorder elements in a sequence, and others, like min and max, that return order-related information.
3. *Numeric algorithms*, which perform mathematical operations, such as accumulate and inner_product.

The header <algorithm> declares function templates for the algorithms in the first two groups, while those in the third are found in <numeric>. The program in Listing 15.3 illustrates selected algorithms (output in Listing 15.4).

Listing 15.3 Illustrates various algorithms

```cpp
// algs.cpp:  Illustrates various algorithms
#include <algorithm>
#include <numeric>
#include <iostream>
#include <string>
#include <utility>
using namespace std;

// Function template to print any sequence:
template<class T>
void print_array(T* begin, T* end)
{
    while (begin != end)
        cout << *begin++ << ' ';
    cout << endl;
}

// Function to test an int for odd-ness:
inline bool odd(int n)
{
    return n % 2 == 1;
}

string parity[] = {"even", "odd"};

inline void print_parity(int n)
{
    cout << parity[n%2] << ' ';
}

// Returns 1 if odd; 0 if even:
inline int calc_parity(int n)
{
    return n%2;
}

main()
{
    int a[] = {1,2,3,4,5};
    const int nelems = sizeof a / sizeof a[0];
    int b[nelems];
```

continued

Listing 15.3   (continued)

```
// Copy a to b (must be enough space)
copy(a, a + nelems, b);
cout << "b == ";
print_array(b, b+nelems);

// Test for equality:
cout.setf(ios::boolalpha);
bool test = equal(a, a + nelems, b);
cout << "a == b? " << test << endl;

// Reverse b:
cout << "Reverse b: ";
reverse(b, b + nelems);
print_array(b, b+nelems);
test = equal(a, a + nelems, b);
cout << "a == b? " << test << endl;

// sort b:
sort(b, b + nelems);
print_array(b, b+nelems);
test = equal(a, a + nelems, b);
cout << "a == b? " << test << endl;

// Sum elements of a:
int sum = 0;
cout << "sum == "
     << accumulate(a, a + nelems, sum)
     << endl;

// Count 3's in b:
int n3 = count(b, b + nelems, 3);
cout << "# = 3's in b: " << n3 << endl;

// Count odd numbers in b:
int nodd = count_if(b, b + nelems, odd);
cout << "# odd's in b: " << nodd << endl;
cout << endl;

// Replace b with parity values:
for_each(a, a + nelems, print_parity);
cout << endl;
transform(b, b + nelems, b, calc_parity);
print_array(b, b+nelems);
}
```

Listing 15.4 Output from the program in Listing 15.3

```
b == 1 2 3 4 5
a == b? true

Reverse b: 5 4 3 2 1
a == b? false

1 2 3 4 5
a == b? true

sum of a == 15

# = 3's in b: 1
# odd's in b: 3

odd even odd even odd
1 0 1 0 1
```

Summary

- Algorithms are the "stuff" of computer science.
- The algorithms in the standard C++ library are *function templates*, most of which process a sequence of objects delimited by a [begin, end) range, where end points just beyond the last element to be processed.
- The standard algorithms fall into one of three categories: general sequence operations, sorting-related operations, and numeric operations.
- A *function object* is a instance of a class that defines operator.
- An *adaptable function object* contains type definitions for its argument and return types.
- Standard function objects implement generators, unary functions, and binary functions.
- A *predicate* is a function (or function object) that returns a bool.
- A *function object adapter* is a function template that takes one or more function objects and other optional values as parameters and returns a new function object.
- By combining function objects with function object adapters, you can customize algorithm predicates, often without ever having to write a function yourself.

References

1. Sedgewick, *Algorithms,* Addison-Wesley, 1983, p. 4.
2. Knuth, *The Art of Computer Programming,* Second Edition, Vol. 1, "Fundamental Algorithms," Addison-Wesley, 1973, p. 2.
3. See, for example, Aho et al., *The Design and Analysis of Computer Algorithms,* Addison-Wesley, 1974.
4. Perhaps I'm being a little bold giving this "law" a name, but it's about time someone did. See Koenig, *Ruminations on C++,* Addison-Wesley, 1997, p. 151.

Containers and Iterators

A *container*, sometimes called a *collection*, is an object that holds other objects. In a limited sense, therefore, a `struct` is a container, but the most useful types of containers allow you to add members at runtime and to traverse the collection of objects in some order. The container most widely used over the years has certainly been the *array*. Arrays are particularly handy when you need to directly access an object by its position number. They are not so handy, however, when you need to add or remove elements to or from any position other than the end. Another drawback, of course, is that you must specify in advance the maximum number of elements an array can hold. To overcome the size issue, the standard library defines a `vector` template that instantiates an array-like container to which you may append as many elements as you like.

The following program uses a `vector` of strings to hold the tokens separately in a text file:

```
// vec1.cpp
#include <iostream>
#include <vector>
#include <algorithm>
#include <string>
using namespace std;

main()
{
    vector<string> tokens;
    string token;

    // Read tokens; fill vector
    while (cin >> token)
        tokens.push_back(token);
```

```
        int ntok = tokens.size();
        cout << "There are " << ntok << " tokens:\n";
        for (int i = 0; i < ntok; ++i)
            cout << i << ": " << tokens[i] << endl;
    }
```

```
// Input:
how now brown cow
```

```
// Output:
There are 4 tokens:
0: how
1: now
2: brown
3: cow
```

The line

```
vector<string> tokens;
```

declares `tokens` to be a vector of strings, but you can declare vectors of any concrete **type**. The `push_back` member function appends a new element to the end of the vector.

To further illustrate the utility of the `vector` template, consider the command-line argument facility of standard C/C++. You normally obtain arguments that the user types on the command line via arguments to `main`:

```
main(int argc, char* argv[])
```

If your users repeatedly invoke programs with long argument lists, they might prefer to store the argument tokens in a file, so that when they enter the command line

```
prog @arg_file
```

the "at" sign (`@`) tells you to look in the file `arg_file` for those tokens. And since you're opening files anyway, why not allow them to nest files? For example, if `arg_file` contained

```
arg1
@file2
arg2
```

and `file2` held

```
arg3
arg4
```

then typing `prog @arg_file` on the command line should be equivalent to the following user command.

```
prog arg1 arg3 arg4 arg2
```

Using vector, it is a simple matter to create a class, call it Arglist, that expands these *indirect files* automatically:

```
#include <string>
#include <vector>
using std::string;
using std::vector;

class Arglist
{
public:
    Arglist(size_t, char **);
    size_t count() const;
    const string& operator[](size_t) const;

private:
    vector<string> args;      // holds args

    void expand(char *);      // reads a file
    void add(char *);         // appends an arg
};
```

An Arglist object uses a vector of strings, which it initializes by processing the argc/argv pair represented by its arguments, opening files as needed. The following program uses an Arglist to print its expanded argument list, one argument per line:

```
#include <iostream>
#include "arglist.h"

main(int argc, char* argv[])
{
    Arglist args(--argc, ++argv); // ignore prog. name
    for (int i = 0; i < args.count(); ++i)
        cout << "arg[" << i << "] == " << args[i] << endl;
}
```

Three of Arglist's five member functions merely delegate their responsibility to the vector args:

```
size_t Arglist::count() const
{
    return args.size();
}


const string& Arglist::operator[](size_t i) const
{
    return args[i];
}
```

```
void Arglist::add(char* arg)
{
    args.push_back(arg);
}
```

The interesting work is done in expand, which processes each argument in a file, opening nested files recursively as needed:

```
#include <fstream>
using namespace std;

void Arglist::expand(char* fname)
{
    ifstream f(fname);
    char token[64];

    while (f >> token)
        if (token[0] == '@')
            expand(token+1);
        else
            add(token);
}
```

The Arglist constructor just calls expand or add, depending on whether the original arguments typed by the user have a leading @-character:

```
Arglist::Arglist(size_t arg_count, char **arg_vec)
{
    for (int i = 0; i < arg_count; ++i)
        if (arg_vec[i][0] == '@')
            expand(arg_vec[i]+1);
        else
            add(arg_vec[i]);
}
```

Standard Containers

The standard library offers three categories of containers: *basic sequence containers, container adapters,* and *associative containers.* The basic sequences, vector, list, and deque, are ordered data structures with their own unique characteristics. Both vector and deque (an abbreviation for "double-ended queue," pronounced "deck") are array-like data structures optimized for random access (i.e., they provide constant-time access to any sequence element, and they overload operator[]). A vector provides constant-time insertion and deletion of elements only at the end of its sequence, while a deque does so at both the beginning and the end. A list is a doubly linked list data structure that supports constant-time insertions and deletions anywhere in its sequence, and it is the container of choice when insertions or deletions occur other than at the ends, especially when only sequential access is required.

All standard containers have *value semantics*, meaning that they have operators and constructors that enable them to be compared (at least for equality), passed and returned by value, and assigned. More importantly, they expect the objects they contain to have value semantics, because they store copies of the objects you give them and routinely copy and assign them as needed. All containers also define the following member functions:

```
size_type size() const;        // current # of elements
size_type max_size() const;    // max # of elements possible
bool empty() const;            // size() == 0?
```

The `size_type` is an unsigned integral type which operates like `size_t`, and is defined appropriately by each container. The sequence containers also define functions to `insert` and `erase` elements at arbitrary positions, as well as the following operations (`T` is the contained object type):

```
void resize(size_type, T = T());   // expand or truncate
T& front() const;                  // return the first element
T& back() const;                   // return the last element
void push_front(const T&);         // insert at front (not
                                   // supported by vector)
void push_back(const T&);          // append to end
void pop_front();                  // remove first element (not
                                   // supported by vector)
void pop_back();                   // remove last element
T& at(size_type n);                // return nth element (not
                                   // supported by list)
```

You may wonder why `list` does not provide member functions to navigate its sequence. The answer to that question also explains why the standard containers explicitly define only a very few of the standard algorithms, such as those discussed in Chapter 15. The answer is *iterators*.

Iterators

An *iterator* is a generalization of a pointer that supports sequence traversal. To visit each element in a `list`, for example, you could do the following:

```
list<T> lst;
// insert some elements, then:
list<T>::iterator p = lst.first();
while (p != lst.end())
{
    // Process current element (*p), then:
    ++p;
}
```

All containers define types `iterator` and `const_iterator`, which support copy, assign, and compare-for-equality operations, and overload at least `operator*`, `operator++` (both flavors), and `operator->`, so you can use normal pointer syntax to process a sequence. The member function first returns an iterator that points at the first element, and the member function end points one past the last element, thus defining a range as required by the standard algorithms. To count all the instances of 3 in a list of integers, for example, you can use count, like this:

```
int n = count(lst.first(), lst.end(), 3);
```

The algorithms in the standard library are actually specified in terms of iterators. The find algorithm, for example, is implemented something like the following:

```
template<class Iterator, class T>
Iterator find(Iterator begin, Iterator end, const T& v)
{
    while (begin != end)
    {
        if (*begin == v)
            break;
        ++end;
    }
    return end;
}
```

It is this arrangment of containment, iteration, and algorithms into separate concepts, coupled with the flexibility of templates, that makes the standard C++ library stand alone as the most powerful general-purpose library ever conceived. Algorithms apply to sequences of built-in arrays as well as sophisticated containers. Containers can manage collections of virtually any concrete type (even other containers). Iterators are the glue that connects containers and algorithms.

Note that find expects Iterator to support only three operations: operator!=, operator*, and operator++. Other algorithms may require other features, such as operator-- for reverse traversal, or operator[] for random access. The standard library divides iterators into five different categories so that an algorithm can publish its iteration requirements, or so you can provide different versions of an algorithm for different situations.

Iterator Taxonomy

The five iterator categories are:

1. Input
2. Output
3. Forward
4. Bidirectional
5. Random access.

Input and output iterators support copying, equality comparison (operator==, operator!=), dereferencing (operator*), and single-pass-only traversal via operator++ and operator++(int). They differ in what they let you do with a dereferenced object: Input iterators yield a read-only reference; output iterators, a write-only one. Like many of the standard algorithms, find expects an input iterator. For documentation purposes, its implementation would be more effectively rendered as

```
template<class InputIterator, class T>
InputIterator find(InputIterator begin, InputIterator end, const T& v)
{
    while (begin != end)
    {
        if (*begin == v)
            break;
        ++end;
    }
    return end;
}
```

A *forward* iterator allows multiple passes through a sequence with both read and write capability, and hence can substitute for either an input or output iterator. The unique algorithm, for instance, removes all but the first of runs of consecutive duplicate elements from its sequence. The call

```
list<T>::iterator p = unique(lst.first(), lst.end());
```

rearranges lst by shuffling nonduplicates upward in the sequence, overwriting the duplicates as it goes, and returns a past-the-end iterator delimiting the sequence of surviving objects. Since it needs to both read and write lst elements, it requires a forward iterator. If a less capable iterator is provided, a compile error will indicate a missing operation.

A *bidirectional* iterator can stand in for a forward iterator, but it also supports backward traversal of sequence elements via operator--() and operator--(int). One way to traverse a list backward, therefore, would look like this:

```
// Traverse backward via operator--:
list::iterator p<T> = lst.end();
while (p > lst.begin())
{
    --p;                            // "advances" backward
    // process *p, then:
    if (p == lst.begin())
        break;
}
```

Containers that support a bidirectional iterator also define the member functions rbegin and rend, which return *reverse iterators*, providing a better way to traverse a list backward, namely

```
// Traverse backward via a reverse_iterator:
list::reverse_iterator<T> p = lst.rbegin();
while (p != lst.rend())
{
    // process *p, then:
    ++p;                            // "advances" backward
}
```

As you might expect, the `reverse` algorithm requires a bidirectional iterator, since the most efficient generic implementation uses two iterators, one at each end, that move in opposite directions until they meet in the middle of a sequence.

A *random access* iterator is a bidirectional iterator that simulates pointer arithmetic in constant time via the usual operators: `operator+(int)`, `operator+=(int)`, `operator-(int)`, `operator-=(int)`, `operator[](int)`, `operator<`, `operator<=`, `operator>`, and `operator>=`. The generic `sort` algorithm requires random access iterators, since it needs to swap elements to rearrange them. Since a `list` cannot have a random access iterator, it has its own `sort` member function. In general, if a generic algorithm either does not apply to or is not optimally efficient for a container, a custom version appears as a member function for that container. Other algorithms optimized for `list` include `merge`, `remove`, and `unique`.

Special-Purpose Iterators

In Chapter 15, all examples that wrote to array sequences operated in *overwrite mode*, meaning that the target array needed to have enough space to receive the output. In the following example, the attempt to copy elements from a `vector<int>` to an empty one would fail at runtime:

```
vector<int> v1;
// fill v1, then:
vector<int> v2;
copy(v1.begin(), v1.end(), v2.begin());      // error
```

Fortunately, there is a way to have the standard containers operate in *insert mode* to allow an algorithm to add new objects anywhere in an existing sequence. An *insert iterator* is an output iterator that replaces all invocations of `operator*` with an appropriate insert operation for its container. The `back_inserter` function template creates such an iterator for its container argument that replaces all output operations with a call to `push_back`. The following `copy` statement fixes the problem with the previous example:

```
copy(v1.begin(), v1.end(), back_inserter(v2));
```

There is also a `front_inserter` template, which of course works only for deque and `list` because vector doesn't support `push_front`. A more general version, `inserter`, inserts objects at a given location in first-in-first-out order; for example,

```
// Insert objects starting before the nth element of lst2:
copy(lst1.begin(), lst1.end(), inserter(lst2, lst2.begin() + n));
```

There are also special iterators for stream I/O. An `ostream_iterator` is an output iterator that inserts objects into an output stream. The following statement, for example, prints `vector<int>` elements to `cout`, each separated by a space:

```
copy(v1.begin(), v1.end(), ostream_iterator<int>(cout, " "));
```

An `istream_iterator` is an input iterator that reads elements from an input stream. To populate a `vector` of `int`s, for example, you could use `copy`, as in

```
copy(istream_iterator<int>(cin), istream_iterator<int>(),
    back_inserter(v1));
```

The `istream_iterator` created with an empty argument list acts as a past-the-end iterator when end-of-file is reached.

The program in Listing 16.1 illustrates most of the concepts discussed to this point. It uses a vector of vectors, in particular a `vector<vector<char>>`, to store a grid of characters representing the first quadrant in the x-y plane. Each `vector<char>` in `grid` is a row that corresponds to a fixed value of y. This row orientation makes horizontal printing convenient, but it requires a counterintuitive y-x (vs. x-y) indexing scheme, hence the statement

```
grid[f(x)][x] = '*'; // y coordinate is first
```

Listing 16.1   Uses a vector of vectors to produce a graph

```
// grid.cpp: Stores an x-y graph in a grid of chars
#include <vector>
#include <iostream>
#include <iterator>
using namespace std;

namespace
{
    typedef vector<char> row_type;
    typedef vector<row_type> grid_type;
    const int xmax = 15;          // # of columns
    const int ymax = xmax;        // # of rows
}

main()
{
    void print_grid(const grid_type&);
    double f(double);             // Function to graph
    grid_type grid;               // A vector of rows

    // Initialize y-axis and clear 1st quadrant:
    grid.reserve(ymax);
    row_type blank_row(xmax);
    blank_row[0] = '|';
    for (int y = 0; y < ymax; ++y)
        grid.push_back(blank_row);
```

Listing 16.1 (continued)

```
    // Initialize x-axis:
    grid[0][0] = '+';
    for (int x = 1; x < xmax; ++x)
        grid[0][x] = '-';

    // Populate with points of f():
    for (int x = 0; x < xmax; ++x)
        grid[f(x)][x] = '*';            // row-oriented

    print_grid(grid);
}

double f(double x)
{
    // Contrived to fix within grid!
    return x * x / ymax + 1.0;
}

void print_grid(const grid_type& grid)
{
    grid_type::const_reverse_iterator yp;
    for (yp = grid.rbegin(); yp != grid.rend(); ++yp)
    {
        // Print a row:
        copy(yp->begin(), yp->end(), ostream_iterator<char>(cout, ""));
        cout << endl;
    }
}

// Output:
|             *
|
|              *
|
|            *
|           *
|
|         *
|        *
|       *
|      *
|     *
|   **
****
+--------------
```

To avoid range errors, the function being graphed in this example is conditioned to fit within the limits of `grid`. The function `vector::reserve` requests that sufficient space for a given number of elements be allocated all at once to avoid the costly reallocations that might naturally occur when inserting elements one at a time.

Container Adapters

The container adapters, `queue`, `stack`, and `priority_queue`, are high-level data structures that use a sequence for their implementation. A `stack`, for example, can be based on a `deque`, `list`, or `vector`, depending on how you declare it:

```
// Declare a stack of strings that uses an underlying vector:
stack< string, vector<string> > string_stack;
```

If you omit the second template argument, `queue<T>` and `stack<T>` use a `deque<T>`, and `priority_queue<T>` uses a `vector<T>`. You can also use an existing sequence by making it a constructor argument:

```
deque<int> d;
// Populate d, then:
queue<int> q(d);            // Treat d as a queue
```

You can use containers of your own design as support sequences, provided that they offer the member functions that the adapters expect.

These containers are called adapters because they adapt a sequence to a specific use by presenting a more restricted interface to users (in particular, they do not provide iterators). A `stack`, for example, has only the member functions you would expect for a last-in-first-out structure:

```
bool empty() const;
size_type size() const;
value_type& top();
const value_type& top() const;          // value_type is the
                                        // contained type (T)
void push(const value_type& x);
void pop();
```

These functions just invoke the corresponding operation on the underlying sequence (e.g., `pop` calls `pop_front`). Instead of `top`, queue defines `front` and `back`, and its push method does a `push_back` on the underlying sequence, whereas pop calls `pop_front`, as expected. Since `vector` does not support `pop_front`, it cannot support a `queue` adapter. A `priority_queue` implements a classic *heap* data structure, whose pop method returns the minimum value with respect to some predicate (`less<T>` by default).

Associative Containers

The associative containers are set, multiset, map, and multimap. A set is a container that holds unique keys and supports *insert* and *test-for-membership* operations. A map, also called a *dictionary* or an *associative array*, associates unique keys with companion objects by pairing the two together and storing those pairs in some data structure. The associative containers multiset and multimap do not require the keys to be unique, and they provide means to traverse the multiple values of equivalent keys.

Although ordering is not an intrinsic quality of these data structures, they order their elements according to a predicate that you optionally provide as a constructor argument (which defaults to less<T>) so that you can treat them as sequences. The standard library also specifies that you can search associative containers for keys in logarithmic time (see "Complexity," first section of Chap. 15). A typical implementation uses some type of tree structure to fulfill these requirements. These containers also provide custom versions of basic algorithms, such as find and count, which operate more efficiently than the generic versions.

The program in Listing 16.2 illustrates a set of strings. Note that the attempt to insert "Tennessee" twice was ignored. The map example in Listing 16.3 shows two ways to insert pairs. One way is to call the insert member function with a pair. The pair template (with members first and second) is part of the standard library; element_type in this case is a pair<string, string>. The other is to use operator[] with a key as the index. Note that the ordering is ascending lexicographical order in both examples, since the default ordering predicate is less<string>. Note also that map<string>::operator[] overwrote "Nashville" with "Knoxville". A call to insert on an existing key, on the other hand, would have been ignored.

Applications

The power of the standard library is best appreciated by studying realistic examples. Listing 16.4 contains a *file inclusion* program. It reads text lines and echoes them to standard output, except for lines that begin with the token #include. For these lines the program substitutes the contents of the files indicated by the next token, like the C/C++ preprocessor does, and repeats the process recursively for nested files, but *only* for files not currently being processed. The program uses a set to keep track of the active files.

The program in Listing 16.5 is a cross-reference–listing generator. It reads tokens from text files, keeping track of the line number where each token occurs. Since tokens need only be listed once, and their line numbers likewise, I use a map that pairs a string with a set of line numbers. Note the simplicity of the inner while loop that populates the map. The line

```
m.insert(make_pair(token,val_type()));
```

inserts an empty set the first time a token appears; subsequent assignments are ignored. The next line retrieves the set associated with a token, then uses it as an lvalue to store the new line number (but again, duplicates are ignored). The library function template make_pair creates pairs on the fly.

Listing 16.2 Illustrates a set of strings

```cpp
// set.cpp
#include <iostream>
#include <set>
#include <string>
using namespace std;

main()
{
    // Populate a set:
    set<string> s;
    s.insert("Alabama");
    s.insert("Georgia");
    s.insert("Tennessee");
    s.insert("Tennessee");

    // Print it out:
    set<string>::iterator p = s.begin();
    while (p != s.end())
        cout << *p++ << endl;      cout << endl;
    // Do some searches:
    string key = "Alabama";
    p = s.find(key);
    cout << (p != s.end() ? "found " : "didn't find ")
         << key << endl;

    key = "Michigan";
    p = s.find(key);
    cout << (p != s.end() ? "found " : "didn't find ")
         << key << endl;
}

// Output:
Alabama
Georgia
Tennessee
found Alabama
didn't find Michigan
```

Listing 16.3 Maps strings to strings

```cpp
// map.cpp
#include <iostream>
#include <map>
#include <string>
using namespace std;
```

Listing 16.3   (continued)

```
main()
{
    // Convenient typedefs:
    typedef map<string, string, greater<string>()> map_type;
    typedef map_type::value_type element_type;
    // Insert some elements (two ways):
    map_type m;
    m.insert(element_type(string("Alabama"),string("Montgomery")));
    m["Georgia"] = "Atlanta";
    m["Tennessee"] = "Nashville";
    m["Tennessee"] = "Knoxville";

    // Print the map:
    map_type::iterator p = m.begin();
    while (p != m.end())
    {
        element_type elem = *p++;
        cout << '{' << elem.first << ',' << elem.second << "}\n";
    }
    cout << endl;

    // Retrieve via a key:
    cout << '"' << m["Georgia"] << '"' << endl;
    cout << '"' << m["Texas"] << '"' << endl;
}

// Output:
{Alabama,Montgomery}
{Georgia,Atlanta}
{Tennessee,Knoxville}
"Atlanta"
""
```

Listing 16.4   A recursion-safe file includer

```
// include.cpp: Nested file inclusion
#include <iostream>
#include <fstream>
#include <sstream>
#include <set>
#include <string>
using namespace std;
```

continued

Listing 16.4   (continued)

```
// List of active filenames:
set<string> files;
void include(const string&);

main(int argc, char* argv[])
{
    if (argc > 1)
        try
        {
            include(argv[1]);
        }
        catch (string& s)
        {
            cerr << s << endl;
        }
}

void include(const string& fname)
{
    // Open file; add to list:
    ifstream f(fname.c_str());
    if (!f)
        throw string("error opening file: ") + fname;
    files.insert(fname);

    // Process file:
    string line;
    while (getline(f, line, '\n'))
    {
        // Inspect first token:
        istringstream is(line);
        string word;
        is >> word;

        if (word == "#include")
        {
            // Attempt to include nested file:
            string nested;
            is >> nested;
            if (files.find(nested) == files.end())
                include(nested);
            // else file is ignored
        }
        else
            cout << line << endl;
    }

    // Remove filename from list:
    files.erase(fname);
}
```

Listing 16.5 A cross-reference listing generator

```cpp
// xref.cpp:  Prints line numbers where each word occurs
#include <iostream>
#include <iomanip>
#include <string>
#include <set>
#include <map>
using namespace std;

namespace
{
    typedef set<int> val_type;
    typedef map<string, val_type> map_type;
    const int WORD_WIDTH = 15;
}

main()
{
    string next_token(const string&, int&);
    void print_list(const val_type&);

    map_type m;
    string line;
    int lineno = 0;

    // Read each line:
    while (getline(cin,line,'\n'))
    {
        ++lineno;

        // Process each word in line:
        int pos = 0;
        string token;
        while (!(token = next_token(line,pos)).empty())
        {
            // Populate the map:
            m.insert(make_pair(token,val_type()));
            m[token].insert(lineno);
        }
    }

    // Print results:
    cout << "No. of distinct words: " << m.size() << endl;
    cout.setf(ios::right, ios::adjustfield);
    for (map_type::const_iterator p = m.begin(); p != m.end(); ++p)
```

continued

Listing 16.5   (continued)

```
    {
        cout << setw(WORD_WIDTH) << p->first << setw(0) << ": ";
        print_list(p->second);
        cout << endl;
    }
}

void print_list(const val_type& v)
{
    const int NUM_WIDTH = 5;
    const int INDENT = WORD_WIDTH + 2;
    const int NUMS_PER_LINE = 8;

    val_type::const_iterator p = v.begin();
    for (int i = 0; p != v.end(); ++i, ++p)
    {
        cout << setw(NUM_WIDTH) << *p;

        // Start a new line, if needed:
        if ((i+1) % NUMS_PER_LINE == 0 && i < v.size()-1)
        {
            cout << endl << setw(INDENT) << ' ';
        }
    }
}

string next_token(const string& s, int& pos)
{
    static const string bad_chars =
        " \t\n\v\a\f`~!@#$%^&*()=+[{"
        "]}\\|;:'\",<.>/?-1234567890";

    // Extract next token delimited by "bad_chars":
    int begin = s.find_first_not_of(bad_chars,pos);
    int end = s.find_first_of(bad_chars,begin);
    pos = end;
    if (begin == string::npos)
        return string("");
    else if (end == string::npos)
        return s.substr(begin);
    else
        return s.substr(begin, end-begin);
}
```

The program in Listing 16.6 is a variation on UNIX's `uniq` filter, which removes adjacent duplicate lines from a text file, similarly to what the `unique` algorithm does to containers. My version, however, removes all duplicates, not just adjacent ones. For example, if the input file contains

```
each
peach
pear
plum
i
spy
tom
thumb
tom
thumb
in
the
cupboard
i
spy
mother
hubbard
```

then the second occurrences of the words `tom`, `thumb`, `i`, and `spy` will be removed. The program performs this feat by first sorting the lines indirectly through an index. Before sorting, it initializes `idx` to the identity vector, that is, the sequence `{0, 1, ... <nlines-1>}`. It then

Listing 16.6   Removes repeated lines

```cpp
// uniq.cpp: Prints unique lines from unsorted input.
// Prints only the first of repeated lines.
// This version compares lexicographically.
// File must fit in memory.

#include <algorithm>
#include <iostream>
#include <string>
#include <vector>
using namespace std;

namespace
{
    vector<string> lines;
```

continued

Listing 16.6 (continued)

```
    // Sort Predicates:
    bool less_by_idx(int a, int b)
    {
        return lines[a] < lines[b];
    }

    bool equal_by_idx(int a, int b)
    {
        return lines[a] == lines[b];
    }
}

main()
{
    vector<int> idx;

    // Read lines into memory:
    string line;
    int nlines = 0;
    for ( ; getline(cin, line, '\n'); ++nlines)
    {
        lines.push_back(line);
        idx.push_back(nlines);          // Identity map
    }

    stable_sort(idx.begin(), idx.end(), less_by_idx);

    // Remove indexes to duplicate lines:
    vector<int>::iterator uniq_end = unique(idx.begin(),
                                            idx.end(),
                                            equal_by_idx);

    // Restore correct order of remaining lines:
    sort(idx.begin(), uniq_end);

    // Output unique lines:
    int nuniq = uniq_end - idx.begin();
    for (int i = 0; i < nuniq; ++i)
        cout << lines[idx[i]] << endl;

    cerr << "Number of input lines: "
         << nlines << endl;
    cerr << "Number of repeated lines: "
         << nlines-nuniq << endl;
    cerr << "Number of unique lines: "
         << nuniq << endl;
}
```

sorts idx based on how the corresponding strings in lines compare, via the function object less_by_index. Although it's not necessary with this particular data, I use stable_sort, which leaves items with equal keys in their original relative order in case you want to adapt this program for sort keys that are a subset of a larger object. The unique algorithm then removes the indexes for which the corresponding text line are adjacent duplicates (using equal_by_idx to determine equality), after which sort restores the original order of the surviving indexes.

Non-STL Containers

The algorithms, containers, and iterators discussed so far in this and the previous chapter were presented to the C++ standardization committee as a package entitled "The Standard Template Library" (STL). Before STL, the committee's library group was working on a number of useful but lesser-endowed container classes, most of which STL supplanted. Only two pre-STL containers survived: bitset and valarray. The container bitset provides methods for manipulating a fixed-size but arbitrarily large collection of bits (see Chap. 9). The container valarray, originally named num_array, supports the sophisticated matrix manipulation techniques commonly found in complex numeric computations. Neither bitset nor valarray are full-fledged containers in the STL sense (e.g., they do not support containers).

Theoretically, a valarray can hold a sequence of any type of object, but it is optimized for handling numbers and its operations are mostly mathematical. The following excerpt initializes a valarray, v1, from an array of doubles:

```
// Initialize a valarray as an identity vector:
#include <valarray>

const int N = 10;
const double values[N] = {0,1,2,3,4,5,6,7,8,9};
const valarray<double> v1(values, N);

// v1 == 0 1 2 3 4 5 6 7 8 9
```

Basic valarray operations include logical shifting of its elements up or down; finding the maximum, minimum, sum; and raising each element to a power. Assume the existence of a function print_array in the following:

```
// Basic operations:
print_array("shift(3)",v1.shift(3));
print_array("cshift(3)",v1.cshift(3));     // circular
cout << "min: " << v1.min() << endl;
cout << "max: " << v1.max() << endl;
cout << "sum: " << v1.sum() << endl;
print_array("pow ^ 2",pow(v1,2.0));
```

```
// Output:
shift(3): 3 4 5 6 7 8 9 0 0 0
cshift(3): 3 4 5 6 7 8 9 0 1 2
min: 0
max: 9
sum: 45
pow ^ 2: 0 1 4 9 16 25 36 49 64 81
```

The valarray overloads most of the standard mathematical functions in <math.h>.

A slice is an object that represents a subsequence of a valarray, defined by its *starting point*, *length*, and *stride*, the latter being the distance between the elements of interest in the host valarray. The following example defines a slice starting at position 1, of size 3, with a stride of 3. When used as an index for v1, the host elements indicated by the slice are extracted into a temporary valarray.

```
slice s(1,3,3);
print_array("v1[s]", v1[s]);

// Output:
v1[s]: 1 4 7
```

A gslice (*generalized slice*) defines more complex subsequences. In the example that follows, gs specifies a subsequence which is itself a collection of two subsequences: one with a length of 2 (len[0]) and a stride of 3 (stride[0]), the other with a length of 3 (len[1]) and stride of 2 (stride[1]), both starting at position 1. Indexing v1 with gs combines these two subsequences ({1 3 5} and {4 6 8}) into one temporary valarray result.

```
// Generalized slice:
valarray<size_t> len(2);        // length vector
len[0] = 2;
len[1] = 3;
valarray<size_t> stride(2);     // stride vector
stride[0] = 3;
stride[1] = 2;
gslice gs(1, len, stride);
print_array("v1[gs]", v1[gs]);
cout << endl;

// Output:
v1[gs]: 1 3 5 4 6 8
```

The template parameter for the length and stride arrays that define the gslice must be size_t.

You can also use a `valarray<bool>` as a mask to extract elements, as in

```
// Masking:
valarray<bool> mask(5);
mask[1] = mask[2] = mask[4] = true;
print_array("v1[mask]", v1[mask]);

// Output:
v1[mask]: 1 2 4
```

or a `valarray<size_t>` to select elements by index:

```
// Indirect indexing:
valarray<size_t> idx(4);
idx[0] = 2;
idx[1] = 2;
idx[2] = 3;
idx[3] = 6;
print_array("v1[idx]", v1[idx]);

// Output:
v1[idx]: 2 2 3 6
```

As if all of this weren't enough, you can use any of these indexing schemes to assign to a valarray as well; for example,

```
// Assignment:
valarray<char> v2("each peach pear plum", 20);
valarray<char> caps("EPPP", 4);
idx[0] = 0;
idx[1] = 5;
idx[2] = 11;
idx[3] = 16;
v2[idx] = caps;
print_array("after v2[idx] = caps", v2);

// Output:
after v2[idx] = caps: E a c h   P e a c h   P e a r   P l u m
```

Summary

- Standard containers can hold objects of any concrete type, including other containers. Concrete types are types that have *value semantics*, meaning they can be copied, assigned, and compared for equality or inequality.
- Standard containers fall into one of three categories: *basic sequences, container adapters,* or *associative containers*.

- The *basic sequences* are `vector`, `deque`, and `list`. They differ chiefly in where they allow efficient insertion and deletion of elements, and in what kind of iterators they support.
- An *iterator* is a generalization of a pointer that lets you traverse a sequence with normal C/C++ pointer syntax. The power of the standard C++ library lies in treating algorithms, containment, and sequence traversal as separate but cooperating concepts. Iterators are the *glue* that connects algorithms and containers in a generic way.
- Iterators fall into one of five categories: *input, output, forward, bidirectional,* and *random access*.
- The standard library specifies algorithms in terms of the types of iterators they require. Containers that do not support an algorithm's iterator requirements often define their own version (e.g., `list<T>::sort`).
- The *container adapters* are `stack`, `queue`, and `priority_queue`. Container adapters wrap basic sequences in a more restrictive interface to implement a higher level of data abstraction.
- The *associative containers* are `set`, `multiset`, `map`, and `multimap`. Associative containers `set` and `map` store only unique keys, whereas the other two permit equivalent keys. These containers support fast (viz. logarithmic) retrieval of keys and can be treated as sequences per a user-defined ordering.
- The special-purpose containers `bitset` and `valarray` do not support the container-iterator-algorithm theme like the other standard containers do.

Text Processing

Most functions in the standard C library are engi-
neered to do one simple task well. Two exceptions to this rule are scanf and printf. They
attempt to handle most of what needs to be done with the input and output of text, which is no
simple task! Although they are usually the first functions a C programmer learns to use, they are
among the last to be mastered. This chapter illustrates some of the finer points of these and other
text-processing functions, as well as the standard C++ string class.

scanf

Since most text input items seem to be separated by whitespace, scanf consumes runs of
optional whitespace for each space character in its format string. There is never a need to have
two consecutive space characters in a scan format. For example, the statements

```
int n;
char c;
scanf("%d %c",&n,&c);
```

read an integer, followed by any amount of whitespace (including none at all), and finally a single, nonwhitespace character (the scan is not completed until a nonwhitespace character is
found). This means that whether the input stream contains

```
123a
```

or

```
123
a
```

either way, n == 123 and c == a.

The following program allows you to separate input items by commas instead:

```
#include <stdio.h>

main()
{
    int n;
    char c;

    while (scanf("%d , %c%*c",&n, &c) == 2)
        printf("%d, %c\n",n,c);
    return 0;
}
```

With the following input:

```
123,a
123 , a
123
,
a
123a
```

the output is:

```
123, a
123, a
123, a
<error>
```

Nonwhite characters in a scan format, such as the comma here, must correspondingly appear in the input stream. If not, as is the case with the last example input line, scanf returns EOF as an error indicator (it normally returns the number of arguments successfully read). Note the white-space around the comma in the format string. Without this, only the first input line would have succeeded.

The occurrence of "%*c" is an example of *assignment suppression*, meaning that the corresponding input is consumed but not stored. Its purpose here is to consume the newline character (I assume that the character 'a' is followed immediately by a carriage return). Suppressed arguments do not contribute to the argument count returned by scanf. When programs that use scanf run interactively, it is easy to get out of sync with the user. For example, if the user enters

```
123,abc
```

by mistake, the program will fail when it encounters the 'c' (the 'b' being consumed by assignment suppression). With interactive programs, it is better to read an entire line, and then scan that line with sscanf.

The following program ignores extraneous input, reports incorrect input, and then continues execution until the user signals an end-of-file. It is also possible to control the size of the items read by adding a field width to the format descriptor (see Listing 17.1).

Listing 17.1 Controls input field width

```c
#include <stdio.h>

main()
{
    char *s = "hello there 12345.67089";
    char s1[6], s2[6], s3[6];
    int n1, n2, nargs;
    float f;

    nargs = sscanf(s,"%20s%3s%s%3d%5f%d",
        s1,s2,s3,&n1,&f,&n2);
    printf("%d: %s,%s,%s,%d,%f,%d\n",
        nargs,s1,s2,s3,n1,f,n2);
    return 0;
}
```

Output
6: hello,the,re,123,45.669998,89

```c
#include <stdio.h>
#define MAXLINE 80

main()
{
    int n;
    char c, buf[MAXLINE+1];

    while (gets(buf))
        if (sscanf(buf,"%d , %c",&n, &c) == 2)
            printf("%d, %c\n",n,c);
        else
            printf("Invalid input: \"%s\"\n",buf);
    return 0;
}
```

It is often convenient to control what type of characters are read into certain variables. This is done with a *scanset*, which is a format descriptor consisting of the set of desired characters enclosed in brackets. The example in Listing 17.2 uses this technique to read a string of binary digits. Scansets differ from other format descriptors in that they do not skip initial whitespace. Listing 17.3 has a function, fgetb, that uses a scanset to read a binary number from an input stream. Using the same input as in Listing 17.2, the output from Listing 17.3 would be

The number was 22

Listing 17.2   Controls input via a scanset

```
#include <stdio.h>

#define MAXLINE 80

main()
{
    char bin[MAXLINE+1];
    int n, nargs = scanf("%[01]%d",bin,&n);

    printf("nargs: %d, bin: %s, n: %d\n",nargs,bin,n);
    return 0;
}

/* Input: */
1011035

/* Output: */
nargs: 2, bin: 10110, n: 35
```

Scansets are also useful when input occurs in a fixed format, such as in database applications. The following little program expects a line with four input items: a string, followed by two integers, followed by another string, all separated by commas.

```
#include <stdio.h>
main()
{
    char s1[BUFSIZ], s2[BUFSIZ];
    int n1, n2;

    scanf(" %[^,],%i ,%i , %[^\n]",s1,&n1,&n2,s2);
    printf("%s,%d,%d,%s\n",s1,n1,n2,s2);
    return 0;
}

/* Input: */
key 1,0x20,10,value one

/* Output: */
key 1,32,10,value one
```

When a circumflex occurs as the first element of a scanset, it reverses its meaning: The scan should then collect characters that are *not* in the scanset. In plain English, the scan format above

Listing 17.3   Illustrates a function that reads binary numbers

```c
#include <stdio.h>
#include <string.h>
#include <limits.h>          /* For CHAR_BIT */
#include <assert.h>

#define MAXBITS (sizeof(int) * CHAR_BIT - 1)

int fgetb(FILE *fp)
{
    int i;
    unsigned sum = 0, value = 1;
    char buf[BUFSIZ];
    assert(fp);

    if (fscanf(fp," %[01]",buf) != 1 || strlen(buf) > MAXBITS)
        return EOF;

    for (i = strlen(buf) - 1; i >= 0; --i)
    {
        if (buf[i] == '1')
            sum += value;
        value *= 2;
    }
    return sum;
}

main()
{
    int n = fgetb(stdin);
    printf("The number was %d\n",n);
    return 0;
}
```

says, "Skip any initial whitespace; then build a string consisting of all characters up to the next comma; then ignore that comma; read two integers, ignoring the intervening comma; then skip any whitespace; finally, collect all the remaining characters in the line as a string." The "%i" format descriptor reads integers according to their base prefixes (i.e., "0x" for hexadecimal, "0" for octal, decimal otherwise).

Listing 17.4 illustrates a use for the "%n" descriptor, which stores the total number of input characters consumed so far into a variable pointed to by the argument in the variable list. It extracts tokens (in this case, strings separated by whitespace) from standard input, but on a line-by-line basis.

Listing 17.4   Illustrates the %n edit descriptor

```c
#include <stdio.h>

main()
{
    char buf[BUFSIZ];
    int nlines;

    for (nlines = 0; gets(buf) != NULL; ++nlines)
    {
        int temp, offset = 0;
        char s[BUFSIZ];

        printf("Line %d: ",nlines+1);
        while (sscanf(buf+offset,"%s%n",s,&temp) == 1)
        {
            printf("$%s$ ",s);
            offset += temp; /* Track position in line */
        }
        putchar('\n');
    }
    return 0;
}

/* Executing this program with its own text as input gives this result: */

Line  1: $#include$ $<stdio.h>$
Line  2:
Line  3: $main()$
Line  4: ${$
Line  5: $char$ $buf[BUFSIZ];$
Line  6: $int$ $nlines;$
Line  7:
Line  8: $for$ $(nlines$ $=$ $0;$ $gets(buf)$ $!=$ $NULL;$ $++nlines)$
Line  9: ${$
Line 10: $int$ $temp,$ $offset$ $=$ $0;$
Line 11: $char$ $s[BUFSIZ];$
Line 12:
Line 13: $printf("Line$ $%2d:$ $",nlines+1);$
Line 14: $while$ $(sscanf(buf+offset,"%s%n",s,&temp)$ $==$ $1)$
Line 15: ${$
Line 16: $printf("$%s$$ $",s);$
Line 17: $offset$ $+=$ $temp;$ $/*$ $Track$ $position$ $in$ $line$ $*/$
Line 18: $}$
Line 19: $putchar('\n');$
Line 20: $}$
Line 21: $return$ $0;$
Line 22: $}$
```

printf

The quintessential "first program" for the student of C is some variant of "Hello, world":

```
/* hello.c:    A first program */
#include <stdio.h>

main()
{
    printf("Hello, world\n");
}
```

This provides a point of departure for discussing basic syntax and program layout, the notion of include files, and most importantly, how to produce output. Most programmers spend their first hours of C exploration discovering the ins and outs of printf. But mastering this most flexible of functions requires more than just a few hours. Consider the output from the following statements:

```
printf("|%5.4d|  |%-5.3s|  |%5.0f|\n",123, "a string", 45.6);
printf("|%+5d|  |%+5d|  |% 5d|  |% 5d|\n",123, 123, 123, 123);
printf("|%#5o|  |%#5x|  |%#5.0f|\n", 15, 15, 15.0);

// Output:
| 0123|  |a s  |  |   46|
| +123|  | -123|  |  123|  | -123|
|  017|  |  0xf|  |  15.|
```

The first statement illustrates the effect of precision (specified with a decimal point followed by an integer). For an integer, it specifies the *minimum* number of digits to be displayed. All this really means is that leading zeroes will appear if necessary to fill out the given precision. With strings, the precision specifies the *maximum* number of characters of the string to display (note that this example left-justifies the result because of the "-" flag). A precision of zero causes a floating point number to be rounded to the nearest integer and displayed without a decimal point. To display a decimal point but no subsequent decimal digits, use the "#" flag, as shown in the third statement. The "+" flag always causes a sign to be displayed, whereas the " " flag substitutes a space for the plus sign. The "#" flag prints an integer with its characteristic notation (viz., a leading "0" for octal, a leading "0x" for hexadecimal, and a decimal point for real numbers). Under all circumstances, all significant digits are displayed, even if the field width (and precision in the case of integers) is exceeded.

It is often convenient to format a string and save it for repeated use, instead of sending it to an output device immediately. This is traditionally called *in-core formatting* and is supported by the sprintf function. The following statement builds a date string in a character array:

```
char s[9];
sprintf(s,"%2d/%02d/%02d",mon,day,year);
```

The function `sprintf` always appends a terminating zero byte to the formatted string. It returns the number of characters formatted (not including the terminating null). In the following program `sprintf` appends trailing blanks to a string, filling it out to a specified size.

```
/* pad.c:    Add trailing blanks to a string */
#include <stdio.h>
#include <string.h>

char *pad(char *s, int size)
{
    int len = strlen(s);
    if (s && len < size)
        sprintf(s+len,"%*c",size-len,' ');
    return s;
}
```

This program also illustrates how to specify a variable-length format in C. The `"*"` edit descriptor can appear as a width or a precision specifier. It indicates that the next argument in the print list (which must be an `int`) should be used as the field width (or precision). The preceding `if`-statement is necessary; otherwise a single blank will always be printed, even if `size-len` is zero.

Variable-length format is also useful when formatting reports or screen output. Instead of allowing long lines to wrap, it is usually preferable to truncate them and then provide some other way (like scrolling) to view the suppressed data. The following segment displays a line on screen without wrapping:

```
#define WIDTH 80
. . .
fprintf(stderr,"%-.*s",WIDTH,line);
```

while this statement right-justifies a row in a report:

```
fprintf(f,"%*.*s\n",WIDTH,WIDTH,line);
```

While `printf` provides some support for zero and blank padding, it is often not enough. For example, in financial applications it is convenient to specify an arbitrary pad character (like asterisks for check protection). Listing 17.5 shows a function, `align`, that places a string into a field with left, right, or center justification and that pads with a user-supplied character.

The following calls to `align`

```
align(s,10,'*',LEFT,"123.45")
align(s,10,'*',CENTER,"123.45")
align(s,10,'*',RIGHT,"123.45")
```

build inside `s[]` the following strings, respectively:

```
123.45****
**123.45**
****123.45
```

Listing 17.5   Aligns a string within a user-supplied field

```
/* align.c: Align a string within a background */

#include <string.h>

#define LEFT (-1)
#define CENTER 0
#define RIGHT 1

#define min(x,y) ((x) <= (y) ? (x) : (y))

char *align(char *buf,int width,char fill,int justify,char *data)
{
    char *p;

    /* Truncate, if necessary */
    int dlen = min(width,strlen(data));

    /* Populate with fill character */
    memset(buf,fill,width);
    buf[width] = '\0';

    /* Calculate starting point */
    if (justify == LEFT)
        p = buf;
    else if (justify == CENTER)
        p = buf + (width-dlen)/2;
    else
        p = buf + width-dlen;

    /* Insert the data there */
    memcpy(p,data,dlen);
    return buf;
}
```

Substrings

Much of text processing concerns itself with substrings—finding or extracting strings that are embedded within lines of text. The program find1.c in Listing 17.6 prints all lines from a text file that contain a given string.

Applying find1 to its own source file with "search" as the search string (argv[1]) gives the following output:

```
char *search_str;
search_str = argv[1];
    if (strstr(line,search_str))
```

Listing 17.6   Extracts lines from a text file

```
/* find1.c:     Extract lines from a file */

#include <stdio.h>
#include <string.h>

#define WIDTH 128

main(int argc, char *argv[])
{
    char line[WIDTH];
    char *search_str;

    if (argc == 1)
        return 1;        /* Search string required */
    search_str = argv[1];

    while (gets(line))
        if (strstr(line,search_str))
            puts(line);

    return 0;
}
```

The find1 program calls the function strstr to determine if one string is a substring of another. The strstr(s1,s2) returns a pointer to the first occurrence of s2 in s1, if it exists, or NULL if it doesn't. Only exact matches succeed (which is why the line with the comment "/* Search ... " didn't print). To ignore case in the search, convert copies of the strings to the same case, as the program find2.c illustrates in Listing 17.7. Processing find1.c with the find2 program now gives all occurrences of the search string, regardless of case:

```
char *search_str;
    return 1;   /* Search string required */
search_str = argv[1];
    if (strstr(line,search_str))
```

Although most compilers provide the function strlwr, it is not a standard library function. However, you can easily write it yourself as follows:

```
/* strlwr.c:    Convert a string to lower case */
#include <ctype.h>
```

```
char *strlwr(char *s)
{
    if (s != NULL)
    {
        char *p;

        for (p = s; *p; ++p)
            *p = tolower(*p);
    }
    return s;
}
```

Many classic programs are command driven; that is, they sequentially process lines of text representing user instructions. (This is how the command interpreters in the DOS and UNIX shells work, of course.) Each line is parsed into its components, usually called *tokens*. The

Listing 17.7 Same as Listing 17.6 except ignores case in letters

```
/* find2.c:    A case-insensitive substring search */

#include <stdio.h>
#include <string.h>

#define WIDTH 128

main(int argc, char *argv[])
{
    char line[WIDTH], lline[WIDTH];
    char *search_str;

    if (argc == 1)
        return 1;    /* Search string required */
    search_str = argv[1];
    strlwr(search_str);

    while (gets(line))
    {
        strlwr(strcpy(lline,line));
        if (strstr(lline,search_str))
            puts(line);
    }

    return 0;
}
```

Listing 17.8 Extracts tokens by ignoring space and punctuation

```
/* token1.c:      Parse input strings into tokens */

#include <stdio.h>
#include <string.h>

main()
{
    char s[81], *break_set =
       " \t\n\f\v\\\"~!@#$%^&*()-_=+`'[]{}|;:/?.,<>";

    while (gets(s) != NULL)
    {
        char *tokp, *sp = s;

        while ((tokp = strtok(sp,break_set)) != NULL)
        {
            puts(tokp);
            sp = NULL;      /* continue in this string */
        }
    }
    return 0;
}

/* Input: */
This is 1just2a3test#.
Good-bye.

/* Output: */
This
is
1just2a3test
Good
bye
*/
```

library function `strtok` recognizes tokens as substrings scattered among separators (sometimes called *break characters*). It skips any leading separators and then collects characters as a substring until another separator is encountered. The program in Listing 17.8 extracts tokens by ignoring space and punctuation characters. It first calls `strtok` with a pointer to the beginning of the line to be parsed. The library function `strtok` inserts a null character directly into the string to delimit the first token (overwriting the space after the `'s'` in `"This"`), sets its internal pointer to the character after that null character (the `'i'` in "is"), and returns a pointer to the beginning of the first token (the `'T'` in "This"):

T	h	i	s	\0	i	s		l	j	u	s	t	...

When you call `strtok` with a `NULL` first argument, it picks up where it left off (the `'i'` in `"is"`). When it can no longer find any tokens, `strtok` itself returns `NULL`. Note that you can change the break set at runtime with each call to `strtok`, which makes this parsing scheme somewhat more flexible than using `sscanf`.

To ignore digits as well as space and punctuation, we merely add them to the break set string. It doesn't take long, however, to realize that break sets can become quite unwieldy. It is often easier to specify the characters that constitute tokens rather than to separate them. Listing 17.9 introduces such a function, `strtokf`, which is similar to `strtok` except that it recognizes tokens via a user-supplied function that identifies acceptable characters. The program in Listing

Listing 17.9 Recognizes tokens via a user-defined function

```
/* strtokf.c:      Collect tokens via a function */

#include <stdio.h>
#include <string.h>

static char *sp = NULL;     /* Internal string position */

char *strtokf(char *s, int (*f)(char))
{
    if (s != NULL)
        sp = s;             /* Remember string address */
    if (sp == NULL)
        return NULL;        /* No string supplied */

    /* Skip leading, unwanted characters */
    while (*sp != '\0' && !f(*sp))
        ++sp;
    s = sp;                 /* Token starts here */

    /* Build token */
    while (*sp != '\0' && f(*sp))
        ++sp;
    if (*sp != '\0')
        *sp++ = '\0';       /* Insert string terminator */

    return strlen(s) ? s : NULL;
}
```

Listing 17.10   Uses `strtokf` to extract tokens

```
/* token2.c: Parse input strings via strtokf() */

#include <stdio.h>
#include <ctype.h>

char *strtokf(char *, int (*)(char));
static int filter(char);

main()
{
    char s[81];

    while (gets(s))
    {
        char *tokp, *sp = s;

        while ((tokp = strtokf(sp,filter)) != NULL)
        {
            puts(tokp);
            sp = NULL;
        }
    }
    return 0;
}

static int filter(char c)
{
    return isalpha(c);
}
```

17.10 uses `strtokf` to extract alphabetic tokens from the same input as in the previous example. This time the output is

```
This
is
just
a
test
Good
bye
```

Another common parsing practice locates specific delimiting characters in a string, similar to the `scanf` technique in the beginning of this chapter (this is especially useful for parsing filenames). The standard library provides this capability via the two functions

```
char *strchr(char *s, char c);
char *strrchr(char *s, char c);
```

The function `strchr` returns a pointer to the first occurrence of 'c' in 's,' and `strrchr` returns a pointer to the last occurrence (the extra `'r'` in its name signals that it searches from the "rear"). Both functions return `NULL` if the character is not found. The program in Listing 17.11 uses `strchr` to extract fields separated by commas.

The function `strchr` is particularly useful in cases like this where the delimiters can occur adjacent to one another. For example, the input line

```
, , ,
```

would be passed over by `strtok` as a stream of break characters.

Listing 17.11   Uses `strchr` to extract comma-separated fields

```
/* token3.c:    Read comma-delimited fields */

#include <stdio.h>
#include <string.h>

main()
{
    char s[BUFSIZ];

    while (gets(s))
    {
        char *p, *sp = s;
        int nchars;

        do
        {
            /* Make p point at next comma, or '\0'*/
            if ((p = strchr(sp,',')) == NULL)
                p = sp + strlen(sp);
            nchars = p - sp;

            /* Print the field */
            if (sp > s)
                putchar(',');
            printf("\"%.*s\"",nchars,sp);

            /* Position at start of next field */
            sp = p+1;
        } while (*p != '\0');

        putchar('\n');
    }
```

continued

Listing 17.11   (continued)

```
    return 0;
}

/* Input: */
a one,2,a three,4
  a one , 2 , a three , 4
a one,2,a three,
a one,2,,
a one,,,
,,,
a one

/* Output: */
"a one","2","a three","4"
"  a one "," 2 "," a three "," 4"
"a one","2","a three",""
"a one","2","",""
"a one","","",""
"","","",""
"a one"
```

The Standard C++ String Class

If you've done a noticeable amount of text processing with the standard C library, you've more than likely encountered the joys of dynamic memory. Whenever you add text to a C-style string, the array of characters that holds it usually has to grow to make room. Text processing therefore becomes an exercise in heap management, and all of a sudden things aren't fun anymore. The standard C++ string class was designed to put the fun back into string handling by taking care of memory management for you. You can insert, append, and remove text as well as concatenate existing strings into a new string without so much as a `malloc` or a `new` on your part. The program in Listing 17.12 illustrates some of the basic operations of the string class, including searching for and inserting substrings. The `resize` method causes a string to shrink or grow, adding spaces if necessary. Like most functions in the string class, the `find` function is overloaded to take a character, `char*`, or another string as an argument.

The program in Listing 17.13 extracts tokens from a string by repeated calls to my function `next_token`, which behaves like `strtok`. The function `next_token` skips break characters by calling `find_first_not_of` to locate the first character of a token. It then starts from there and calls `find_first_of` to find the next break character. Everything in between is the token. The important distinction between `next_token` and `strtok`, of course, is that the latter

Listing 17.12   Illustrates common string class functions

```cpp
#include <iostream>
#include <string>

using namespace std;

main()
{
    string s1("Mary had a little lamb"),
           s2 = "Old McDonald had a farm";

    // Test some operators
    string s3 = s1 + ", but " + s2;
    cout << s3 << endl;
    s3.resize(s1.length());
    cout.setf(ios::boolalpha);
    cout << "s1 == s3? " << (s1 == s3) << endl;

    // Search and insert
    size_t pos = s2.find("farm");
    s2.insert(pos,"little ");
    cout << "s2 == " << s2 << endl;

    // Subscripting
    s1[s1.length()-1] = 'p';
    cout << "s1 == " << s1 << endl;
    return 0 ;
}

// Output:
Mary had a little lamb, but Old McDonald had a farm
s1 == s3? true
s2 == Old McDonald had a little farm
s1 == Mary had a little lamp
```

is destructive, while next_token leaves the original string untouched. Table 17.1 summarizes the searching functions in the string class, along with their C-library equivalents.

The program in Listing 17.14 replaces all occurrences of a given string with another in the standard input file. One of the most useful features declared in the <string> header is the global function getline. This function reads from an input stream into a string up to a break character, which you supply and it consumes and discards. With getline you no longer have to guess how long your input buffers need to be—it does all of the memory management for you!

Listing 17.13   Extract tokens from a string

```cpp
// extract.cpp: Extract tokens
#include <iostream>
#include <string>

using namespace std;

string next_token(const string&, int&);
string bad_chars = "`1234567890-=~!@#$%^&*()_+[]"
                   "\\{}|;':\",./<>?\t\v\a\n ";        // note space!

main()
{
    string s = "this is 1just2a3test#.";
    int pos = 0;
    string token;
    while (!(token = next_token(s,pos)).empty())
        cout << token << endl;
}

string next_token(const string& s, int& pos)
{
    int begin = s.find_first_not_of(bad_chars,pos);
    int end = s.find_first_of(bad_chars,begin);
    pos = end;

    if (begin == string::npos)
        return string();
    else if (end == string::npos)
        return s.substr(begin);
    else
        return s.substr(begin, end-begin);
}

// Output:
this
is
just
a
test
```

Table 17.1   Equivalent string search functions in C++ and C

C++ string class member function	*Standard C library function*
find	`strstr, strchr`
rfind	`strrchr`
find_first_of	`strcspn, strpbrk` (See Chap. 4)
find_first_not_of	`strspn` (See Chap. 4)
find_last_of	(none)
find_last_not_of	(none)

Listing 17.14   Replaces all occurrences of a string in a file

```cpp
// replace.cpp: Replaces substrings
#include <iostream>
#include <string>

using namespace std;

string replace_all(const string& s,
                   const string& from,
                   const string& to)
{
    string buf = s;          // Copy to return
    int pos = 0;
    while ((pos = buf.find(from,pos)) != string::npos)
    {
        buf.replace(pos,from.size(),to);
        ++pos;
    }
    return buf;
}

main(int argc, char* argv[])
{
    if (argc >= 3)
    {
        string line;
        while (getline(cin,line,'\n'))
            cout << replace_all(line,argv[1],argv[2])
                << endl;
    }
}
```

String Streams

Classic C++ supports in-core formatting with `ostrstream` and `istrstream`, which treat an underlying `char` array as a stream. For example, the following excerpt uses an `ostrstream` to build a string with an embedded numeric value:

```
#include <iostream.h>
#include <strstream.h>

int id = 100;
char buf[BUFSIZ];
ostrstream os(buf);
os << "the id is " << id << ends;
cout << buf << endl;               // prints "the id is 100"
```

There is also a version of `ostrstream` that sizes itself automatically for you. As the following excerpt illustrates, when you call `ostrstream::str()` to get a pointer to the string that has been built, you are responsible for that dynamic data. You must either `delete` it, or give the responsibility back to the `ostrstream` object with the `freeze` function:

```
#include <iostream.h>
#include <strstream.h>

int id = 100;
ostrstream os;                      // no buffer supplied!
os << "the id is " << id << ends;
cout << os.str() << endl;           // prints "the id is 100"
os.rdbuf()->freeze(0);              // Throw the hot potato back
```

The standard C++ library also provides classes `ostringstream` and `istringstream` that enables I/O with strings instead of `char` arrays, so you don't have to worry about buffer sizes and memory leaks. The example above with `ostringstream` comes out as:

```
#include <iostream>
#include <sstream>
#include <string>

using namespace std;

int id = 100;
ostringstream os;                   // no buffer supplied!
os << "the id is " << id;           // ends not needed; nor freeze later
cout << os.str() << endl;           // prints "the id is 100"
```

The program in Listing 17.15 attaches an `istringstream` to a string and parses tokens from it separated by commas. Note the use of `getline` with a comma delimiter to read the first token.

Listing 17.15   Illustrates an input string stream

```
// sstream.cpp: Parse comma-delimited fields in a string
#include <iostream>
#include <sstream>
#include <string>

using namespace std;

main()
{
    string s = "key 1,0x20,10,value one";

    istringstream is(s);
    string key, value;
    int num1, num2;
    char comma;

    // Parse input line:
    getline(is,key,',');
    is >> hex >> num1 >> comma;
    is >> dec >> num2 >> comma;
    getline(is,value,'\n');

    cout << '"' << key << '"' << comma
         << num1 << comma
         << num2 << comma
         << '"' << value << '"'
         << endl;
}

// Output:
"key 1",32,10,"value one"
```

Wide Strings

The string class is an instantiation of a template called `basic_string`, which actually does all the work of text processing. In fact, you should find a declaration something like the following in the `<string>` header (modulo an extra template argument or two):

```
typedef basic_string<char> string;
```

As long as the template argument to basic_string represents a "char-like" class (i.e., something you can do char-like operations on: assignment, equality, and relational comparisons; stream

I/O; etc.), then you can have "strings" of that type for free! Another important flavor of `basic_string` that comes with the standard library is a *wide string*:

```
typedef basic_string<wchar_t> wstring;
```

In C++ `wchar_t` is a first-class type meant to represent *wide characters*, which on most platforms are 16-bit unsigned integers. This makes `wstring`, and the corresponding wide stream classes (`wistream`, `wostream`, etc.) suitable for internationalized development using the Unicode character encoding. See Chapter 5 for more on `wchar_t` and Unicode.

Summary

- Before you write off `scanf` and `printf` as not cool, take a look at all the powerful formatting commands you might miss. They do some things that C++ streams just can't (e.g., scansets).
- In interactive applications it is usually better to read a line at a time and then parse each line as necessary.
- The functions defined in <stdio.h> and <string.h> are handy when your strings don't require memory management.
- The most important feature of the standard C++ string class is *memory management*.
- The standard C++ library supports strings of any "char-like" type via the `basic_string` template.
- Wide strings and streams, coupled with environmental support for Unicode, facilitate international programming.

CHAPTER 18

File Processing

$\mathbf{F}$ ile systems differ greatly from one environment to another. Because there is no universal approach to issues such as directory structure, filenames, I/O modes, or file locking, it is sometimes difficult to write portable programs that use files. This chapter illustrates some of the most commonly used file I/O functions from the C and C++ libraries and also discusses a number of file-processing functions from the POSIX standard.

Filters

The following short program copies a line at a time from standard input to standard output:

```
/* copy1.c */
#include <stdio.h>

main()
{
    char s[BUFSIZ];

    while (gets(s))
        puts(s);
    return 0;
}
```

Defined in <stdio.h>, BUFSIZ is the size of the internal buffers used by many standard I/O functions and is a good choice for the size of your buffers, unless you have a good reason to do differently. Unless you instruct otherwise, the standard I/O functions perform buffered I/O, meaning that data is collected and then transferred a buffer at a time for efficiency.

A C++ streams version of the preceding example might look like this:

```
// copy1.cpp
#include <iostream>
#include <string>
using namespace std;
```

```
main()
{
    string s;

    while (getline(cin, s))
        cout << s << endl;
}
```

The C++ version has the advantage that it doesn't need to worry about buffer size—the `getline` function automatically allocates memory as needed to hold an input line.

On command line–oriented operating systems like MSDOS and UNIX, these programs are more interesting than they appear. In conjunction with *redirection* you can create a file from the console:

```
C:> copy1 >file1
```

After entering the lines of text, enter Ctrl-Z (in MSDOS; Ctrl-D in UNIX) on a line by itself to signal the end of input. To make a copy of an existing file, enter

```
C:> copy1 <file1 >file2
```

A program like this one that reads only from standard input and writes only to standard output is called a *filter*.

It is also possible to redirect from within the program itself via the `freopen` library function, which disconnects an open file pointer from its file and connects it to a new one. The program in Listing 18.1 disconnects `stdin` and/or `stdout` from the console and connects them to the files entered on the command line. You could invoke `copy2` without explicit redirection like this:

```
C:> copy2 file1 file2
```

The names of the files become arguments to `main`. Using `freopen` is convenient because you don't have to explicitly open and close files, but it disallows any interaction with the user (since the console has been redirected to files). Most interactive applications, however, require both file and console I/O. The version in Listing 18.2 shows how to open files explicitly—no redirection is performed, and both filenames are required.

The function `fgets` differs from `gets` in that it needs to know how big your buffer is (`gets` just assumes there is enough room). It reads up to one less than that many characters so it can append a `'\0'`, and it keeps the newline character in the string it returns (if there's room; `gets` always discards it). Their respective companion output functions act as you would expect: `puts` appends a newline to output, and `fputs` does not.

Both `fgets` and `gets` return NULL upon end-of-file or error; any additional error-checking is not usually required. You should, however, do explicit checks for output errors, especially on a PC-like system where running out of disk space is not uncommon (on floppy diskettes, for

Listing 18.1 A copy filter that allows optional redirection

```c
/* copy2.c */

#include <stdio.h>
#include <stdlib.h>

main(int argc, char *argv[])
{
    char s[BUFSIZ];

    /* Open optional input file */
    if (argc > 1)
        if (freopen(argv[1],"r",stdin) == NULL)
            return EXIT_FAILURE;

    /* Open optional output file */
    if (argc > 2)
        if (freopen(argv[2],"w",stdout) == NULL)
            return EXIT_FAILURE;

    while (gets(s))
        puts(s);
    return EXIT_SUCCESS;
}
```

Listing 18.2 Copies files via explicit file pointers

```c
/* copy3.c */
#include <stdio.h>
#include <stdlib.h>

main(int argc, char *argv[])
{
    if (argc == 3)
    {
        char s[BUFSIZ];
        FILE *inf, *outf;

        if ((inf = fopen(argv[1],"r")) == NULL)
            return EXIT_FAILURE;

        if ((outf = fopen(argv[2],"w")) == NULL)
            return EXIT_FAILURE;

        while (fgets(s,BUFSIZ,inf))
            fputs(s,outf);
```

continued

Listing 18.2   (continued)

```
            fclose(inf);
            fclose(outf);
            return EXIT_SUCCESS;
        }
        else
            return EXIT_FAILURE;
}
```

example). You do this with a call to `ferror`. For example, you should replace the `while` loop in Listing 18.2 with the following:

```
/* copy4.c */
    ...
            while (fgets(buf,BUFSIZ,inf))
            {
                fputs(buf,outf);
                fflush(outf);
                if (ferror(outf))
                    return EXIT_FAILURE;
            }
    ...
```

Since file I/O is buffered, you must flush the output buffer before checking for an error. Once the error state of a file is set, it remains unchanged until you reset it by calling `clearerr` or `rewind`.

Listing 18.3 has a C++ version of Listing 18.2. File stream constructors automatically open the files indicated by their string arguments. When a stream appears in a boolean expression, it returns false if an error or end-of-file has occurred. The `getline` function returns its stream argument, so you can test it the same way.

Binary Files

The examples so far work only with text files (i.e., files of lines delimited by `'\n'`). In order to copy any file whatsoever, such as an executable program, it is necessary to open the file in *binary mode*. In *text mode* under MSDOS, each newline character in memory is replaced with a `"\r\n"` pair (CRLF) on the output device, while the process is reversed during input (this is a carryover from ancient CP/M days). In addition, a Ctrl-Z is interpreted as end-of-file, so it is impossible to read past a Ctrl-Z in text mode. In binary mode no such translations are made—the data in memory and on disk are the same.

The program in Listing 18.4 can copy any type of file. A `"b"` appended to the usual open mode indicates binary mode. The functions `fread` and `fwrite` read and write blocks of data, and they return the number of blocks (not bytes) successfully processed. In the example in Listing 18.4, the items just happen to be bytes (i.e., blocks of length 1). When `fwrite` returns a

Listing 18.3 A C++ version of Listing 18.2

```cpp
// copy3.cpp
#include <iostream>
#include <fstream>
#include <string>
using namespace std;

main(int argc, char *argv[])
{
    if (argc == 3)
    {
        string s;
        ifstream inf(argv[1]);
        ofstream outf(argv[2]);
        if (!inf || !outf)
            return;

        while (getline(inf,s))
            outf << s << endl;
    }
}
```

Listing 18.4 Copies binary files

```c
/* copy5.c */
#include <stdio.h>
#include <stdlib.h>

main(int argc, char *argv[])
{
    if (argc == 3)
    {
        char buf[BUFSIZ];
        FILE *inf, *outf;

        if ((inf = fopen(argv[1],"rb")) == NULL)
            return EXIT_FAILURE;

        if ((outf = fopen(argv[2],"wb")) == NULL)
            return EXIT_FAILURE;

        while (!feof(inf))
        {
            int nitems = fread(buf,1,BUFSIZ,inf);
```

continued

Listing 18.4   (continued)

```
            if (fwrite(buf,1,nitems,outf) != nitems)
                return EXIT_FAILURE;
        }

        fclose(inf);
        fclose(outf);
        return EXIT_SUCCESS;
    }
    else
        return EXIT_FAILURE;
}
```

number less than the number of items requested, you know that a write error has occurred, in which case an explicit call to `ferror` isn't necessary. Any noncharacter data written by `fwrite` is stored in binary on the output device and is generally not meant for human eyes. C++ streams have `read` and `write` methods that behave analogously to `fread` and `fwrite` (see Listing 18.5). The function `istream::gcount` in Listing 18.5 returns the "get count," the number of bytes transferred by `istream::read`.

Record Processing

The functions `fread` and `fwrite` are suitable for processing files of fixed-length records. The program in Listing 18.6 populates a file from keyboard input (terminated by Ctrl-Z) and then randomly accesses certain records. I've often used `stderr` for printing prompts because it is always attached to the console and is unbuffered on most systems.

A `"+"` in the open mode request indicates update mode, which means that both input and output are allowed on the file. You must separate input and output operations, however, with a call to `fflush` or to some file-positioning command, such as `fseek` or `rewind`. The command `fseek` positions the read/write cursor a given number of bytes from the beginning of the file (`SEEK_SET`), from the end of the file (`SEEK_END`), or from the current position (`SEEK_CUR`). The command `rewind` is equivalent to `fseek(f,0L,SEEK_SET)`. Arbitrary byte positions passed to `fseek` only make sense in binary mode, since in text mode there may be embedded characters you know nothing about. The function `ftell` returns the current position in a file, which value can be passed to `fseek` to return to that position. (This synchronized use of `fseek` and `ftell` works even in text mode.) Since `fseek` and `ftell` take a `long` integer argument for the file position, they are limited in the size of file they can correctly traverse. If your system supports larger file position values, you can randomly traverse them via the library functions `fgetpos` and `fsetpos`, which traffic in values of type `fpos_t`, a type that may or may not be an integral value.

The program in Listing 18.7 puts `fgetpos` and `fsetpos` to good use in a simple four-way scrolling browser for large files. It keeps only one screen's worth of text in memory. If you want to scroll up or down through the file, it reads (or rereads) the adjacent text and displays it. When

Listing 18.5 A C++ version of Listing 18.4

```cpp
// copy5.cpp
#include <iostream>
#include <fstream>
#include <stdlib.h>
using namespace std;

main(int argc, char *argv[])
{
    if (argc == 3)
    {
        char buf[BUFSIZ];

        ifstream inf(argv[1], ios::in | ios::binary);
        ofstream outf(argv[2], ios::out | ios::binary);

        while (inf)
        {
            inf.read(buf,BUFSIZ);
            outf.write(buf,inf.gcount());
            if (!outf)
                return EXIT_FAILURE;
        }
        return inf.fail() ? EXIT_FAILURE : EXIT_SUCCESS;
    }
    else
        return EXIT_FAILURE;
}
```

Listing 18.6 Processes fixed-length record files

```c
/* records.c: Illustrates file positioning */
#include <stdio.h>
#include <string.h>
#include <stdlib.h>

#define MAXRECS 10

struct record
{
    char last[16];
    char first[11];
    int age;
};
```

continued

Listing 18.6   (continued)

```
static char *get_field(char *, char *);

main()
{
    int nrecs;
    char s[81];
    struct record recs[MAXRECS], recbuf;
    FILE *f;

    /* Carefully store records */
    for (nrecs = 0; nrecs < MAXRECS && get_field("Last",s); ++nrecs)
    {
        strncpy(recs[nrecs].last,s,15)[15] = '\0';
        get_field("First",s);
        strncpy(recs[nrecs].first,s,10)[10] = '\0';
        get_field("Age",s);
        recs[nrecs].age = atoi(s);
    }

    /* Write records to file */
    if ((f = fopen("recs.dat","w+b")) == NULL)
        return EXIT_FAILURE;
    if (fwrite(recs,sizeof recs[0],nrecs,f) != nrecs)
        return EXIT_FAILURE;

    /* Position at last record */
    fseek(f,(nrecs-1)*sizeof(struct record),SEEK_SET);
    fread(&recbuf,1,sizeof(struct record),f);
    printf("last: %s, first: %s, age: %d\n",
      recbuf.last,recbuf.first,recbuf.age);

    /* Position at first record */
    rewind(f);
    fread(&recbuf,1,sizeof(struct record),f);
    printf("last: %s, first: %s, age: %d\n",
      recbuf.last,recbuf.first,recbuf.age);

    return EXIT_SUCCESS;
}

static char *get_field(char *prompt, char *buf)
{
    /* Prompt for input field */
    fprintf(stderr,"%s: ",prompt);
    return gets(buf);
}
```

Listing 18.6   (continued)

```
/* Output: */
Last: Lincoln
First: Abraham
Age: 188
Last: Bach
First: Johann
Age: 267
Last: Tse
First: Lao
Age: 3120
last: Tse, first: Lao, age: 3120
last: Lincoln, first: Abraham, age: 188
```

Listing 18.7   A simple 4-way scrolling file browser

```cpp
// view.cpp:  A simple 4-way-scrolling file browser
//
// Displays a text file according to
// the following interactive commands:
//
//        N          Next screen
//        P          Previous screen
//        T          Top of file
//        B          Bottom of file
//        L          Scroll Left
//        R          Scroll Right
//        Q,X        Quit (eXit)
//

#include <cstdlib>
#include <cstdio>
#include <cstring>
#include <cctype>
#include <stack>        // STL container

using namespace std;

namespace
{
    const int NROWS = 24;       // Height of screen - 1
    const int NCOLS = 79;       // Width of screen - 1
    const int HORIZ = 20;       // Horiz. scroll increment
```

continued

Listing 18.7   (continued)

```
    // Buffer for current screen
    char Screen[NROWS][BUFSIZ];

    size_t
        Nlines,        // Number of lines to display
        Offset = 0;    // Horizontal display offset

    void read_a_screen(FILE* f)
    {
        clearerr(f);      // Reset possible EOF condition
        for (int i = 0; i < NROWS && fgets(Screen[i],BUFSIZ,f); ++i)
            Screen[i][strlen(Screen[i])-1] = '\0';
        Nlines = i;
    }

    void display(void)
    {
        // Add your code to clear screen and home the cursor here.

        // Display a screenful of text:
        for (int i = 0; i < Nlines; ++i)
            if (Offset < strlen(Screen[i]))
                fprintf(stderr,"%-.*s\n",NCOLS,Screen[i]+Offset);
            else
                fputc('\n',stderr);
    }
}

main(int argc, char *argv[])
{
    stack<fpos_t> stk;
    FILE* f;
    fpos_t top_pos;

    // Open input file:
    if (argc == 1 || (f = fopen(argv[1],"r")) == NULL)
    {
        fputs("Error opening file.\n",stderr);
        return EXIT_FAILURE;
    }

top:
    // Display initial screen:
    rewind(f);
    fgetpos(f,&top_pos);
    read_a_screen(f);
    display();
```

Listing 18.7   (continued)

```
for (;;)
{
    int c = getchar();
    switch(toupper(c))
    {
        case 'N':
            if (!feof(f))
            {
                stk.push(top_pos);
                fgetpos(f,&top_pos);
                read_a_screen(f);
            }
            display();
            break;

        case 'P':
            if (!stk.empty())
            {
                top_pos = stk.top();
                stk.pop();
                fsetpos(f,&top_pos);
                read_a_screen(f);
            }
            display();
            break;

        case 'T':
            while (!stk.empty())
                stk.pop();
            goto top;

        case 'B':
            while (!feof(f))
            {
                stk.push(top_pos);
                fgetpos(f,&top_pos);
                read_a_screen(f);
            }
            display();
            break;

        case 'L':
            if (Offset > 0)
                Offset -= HORIZ;
            display();
            break;
```

continued

Listing 18.7   (continued)

```
            case 'R':
                if (Offset < BUFSIZ-HORIZ)
                    Offset += HORIZ;
                display();
                break;

            case 'Q':
            case 'X':
                return EXIT_SUCCESS;
        }

        if (c != '\n')
            (void) getchar();    // Eat '\n'
    }
}
```

scrolling down (i.e., forward) through the file, the file position of the data on the screen is pushed onto a stack, and the program reads the next screenful from the current file position. To scroll up, it retrieves the file position of the previous screen from the stack. Although this is the crudest of algorithms for viewing text, it can view a file of any size, and it performs acceptably on systems that cache disk operations (really!). C++ streams have the following types and operations that correspond to the C ones we have been discussing:

C	C++
fpos_t	streampos
fgetpos	tellg (input), tellp (output)
fsetpos	seekg (input), seekp (output)

Temporary Files

When your program requires a scratch file for temporary processing, you need a unique name for that file. If the name isn't important to you, let tmpnam do the work of creating the filename for you:

```
char fname[L_tmpnam];
tmpnam(fname);
f = fopen(fname,...
```

the tmpnam function will supply at least TMP_MAX unique names before it starts repeating. The macros L_tmpnam and TMP_MAX are defined in stdio.h. Don't forget to delete the file by calling remove before your program terminates

```
remove(fname);
```

If you don't need to know the name of a temporary file but just want access to one, you can use the `tmpfile` function to get a file pointer to a temporary file. It returns a pointer to a file opened with mode `"wb+"` (this is usually adequate for scratch files). The best part is that the file is deleted automatically when the program terminates normally (i.e., if `abort` wasn't called).

Portability

It is always easier to move applications from one platform to another than it is to rewrite them ("move" meaning "copy and recompile"). Such portability is possible only if purveyors of technology agree to do things the same way. Industry standards are the specification of such agreements. I have made an effort in this book to write portable code. With rare exceptions, all of the program examples will run identically on any platform with either an ANSI/ISO-compliant C compiler or a compiler that complies with CD2 of the ANSI/ISO C++ Standards Committee ("Committee Draft 2", which is essentially "Standard C++").

But a standard can only go so far. None of my example programs take advantage of today's sophisticated user interfaces or file systems. Such mechanisms vary widely across platforms and cannot be standardized at the programming language level, and many applications need access to their operating environment beyond what standard C and C++ provide. If only there were a way to use the services of your operating system without destroying portability!

POSIX

In the early 1980s an organization called `/usr/group` (the UNIX Users' association, now called Usenix) began an effort to standardize both C and the C programming environment. Much of what they defined applied to all environments and became the basis for the standard C library. Another part of their work resulted in a set of functions to access UNIX system services (UNIX was the most common C programming environment at the time). These functions constitute the C language bindings of what now is called POSIX (Portable Operating System Interface). Fortunately, many environments, including Windows NT, OpenVMS, and the many flavors of UNIX, provide most or all of these functions. This suggests a simple recipe for maximizing portability:

1. Program in standard C.
2. If Step 1 is too restrictive, use only POSIX-compliant functions.
3. If Steps 1 and 2 aren't possible, isolate system-dependent code in separate modules. This will minimize how much code you'll have to rewrite when porting to another system. There are cross-platform tools available that may do some of this work for you.

There is of course much more to POSIX than C language bindings (bindings for other languages and a specification for a command shell, for example). The rest of this chapter illustrates most of the POSIX functions that pertain to file processing.

File Descriptors

The definition of the FILE structure in the <stdio.h> header in your environment should contain an integer that represents a *file descriptor* (look for a member named something like fd, _file, or fildes). A file descriptor, also called a *file handle*, is a unique, nonnegative integer assigned by the native file system that identifies an access path into a file. POSIX file access functions use file handles instead of file pointers to perform basic operations comparable to those offered in the standard C library, but with less overhead. (A comparison of POSIX and standard C functions is in Table 18.1. Other POSIX file access functions are listed in Table 18.2.

Copying Files via Descriptors

The program cat.c in Listing 18.8 concatenates the files indicated on the command line to standard output. For example, the command

```
cat file1 file2 >file3
```

combines file1 and file2 into a new file, file3. This program uses standard C functions for reading and writing. The only POSIX functions are in the line

```
FILE *std_out = fdopen(fileno(stdout),"wb");
```

Table 18.1 A correspondence between POSIX and Standard C file access functions

POSIX	Standard C
close	fclose
creat	fopen
dup2	freopen
lseek	fseek
open	fopen
read	fread
tell	ftell
write	fwrite

Table 18.2 Other POSIX file access functions

Function	Description
access	Check file existence and permissions
dup	Duplicate a file handle (in synch with original)
chmod	Change file permissions
fdopen	Associates a FILE * with a file handle
fileno	Extracts the file handle from a FILE *
fstat	Get file info (from a FILE *)
stat	Get file info (from a filename)
unlink	Same as remove() on non-UNIX systems

Listing 18.8   Concatenates files to standard output

```c
/* cat.c:      concatenate files */
#include <stdio.h>
#include <stdlib.h>

void copy(FILE *, FILE *);

main(int argc, char *argv[])
{
    int i;
    FILE *f;
    FILE *std_out = fdopen(fileno(stdout),"wb");

    if (std_out == NULL)
        return EXIT_FAILURE;
    for (i = 1; i < argc; ++i)
    {
        if ((f = fopen(argv[i],"rb")) == NULL)
            fprintf(stderr,"cat: Can't open %s\n",argv[i]);
        else
        {
            copy(f,std_out);
            fclose(f);
        }
    }
    return EXIT_SUCCESS;
}

void copy(FILE *from, FILE *to)
{
    int count;
    static char buf[BUFSIZ];

    while (!feof(from))
    {
        count = fread(buf,1,BUFSIZ,from);
        if (ferror(from))
            exit(EXIT_FAILURE);
        fwrite(buf,1,count,to);
        if (ferror(to))
            exit(EXIT_FAILURE);
    }
}
```

This line enables writing to standard output in binary mode, in case one of the user files is not a text file. It associates a new file pointer with standard output, but no new handle is created; in other words, the file pointers `stdout` and `std_out` share the same file handle.

The function `filecopy` in Listing 18.9 opens an input and an output file in binary mode. The `open` system call returns a file handle, or –1 if the open fails (most POSIX functions return –1 upon failure). The flags used to define `INPUT_MODE` and `OUTPUT_MODE` are defined in the POSIX header `<fcntl.h>`. The third argument in the `open` of the output file is the file protection: It specifies that if the file doesn't already exist, it should not be write protected. (`S_IWRITE` is defined in `<sys/stat.h>`.) Any include file prefixed with `sys/` is a POSIX include file (although many, such as `<io.h>` and `<fcntl.h>`, have no such prefix). On most systems you need to include `<sys/types.h>` before `<sys/stat.h>`. The `read` and `write` functions both return the number of bytes transferred.

The program in Listing 18.10 uses `filecopy` to copy one or more files to a given directory. The `stat` function fills a structure with basic file information, including these members:

`st_mode`   file mode (directory indicator, file permissions)

`st_size`   file size in bytes

`st_mtime` time of last data modification

Testing `st_mode` with the mask `S_IFDIR` (from `<sys/stat.h>`) determines whether the file is a directory. The forward slash character is a directory separator for pathnames in all POSIX systems (note the `sprintf` statement in function `cp`). It is only in the command line of the MSDOS shell (COMMAND.COM) that a backslash character is required as the separator character. Both slash characters are totally interchangeable within MSDOS programs. For maximum portability, the names of files and directories should only use characters from the portable filename character set: alphanumerics, the period, and the underscore.

Reading Directory Entries

The most widely used operating systems that support C and C++ development today have a hierarchical directory structure. POSIX defines functions to create, delete, and navigate among directories, as well as functions to read the entries in a directory (see Table 18.3). The program in Listing 18.11 prints a listing of the current directory to standard output. To read a directory, you must first get a pointer to a `DIR` structure with the `opendir` function. Successive calls to `readdir` return a pointer to a `struct dirent` structure (which contains the entry name) or `NULL` when all entries have been read. These structures and functions are declared in `<dirent.h>`.

As shown in Listing 18.11, `list` displays the name, permissions, size, and time of last modification for each file. The legend for the file permissions is

d   the entry is itself a directory

r   the user has read permission

w   the user has write permission

Listing 18.9   Copies files via handles

```
/* filecopy.c:   Low-level file copy */
#include <io.h>
#include <sys/types.h>
#include <sys/stat.h>
#include <fcntl.h>

#define BUFSIZ 512
#define INPUT_MODE   (O_RDONLY | O_BINARY)
#define OUTPUT_MODE (O_WRONLY | O_BINARY | O_CREAT)

int filecopy(char *from, char *to)
{
    int status = -1;
    int fd1 = open(from,INPUT_MODE);
    int fd2 = open(to,OUTPUT_MODE,S_IWRITE);

    if (fd1 >= 0 && fd2 >= 0)
    {
        int nbytes;
        static char buffer[BUFSIZ];

        status = 0;
        while ((nbytes = read(fd1,buffer,BUFSIZ)) > 0)
        {
            if (write(fd2,buffer,nbytes) != nbytes)
            {
                /* Write error */
                status = -1;
                break;
            }
        }

        /* Was there a read error? */
        if (nbytes == -1)
            status = -1;
    }

    if (fd1 >= 0)
        close(fd1);
    if (fd2 >= 0)
        close(fd2);
    return status;
}
```

Listing 18.10   Copies files to a directory

```
/* cp.c:      Copy files */
#include <stdio.h>
#include <stdlib.h>
#include <sys/types.h>
#include <sys/stat.h>

extern int filecopy(char *, char *);
static void cp(char *, char *);

main(int argc, char *argv[])
{
    int i;
    struct stat finfo;
    char *target = argv[argc-1];

    /* Make sure target is a directory */
    if (argc < 3)
    {
        fputs("Too few arguments.\n",stderr);
        return EXIT_FAILURE;
    }
    if (stat(target,&finfo) || !(finfo.st_mode & S_IFDIR))
    {
        fprintf(stderr,"%s is not a valid directory\n",target);
        return EXIT_FAILURE;
    }

    /* Copy files */
    for (i = 1; i < argc-1; ++i)
        cp(argv[i],target);
    return EXIT_SUCCESS;
}

static void cp(char *file, char *target)
{

    static char newfile[FILENAME_MAX];

    /* Combine target and source file for a full pathname */
    sprintf(newfile,"%s/%s",target,file);
    fprintf(stderr,"copying %s to %s\n",file,newfile);
    if (filecopy(file,newfile) != 0)
        fputs("cp: Copy failed\n",stderr);
}

// Sample Execution:
C:> md temp
C:> cp cp.c cp.exe temp
copying cp.c to temp/cp.c
copying cp.exe to temp/cp.exe
```

Table 18.3 POSIX directory access functions

Function	Description
chdir	Change the current working directory
closedir	Stop reading a directory
getcwd	Get name of the current working directory
mkdir	Create a new directory
opendir	Open a directory for reading
readdir	Get the next directory entry
rewinddir	Reset directory read pointer back to the beginning
rmdir	Delete a directory (must be empty)

Listing 18.11 Lists entries in the current directory

```
/* list.c:  Print a directory listing */
#include <stdio.h>
#include <dirent.h>
#include <sys/types.h>
#include <sys/stat.h>
#include <time.h>
#include <string.h>
#include <assert.h>

static char *attr_str(short attr);

main()
{
    DIR *dirp = opendir(".");  /* Current dir */
    struct dirent *entry;

    assert(dirp);
    while ((entry = readdir(dirp)) != NULL)
    {
        struct stat finfo;

        stat(entry->d_name,&finfo);
        printf(
                "%-12.12s   %s %8ld  %s",
                strlwr(entry->d_name),
                attr_str(finfo.st_mode),
                finfo.st_size,
                ctime(&finfo.st_mtime)
              );
    }
    closedir(dirp);
    return 0;
}
```

continued

Listing 18.11   (continued)

```
static char *attr_str(short attr)
{
    static char s[4];

    strcpy(s,"---");
    if (attr & S_IFDIR)
        s[0] = 'd';
    if (attr & S_IREAD)
        s[1] = 'r';
    if (attr & S_IWRITE)
        s[2] = 'w';
    return s;
}

/* Sample Output:*/
.                 dr-         0  Fri May 02 04:13:06 1997
..                dr-         0  Fri May 02 04:05:26 1997
cat.c             -rw       875  Fri May 02 03:50:26 1997
cat.exe           -rw     61440  Fri May 02 03:50:31 1997
cp.c              -rw      1072  Fri May 02 04:00:51 1997
cp.exe            -rw     61440  Fri May 02 04:02:02 1997
filecopy.c        -rw       970  Fri May 02 04:01:54 1997
list.c            -rw       968  Fri May 02 04:12:04 1997
list.exe          -rw     61440  Fri May 02 04:12:21 1997
```

The first two entries are special: "." refers to the current directory and ".." to its parent. These are created by the file system so you can't alter them directly (hence no 'w' permission is displayed). The root directory is referred to by the token / in POSIX functions (and optionally by \\ in MSDOS's). Since the modification time is a standard time value (time_t), I use the standard C function ctime to display it. (Chapter 19 explains standard C's time functions.)

Redirecting Standard Error

When you enter a command such as

```
cat file1 file2 >file3
```

the command shell disconnects the internal file handle for standard output from the console and connects it to file3 before it loads the program cat. When cat terminates, the shell reconnects the handle to the console. Listing 18.12 shows how to do the same thing with stderr. The function redir_stderr does the following:

1. Gets a handle to the new destination by calling open.
2. Creates a new handle to the original destination with dup (this is for restoring it later).

3. Redirects the output by disconnecting it from the original destination and connecting it to the new one (this is what dup2 does).

When you don't need the redirection anymore, call restore_stderr to

1. Redirect standard error back to its original destination
2. Discard the duplicate handle.

A handle created with dup is "synchronized" with the original, so that if you change file position with lseek on one handle, the position is updated for the other handle as well.

You may be wondering why you can't just use a call to freopen to redirect standard error. This works fine within a single program, but freopen has no effect if you initiate another

Listing 18.12   Redirects standard error

```
/* stderr.c:    Redirect stderr */
#include <stdio.h>
#include <io.h>
#include <fcntl.h>
#include <sys/types.h>
#include <sys/stat.h>

static int old_handle = -1;

int redir_stderr(char *fname)
{
    int fd = open(fname,O_WRONLY|O_CREAT|O_TEXT,S_IWRITE);
    if (fd >= 0)
    {
        int err_handle = fileno(stderr);
        old_handle = dup(err_handle);
        dup2(fd,err_handle);
        close(fd);
    }
    return fd;
}

void restore_stderr(void)
{
    if (old_handle != -1)
    {
        dup2(old_handle,fileno(stderr));
        close(old_handle);
        old_handle = -1;
    }
}
```

program from within your program (using `system`, say), because only the local file pointer changes. To have such changes persist across subprocesses you must use `dup2`.

The program `ddir.c` in Listing 18.13 illustrates most of the POSIX concepts discussed above. It deletes an entire directory tree by following these steps:

1. Make the root of the tree the current working directory
2. Delete all files within that directory with a shell command (in this case the MSDOS `del` command)
3. Any entry left in the directory is one of the following:
   a. *protected file*—lower the protection with `chmod` and delete the file explicitly with `unlink` (you can use `remove` in MSDOS, but you shouldn't in UNIX; `unlink` works for both)

Listing 18.13 Deletes a directory tree

```
/* ddir.c:  Remove subdirectory tree (Borland C only!) */
#include <stdio.h>
#include <stdlib.h>
#include <io.h>
#include <sys/stat.h>
#include <dirent.h>
#include <dir.h>

main(int argc, char **argv)
{
    void rd(char*);
    char *old_path = getcwd(NULL,64);

    /* Delete the directories */
    while (--argc)
        rd(*++argv);

    /* Restore directory */
    chdir(old_path);
    free(old_path);
    return 0;
}

void rd(char* dir)
{
    extern int redir_stderr(char* fname);
    extern void restore_stderr(void);
    void erase_dir(void);

    /* Log onto the directory to be deleted */
    chdir(dir);
```

    b. *subdirectory*—recursively repeat the whole process starting with Step 1 on the subdirectory

  4. Ascend to the parent directory and delete the directory in question with `rmdir`.

If any files can't be deleted (or if there are none to delete), some versions of MSDOS send a message to standard error. I redirect standard error to the `nul` device before calling `system` so these messages will not appear.

Listing 18.13 (continued)

```
    /* Delete all normal files via OS shell (DOS version) */
    redir_stderr("nul");
    system("del /q *.* > nul");
    restore_stderr();

    /* Delete any remaining directory entries */
    erase_dir();

    /* Remove the directory from its parent */
    chdir("..");
    rmdir(dir);
}

static void erase_dir(void)
{
    DIR* dirp;
    struct dirent* entry;
    struct stat finfo;

    /* Erase what's left in the current directory */
    dirp = opendir(".");
    while ((entry = readdir(dirp)) != NULL)
    {
        if (entry->d_name[0] == '.')
            continue;
        stat(entry->d_name, &finfo);
        if (finfo.st_mode & S_IFDIR)
            rd(entry->d_name);        /* Subdirectory */
        else
        {
            /* Enable delete of file, then do it */
            chmod(entry->d_name, S_IWRITE);
            unlink(entry->d_name);
        }
    }
    closedir(dirp);
}
```

Encapsulating Directory Operations

As usual, C++ can make life a lot easier. Listings 18.14 and 18.15 have the definition of a `Directory` class that hides the details of the POSIX data structures. The constructor automatically opens the directory and positions at the first entry, and the destructor closes the directory. Listings 18.16 and 18.17 show how straightforward the `list` and `ddir` programs are if you use this class.

Listing 18.14   Header file for the `Directory` class

```
// mydir.h: A Directory Navigating class
#include <string>
#include <exception>
#include <sys/stat.h>
#include <dirent.h>
#include <dir.h>
#include <assert.h>

using std::string;
using std::exception;

class DirError : public exception
{
public:
    DirError(const string& s) : exception(s)
    {}
};

class Directory
{
public:
    // Creators:
    Directory(const string&);
    ~Directory();

    // Navigators:
    void rewind();
    void next();
    bool eof() const;

    // Info on directory entries:
    string entry_name() const;
```

Listing 18.14   (continued)

```cpp
    long entry_size() const;
    int entry_attrs() const;
    time_t entry_time() const;
    bool entry_isdir() const;

private:
    DIR* dirp;
    struct dirent* entry;
    struct stat info;

    void do_stats();
};

inline Directory::~Directory()
{
    assert(dirp);
    closedir(dirp);
}

inline bool Directory::eof() const
{
    return entry == NULL;
}

inline void Directory::next()
{
    assert(dirp);
    entry = readdir(dirp);
    if (entry)
        do_stats();
}

inline void Directory::rewind()
{
    assert(dirp);
    rewinddir(dirp);
    next();
}

inline bool Directory::entry_isdir() const
{
    assert(dirp);
    return info.st_mode & S_IFDIR;
}
```

Listing 18.15 `Directory` class implementation file

```cpp
// mydir.cpp
#include "mydir.h"

Directory::Directory(const string& s)
{
    dirp = opendir(s.c_str());
    if (!dirp)
        throw DirError("invalid directory");
    next();
}

string Directory::entry_name() const
{
    assert(dirp);
    if (eof())
        throw DirError("no entry available");
    return entry->d_name;
}

int Directory::entry_attrs() const
{
    assert(dirp);
    if (eof())
        throw DirError("no entry available");
    return info.st_mode;
}

long Directory::entry_size() const
{
    assert(dirp);
    if (eof())
        throw DirError("no entry available");
    return info.st_size;
}

time_t Directory::entry_time() const
{
    assert(dirp);
    if (eof())
        throw DirError("no entry available");
    return info.st_mtime;
}

void Directory::do_stats()
{
    if (stat(entry->d_name, &info) == -1)
        throw DirError("file info not available");
}
```

Listing 18.16 C++ version of Listing 18.10

```cpp
// list.cpp:  Prints a directory listing
#include <iostream>
#include <iomanip>
#include <sys/stat.h>
#include <time.h>
#include <string>
#include "mydir.h"

using namespace std;

string attr_str(int attr);

main()
{
    Directory d(".");
    while (!d.eof())
    {
        time_t t = d.entry_time();
        cout.setf(ios::left, ios::adjustfield);
        cout << setw(15) << d.entry_name().substr(0,12);
        cout << setw(4) << attr_str(d.entry_attrs());
        cout.setf(ios::right, ios::adjustfield);
        cout << setw(8) << d.entry_size() << "   ";
        cout << ctime(&t);        // includes newline
        d.next();
    }
}

string attr_str(int attr)
{
    string result(attr & S_IFDIR ? "d" : "-");
    result += attr & S_IREAD ? "r" : "-";
    result += attr & S_IWRITE ? "w" : "-";
    return result;
}
```

Listing 18.17   C++ version of Listing 18.13

```cpp
// ddir.cpp
#include <iostream>
#include <string>
#include <stdexcept>
#include <stdlib.h>
#include <dir.h>
#include <io.h>
#include "mydir.h"

using namespace std;

extern "C" int redir_stderr(char *);
extern "C" void restore_stderr(void);

main(int argc, char **argv)
{
    char *old_path = getcwd(NULL,64);
    void rd(const string&);

    try
    {
        while (−argc)
            rd(*++argv);
    }
    catch (exception& x)
    {
        cerr << x.what() << endl;
        return EXIT_FAILURE;
    }

    chdir(old_path);
    free(old_path);
    return EXIT_SUCCESS;
}

void rd(const string& dir)
{
    void erase_dir(void);

    chdir(dir.c_str());
    redir_stderr("nul");
    system("del /q *.* > nul");
    restore_stderr();

    erase_dir();
```

Listing 18.17   (continued)

```
    chdir("..");
    rmdir(dir.c_str());
}

static void erase_dir(void)
{
    Directory d(".");
    for (; !d.eof(); d.next())
    {
        string dname = d.entry_name();
        if (dname[0] == '.')
            continue;
        if (d.entry_isdir())
            rd(dname);
        else
        {
            chmod(dname.c_str(),S_IWRITE);
            unlink(dname.c_str());
        }
    }
}
```

Summary

- Not all file operations port across platforms. Those that generally do are in the standard C and C++ libraries.
- A *filter* reads only from standard input and writes only to standard output. Filters are powerful tools in environments that support I/O *redirection*.
- Don't forget to check for output when writing files—you may overrun the output media.
- Some environments distinguish between *text* and *binary* files. Block I/O and random file positioning require binary mode.
- If the standard libraries don't meet your file processing needs, try to use POSIX-compliant file operations. Failing that, isolate platform dependencies in separate modules to facilitate the porting process.
- As always, consider using C++ to encapsulate lower-level concepts and operations.

Time and Date Processing

Most operating systems have some way of keeping track of the current date and time. The C language makes this information available in various formats through the library functions defined in <time.h>. The time function returns a value of type time_t (usually a long), an implementation-dependent encoding of the current date and time. You can pass this value to other functions, such as localtime, for more specific information. The following example prints the current date and time in various formats:

```
/* tformat.c */
#include <stdio.h>
#include <time.h>

main()
{
    time_t tval;
    struct tm *now;
    char buf[BUFSIZ];
    char *fancy_format =
        "Or getting really fancy:\n"
        "Today is %A, %B %d, day %j of %Y,\n"
        "and the time is %I:%M %p";

    /* Get current date and time */
    tval = time(NULL);
    now = localtime(&tval);

    printf("The current date and time: %d/%02d/%02d %d:%02d:%02d\n\n",
            now->tm_mon+1, now->tm_mday, now->tm_year,
            now->tm_hour, now->tm_min, now->tm_sec);
    printf("Or in default system format: %s\n", ctime(&tval));
    strftime(buf, sizeof buf, fancy_format, now);
    puts(buf);
    return 0;
}
/* Output: */
The current date and time: 3/27/97 16:58:11
```

```
Or in default system format: Thu Mar 27 16:58:11 1997
```

```
Or getting really fancy:
Today is Thursday, March 27, day 086 of 1997,
and the time is 04:58 PM
```

The `localtime` function breaks the encoded time down into the following components:

```
struct tm
{
    int tm_sec;        /* seconds (0 - 60) */
    int tm_min;        /* minutes (0 - 59) */
    int tm_hour;       /* hour of the day (0 - 23) */
    int tm_mday;       /* day of the month (1 - 31) */
    int tm_mon;        /* months since January (0 - 11)!!! */
    int tm_year;       /* years since 1900 */
    int tm_wday;       /* day of the week (0 - 6) */
    int tm_yday;       /* days since January 1 (0 - 365) */
    int tm_isdst;      /* whether daylight savings is in effect */
};
```

The `localtime` function returns a pointer to a static structure; therefore only one such structure at a time is available in a program without making a copy. The `ctime` function returns a pointer to a static string which describes the complete time and date in a standard format and terminates with a newline character. The `strftime` formats a string according to user specifications. For example, the `%A` descriptor represents the name of the day of the week. (See Table 19.1 for the complete list of format descriptors).

The next sample program shows how to do simple date/time arithmetic:

```
/* tmath.c: Calculate a future date and elapsed program time */
#include <stdio.h>
#include <stdlib.h>
#include <time.h>

main()
{
    time_t start, stop;
    struct tm *now;
    int ndays;

    /* Get current date and time */
    time(&start);
    now = localtime(&start);

    /* Enter an interval in days */
    fputs("How many days from now? ",stdout);
    fflush(stdout);
    if (scanf("%d", &ndays) != 1)
        return EXIT_FAILURE;
```

```
        now->tm_mday += ndays;
        if (mktime(now) != -1)
            printf("\nNew date: %s", asctime(now));
        else
            puts("Sorry. Can't encode your date.");

        /* Compute elapsed program time */
        time(&stop);
        printf("Elapsed program time in seconds: %f\n",
               difftime(stop,start));
        return EXIT_SUCCESS;
}


/* Output: */
How many days from now? 45
New date: Sun May 11 17:01:47 1997
Elapsed program time in seconds: 1.000000
```

Note also the alternate syntax for the `time` function in the above example (viz., the address of the `time_t` parameter is passed instead of being used as a return value). The `mktime` function alters a `struct tm` structure so that the date and time values are within the proper ranges, after which it updates the day-of-week (`tm_wday`) and day-of-year (`tm_yday`) fields. The `mktime` function can fail if the indicated date is not representable. This happens when the date in question precedes your implementation's *reference date*. For example, a typical DOS/Windows-based compiler cannot encode dates before January 1, 1970, but VAX C's reference date is in the mid-1800s. Dates far in the future can also fail to encode. See the

Table 19.1   `strftime` format descriptors

%A, %a	full/abbreviated weekday name (*Saturday/Sat*)
%B, %b	full/abbreviated month name (*April/Apr*)
%c	date and time (*Apr 12 12:38:03 1997*)
%d	day of month (*12*)
%H	hour (24-based: *12*)
%I	hour (12-based: *12*)
%j	day of year (*102*)
%m	month of year (1-based: *4*)
%M	minutes of the hour (*38*)
%p	AM/PM (*PM*)
%S	seconds of the minute (*03*)
%U	week of the year (Sunday-based: *14*)
%w	day of week (Sunday is 0: *6*)
%W	week of the year (Monday-based: *14*)
%x	date (*Apr 12 1997*)
%X	time (*12:38:03*)
%y	year of the century (*97*)
%Y	year (*1997*)
%Z	time zone (if supported:)

description of time in your compiler's reference manual for the limitations of your platform. The asctime function returns the standard string for the time represented in the passed struct tm structure, so ctime(&tval) is equivalent to asctime(localtime(&tval)). The difftime function returns the difference in seconds between two encodings as a double.

Sometimes it is useful to process dates outside the reference scope of your system, or to calculate the interval between two dates in units other than seconds. In this case you ought to devise your own date encoding. The program in Listings 19.1–19.3 shows one technique for determining the number of years, months, and days between two dates, using a simple year/month/day encoding (note that leap years are taken into account). For brevity, this program assumes that the dates are valid and that the first date entered precedes the second. Following the lead of the functions in time.h, the function date_interval returns a pointer to a static Date structure.

Julian Day Encoding

While the date_interval function accommodates our common notion of age, greater precision in date arithmetic is often needed. Banks need to be able calculate interest to the day, for example. Astronomers use the notion of a *Julian day* to simplify date calculations. The Julian

---

Listing 19.1 A simple date structure

```
/* date.h: A simple encoding for dates */
struct DATE
{
    int year;      /* Full date (e.g., 1992, not 92) */
    int month;     /* 1 - 12 */
    int day;       /* 1 - 31 */
};
typedef struct DATE Date;

Date* date_interval(Date *, Date *);
```

Listing 19.2 Calculates duration between two dates

```
/* date.c: Calculate duration between two dates */
#include <assert.h>
#include "date.h"

#define isleap(y) ((y)%4 == 0 && (y)%100 != 0 || (y)%400 == 0)

/* Days per month for non-leap and leap years: */
static int Daytab[2][13] =
{
    {0, 31, 28, 31, 30, 31, 30, 31, 31, 30, 31, 30, 31},
    {0, 31, 29, 31, 30, 31, 30, 31, 31, 30, 31, 30, 31}
};
```
continued

Listing 19.2   (continued)

```c
Date* date_interval(Date *d1, Date *d2)
{
    static Date result;
    int months, days, years, prev_month, year2;

    /* Compute the interval - assume d1 precedes d2 */
    years = d2->year - d1->year;
    assert(years > 0);
    months = d2->month - d1->month;
    days = d2->day - d1->day;

    /* Do the obvious corrections (must adjust days before months!) -
     *
     * This is a loop in case the previous month is February,
     * and days < -28.
     */
    prev_month = d2->month - 1;
    year2 = d2->year;
    while (days < 0)
    {
        /* Borrow from the previous month */
        if (prev_month == 0)
        {
            prev_month = 12;
            --year2;
        }
        --months;
        days += Daytab[isleap(year2)][prev_month--];
    }

    if (months < 0)
    {
        /* Borrow from the previous year */
        --years;
        months += 12;
    }
    /* Prepare output */
    result.month = months;
    result.day = days;
    result.year = years;
    return &result;
}
```

Listing 19.3 Tests the date-interval function

```
/* tdate.c: Test date_int() */
#include <stdio.h>
#include "date.h"

main()
{
    Date d1, d2, *result;

    /* Read in two dates - assume first precedes second */
    fputs("Enter a date, MM/DD/YY> ",stdout);
    fflush(stdout);
    if (scanf("%d/%d/%d%*c",&d1.month,&d1.day,&d1.year) != 3)
        return 1;

    fputs("Enter a later date, MM/DD/YY> ",stdout);
    fflush(stdout);
    if (scanf("%d/%d/%d%*c",&d2.month,&d2.day,&d2.year) != 3)
        return 1;

    /* Compute interval in years, months, and days */
    result = date_interval(&d1, &d2);
    printf("years: %d, months: %d, days: %d\n",
            result->year, result->month, result->day);
    return 0;
}

/* Output: */
Enter a date, MM/DD/YY> 5/1/1954
Enter a later date, MM/DD/YY> 3/27/1997
years: 42, months: 10, days: 26
```

Day method was developed by Joseph Scaliger (ca. 1577 A.D.) as a means of assigning consecutive numbers to the days of recorded time. The Julian day number of a day is the number of days elapsed since midnight on January 1st, 4713 B.C. (The name "Julian" here derives not from the Julian calendar, but from the name of Scaliger's father.)

The Julian calendar system, developed in 45 B.C., upon which our Gregorian calendar is based, assumed a year to be 365 days, and therefore defined a year to be 365 days with a leap year every four years. It turns out, however, that the solar year varies from year to year, and is actually closer to 365.242 days on average. By 1582 it became quite apparent that something was wrong with the Julian calendar system, since the vernal equinox was about 10 days ahead of schedule. It was determined at that time that a better method to keep the years in synch with nature would be to correct the leap year criterion to omit years divisible by 100, except those divisible by 400, hence the formula for isleap in Listing 19.2. To get things back on track, Pope Gregory proclaimed Thursday, October 4, 1582 A.D., as the end of the Julian Calendar. The next day was named Friday, October 15, 1582 A.D., the beginning of the era of the Gregorian calendar.

Listings 19.4 through 19.6 define a large number of functions for date processing, including the functions `GregToJul` and `JulToGreg`, which convert a Gregorian date to and from a Julian date, respectively. The algorithm used here was adapted from an article in the *C Users Journal*,[1] and uses only integer arithmetic, so it is more efficient than the astronomer's version that resolves to portions of a second during a day by using real arithmetic. These algorithms are exact to the day for all dates after October 15, 1582. For positive years preceding this date, they can differ by as much as 10 days from the true astronomical value, and dates B.C. can be off by as much as a year. `JulToGreg` restores any original date transformed by `GregToJul` without error; however, any other use on dates before October 15, 1582, such as subtracting two Julian day numbers to determine the number of elapsed days, or calling `DayOfWeek`, may yield erroneous results. For simplicity, I have disallowed any dates prior to 1583. Listing 19.7 illustrates various functions from the `DateStuff` namespace.

Listing 19.4   Declaration for date classes and functions

```
// datefwd.h
#if !defined(DATEFWD_H)
#define DATEFWD_H

#include <limits.h>
#include <string>

namespace DateStuff
{
    // Constants and Data:
    enum YearLimits {MIN_YEAR = 1583, MAX_YEAR = INT_MAX};
    enum Days {MONDAY, TUESDAY, WEDNESDAY, THURSDAY,
               FRIDAY, SATURDAY, SUNDAY, DAY_ERROR};
    enum Months {MONTH_ERROR, JANUARY, FEBRUARY, MARCH, APRIL, MAY, JUNE,
                 JULY, AUGUST, SEPTEMBER, OCTOBER, NOVEMBER, DECEMBER};

    // Classes: (explained later)
    struct Duration;
    class  Year;
    class  YMonth;
    class  Date;
    class  FullDate;
    class  Date_Exception;

    // Generic Date Functions:

    // System Date:
    void Today(int&, int&, int&);

    // Leap Test:
    bool IsLeap(int y);
```

Listing 19.4 (continued)

```
// Other Validity Checks:
bool IsValidYear(int y);
bool IsValidMonth(int m);
bool IsValidDay(int m, int d);
bool IsValidYMDay(int y, int m, int d);

// Various Computations:
int  Compare(int y1, int m1, int d1,
             int y2, int m2, int d2);
int  DayOfWeek(int y, int m, int d);
int  DayOfYear(int y, int m, int d);
int  EndOfMonth(int y, int m);
int  EndOfYear(int y);
void NthDay(int n, int y, int& m, int& d);
int  NthWeekDay(int n, int wd, int y, int m);
int  DaysInPrevMonth(int y, int m);
int  DaysInNextMonth(int y, int m);
int  GetDaysInMonth(bool isLeap, int m);
int  GetDaysToDate(bool isLeap, int m);

int  FirstSat(int dow);
int  FirstSatOfMonth(int y, int m);
int  FirstSatOfYear(int y);

int  AbsoluteWeek(int doy);
int  AbsoluteWeekOfMonth(int y, int m, int d);
int  AbsoluteWeekOfYear(int y, int m, int d);
int  CommonWeek(int s, int doyom);
int  CommonWeekOfMonth(int y, int m, int d);
int  CommonWeekOfYear(int y, int m, int d);
void NthCommonWeek(int n, int y, int& doy1, int& doy2);
int  NumCommonWeeks(int y);

void AddYears(int yrs, int& y, int& m, int& d);
void SubtractYears(int yrs, int& y, int& m, int& d);
void AddMonths(int mths, int& y, int& m, int& d);
void SubtractMonths(int mths, int& y, int& m, int& d);
long MonthsBetween(int y1, int m1, int y2, int m2);
void AddDays(int days, int& y, int& m, int& d);
void SubtractDays(int days, int& y, int& m, int& d);
long DaysBetween(int y1, int m1, int d1, int y2, int m2, int d2);
void AddWeekDays(int wdays, int& y, int& m, int& d);
void SubtractWeekDays(int wdays, int& y, int& m, int& d);
long WeekDaysBetween(int y1, int m1, int d1, int y2, int m2, int d2);
void AddWeeks(int wks, int& y, int& m, int& d);
void SubtractWeeks(int wks, int& y, int& m, int& d);
long WeeksBetween(int y1, int m1, int d1, int y2, int m2, int d2);
```

continued

Listing 19.4   (continued)

```
        Duration Age(int y, int m, int d);
        Duration AgeBetween(int y1, int m1, int d1,
                            int y2, int m2, int d2);

        // Julian Day Conversions:

        long GregToJul(int y, int m, int d);
        void JulToGreg(long jd, int& y, int& m, int& d);
        int  DayOfWeek(long jd);
        int  DayOfYear(long jd);

        // Other Conversions:
        using std::string;
        string ToString(int y, int m, int d);
        void   FromString(const string& str, int& y, int& m, int& d);

        // Misc.
        void ResolveMonths(long mths, int& y, int& m);
        void CheckY(int y);
        void CheckYM(int y, int m);
        void CheckYMD(int y, int m, int d);
}

#endif
```

Listing 19.5   A module of Date functionality

```
// DateStuff.h:
#if !defined(DATESTUF_H)
#define DATESTUF_H

#include <assert.h>
#include "datefwd.h"
#include "xcept.h"using std::string;

namespace DateStuff
{
    // Classes:
    struct Duration
    {   int m_Year;
        int m_Month;
        int m_Day;
        Duration(int y = 0, int m = 0, int d = 0)
        {
            m_Year = y;
            m_Month = m;
            m_Day = d;
        }
    };
```

Listing 19.5 (continued)

```cpp
// Exception class:
using std::exception;
class Date_Exception : public exception

{
public:
    Date_Exception(int cod, const string& msg = "")
        : exception((s_ErrorStrings[cod] + ":" + msg).c_str())
    {
        assert(BEGIN <= cod && cod < END);
    }
    enum {BEGIN = 200};
    enum {DATE_ERROR = BEGIN, YEAR_ERROR, MONTH_ERROR,
          DAY_ERROR, RANGE_ERROR, BIRTHDAY_ERROR,
          END, NUM_ERRORS = END - BEGIN};

protected:
    string ErrorString(int) const;     // Override

private:
    static string s_ErrorStrings[NUM_ERRORS];
};

// Inlines:
inline bool IsLeap(int y)
{
    // Determines if year is a leap year (returns 1 or 0)
    return !!(y % 4 == 0 && y % 100 != 0 || y % 400 == 0);
}

inline bool IsValidYear(int y)
{
    return MIN_YEAR <= y && y <= MAX_YEAR;
}

inline bool IsValidMonth(int m)
{
    return 1 <= m && m <= 12;
}

inline bool IsValidYMonth(int y, int m)
{
    return IsValidYear(y) && IsValidMonth(m);
}

inline bool IsValidDay(int m, int d)
{
    return IsValidMonth(m) &&
           1 <= d && d <= GetDaysInMonth(true,m);
}
```

continued

Listing 19.5   (continued)

```cpp
inline bool IsValidYMDay(int y, int m, int d)
{
    return IsValidYMonth(y,m) &&
            1 <= d && d <= EndOfMonth(y, m);
}

inline int DayOfWeek(long jd)
{
    return int(jd % 7L);   // See enum Days above.
}

inline int DayOfWeek(int y, int m, int d)
{
    CheckYMD(y,m,d);
    return int(GregToJul(y, m, d) % 7);
}

inline int DayOfYear(long jd)
{
    int y, m, d;
    JulToGreg(jd, y, m, d);
    return DayOfYear(y, m, d);
}

inline int DayOfYear(int y, int m, int d)
{
    CheckYMD(y,m,d);
    return int(GetDaysToDate(IsLeap(y),m) + d);
}

inline int EndOfMonth(int y, int m)
{
    CheckYM(y,m);
    return GetDaysInMonth(IsLeap(y),m);
}

inline int EndOfYear(int y)
{
    CheckY(y);
    return GetDaysToDate(IsLeap(y),13);
}

inline int AbsoluteWeek(int d)
{
    assert(1 <= d && d <= 366);
    return (d - 1) / 7 + 1;
}
```

Listing 19.5   (continued)

```
inline int AbsoluteWeekOfYear(int y, int m, int d)
{
    CheckYMD(y,m,d);
    return AbsoluteWeek(DayOfYear(y,m,d));
}

inline int AbsoluteWeekOfMonth(int y, int m, int d)
{
    CheckYMD(y,m,d);
    return AbsoluteWeek(d);
}

inline int CommonWeekOfMonth(int y, int m, int d)
{
    CheckYMD(y,m,d);
    return CommonWeek(FirstSatOfMonth(y,m), d);
}

inline int CommonWeekOfYear(int y, int m, int d)
{
    CheckYMD(y,m,d);
    return CommonWeek(FirstSatOfYear(y), DayOfYear(y,m,d));
}

inline int FirstSatOfYear(int y)
{
    CheckY(y);
    return FirstSat(DayOfWeek(y,1,1));
}

inline int FirstSatOfMonth(int y, int m)
{
    CheckYM(y,m);
    return FirstSat(DayOfWeek(y,m,1));
}

inline int Compare(int y1, int m1, int d1, int y2, int m2, int d2)
{
    // Returns the # of days between two dates (signed)
    return GregToJul(y1,m1,d1) - GregToJul(y2,m2,d2);
}

inline long DaysBetween(int y1, int m1, int d1, int y2, int m2, int d2)
{
    // A synonym for Compare.
    return Compare(y1,m1,d1,y2,m2,d2);
}
```
                                                                        continued

Listing 19.5   (continued)

```
inline int NumCommonWeeks(int y)
{
    CheckY(y);
    return (EndOfYear(y) - FirstSatOfYear(y) - 1) / 7 + 2;
}

inline long MonthsBetween(int y1, int m1, int y2, int m2)
{
    CheckYM(y1,m1);
    CheckYM(y2,m2);
    return (y1 - y2)*12L + m1 - m2;
}

inline void AddDays(int days, int& y, int& m, int& d)
{
    CheckYMD(y,m,d);
    JulToGreg(GregToJul(y,m,d) + days, y, m, d);
}
inline void SubtractDays(int days, int& y, int& m, int& d)
{
    CheckYMD(y,m,d);
    JulToGreg(GregToJul(y,m,d) - days, y, m, d);
}

inline void AddWeeks(int wks, int& y, int& m, int& d)
{
    CheckYMD(y,m,d);
    AddDays(wks*7,y,m,d);
}

inline void SubtractWeeks(int wks, int& y, int& m, int& d)
{
    CheckYMD(y,m,d);
    SubtractDays(wks*7,y,m,d);
}

inline long WeeksBetween(int y1, int m1, int d1, int y2, int m2, int d2)
{
    CheckYMD(y1,m1,d1);
    CheckYMD(y2,m2,d2);
    return DaysBetween(y1,m1,d1,y2,m2,d2) / 7L;
}

}   // end namespace DateStuff

#endif
```

Listing 19.6   A module of Date functionality (continued)

```cpp
// datestuf.cpp
#include "datestuf.h"
#include <time.h>
#include <stdlib.h>
#include <algorithm>      // for min(), swap()

using std::min;

namespace DateStuff
{
    static const int DaysInMonth[][13] =
    {
        {0, 31, 28, 31, 30, 31, 30, 31, 31, 30, 31, 30, 31},
        {0, 31, 29, 31, 30, 31, 30, 31, 31, 30, 31, 30, 31}
    };

    static const int DaysToDate[][13] =
    {
        {0, 31, 59, 90, 120, 151, 181, 212, 243, 273, 304, 334, 365},
        {0, 31, 60, 91, 121, 152, 182, 213, 244, 274, 305, 335, 366}
    };
}

int DateStuff::GetDaysInMonth(bool isLeap, int m)
{
    assert(isLeap == 0 || isLeap == 1);
    if (!IsValidMonth(m))
        Throw(Date,MONTH_ERROR);
    return DaysInMonth[isLeap][m];
}

int DateStuff::GetDaysToDate(bool isLeap, int m)
{
    // m must be in [1,13]
    assert(isLeap == 0 || isLeap == 1);
    if (m < 1 || 13 < m)
        Throw(Date,MONTH_ERROR);
    return DaysToDate[isLeap][m-1];
}

long DateStuff::GregToJul(int year, int month, int day)
{
    // Converts Gregorian calendar date to integral Julian day number
    CheckYMD(year, month, day);
    long m = long(month);
    long d = long(day);
    long y = long(year);
```

continued

Listing 19.6   (continued)

```
    return d - 32075L
          + 1461L * (y + 4800 + (m - 14L)/12L) / 4L
          +  367L * (m - 2L - (m - 14L)/12L * 12L) / 12L
          -    3L * ((y + 4900L + (m - 14L)/12L) / 100L) / 4L;
}

void DateStuff::JulToGreg(long jday, int& year, int& month, int& day)
{
    // Converts Julian day number to Gregorian calendar date
    long t1 = jday + 68569L;
    long t2 = 4L*t1 / 146097L;
    t1 -= (146097L*t2 + 3L) / 4L;

    long y = 4000L*(t1 + 1)/1461001L;
    t1 = t1 - 1461L*y/4L + 31;

    long m = 80L *t1/2447L;
    day = int(t1 - 2447L*m/80L);

    t1 = m / 11L;
    month = int(m + 2L - 12L*t1);

    year = int(100L * (t2 - 49L) + y + t1);
}

void DateStuff::NthDay(int n, int year, int& month, int& day)
{
    CheckY(year);
    if (n < 1 || 366 < n)
        Throw(Date,DAY_ERROR);

    int row = IsLeap(year);
    if (n > DaysToDate[row][12])
        Throw(Date,RANGE_ERROR);

    for (month = 0; month < 13; ++month)
        if (DaysToDate[row][month] >= n)
            break;

    if (DaysToDate[row][month] > n)
        day = int(n - DaysToDate[row][month-1]);
    else
        day = int(DaysToDate[row][month] - DaysToDate[row][month-1]);
}

int DateStuff::NthWeekDay(int n, int weekDay, int year, int month)
{
    CheckYM(year,month);
    if (!(1 <= n && n <= 5) ||
        !(MONDAY <= weekDay && weekDay <= SUNDAY))
        Throw(Date,DAY_ERROR);
```

Listing 19.6   (continued)

```cpp
    // Find the first occurrence of desired week day:
    long jday = GregToJul(year, month, 1);
    while (int(jday % 7L) != weekDay)
        ++jday;

    // Advance by weeks to nth occurrence of desired week day:
    for (int weekno = 1; weekno < n; ++weekno)
        jday += 7L;

    // Convert Julian to Gregorian and return the day
    int day;
    int tempmonth = month;
    JulToGreg(jday, year, month, day);
    if (month != tempmonth)
        Throw(Date,RANGE_ERROR);
    return day;
}

int DateStuff::DaysInPrevMonth(int year, int month)
{
    CheckYM(year,month);
    if (month == 1)
    {
        --year;
        month = 12;
    }
    else
        --month;
    return DaysInMonth[IsLeap(year)][month];
}

int DateStuff::DaysInNextMonth(int year, int month)
{
    CheckYM(year,month);
    if (month == 12)
    {
        ++year;
        month = 1;
    }
    else
        ++month;
    return DaysInMonth[IsLeap(year)][month];
}
```

continued

Listing 19.6   (continued)

```
string
DateStuff::Date_Exception::s_ErrorStrings[Date_Exception::NUM_ERRORS] =
{
    "Invalid Date",
    "Invalid Year",
    "Invalid Month",
    "Invalid Day",
    "Range error",
    "Invalid Birthday"
};

string DateStuff::Date_Exception::ErrorString(int cod) const
{
    assert(BEGIN <= cod && cod < END);
    return s_ErrorStrings[cod-BEGIN];
}

int DateStuff::FirstSat(int dow)
{
    // Computes the ordinal of the first
    // Saturday, given the day of week of
    // the first day (of either month or year).
    // NOTE: This assumes MONDAY == 0 ... SUNDAY == 6
    assert(MONDAY <= dow && dow <= SUNDAY);
    if (dow == SUNDAY)
        return 7;
    else if (dow == SATURDAY)
        return 1;
    else
        return SATURDAY - dow + 1;
}

int DateStuff::CommonWeek(int s, int d)
{
    // s is the ordinal of the first Saturday
    // (of either month or year).
    // d is the ordinal of the corresponding
    // day (of either month or year).
    // See also: CommonWeekOfMonth, CommonWeekOfYear.
    assert(1 <= s && s <= 7);
    assert(1 <= d && d <= 366);
    if (d <= s)
        return 1;
    else
        return 2+(d-s-1)/7;
}
```

Listing 19.6   (continued)

```
void DateStuff::Today(int& y, int& m, int& d)
{
    time_t tval = time(0);
    struct tm *tmp = localtime(&tval);

    d = tmp->tm_mday;
    m = tmp->tm_mon + 1;
    y = tmp->tm_year + 1900;
}

void DateStuff::NthCommonWeek(int n, int y, int& doy1, int& doy2)
{
    if (!(1 <= doy1 && doy1 <= EndOfYear(y)) ||
        !(1 <= doy2 && doy2 <= EndOfYear(y)))
        Throw(Date,DAY_ERROR);

    int s = FirstSatOfYear(y);
    if (n <= 1)
    {
        doy1 = 1;
        doy2 = s;
    }
    else
    {
        int nc = NumCommonWeeks(y);
        if (n > nc)
            n = nc;
        doy1 = s + 1 + 7*(n - 2);
        doy2 = (n == nc) ? EndOfYear(y) : s + 7*(n-1);
    }
}

void DateStuff::AddYears(int yrs, int& y, int& m, int& d)
{
    CheckYMD(y,m,d);
    if (y > MAX_YEAR - yrs)
        Throw(Date,RANGE_ERROR);
    y += yrs;
    d = min(d, EndOfMonth(y,m));     // Guard against leap change
}

void DateStuff::SubtractYears(int yrs, int& y, int& m, int& d)
{
    CheckYMD(y,m,d);
    if (y < MIN_YEAR + yrs)
        Throw(Date,RANGE_ERROR);
    y -= yrs;
    d = min(d, EndOfMonth(y,m));     // Guard against leap change
}
```

continued

Listing 19.6   (continued)

```
void DateStuff::AddMonths(int mths, int& y, int& m, int& d)
{
    CheckYMD(y,m,d);
    ResolveMonths(y*12 + m + mths, y, m);
    d = min(d, EndOfMonth(y,m));
}

void DateStuff::SubtractMonths(int mths, int& y, int& m, int& d)
{
    CheckYMD(y,m,d);
    ResolveMonths(y*12 + m - mths, y, m);
    d = min(d, EndOfMonth(y,m));
}

void DateStuff::AddWeekDays(int wdays, int& y, int& m, int& d)
{
    CheckYMD(y,m,d);
    // NOTE: This algorithm uses the fact that MONDAY == 0

    // Back-up to nearest weekday:
    int dayno = DayOfWeek(y,m,d);
    if (dayno > FRIDAY)
    {
        SubtractDays(dayno - FRIDAY,y,m,d);
        dayno = FRIDAY;
    }

    // Advance by weeks first:
    if (wdays >= 5)
        AddWeeks(wdays / 5,y,m,d);

    // Now advance the rest of the days:
    int extra = int(wdays % 5);
    if (dayno + extra > FRIDAY)
        extra += 2;      // Skip weekend
    if (extra > 0)
        AddDays(extra,y,m,d);
}

void DateStuff::SubtractWeekDays(int wdays, int& y, int& m, int& d)
{
    CheckYMD(y,m,d);
    // NOTE: This algorithm uses the fact that MONDAY == 0
```

Listing 19.6   (continued)

```
    // Advance to nearest weekday:
    int dayno = DayOfWeek(y,m,d);
    if (dayno > FRIDAY)
    {
        AddDays(7 - dayno,y,m,d);
        dayno = MONDAY;
    }

    // Subtract weeks first:
    SubtractWeeks(wdays / 5,y,m,d);

    // Now back up the rest of the days:
    int extra = int(wdays % 5);
    if (dayno - extra < MONDAY)
        extra += 2;      // Skip weekend
    SubtractDays(extra,y,m,d);
}

long DateStuff::WeekDaysBetween(int y1, int m1, int d1,
                               int y2, int m2, int d2)
{
    CheckYMD(y1,m1,d1);
    CheckYMD(y2,m2,d2);

    // Back up to nearest weekday:
    int dayno1 = DayOfWeek(y1,m1,d1);
    if (dayno1 > FRIDAY)
    {
        SubtractDays(dayno1 - FRIDAY,y1,m1,d1);
        dayno1 = FRIDAY;
    }
    int dayno2 = DayOfWeek(y2,m2,d2);
    if (dayno2 > FRIDAY)
    {
        SubtractDays(dayno2 - FRIDAY,y2,m2,d2);
        dayno2 = FRIDAY;
    }

    long weeks = WeeksBetween(y1,m1,d1,y2,m2,d2);
    int extra = int(dayno2 - dayno1);
    long days = weeks*5 + extra;
    return days;
}
```

continued

Listing 19.6   (continued)

```
DateStuff::Duration DateStuff::Age(int y, int m, int d)
{
    int y2, m2, d2;
    Today(y2,m2,d2);
    return AgeBetween(y,m,d,y2,m2,d2);
}


DateStuff::Duration DateStuff::AgeBetween(int y1, int m1, int d1,
                                          int y2, int m2, int d2)
{
    // Find order of two dates:
    int order = Compare(y1,m1,d1,y2,m2,d2);
    if (order == 0)
        return Duration(0,0,0);
    else if (order > 0)
    {
        // Make date1 precede date2:
        using std::swap;
        swap(y1, y2);
        swap(m1, m2);
        swap(d1, d2);
    }

    int years = y2 - y1;
    int months = m2 - m1;
    int days = d2 - d1;
    assert(years > 0 || years == 0 && months > 0 ||
            years == 0 && months == 0 && days > 0);

    int lastMonth = m2;
    int lastYear = y2;
    while (days < 0)
    {
        // Borrow from month:
        assert(months > 0);
        days += DaysInPrevMonth(lastYear, lastMonth--);
        --months;
        // This is a loop in case one is borrowing from
        // February, and therefore doesn't get enough days
        // to make 'days' go non-negative. This loop
        // will never iterate more than twice.
    }
```

Listing 19.6   (continued)

```
    if (months < 0)
    {
        // Borrow from year:
        assert(years > 0);
        months += 12;
        --years;
    }

    return Duration(years,months,days);
}

void DateStuff::ResolveMonths(long months, int& y, int& m)
{
    assert(months > 1582*12);

    if (months < 0)
        months = -months;
    y = int(months / 12);
    m = int(months % 12);
    if (m == 0)
        m = 12;
    if (!IsValidYMonth(y,m))
        Throw(Date,RANGE_ERROR);
}

void DateStuff::FromString(const string& s, int& y, int& m, int& d)
{
    y = atoi(s.substr(0,4).c_str());
    m = atoi(s.substr(4,2).c_str());
    d = atoi(s.substr(6,2).c_str());
    if (!IsValidYMDay(y,m,d))
        Throw(Date,DATE_ERROR);
}

void DateStuff::CheckYMD(int y, int m, int d)
{
    if (!IsValidYMDay(y,m,d))
        Throw(Date,DATE_ERROR);
}

void DateStuff::CheckYM(int y, int m)
{
    if (!IsValidYMonth(y,m))
        Throw(Date,DATE_ERROR);
}
```

continued

Listing 19.6   (continued)

```
void DateStuff::CheckY(int y)
{
    if (!IsValidYear(y))
        Throw(Date,DATE_ERROR);
}

string DateStuff::ToString(int y, int m, int d)
{
    char buf[9];
    sprintf(buf,"%04d%02d%02d",y,m,d);
    return string(buf);
}
```

Listing 19.7   Illustrates various date functions

```
// tdstuf.cpp

#include "datestuf.h"
#include <iostream>

const char* DayText[] = {"Monday", "Tuesday", "Wednesday",
    "Thursday", "Friday", "Saturday", "Sunday"};

using namespace DateStuff;

main()
{
    int year = 1997;
    int month = 4;
    int day = 1;

    cout.setf(ios::boolalpha);
    cout << "Date: " << month << '/' << day << '/' << year << endl;
    cout << "Leap year? " << IsLeapYear(year) << endl;
    cout << "Day of week: " << DayText[DayOfWeek(year, month, day)] << endl;
    cout << "Day of year: " << DayOfYear(year, month, day) << endl;
    cout << "Days in month: " << EndOfMonth(year, month) << endl;
    cout << "Days in previous month: " << DaysInPrevMonth(year, month)
        << endl;
    cout << "Days in next month: " << DaysInNextMonth(year, month) << endl;
    cout << "3rd Saturday of month: " << NthWeekDay(3,SATURDAY,year,month)
        << endl;
```

Listing 19.7   (continued)

```
    long jday = GregToJul(year,month,day);
    cout << "Julian day number: " << jday << endl;
    int year2, month2, day2;
    JulToGreg(jday + 100,year2,month2,day2);
    cout << "100 days from now: " << month2 << '/' << day2 << '/' << year2
        << endl;
}

// Output:
Date: 4/1/1997
Leap year? false
Day of week: Tuesday
Day of year: 91
Days in month: 30
Days in previous month: 31
Days in next month: 31
3rd Saturday of month: 19
Julian day number: 2450540
100 days from now: 7/10/1997
```

Date Classes for Real Work

It would be a simple matter at this point to define a C++ date class that holds either a Julian day number, or a year/month/day triple, with the ability to determine the day or week of the year, or find the duration between two dates in terms of days, weeks, months, or years. Business data processing often has even more complicated requirements, however. Sometimes you have only a year, or a year and a month, perhaps, yet you can still perform many important functions on such *partial dates*. The remainder of this chapter implements classes to accommodate complex business requirements, including the handling of partial dates.

The Date classes described below process Gregorian dates from January 1, 1583 through December 31, 2,147,483,647 in a 32-bit environment, and provide the following services:

- Test a year for "leapness"
- What is a date's day-of-week
- What is a date's day-of-year
- What is a date's absolute week of year or month
- What is a date's common week of year or month
- Find the nth common week of the year
- How many days in a month
- How many days in a year
- What date is the nth weekday (e.g., 3rd Wednesday) of a month in a given year

• Convert a year/month/day triad to and from a string of numeric characters
• Compare dates relationally
• Add/subtract the following to/from a date:
—Years
—Months
—Weeks
—Days
—Weekdays (M–F)
• Compute the duration between two dates. Give the answer in terms of age (year, months, and days) or as one of the following: years, months, weeks, days or weekdays (e.g., YearsBetween, WeekDaysBetween, etc.).

To handle partial dates, Date needs to accept a year, a year and a month, or a year, month, and day, so it needs a constructor like:

```
Date(int y = 0, int m = 0, int d = 0);
```

This particular constructor also allows an *empty date*, meaning no information is available, which often happens in real applications. We expect such a Date class to "do the right thing" when we ask it to find the duration between two dates, whether they're empty, partial, or full, so we need to decide what the "right thing" is. First off, empty dates don't make sense in date operations, so all such attempts will cause an exception to be thrown. Secondly, when two Date objects appear in an operation, such as finding the duration between them, the "lowest common denominator" among them will determine the outcome. For example, the calculation below should return 3 *months*, since d2, which represents January 1997, knows nothing about days.

```
Date d1(1997,4,12), d2(1997,1);
int diff = d1 - d2;    // Knows to return months
```

It would certainly suffice to have the methods of the Date class contain all the logic to handle every possible combination of partial dates in its computations, but it is often a good idea to encapsulate logical concepts in *classes* wherever possible. Accordingly, I will define a hierarchy of implementation classes that the Date class can call upon to do the "right thing" as needed, as Figure 19.1 depicts.

The Year class contains methods to compare, add, and subtract years. A YMonth (for "Year & Month") object can substitute for a Year, where a year alone is concerned, but also traffics in months.

Since the duration between two partial dates can have any combination of years, months, and days, I have defined a Duration class to handle such return values. Following the advice of Chapter 13, I have also defined Date_Exception, an exception class for this date component.

The Year class is defined in Listings 19.8 and 19.9. Note the declarations for AddYears and SubtractYears. These are virtual functions because YMDay must override them to correctly handle leap years.

Figure 19.1   Class diagram for the date classes

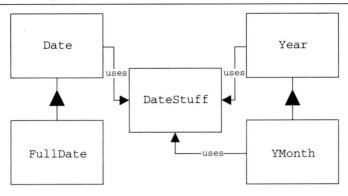

Listing 19.8   Interface for the `Year` class

```
// year.h
#if !defined(YEAR_H)
#define YEAR_H

#include "datestuf.h"

namespace DateStuff
{

class Year
{
public:
    Year();                     // current year
    Year(int);
    Year(const string&);        // picks off first 4 digits

    // Accessors
    int GetYear() const;

    // Comparison
    int Compare(const Year& right) const;
    bool operator==(const Year& right) const;
    bool operator!=(const Year& right) const;
    bool operator<(const Year& right) const;
    bool operator>(const Year& right) const;
    bool operator<=(const Year& right) const;
    bool operator>=(const Year& right) const;

    // Arithmetic
    int operator-(const Year& right) const;
```

continued

Listing 19.8   (continued)

```cpp
    // Other Operations
    virtual void AddYears(int years);
    virtual void SubtractYears(int years);
    int YearsBetween(const Year& right) const;
    Duration AgeBetween(const Year& right) const;
    Duration Age() const;
    int EndOfYear() const;

    string ToString() const;
    bool IsValid() const;
    bool IsEmpty() const;

protected:
    int m_Year;
};

inline int Year::GetYear() const
{
    return m_Year;
}

inline int Year::Compare(const Year& right) const
{
    return m_Year - right.m_Year;
}

inline bool Year::operator==(const Year& right) const
{
    return Compare(right) == 0;
}

inline bool Year::operator!=(const Year& right) const
{
    return Compare(right) != 0;
}

inline bool Year::operator<(const Year& right) const
{
    return Compare(right) < 0;
}

inline bool Year::operator>(const Year& right) const
{
    return Compare(right) > 0;
}
```

Listing 19.8   (continued)

```
inline bool Year::operator<=(const Year& right) const
{
    return Compare(right) <= 0;
}

inline bool Year::operator>=(const Year& right) const
{
    return Compare(right) >= 0;
}

inline int Year::operator-(const Year& right) const
{
    return Compare(right);
}


inline Duration Year::AgeBetween(const Year& right) const
{
    return Duration(YearsBetween(right));
}

inline int Year::YearsBetween(const Year& right) const
{
    int diff = int(right.m_Year - m_Year);
    return int(diff >= 0 ? diff : -diff);
}

inline bool Year::IsValid() const
{
    return MIN_YEAR <= m_Year && m_Year <= MAX_YEAR;
}
inline bool Year::IsEmpty() const
{
    return m_Year == 0;
}

inline string Year::ToString() const
{
    return IsEmpty() ? string()
                     : DateStuff::ToString(m_Year,0,0);
}

} // namespace Date

#endif
```

Listing 19.9   Implementation for the `Year` class

```cpp
// year.cpp
#include "year.h"
#include <time.h>

using namespace DateStuff;

Year::Year()
{
    // Get current year:
    time_t tval = time(0);
    struct tm *tmp = localtime(&tval);

    m_Year = int(tmp->tm_year + 1900);
}

Year::Year(int y)
{
    m_Year = y;
    if (!IsEmpty() && !IsValid())
        Throw(Date,YEAR_ERROR);
}

Year::Year(const string& s)
{
    m_Year = int(atoi(s.substr(0,4).c_str()));
    if (!IsEmpty() && !IsValid())
        Throw(Date,YEAR_ERROR);
}

void Year::AddYears(int y)
{
    if (m_Year > MAX_YEAR - y)
        Throw(Date,RANGE_ERROR);
    m_Year += y;
}

void Year::SubtractYears(int y)
{
    if (m_Year < MIN_YEAR + y)
        Throw(Date,RANGE_ERROR);
    m_Year -= y;
}

Duration Year::Age() const
{
    return AgeBetween(Year());
}
```

Listing 19.9   (continued)

```
int Year::EndOfYear() const
{
    if (!IsValid())
        Throw(Date,YEAR_ERROR);
    return DateStuff::EndOfYear(m_Year);
}
```

YMonth (Listings 19.10 and 19.11) adds functionality to handle months and quarters, and its operator- returns the number of months between two dates. Since a YMonth *is-a* Year, it passes responsibility to Year when it makes sense to do so (see the functions Compare and IsValid).

Listing 19.10   Interface for the YMonth class

```
// ymonth.h
#if !defined(YMONTH_H)
#define YMONTH_H

#include "year.h"

namespace DateStuff
{

class YMonth : public Year
{
    typedef Year Super;

public:
    YMonth();
    YMonth(int y, int m);
    YMonth(const string& s);

    // Accessors
    int GetMonth() const;

    // Comparison
    int  Compare(const YMonth& right) const;
    bool operator==(const YMonth& right) const;
    bool operator!=(const YMonth& right) const;
    bool operator<(const YMonth& right) const;
    bool operator>(const YMonth& right) const;
    bool operator<=(const YMonth& right) const;
    bool operator>=(const YMonth& right) const;
```

continued

Listing 19.10   (continued)

```
    // Arithmetic
    long operator-(const YMonth& right) const;

    // Other Operations
    virtual void AddMonths(long months);
    virtual void SubtractMonths(long months);
    long MonthsBetween(const YMonth& right) const;
    Duration AgeBetween(const YMonth& right) const;
    Duration Age() const;
    int EndOfYear() const;
    int EndOfMonth() const;
    int DaysInPrevMonth() const;
    int DaysInNextMonth() const;

    string ToString() const;
    bool IsValid() const;
    bool IsEmpty() const;

    static Duration AgeBetween(const YMonth& first,
                               const YMonth& last);

protected:
    int m_Month;

private:
    void Resolve(long months);
};


inline int YMonth::GetMonth() const
{
    return m_Month;
}

inline int YMonth::Compare(const YMonth& right) const
{
    int diff = Super::Compare(right);
    return (diff == 0) ? m_Month - right.m_Month : diff;
}

inline bool YMonth::operator==(const YMonth& right) const
{
    return Compare(right) == 0;
}

inline bool YMonth::operator!=(const YMonth& right) const
{
    return Compare(right) != 0;
}
```

Listing 19.10   (continued)

```cpp
inline bool YMonth::operator<(const YMonth& right) const
{
    return Compare(right) < 0;
}

inline bool YMonth::operator>(const YMonth& right) const
{
    return Compare(right) > 0;
}

inline bool YMonth::operator<=(const YMonth& right) const
{
    return Compare(right) <= 0;
}

inline bool YMonth::operator>=(const YMonth& right) const
{
    return Compare(right) >= 0;
}

inline long YMonth::operator-(const YMonth& right) const
{
    return (m_Year - right.m_Year)*12L + m_Month - right.m_Month;
}

inline long YMonth::MonthsBetween(const YMonth& right) const
{
    long diff = (right - *this);
    return diff >= 0 ? diff : -diff;
}

inline void YMonth::AddMonths(long m)
{
    Resolve(m_Year*12L + m_Month + m);
}

inline void YMonth::SubtractMonths(long m)
{
    Resolve(m_Year*12L + m_Month - m);
}

inline Duration YMonth::AgeBetween(const YMonth& right) const
{
    return AgeBetween(right, *this);
}
```

continued

Listing 19.10   (continued)

```
inline bool YMonth::IsValid() const
{
    return Super::IsValid() &&
           1 <= m_Month && m_Month <= 12;
}

inline bool YMonth::IsEmpty() const
{
    return Super::IsEmpty() && m_Month == 0;
}

inline string YMonth::ToString() const
{
    char buf[23];     // 2 ints + 1
    sprintf(buf,"%04d%02d",m_Year,m_Month);
    return IsEmpty() ? string() : string(buf);
}

inline void YMonth::Resolve(long months)
{
    DateStuff::ResolveMonths(months,m_Year, m_Month);
}

inline Duration YMonth::AgeBetween(const YMonth& p1,
                                   const YMonth& p2)
{
    return DateStuff::AgeBetween(p1.m_Year, p1.m_Month, 0,
                                 p2.m_Year, p2.m_Month, 0);
}

} // namespace DateStuff

#endif
```

Listing 19.11   Implementation for the YMonth class

```
// ymonth.cpp
#include "ymonth.h"
#include <time.h>

using namespace DateStuff;

YMonth::YMonth()
{
    // Get current year:
    time_t tval = time(0);
    struct tm *tmp = localtime(&tval);

    m_Month = int(tmp->tm_mon + 1);
}
```

Listing 19.11   (continued)

```
YMonth::YMonth(int y, int m)
      : Year(y)

{
    m_Month = m;
    if (!IsEmpty() && !IsValid())
        Throw(Date,MONTH_ERROR);
}

YMonth::YMonth(const string& s)
      : Year(s)
{
    m_Month = int(atoi(s.substr(4,2).c_str()));
    if (!IsEmpty() && !IsValid())
        Throw(Date,MONTH_ERROR);
}

Duration YMonth::Age() const
{
    return AgeBetween(*this, YMonth());
}

int YMonth::EndOfYear() const
{
    if (!IsValid())
        Throw(Date,MONTH_ERROR);
    return DateStuff::EndOfYear(m_Year);
}

int YMonth::EndOfMonth() const
{
    if (!IsValid())
        Throw(Date,MONTH_ERROR);
    return DateStuff::EndOfMonth(m_Year, m_Month);
}

int YMonth::DaysInPrevMonth() const
{
    if (!IsValid())
        Throw(Date,MONTH_ERROR);
    return DateStuff::DaysInPrevMonth(m_Year, m_Month);
}

int YMonth::DaysInNextMonth() const
{
    if (!IsValid())
        Throw(Date,MONTH_ERROR);
    return DateStuff::DaysInNextMonth(m_Year, m_Month);
}
```

Class `Year` and object `YMonth` are not intended for use other than by the `Date` and `Full-Date` classes. As you can see in Listings 19.12 and 19.13, the `Date` functions determine the greatest precision that applies to all their arguments and then delegate the real work to `Year`, or `YMonth`, as required. For example, the function `AddDays` knows that only a `Date` with a valid year, month, and day can meet its request, so it checks its argument and throws an exception if it isn't a valid `YMDay`. The `AgeBetween` member function creates temporaries of the correct type and calls the appropriate `AgeBetween` method automatically. The `Date` class also provides string conversions. This is convenient since we actually store dates as strings in YYYYMMDD format in our databases, where the day, both the month and the day, or all three parts can be missing. In Listings 19.14 and 19.15, `FullDate` is a specialization of `Date` that requires a valid year, month, and day in all its instances. Because of the way these classes are designed, `FullDate` just needs to enforce this in its constructors, and everything else takes care of itself. The program in Listing 19.16 illustrates `Date` and `FullDate` functionality.

Listing 19.12   Interface for the `Date` class

```
// date.h
#if !defined(DATE_H)
#define DATE_H

#include "datestuf.h"
#include "year.h"
#include "ymonth.h"

namespace DateStuff
{

class Date
{
public:
    Date(int = 0, int = 0, int = 0);
    Date(const string&);
    Date(const Year&);
    Date(const YMonth&);

    // Additional assignment (for efficiency):
    Date& operator=(const string&);
    Date& operator=(const Year&);
    Date& operator=(const YMonth&);

    // Accessors:
    int GetYear() const;
    int GetMonth() const;
    int GetDay() const;
```

Listing 19.12 (continued)

```
// Tests:
bool IsValidYear() const;
bool IsValidYMonth() const;
bool IsValidYMDay() const;
virtual bool IsValid() const; // one of the above 3
bool IsEmpty() const;

// Comparison:
int  Compare(const Date&) const;
bool operator==(const Date&) const;
bool operator!=(const Date&) const;
bool operator<(const Date&) const;
bool operator>(const Date&) const;
bool operator<=(const Date&) const;
bool operator>=(const Date&) const;

// Basic calculations:
void AddYears(int);
void SubtractYears(int);
int YearsBetween(const Date&);
void AddMonths(long);
void SubtractMonths(long);
long MonthsBetween(const Date&) const;
void AddDays(long);
void SubtractDays(long);
long DaysBetween(const Date&) const;
void AddWeeks(long weeks);
void SubtractWeeks(long weeks);
long WeeksBetween(const Date&) const;
void AddWeekDays(long days);
void SubtractWeekDays(long days);
long WeekDaysBetween(const Date& right) const;
Duration operator-(const Date&) const;

// Special Requests:
int DayOfWeek() const;
int DayOfYear() const;
int EndOfMonth() const;
int EndOfYear() const;
Duration AgeBetween(const Date&) const;
Duration Age() const;
static Date Today();

// Conversions:
string ToString() const;
```

continued

Listing 19.12   (continued)

```
protected:
    int m_Year;
    int m_Month;
    int m_Day;
};

inline Date::Date(const Year& y)
{
    m_Year = y.GetYear();
    m_Month = 0;
    m_Day = 0;
}

inline Date::Date(const YMonth& ym)
{
    m_Year = ym.GetYear();
    m_Month = ym.GetMonth();
    m_Day = 0;
}

inline Date& Date::operator=(const Year& y)
{
    assert(y.IsEmpty() || y.IsValid());
    m_Year = y.GetYear();
    m_Month = 0;
    m_Day = 0;
    return *this;
}

inline Date& Date::operator=(const YMonth& ym)
{
    assert(ym.IsEmpty() || ym.IsValid());
    m_Year = ym.GetYear();
    m_Month = ym.GetMonth();
    m_Day = 0;
    return *this;
}

inline int Date::GetYear() const
{
    return m_Year;
}

inline int Date::GetMonth() const
{
    return m_Month;
}
```

Listing 19.12   (continued)

```
inline int Date::GetDay() const
{
    return m_Day;
}

inline bool Date::IsValidYear() const
{
    return DateStuff::IsValidYear(m_Year);
}

inline bool Date::IsValidYMonth() const
{
    return DateStuff::IsValidYMonth(m_Year,m_Month);
}

inline bool Date::IsValidYMDay() const
{
    return DateStuff::IsValidYMDay(m_Year,m_Month,m_Day);
}

inline bool Date::IsValid() const
{
    return IsEmpty() ||
            (m_Day == 0 && m_Month == 0 && IsValidYear()) ||
            (m_Day == 0 && IsValidYMonth()) ||
            IsValidYMDay();
}

inline bool Date::IsEmpty() const
{
    return m_Day == 0 && m_Month == 0 && m_Year == 0;
}

inline int Date::Compare(const Date& r) const
{
    int ydiff = m_Year - r.m_Year;
    int mdiff = m_Month - r.m_Month;
    return (ydiff == 0) ? ((mdiff == 0) ? m_Day - r.m_Day
                                        : mdiff)
                        : ydiff;
}

inline bool Date::operator==(const Date& r) const
{
    return Compare(r) == 0;
}
```

continued

Listing 19.12   (continued)

```cpp
inline bool Date::operator!=(const Date& r) const
{
    return Compare(r) != 0;
}

inline bool Date::operator<(const Date& r) const
{
    return Compare(r) < 0;
}

inline bool Date::operator>(const Date& r) const
{
    return Compare(r) > 0;
}

inline bool Date::operator<=(const Date& r) const
{
    return Compare(r) <= 0;
}

inline bool Date::operator>=(const Date& r) const
{
    return Compare(r) >= 0;
}

inline Duration Date::operator-(const Date& r) const
{
    return AgeBetween(r);
}

inline string Date::ToString() const
{
    return IsEmpty() ? string()
                     : DateStuff::ToString(m_Year, m_Month, m_Day);
}

inline Date Date::Today()
{
    int y, m, d;
    DateStuff::Today(y,m,d);
    return Date(y,m,d);
}

}    // end namespace DateStuff

#endif
```

Listing 19.13   Implementation for the `Date` class

```cpp
// date.cpp
#include "date.h"

using namespace DateStuff;

Date::Date(int y, int m, int d)
{
    m_Year = y;
    m_Month = m;
    m_Day = d;
    if (!IsEmpty() && !IsValid())
        Throw(Date, DATE_ERROR);
}

Date::Date(const string& s)
{
    // Requires YYYYMMDD
    if (s.size() > 8)
        Throw2(Date, DATE_ERROR, "String too long");

    m_Year = int(atoi(s.substr(0,4).c_str()));
    m_Month = int(atoi(s.substr(4,2).c_str()));
    m_Day = int(atoi(s.substr(6,2).c_str()));
    if (!IsEmpty() && !IsValid())
        Throw(Date, DATE_ERROR);
}

Date& Date::operator=(const string& s)
{
    // Requires left-subset of YYYYMMDD
    if (s.size() > 8)
        Throw2(Date, DATE_ERROR, "String too long");

    m_Year = int(atoi(s.substr(0,4).c_str()));
    m_Month = int(atoi(s.substr(4,2).c_str()));
    m_Day = int(atoi(s.substr(6,2).c_str()));
    if (!IsEmpty() && !IsValid())
        Throw(Date, DATE_ERROR);
    return *this;
}

void Date::AddYears(int years)
{
    if (IsValidYMDay())
    {
        DateStuff::AddYears(years, m_Year, m_Month, m_Day);
    }
```

continued

Listing 19.13   (continued)

```
    else if (IsValidYMonth() || IsValidYear())
    {
        Year y(m_Year);
        y.AddYears(years);
        operator=(y);
    }
    else
        Throw(Date,DATE_ERROR);
}

void Date::SubtractYears(int years)
{
    if (IsValidYMDay())
    {
        DateStuff::SubtractYears(years, m_Year, m_Month, m_Day);
    }

    else if (IsValidYMonth() || IsValidYear())
    {
        Year y(m_Year);
        y.SubtractYears(years);
        operator=(y);
    }
    else
        Throw(Date,DATE_ERROR);
}

int Date::YearsBetween(const Date& r)
{
    if (!IsValid())
        Throw(Date,DATE_ERROR);
    Year me(m_Year);
    Year you(r.m_Year);
    return me.YearsBetween(you);
}

void Date::AddMonths(long months)
{
    if (IsValidYMDay())
    {
        DateStuff::AddMonths(months,m_Year, m_Month, m_Day);
    }
    else if (IsValidYMonth())
    {
        DateStuff::ResolveMonths(m_Year*12L + m_Month + months,
                                 m_Year, m_Month);
    }
```

Listing 19.13 (continued)

```
    else
        Throw(Date,DATE_ERROR);
}

void Date::SubtractMonths(long months)
{
    if (IsValidYMDay())
    {
        DateStuff::SubtractMonths(months,m_Year, m_Month, m_Day);
    }
    else if (IsValidYMonth())
    {
        DateStuff::ResolveMonths(m_Year*12L + m_Month - months,
                             m_Year, m_Month);
    }
    else
        Throw(Date,DATE_ERROR);
}

long Date::MonthsBetween(const Date& r) const
{
    if (!IsValidYMonth() || !r.IsValidYMonth())
        Throw(Date,DATE_ERROR);
    return DateStuff::MonthsBetween(m_Year, m_Month, r.m_Year, r.m_Month);
}

void Date::AddDays(long days)
{
    if (!IsValidYMDay())
        Throw(Date,DATE_ERROR);
    DateStuff::AddDays(days,m_Year, m_Month, m_Day);
}

void Date::SubtractDays(long days)
{
    if (!IsValidYMDay())
        Throw(Date,DATE_ERROR);
    DateStuff::SubtractDays(days,m_Year, m_Month, m_Day);
}

long Date::DaysBetween(const Date& r) const
{
    if (!IsValidYMDay() || !r.IsValidYMDay())
        Throw(Date,DATE_ERROR);
    return DateStuff::DaysBetween(m_Year, m_Month, m_Day,
                             r.m_Year, r.m_Month, r.m_Day);
}
```

continued

Listing 19.13   (continued)

```
void Date::AddWeekDays(long days)
{
    if (!IsValidYMDay())
        Throw(Date,DATE_ERROR);
    DateStuff::AddWeekDays(days, m_Year, m_Month, m_Day);
}

void Date::SubtractWeekDays(long days)
{
    if (!IsValidYMDay())
        Throw(Date,DATE_ERROR);
    DateStuff::SubtractWeekDays(days, m_Year, m_Month, m_Day);
}

long Date::WeekDaysBetween(const Date& r) const
{
    if (!IsValidYMDay() || !r.IsValidYMDay())
        Throw(Date,DATE_ERROR);
    return DateStuff::WeekDaysBetween(m_Year, m_Month, m_Day,
                                      r.m_Year, r.m_Month, r.m_Day);
}

void Date::AddWeeks(long weeks)
{
    if (!IsValidYMDay())
        Throw(Date,DATE_ERROR);
    DateStuff::AddWeeks(weeks, m_Year, m_Month, m_Day);
}

void Date::SubtractWeeks(long weeks)
{
    if (!IsValidYMDay())
        Throw(Date,DATE_ERROR);
    DateStuff::SubtractWeeks(weeks, m_Year, m_Month, m_Day);
}

long Date::WeeksBetween(const Date& r) const
{
    if (!IsValidYMDay() || !r.IsValidYMDay())
        Throw(Date,DATE_ERROR);
    return DateStuff::WeeksBetween(m_Year, m_Month, m_Day,
                                   r.m_Year, r.m_Month, r.m_Day);
}
```

Listing 19.13   (continued)

```
Duration Date::AgeBetween(const Date& r) const
{
    if (!IsValid() || !r.IsValid())
        Throw(Date,DATE_ERROR);

    if (IsValidYMDay() && r.IsValidYMDay())
        return DateStuff::AgeBetween(m_Year, m_Month, m_Day,
                                     r.m_Year, r.m_Month, r.m_Day);
    else if (IsValidYMonth() && r.IsValidYMonth())
        return DateStuff::AgeBetween(m_Year, m_Month, 0,
                                     r.m_Year, r.m_Month, 0);
    else if (IsValidYear() && r.IsValidYear())
        return DateStuff::AgeBetween(m_Year, 0, 0, r.m_Year, 0, 0);
    else
    {
        // Shouldn't get here:
        assert(0);
        return Duration(-1,-1,-1);  // MS requires an explicit return!
    }
}

Duration Date::Age() const
{
    return AgeBetween(Today());
}

int Date::DayOfWeek() const
{
    if (!IsValidYMDay())
        Throw(Date,DATE_ERROR);
    return DateStuff::DayOfWeek(m_Year, m_Month, m_Day);
}

int Date::DayOfYear() const
{
    if (!IsValidYMDay())
        Throw(Date,DATE_ERROR);
    return DateStuff::DayOfYear(m_Year, m_Month, m_Day);
}

int Date::EndOfMonth() const
{
    if (!IsValidYMonth())
        Throw(Date,DATE_ERROR);
    return DateStuff::EndOfMonth(m_Year, m_Month);
}
```

continued

Listing 19.13   (continued)

```
int Date::EndOfYear() const
{
    if (!IsValidYear())
        Throw(Date,DATE_ERROR);
    return DateStuff::EndOfYear(m_Year);
}
```

Listing 19.14   Interface for the `FullDate` class

```
// FullDate.h
#if !defined(FULLDATE_H)
#define FULLDATE_H

#include "date.h"

namespace DateStuff
{

class FullDate : public Date
{
public:
    FullDate();
    FullDate(const string&);
    FullDate(int, int, int);
    FullDate(const Date&);

    bool IsValid() const;
    long ToJul() const;
};

inline FullDate::FullDate()
{
    DateStuff::Today(m_Year, m_Month, m_Day);
}

inline bool FullDate::IsValid() const
{
    return IsEmpty() || DateStuff::IsValidYMDay(m_Year, m_Month, m_Day);
}

inline long FullDate::ToJul() const
{
    return GregToJul(m_Year, m_Month, m_Day);
}

}    // end namespace DateStuff

#endif
```

Listing 19.15 Implementation for the `FullDate` class

```cpp
// fulldate.cpp
#include "fulldate.h"

using namespace DateStuff;

FullDate::FullDate(const string& s)
{
    DateStuff::FromString(s,m_Year,m_Month,m_Day);
    if (!IsEmpty() && !IsValidYMDay())
        Throw(Date,DATE_ERROR);
}

FullDate::FullDate(int year, int month, int day)
{
    m_Year = year;
    m_Month = month;
    m_Day = day;
    if (!IsEmpty() && !IsValidYMDay())
        Throw(Date,DATE_ERROR);
}

FullDate::FullDate(const Date& d)
{
    m_Year = d.GetYear();
    m_Month = d.GetMonth();
    m_Day = d.GetDay();
    assert(IsValid());
}
```

Listing 19.16 Illustrates `Date` and `FullDate` functionality

```cpp
// tdate.cpp:     Tests Date and FullDate
#include <iostream>
#include <stdexcept>
#include "fulldate.h"

using namespace DateStuff;
using namespace std;

void checkDate(int, int, int);
const char* DayText[] = {"Monday", "Tuesday", "Wednesday",
    "Thursday", "Friday", "Saturday", "Sunday"};
```

continued

Listing 19.16   (continued)

```
main()
{
    checkDate(0,3,14);          // Invalid year
    checkDate(1997,0,12);       // Invalid month
    checkDate(1998,13,1);       // Invalid month
    checkDate(97,1,12);         // Invalid year
    checkDate(1999,2,29);       // Invalid day
    checkDate(1900,2,29);       // Invalid day

    Date empty(0,0,0);
    cout << "empty: \"" << empty.ToString() << "\"\n";
    Date empty2("");
    cout << "empty2: \"" << empty2.ToString() << "\"\n";

    Date d1 = string("20000101");
    Date d2(2000,3,1);
    cout << "Day of week for d1: " << d1.ToString() << " == "
        << DayText[d1.DayOfWeek()] << endl;
    cout << "Day of week for d2: " << d2.ToString() << " == "
        << DayText[d2.DayOfWeek()] << endl;

    Date p1(1996,2,29);
    Date p2("20000229");

    cout << "p1 == " << p1.ToString() << endl;
    cout << "p2 == " << p2.ToString() << endl;

    Duration d = p1.AgeBetween(p2);
    cout << "Duration between p1 and p2: "
        << d.year << " years, "
        << d.month << " months, "
        << d.day << " days\n";

    Duration dd = p1.AgeBetween(d2);
    cout << "Duration between p1 and d2 (20000301): "
        << dd.year << " years, "
        << dd.month << " months, "
        << dd.day << " days\n";

    if (p1 < p2)
    {
        p1.AddYears(d.day);
        p1.AddMonths(d.month);
        p1.AddYears(d.year);
    }
```

Listing 19.16 (continued)

```
else if (p1 > p2)
{
    p2.AddYears(d.day);
    p2.AddMonths(d.month);
    p2.AddYears(d.year);
}

cout << "p1 == p2 (after adding Duration(p1,p2)): "
     << (p1 == p2 ? "Yes" : "No")
     << endl;

FullDate today;
Date f(today);
cout << "Today: " << f.ToString() << endl;
f.AddWeekDays(2);
cout << "+2 weekdays: " << f.ToString() << endl;
f.AddWeekDays(10);
cout << "+10 weekdays: " << f.ToString() << endl;
f.AddWeekDays(30);
cout << "+30 weekdays: " << f.ToString() << endl;
f.SubtractWeekDays(30);
cout << "-30 weekdays: " << f.ToString() << endl;
f.SubtractWeekDays(10);
cout << "-10 weekdays: " << f.ToString() << endl;
f.SubtractWeekDays(2);
cout << "-2 weekdays: " << f.ToString() << endl;

cout << "WeekdaysBetween 12/11/96 and 12/13/96: "
     << Date(1996,12,11).WeekDaysBetween(Date(1996,12,13))
     << endl;
cout << "WeekdaysBetween 12/13/96 and 12/27/96: "
     << Date(1996,12,13).WeekDaysBetween(Date(1996,12,27))
     << endl;
cout << "WeekdaysBetween 12/27/96 and 2/7/97: "
     << Date(1996,12,27).WeekDaysBetween(Date(1997,2,7))
     << endl;

FullDate f1(d1), f2(d2);
Duration f12 = f2 - f1;
cout << "d2 - d1 == "
     << f12.year << " years, "
     << f12.month << " months, "
     << f12.day << " days\n";
}
```

continued

Listing 19.16   (continued)

```
void checkDate(int year, int month, int day)
{
    try
    {
        Date(year,month,day);
        cout << "Validity check FAILED" << endl;
    }
    catch (Date_Exception& x)
    {
        cout << "Validity check PASSED (" << x.what() << ')' << endl;
    }
}


// Output:
Validity check PASSED (Invalid Date:DATE.CPP:Line 15)
Validity check PASSED (Invalid Date:DATE.CPP:Line 15)
Validity check PASSED (Invalid Date:DATE.CPP:Line 15)
Validity check PASSED (Invalid Date:DATE.CPP:Line 15)
Validity check PASSED (Invalid Date:DATE.CPP:Line 15)
Validity check PASSED (Invalid Date:DATE.CPP:Line 15)
empty: ""
empty2: ""
Day of week for d1: 20000101 == Saturday
Day of week for d2: 20000301 == Wednesday
p1 == 19960229
p2 == 20000229
Duration between p1 and p2: 4 years, 0 months, 0 days
Duration between p1 and d2 (20000301): 4 years, 0 months, 1 days
p1 == p2 (after adding Duration(p1,p2)): Yes
Today: 19970412
+2 weekdays: 19970415
+10 weekdays: 19970429
+30 weekdays: 19970610
-30 weekdays: 19970429
-10 weekdays: 19970415
-2 weekdays: 19970411
WeekdaysBetween 12/11/96 and 12/13/96: 2
WeekdaysBetween 12/13/96 and 12/27/96: 10
WeekdaysBetween 12/27/96 and 2/7/97: 30
d2 - d1 == 0 years, 2 months, 0 days
```

Calculating the Week of the Year

The *absolute week* of a year (or month) is based on the seven-day period beginning at the first day, and ending at the seventh, which is the first week. Finding the absolute week of a day number is found, therefore, by the simple formula:

```
w = (d - 1) / 7 + 1;
```

where d is the day number. This works for either the week of the year or the week of the month.

    The *common week* is based on a Sunday-to-Saturday duration. The first common week of a year or month begins on the first day, and ends on the first Saturday encountered (which could be the very same day). Intervening weeks go from Sunday to Saturday, and the last week begins on the last Sunday and ends on the last day (which again could be that Sunday). Hence, there are 53 common weeks in a year (except when the first Saturday of a leap year is New Year's Day, in which case there are 54), and 5 common weeks in a month (except when February has 28 days and begins on Sunday, in which case there are 4).

    To compute the common week of the year given the ordinal number of the day, note the following pattern (s denotes the ordinal of the first Saturday of the year):

Week Number	Start Day	End Day
1	1	s
2	$s + 1$	$s + 7$
3	$s + 8$	$s + 14$
n	$s + 1 + 7(n-2)$	$s + 7(n-1)$

For n >= 2, then, you can write

```
s + 1 + 7(n - 2) <= d <= s + 7(n - 1)
```

where d is the day in question. Solving this inequality for n gives:

```
1 + (d - s)/7 <= n <= 2 + (d - s - 1)/7      // integer arithmetic!
```

    These bounds for n are equal when d - s is a multiple of 7, that is, when d is a Saturday. When d is not a Saturday, then the bounds differ by 1. The question then is, which one of the two bounds is the correct value of n? Trying a few dates suggests it is the upper bound (and a computer simulation verifies this). This is consistent with the fact that dates less than 7 can be in the second common week (not possible with the lower bound). The common week of a date d can therefore be determined by the following simple formula:

```
n = 2 + (d - s - 1)/7
```

where d and s have the meanings explained above. This formula also holds for the common week of the month, where d is the day of the month, and s is the ordinal of its first Saturday.

The number of common weeks in a year, as mentioned above, is on rare occasion 54, but usually 53, and can be obtained by setting the formula for the lower bound in the table above equal to the last day of the year (e, which is either 365 or 366) and solving for n:

```
s + 1 + 7(n - 2) = e
```

which gives

```
n = (e - s - 1)/7 + 2
```

Summary

- Use <time.h> functions such as `localtime`, `strftime`, and `difftime` for simple time and date operations.
- Be sure to know the *reference date* for your environment.
- Integer-based Julian day encoding facilitates easy and efficient date computation for a wide range of dates (viz., after October 15, 1582).
- The `Date` and `FullDate` classes handle most common business date processing needs, including *partial dates*.

Reference

1. Burki, David, "Date Conversions," *C Users Journal*, Feb. 1993, pp. 29–34.

CHAPTER 20

Dynamic Memory Management

$\mathbf{A}$s a C/C++ programmer you need to worry about three types of internal storage for program objects: *automatic*, *static*, and *dynamic*. When you define automatic variables inside a block, most compilers generate code to allocate space for those variables on the program stack or in registers. When execution leaves a block, the stack pointer moves back up where it was before entering the block, in effect destroying that block's automatic variables. When execution reenters the block, it creates all automatic variables afresh, with the same initial values as before. Static objects are declared either at file scope or inside a block or namespace with the `static` specifier. They reside at a fixed location in the program's data space and are initialized once before their first use. Dynamic objects are created at runtime by special system calls and reside on the *heap* (or *free store*), a special data area set aside for user-controlled, runtime memory allocation. When you request heap space for an object, you get an address in return. The system reserves the memory at that address for your use until you're through with it. This chapter discusses common techniques for using dynamic memory in C and C++.

Ragged Arrays

The heap comes in handy when you don't know at compiletime how much space you need to store an object or how many objects you will need. For example, a common practice for processing text files in C allocates heap space for each line of text, storing the address in an array of pointers to `char`. The program in Listing 20.1 reads up to `MAXLINES` lines of text into memory and sorts them in ascending order, using `qsort`. (For an explanation of the `qsort` function, see Chap. 15.) As it reads each line, it calls `malloc` (a `<stdlib.h>` function) to get enough heap space to hold the line and its terminating null byte. It stores the address that `malloc` returns in the array `strings`. This flexible storage mechanism is sometimes called a *ragged array*, because it only allocates the memory that each line of text requires, as the following diagram depicts.

Lines to read and sort		Ragged array strings[]
strings[0]	————————————→	n o w \0
strings[1]	————————————→	i s \0
strings[2]	————————————→	t h e \0
strings[3]	————————————→	t i m e \0
etc.		

Listing 20.1   A sort program

```c
/* sort.c: Sort strings */

#include <stdio.h>
#include <stdlib.h>
#include <string.h>
#include <assert.h>

#define MAXLINES 1024

static int scomp(const void *, const void *);

main(int argc, char *argv[])
{
    int i, n;
    char *strings[MAXLINES], buf[BUFSIZ];

    if (argc > 1)
        freopen(argv[1],"r",stdin);

    for (n = 0; n < MAXLINES && fgets(buf,BUFSIZ,stdin); ++n)
    {
        strings[n] = malloc(strlen(buf)+1);
        assert(strings[n]);
        strcpy(strings[n],buf);
    }

    qsort(strings, n, sizeof strings[0], scomp);

    for (i = 0; i < n; ++i)
    {
        fputs(strings[i],stdout);
        free(strings[i]);
    }
    return 0;
}

static int scomp(const void *p1, const void *p2)
{
    char *a = * (char **) p1;
    char *b = * (char **) p2;
    return strcmp(a,b);
}
```

Although there is an overhead penalty of one pointer per line, this is likely to be more efficient than using a two-dimensional storage scheme with a large line length.

Lines to read and sort	Ragged array strings[]	2-d storage strings [][MAXLINE]
strings[0]	n o w \0	n o w \0 ? ? ? ?
strings[1]	i s \0	i s \0 ? ? ? ? ?
strings[2]	t h e \0	t h e \0 ? ? ? ?
strings[3]	t i m e \0	t i m e \0 ? ? ?
etc.		

When you are through with dynamic memory, pass its address as a parameter to `free`, which makes the space available for future calls to `malloc`.

Using the Heap in Standard C

The header `<stdlib.h>` declares four functions for using dynamic memory:

1. `void *malloc(size_t siz);`
   Returns a pointer to the first of `siz` bytes. Usually used for allocating single objects.
2. `void *calloc(size_t nelems, size_t elem_size);`
   Returns a pointer to `nelems*elem_size` bytes, initialized to zero. Usually used for allocating arrays of objects.
3. `void *realloc(void *ptr, size_t siz);`
   Used to expand or shrink a heap allocation. The `ptr` must have originated from a previous call to `malloc`, `calloc`, or `realloc` except that if `ptr` is `NULL`, the result is the same as `malloc(siz)`. If there is enough space for the new allocation, `realloc` copies the original data to the new location, and then returns the new address. If `ptr` is not `NULL`, and `siz` is 0, then `realloc` acts like `free`.
4. `void free(void *ptr);`
   Makes previously allocated heap memory available for reuse. The `ptr` must have been returned by a previous call to one of the above allocation functions. The call `free(NULL)` is a benign, do-nothing call.

The three allocation functions return a `NULL` pointer if the amount of memory requested is not available.

The program in Listings 20.2 and 20.3 illustrates all four functions. It extends the traditional `argc`/`argv` mechanism for reading command-line arguments by allowing you to specify files of arguments. Any program argument that begins with the '@' character names an *indirect file*, a file that contains more arguments. For example, the command

```
getargs @arg.dat
```

causes the file `arg.dat` to be read for more arguments. Such command files can be nested (see Listing 20.4).

Listing 20.2 Illustrates Indirect Files

```
/* getargs.c: Reads files of arguments */
#include <stdio.h>

extern char **arglist(int,char **,int *);
extern void free_arglist(int,char **);

main(int argc, char *argv[])
{
    int i, nargs;
    char **args = arglist(--argc,++argv,&nargs);

    for (i = 0; i < nargs; ++i)
        printf("%d: %s\n",i,args[i]);
    free_arglist(nargs,args);
    return 0;
}

/* Sample Execution:
c:> getargs @arg.dat
0: little
1: lamb
2: where
3: no
4: one
5: along
6: came
7: a
8: spider
9: has
10: gone
11: before
12: little
13: lamb
*/
```

The `arglist` function returns a pointer to a dynamically sized, ragged array of strings, which is the fully expanded list of program arguments. The function `free_args` frees all of the memory used in the creation of the array.

The `arglist` function uses `calloc` to dynamically allocate an array large enough to hold `argc-1` arguments, the original number of arguments on the command line. It calls `add` to insert a new argument into the list. If the array is full, `add` calls `realloc` to increase the size of the array by a predetermined amount (`CHUNK`). Then `add` calls `malloc` to place all argument strings on the heap. The function `expand` processes indirect file arguments. Since indirect files can be

Listing 20.3 Functions to read arguments from indirect files

```c
/* arglist.c:     Recursively reads arguments from files */
#include <stdio.h>
#include <stdlib.h>
#include <string.h>
#include <assert.h>

#define CHUNK 10      /* Reallocation amount */

static char **args; /* The argument list */
static int nleft;    /* Unused argument slots */
static int nargs;    /* Number of arguments */

/* Private Functions */
static void expand(FILE *f);
static void add(char *arg);

char **arglist(int old_nargs, char **old_args, int *new_nargs)
{
    int i;

    /* Initial Allocation */
    args = calloc(old_nargs,sizeof(char *));
    assert(args);
    nleft = old_nargs;
    nargs = 0;

    /* Process each command-line argument */
    for (i = 0; i < old_nargs; ++i)
        if (old_args[i][0] == '@')
        {
            /* Open file of arguments */
            FILE *f = fopen(old_args[i]+1,"r");
            if (f)
            {
                expand(f);
                fclose(f);
            }
        }
        else
            add(old_args[i]);

    *new_nargs = nargs;
    return args;
}
```

continued

Listing 20.3 (continued)

```
void free_arglist(int n, char **av)
{
    int i;
    for (i = 0; i < n; ++i)
        free(av[i]);
    free(av);
}

static void expand(FILE *f)
{
    char token[BUFSIZ];

    while (fscanf(f,"%s",token) == 1)
        if (token[0] == '@')
        {
            FILE *g = fopen(token+1,"r");
            if (g)
            {
                expand(g);
                fclose(g);
            }
        }
        else
            add(token);
}

static void add(char *arg)
{
    if (nleft == 0)
    {
        /* Expand argument list */
        args = realloc(args,(nargs+CHUNK) * sizeof(char *));
        assert(args);
        nleft = CHUNK;
    }

    /* Allocate space for and store argument */
    args[nargs] = malloc(strlen(arg) + 1);
    assert(args[nargs]);
    strcpy(args[nargs++], arg);
    --nleft;
}
```

Listing 20.4 Input files for testing the **arglist** function

---

File arg.dat:

little lamb
@arg2.dat
little
lamb

File arg2.dat:

where no one
@arg3.dat
has gone
before

File arg3.dat:

along came
a
spider

---

nested, expand is a recursive function. If there are no indirect file arguments, then realloc is never called.

The C++ Free Store

As an alternative to the memory management functions in <stdlib.h>, C++ offers the new and delete operators. The word *operators* is key. In C you must explicitly pass the size of the objects you're working with to malloc. Since new is an operator in C++, the compiler figures out how much memory is needed—you just deal with objects. To get a pointer to a dynamic object of any type, just ask for it:

```
T *tp = new T;
```

Using new does two things:

1. Allocates memory for the object
2. Calls the appropriate constructor.

Arrays are easy, too:

```
const size_t SIZE = 100;
T *tap = new T[SIZE];
```

In this case new calls the default constructor to initialize each array element in order of increasing index.

Even multidimensional arrays are a snap. For example, to allocate a two-by-three array, you can do something like:

```
const size_t NROWS = 2;
const size_t NCOLS = 3;
T (*p)[NCOLS] = new T[NROWS][NCOLS];
```

You can now use p with array syntax, as in

```
T t;
...
p[0][1] = t;
```

(If p's declaration syntax is puzzling to you, see Chap. 2).

To dispose of a heap object, you use the delete operator:

```
delete tp;              // scalar version
delete [] tap;          // array version
```

A call to delete invokes the appropriate destructor before deallocating memory. The array version, delete [], destroys the array elements in decreasing index order. It is important to use the correct version of delete when returning memory to the heap.

Deep versus Shallow Copy

The simple string class in Listings 20.5 and 20.6 uses a C-style string to hold its data. Since the string can grow and shrink, the data buffer is allocated on the heap. The test program in Listing 20.7 exposes a problem with this class, however. Somehow a string that is either initialized or assigned from another stays "connected" to the original, so that changing one changes the other. If you look closely at the class definition, you'll notice that I did not define a copy constructor or an assignment operator. A copy constructor has the signature

```
String(const String&);
```

and executes whenever a new String object is initialized with the value of another, as in

```
String t = s;
```

The assignment operator has the following signature:

```
String& operator=(const String&);
```

The compiler automatically generates these functions if you don't. These automatic versions use *memberwise* semantics, however. This means that when you initialize a new string object with another's value, each member of the receiving object is initialized with the value of the corresponding member in the original object. If the data member is an instance of a type that has a copy constructor, that constructor gets called. In the case of String, the data members are built-in types, so the pointer and counter are just copied as scalar values. This results in the following situation:

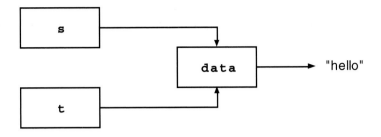

Listing 20.5   Header for a simple `String` class

```
// str.h
#include <stddef.h>

class ostream;

class String
{
public:
    String(const char*);
    ~String();

    char& operator[](size_t pos);
    friend ostream& operator<<(ostream&, const String&);

private:
    char* data;
    size_t count;
    void clone(const char *);
};

inline String::String(const char *s)
{
    clone(s);
}

inline String::~String()
{
    delete [] data;
}

inline char& String::operator[](size_t pos)
{
    return data[pos];
}
```

Listing 20.6   Implementation file for the `String` class

```
// str.cpp
#include <iostream>
#include <string.h>
#include "str.h"

ostream& operator<<(ostream& os, const String& s)
{
    os.write(s.data,s.count);
    return os;
}

void String::clone(const char *s)
{
    count = strlen(s);
    data = new char[count + 1];
    strcpy(data,s);
}
```

Listing 20.7   Exposes the `String` class's shallow copy

```
// tstr.cpp:      Test the C++ string class
#include <iostream>
#include "str.h"

main()
{
    String s = "hello", t = s;

    t[0] = 'j';
    cout << "s == " << s << endl;
    cout << "t == " << t << endl;
}

// Output:
s == jello
t == jello
```

The string objects s and t actually share the underlying C-string buffer, since the compiler-generated copy constructor just copied s.data to t.data. This is called a *shallow copy*. If s should go out of scope before t does, the String destructor will make t.data a dangling pointer:

What you really want is a *deep copy*, which creates a separate copy of the underlying character buffer for each initialization or assignment. This requires a copy constructor and assignment operator to allocate a new buffer for the receiving object, as follows:

```
String(const String& s)
{
    clone(s.data);
}

String& String::operator=(const String& s)
{
    if (this != &s)
    {
        delete [] data;
        clone(s.data);
    }
    return *this;
}
```

In general, when an object contains a pointer to heap memory, you should define a custom copy constructor and assignment operator, as well as a destructor and other constructors as necessary.

Handling Memory Allocation Failure

Before development of the exceptions part of C++, if a new operation failed to allocate an object, it returned a null pointer, just like malloc does in C:

```
T *tp = new T;
if (tp)
    // Use new object
```

C++ now stipulates that a memory-allocation failure results in a bad_alloc exception. The standard library, as well as third-party libraries, may make generous use of the free store. Since a memory allocation request can occur when you least expect it, almost any program you write should be prepared to handle a bad_alloc exception. The obvious way is to supply a handler:

```
catch(const bad_alloc& x)
{
    cerr << "Out of memory: " << x.what() << endl;
    abort();
}
```

If you prefer the classic behavior of returning a null pointer, you can use a special version of the new operator:

```
#include <new>
//...
    T* tp = new (nothrow) T;
    if (tp)
        // use tp...
```

Yet another way of handling out-of-memory conditions is to replace parts of the memory allocation machinery itself. When a memory allocation fails, C++ calls the default new_handler, which in turn throws a bad_alloc exception. You can provide your own handler by passing its address to set_new_handler (see Listing 20.8).

Overriding `new` and `delete`

The standard C++ library defines twelve functions for allocating and deallocating memory. When you use the new operator, it calculates the number of bytes needed and in turn calls one of these functions to allocate those bytes. The twelve functions are:

```
// Scalar versions
void *operator new(size_t);
void *operator new(size_t, const nothrow_t);
void operator delete(void *);
void operator delete(void *, const nothrow_t);

// Array versions
void *operator new[](size_t);
void *operator new[](size_t, const nothrow_t);
void operator delete[](void *);
void operator delete[](void *, const nothrow_t);

// Placement new
void *operator new(size_t, void *);
void *operator new[](size_t, void *);
void operator delete(void*, void*);
void operator delete[](void*, void*);
```

Whenever you allocate an object of a built-in type from the heap, new calls the first oper-ator new above to get the memory. You can easily implement it via malloc (see Listing 20.9). Likewise, deleting a dynamic, built-in object results in a call to ::operator delete(void *). Listing 20.10 also illustrates that you can *override* these functions. Notice that I use printf, *not* cout, in the replacement versions. In many C++ implementations, cout uses the new operator, so if I had used cout inside my operator new I'd have infinite recursion on my hands!

Any function you define with the same signature as one of the first eight functions above replaces the library version of that function in your program. The four placement versions over-

Listing 20.8 Illustrates `set_new_handler`

```cpp
// exhaust1.cpp
#include <iostream>
#include <stdlib.h>
#include <new>

inline void my_handler()
{
    cout << "Memory exhausted" << endl;
    abort();
}

main()
{
    set_new_handler(my_handler);

    for (int i = 0; ; ++i)
    {
        (void) new double[100];
        if ((i+1)%10 == 0)
            cout << (i+1) << " allocations" << endl;
    }
}

// Output:
10 allocations
20 allocations
30 allocations
40 allocations
50 allocations
60 allocations
70 allocations
Memory exhausted
Abnormal program termination
```

load; they're not replaceable like the others. Since so many standard and third-party program components rely on global new and delete, it's rarely a good idea to replace them. You can also replace the various versions of operator new and operator delete on a per-class basis (see "Managing the Heap" below).

Placement new

Sometimes you want to create an object at a predetermined address. The location could be in a region of RAM mapped to some device, or within a class-specific heap. You can construct such

Listing 20.9 Typical implementation of `::operator new` and `::operator delete`

```
// opnew.cpp
#include <stdlib.h>
#include <new.h>

void *operator new(size_t siz)
{
    // Get new_handler
    void (*new_handler)() = set_new_handler(0);
    set_new_handler(new_handler);

    for (;;)
    {
        // Return pointer upon success
        void *p = malloc(siz);
        if (p)
            return p;

        // If there is a handler, call it
        if (new_handler)
            new_handler();
        else
            return 0;
    }
}

void operator delete(void *p)
{
    if (p)
        free(p);
}
```

an object using the *placement* syntax for the `new` operator. For example, to construct a `T` at address `p`, do the following:

```
#include <new>
T *tp = new (p) T;
```

In this case, no version of `operator new` executes, since the memory location is already determined. In fact, the default version of placement `operator new` ignores its size parameter and just returns the address parameter:

```
void *operator new(size_t, void *p)
{
    return p;
}
```

As Listing 20.11 illustrates, you can overload (not override) placement new with as many parameters as you like.

You can use placement new to keep an assignment operator in sync with its copy constructor without duplicating the code that initializes a new object. You explicitly invoke the destructor on the object's this pointer and reconstruct the new copy in place with placement new, like this:

```
T& T::operator=(const T& x)
{
    if (this != &x)
    {
        this->T::~T();
        new (this) T(x);
    }
    return *this;
}
```

Listing 20.10 Overriding `operator new` and `operator delete`

```
// override.cpp
#include <stdio.h>
#include <stdlib.h>
#include <new>

void* operator new(size_t siz)
{
    printf("allocating %d bytes\n",siz);
    return malloc(siz);
}

void operator delete(void *p)
{
    printf("deleting memory at %p\n",p);
    free(p);
}

main()
{
    double *dp = new double;
    delete dp;
}

// Output:
allocating 8 bytes
deleting memory at 007C2C9C
```

Listing 20.11   A placement `operator new` with two arguments

```cpp
// overload.cpp
#include <iostream.h>

void *operator new(size_t siz, void *arg1, int arg2)
{
    cout << "new: siz == " << siz
         << ", arg1 == " << (void *) arg1
         << ", arg2 == " << arg2 << endl;
    return arg1;
}

main()
{
    void *p = (void *) 0x1234;
    int *ip = new (p,100) int;
    cout << "ip == " << (void *) ip << endl;
    return 0;
}

// Output:
new: siz == 2, arg1 == 0x1234, arg2 == 100
ip == 0x1234
```

This clever technique may break down with derived classes, however. For more information, see Pete Becker, "Not All `operator=`'s Are Equal," *C/C++ Users Journal* (May 1997), pp. 91–92.

Managing the Heap

Have you ever wondered how the heap management mechanism knows how much memory to release when you call `free(p)`? Since you don't tell it, it must keep that information somewhere. In most systems that somewhere is right before the pointer p itself, so instead of getting this:

you're really getting this:

p

This overhead can turn out to be rather costly when you allocate a large number of small objects.

Another phenomenon that occurs is *fragmentation*. After allocating many objects and then deleting some, there are gaps in the heap:

Free	Used	Used	Free	Used	Used	Free . . .

Although there is enough space on the heap for another object, it is not contiguous, so an allocation may fail. One way to sidestep these problems is to allocate a large pool of memory and manage it yourself. This can result in critical savings of time and space for container classes.

Placement new is handy for managing class-specific heaps. The program in Listing 20.12 has a class template for an expandable vector. To save overhead, it allocates storage to hold a predetermined number (CHUNK) of elements. Whenever you append an element to the vector, it just constructs that element at the next available location:

```
new (arena + length_++) T(x);
```

It only uses the global operator new when it is time to expand the underlying storage pool.

```
T *new_arena = (T*) ::operator new(sizeof(T) * new_capacity);
```

When it comes time to destroy a single element, you don't want to deallocate any memory, since it is part of the storage arena and can be reused. Instead, you explicitly invoke the destructor:

```
(arena+i)->T::~T();
```

See Listing 20.13 for a program that uses the Vector class.

Avoiding Memory Management

C and C++ get a lot of bad press because it is so easy to mismanage dynamic memory. A good way to finesse those difficulties is to let someone else do the work for you, when possible. For example, instead of reading lines into memory like the sort program in Listing 20.1 does, why not let the standard library do the hard part? The program in Listing 20.14 uses getline to read input lines of arbitrary length, and then stores them in a vector, which handles its own memory. The arglist mechanism introduced above is also lot easier with vectors (see Chap. 16).

Listing 20.12 A `Vector` class template that manages its own heap

```cpp
// Vector.h
#include <iostream>
#include <stddef.h>
#include <stdlib.h>
#include <new>

// The next two functions are just for tracing execution:
inline void *operator new(size_t siz)
{
    cout << ">>> operator new (" << siz << " bytes)" << endl;
    return malloc(siz);
}

inline void operator delete(void *p)
{
    cout << ">>> operator delete: " << (void *) p << endl;
    free(p);
}

template<class T>
class Vector
{
public:
    Vector();
    Vector(size_t);
    ~Vector();

    // Append & subscript:
    Vector<T>& operator+=(const T&);
    T& operator[](size_t);

    // Length-related functions:
    size_t length() const;
    void resize(size_t);
    size_t capacity() const;
    void reserve(size_t);

private:
    T *arena;          // class-specific storage arena
    size_t length_;
    size_t capacity_;

    enum {CHUNK = 10};

    // Disallow copy and assign:
    Vector(const Vector&);
    Vector<T>& operator=(const Vector<T>&);
```

Listing 20.12 (continued)

```cpp
    static size_t next_chunk(size_t n);
};

template<class T>
inline Vector<T>::Vector()
{
    // Intialize an empty vector
    arena = 0;
    length_ = capacity_ = 0;
}

template<class T>
inline Vector<T>::Vector(size_t n)
{
    // Allocate a multiple of CHUNK elements >= n
    length_ = 0;
    capacity_ = next_chunk(n);
    arena = (T *) ::operator new(sizeof(T) * capacity_);
    cout << ">>> arena created at " << (void *) arena << endl;
}

template<class T>
Vector<T>::~Vector()
{
    // Execute destructor for each element
    for (int i = 0; i < length_; ++i)
        (arena+i)->T::~T();

    ::operator delete(arena);
}

template<class T>
inline T& Vector<T>::operator[](size_t pos)
{
    if (pos >= length_)
        throw "bad index in Vector<T>::operator[]";
    return arena[pos];
}

template<class T>
inline size_t Vector<T>::length() const
{
    return length_;
}
```

continued

Listing 20.12 (continued)

```
template<class T>
inline size_t Vector<T>::capacity() const
{
    return capacity_;
}

template<class T>
void Vector<T>::reserve(size_t new_capacity)
{
    // Only allow an increase:
    if (new_capacity > capacity_)
    {
        new_capacity = next_chunk(new_capacity);
        if (new_capacity > capacity_)
        {
            // Copy elements to new space
            T *new_arena = (T*) ::operator new(sizeof(T) *
                               new_capacity);
            cout << ">>> new arena created at "
                 << (void *) new_arena << endl;
            for (int i = 0; i < length_; ++i)
                (void) new (new_arena + i) T(arena[i]);

            // Destroy old vector
            for (i = 0; i < length_; ++i)
                (arena+i)->T::~T();
            delete arena;

            // Update state
            arena = new_arena;
            capacity_ = new_capacity;
        }
    }
}

template<class T>
void Vector<T>::resize(size_t new_length)
{
    // Only allow a decrease:
    if (new_length < length_)
    {
        // Just destroy truncated elements;
        // Don't change capacity
        for (int i = new_length; i < length_; ++i)
            (arena+i)->T::~T();
        length_ = new_length;
    }
}
```

Listing 20.12   (continued)

```
template<class T>
Vector<T>& Vector<T>::operator+=(const T& x)
{
    if (length_ == capacity_)
        reserve(length_ + 1);
    (void) new (arena + length_++) T(x);
    return *this;
}

template<class T>
inline size_t Vector<T>::next_chunk(size_t n)
{
    return ((n + CHUNK - 1) / CHUNK) * CHUNK;
}
```

Listing 20.13   Tests the `Vector` class

```
// tvector.cpp
#include <iostream.h>
#include "Vector.h"

// A user-defined class to test Vector
class Foo
{
    long x;

public:
    Foo() : x(0)
    {
        cout << "Foo::Foo()\n";
    }

    Foo(int i) : x(i)
    {}

    Foo(const Foo& f) : x(f.x)
    {
        cout << "Foo::Foo(const Foo&)\n";
    }

    ~Foo()
    {
        cout << "Foo::~Foo()\n";
    }
```

continued

Listing 20.13   (continued)

```cpp
    friend ostream& operator<<(ostream& os, const Foo& f)
    {
        cout << f.x; return os;
    }
};

main()
{
    // Instantiate a vector of ints
    Vector<int> v(5);
    for (int i = 0; i < 11; ++i)
        v += i;
    for (i = 0; i < v.length(); ++i)
        cout << v[i] << endl;

    // Instantiate a vector of Foo's
    Vector<Foo> v2;
    v2 += 0;
    v2 += 1;
    v2 += 2;
    for (i = 0; i < v2.length(); ++i)
        cout << v2[i] << endl;

    return 0;
}


// Output:
>>> operator new (20 bytes)
>>> arena created at 0x181e
>>> operator new (40 bytes)
>>> new arena created at 0x1836
>>> operator delete: 0x181e
0
1
2
3
4
5
6
7
8
9
10
>>> operator new (40 bytes)
>>> new arena created at 0x1862
Foo::Foo(const Foo&)
```

Listing 20.13   (continued)

```
Foo::~Foo()
Foo::Foo(const Foo&)
Foo::~Foo()
Foo::Foo(const Foo&)
Foo::~Foo()
0
1
2
Foo::~Foo()
Foo::~Foo()
Foo::~Foo()
>>> operator delete: 0x1862
>>> operator delete: 0x1836
```

Listing 20.14   A better version of Listing 20.1

```cpp
// sort.cpp
#include <iostream>
#include <fstream>
#include <string>
#include <vector>
#include <algorithm>

using namespace std;

main(int argc, char *argv[])
{
    vector<string> strings;

    ifstream ifs(argv[1]);
    if (!ifs)
        return 1;

    string line;
    while (getline(ifs,line))
        strings.push_back(line);

    sort(strings.begin(), strings.end());

    for (int i = 0; i < strings.size(); ++i)
        cout << strings[i] << endl;

    return 0;
}
```

Summary

- Use dynamic memory when you don't know ahead of time how much space you need to store an object, or how many objects you'll need.
- The `new` operator calls `operator new` to acquire memory for a dynamic object, and then calls the appropriate constructor. The `delete` operator undoes that by invoking the object's destructor and then calling `operator delete`.
- Be sure to use `delete []` on arrays.
- Check to see if you need to use *deep copy* whenever a class has a pointer data member.
- Remember that memory failure raises a `bad_alloc` exception. Use the `nothrow` version of `new` if you want the classic "return null" behavior. You can further customize memory failure recovery by supplying a *new handler*.
- Use *placement new* to construct an object at a given address.
- To minimize memory fragmentation, consider using a private pool for a homogeneous collection of dynamic objects, such as a container.
- Let the standard library manage memory for you whenever possible.

C/C++ Compatibility

To be true to its mission of type safety, as well as to support object-oriented programming styles, C++ has had to bend some of the rules of the C language. The key incompatibilities between the two languages are summarized below. Even if you're a C programmer, following the C++ rules where possible tends to result in safer programs.

1. **New comment style**. C++ treats all text following the token `//` as a comment.
2. **New keywords**. C++ has added a number of keywords and reserved words to C, disallowing them to be used as user identifiers. The expanded list is as follows:

and	do	not	this
and_eq	double	not_eq	throw
asm	dynamic_cast	operator	true
auto	else	or	try
bitand	enum	or_eq	typedef
bitor	explicit	private	typeid
bool	extern	protected	typename
break	false	public	union
case	float	reinterpret_cast	unsigned
catch	friend	return	using
char	goto	short	virtual
class	if	signed	void
compl	inline	sizeof	volatile
const	int	static	wchar_t
const_cast	long	static_cast	volatile
continue	mutable	struct	xor
default	namespace	switch	xor_eq
delete	new	template	

3. **New punctuators**. New punctuation tokens (see Chaps. 2 and 3) are

```
<:                      %:%:
:>                      ::
<%                      .*
%>                      ->*
%:
```

4. **Type of character literals**. A character literal, such as `'a'`, is of type `char` in C++ (to allow overloading vs. `int`). In C, character literals are type `int`.

5. **The `const`-ness of C-style string literals**. A literal such as "A" is of type `const char*`. In C, it was not `const`. This means that an expression such as

```
char* p = "abc";        // assigning const to non-const
```

is deprecated.

6. **Behavior of `const`**. All `const` integers are true compiletime constants in C++, and as such can be used as array dimensions. All `const` objects declared at file scope have *internal linkage*, allowing them to replace object-like macros in header files (see Chap. 11).

7. **Behavior of `main()`**. The function `main()` cannot be called recursively in C++.

8. **Type-safe linkage**. Functions with different signatures cannot mistakenly be linked (see Chap. 1).

9. **Behavior of `void*`**. Assigning from a pointer to `void` to any other pointer type requires a cast. (See Chap. 10).

10. **Structure tags are type names**. Structure tags are now in the same namespace as type definitions and normal variable names. This allows defining user objects without the `struct` or `class` keywords.

11. **No implicit `int`**. The `int` is no longer assumed as the return type of a function. You must explicitly specify the type of function return values.

12. **Compatibility of `enum` with `int`**. Assigning an `int` to an `enum` requires a cast.

13. **An `enum` is overloadable.** Enumerated types are now distinguished as distinct types in function overloading.

14. **Prototypes required.** Old-style–C function declarations where argument types are declared outside of the argument list are not allowed. All functions must be fully declared or defined before they are called.

15. **Empty argument list == `void`.** A function with no arguments—`f()`, say—is equivalent to `f(void)`.

16. **Structures define a scope.** Nested `struct` definitions belong to the scope where they are defined.

Standard C++ Algorithms

The template arguments in the tables below use the following shorthand:

Abbreviation	Meaning
II	input iterator
OI	output iterator
FI	forward iterator
BI	bi-directional iterator
RI	random access iterator
UOP	unary operation
BOP	binary operation
P	predicate
BinP	binary predicate
Gen	generator
RandGen	random number generator

I've taken some modest liberties with the complexity notation. For example, it is somewhat silly to use the expression O(3*N), but I do so to indicate the operation count will not exceed 3*N. Complexity measures not expressed with "big-Oh" notation represent an exact operation count.

Table B.1   Nonmutating sequence algorithms

Function	Complexity
template<class II, class F> F **for_each**(II first, II last, F f);	N
template<class II, class T> II **find**(II first, II last, const T& value);	O(N)
template<class II, class P> II **find_if**(II first, II last, P pred);	O(N)
template<class FI1, class FI2> FI1 **find_end**(FI1 first1, FI1 last1, FI2 first2, FI2 last2);	O(M*(N−M+1))
template<class FI1, class FI2, class BinP> FI1 **find_end**(FI1 first1, FI1 last1, FI2 first2, FI2 last2, BinP pred);	O(M*(N−M+1))
template<class FI1, class FI2> FI1 **find_first_of**(FI1 first1, FI1 last1, FI2 first2, FI2 last2);	O(M*N)
template<class FI1, class FI2, class BinP> FI1 **find_first_of**(FI1 first1, FI1 last1, FI2 first2, FI2 last2, BinP pred);	O(M*N)
template<class FI> FI **adjacent_find**(FI first, FI last);	O(N)
template<class FI, class BinP> FI **adjacent_find**(FI first, FI last, BinP pred);	O(N)
template<class II, class T> iterator_traits<II>::difference_type **count**(II first, II last, const T& value);	N
template<class II, class P> iterator_traits<II>::difference_type **count_if**(II first, II last, P pred);	N
template<class II1, class II2> pair<II1, II2> **mismatch**(II1 first1, II1 last1, II2 first2);	O(N)
template<class II1, class II2, class BinP> pair<II1, II2> **mismatch**(II1 first1, II1 last1, II2 first2, BinP pred);	O(N)
template<class II1, class II2> bool **equal**(II1 first1, II1 last1, II2 first2);	O(N)
template<class II1, class II2, class BinP> bool **equal**(II1 first1, II1 last1, II2 first2, BinP pred);	O(N)
template<class FI1, class FI2> FI1 **search**(FI1 first1, FI1 last1, FI2 first2, FI2 last2);	O(M*N)
template<class FI1, class FI2, class BinP> FI1 **search**(FI1 first1, FI1 last1, FI2 first2, FI2 last2, BinP pred);	O(M*N)
template<class FI, class Size, class T> FI **search_n**(FI first, FI last, Size count, const T& value);	N*count
template<class FI, class Size, class T, class BinP> FI **search_n**(FI first, FI last, Size count, const T& value, BinP pred);	N*count

Table B.2   Mutating-sequence algorithms

Function	Complexity
template<class II, class OI> OI **copy**(II first, II last, OI result);	N
template<class BI1, class BI2> BI2 **copy_backward**(BI1 first, BI1 last, BI2 result);	N
template<class T> void **swap**(T& a, T& b);	constant
template<class FI1, class FI2> FI2 **swap_ranges**(FI1 first1, FI1 last1, FI2 first2);	N
template<class FI1, class FI2> void **iter_swap**(FI1 a, FI2 b);	constant
template<class II, class OI, class UOP> OI **transform**(II first, II last, OI result, UOP op);	N
template<class II1, class II2, class OI, class BOP> OI **transform**(II1 first1, II1 last1, II2 first2, OI result, BOP op);	N
template<class FI, class T> void **replace**(FI first, FI last, const T& old_value, const T& new_value);	N
template<class FI, class P, class T> void **replace_if**(FI first, FI last, P pred, const T& new_value);	N
template<class II, class OI, class T> OI **replace_copy**(II first, II last, OI result, const T& old_value, const T& new_value);	N
template<class II, class OI, class P, class T> OI **replace_copy_if**(II first, II last, OI result, P pred, const T& new_value);	N
template<class FI, class T> void **fill**(FI first, FI last, const T& value);	N
template<class OI, class Size, class T> void **fill_n**(OI first, Size n, const T& value);	N
template<class FI, class Gen> void **generate**(FI first, FI last, Gen gen);	N
template<class OI, class Size, class Gen> void **generate_n**(OI first, Size n, Gen gen);	N
template<class FI, class T> FI **remove**(FI first, FI last, const T& value);	N
template<class FI, class P> FI **remove_if**(FI first, FI last, P pred);	N
template<class II, class OI, class T> OI **remove_copy**(II first, II last, OI result, const T& value);	N
template<class II, class OI, class P> OI **remove_copy_if**(II first, II last, OI result, P pred);	N

continued

Table B.2   (continued)

Function	Complexity
template<class FI> FI **unique**(FI first, FI last);	N–1
template<class FI, class BinP> FI **unique**(FI first, FI last, BinP pred);	N–1
template<class II, class OI> OI **unique_copy**(II first, II last, OI result);	N
template<class II, class OI, class BinP> OI **unique_copy**(II first, II last, OI result, BinP pred);	N
template<class BI> void **reverse**(BI first, BI last);	N/2
template<class BI, class OI> OI reverse_copy(BI first, BI last, OI result);	N
template<class FI> void **rotate**(FI first, FI middle, FI last);	O(N)
template<class FI, class OI> OI **rotate_copy**(FI first, FI middle, FI last, OI result);	N
template<class RI> void **random_shuffle**(RI first, RI last);	N–1
template<class RI, class RandGen> void **random_shuffle**(RI first, RI last, RandGen& rand);	N–1
template<class BI, class P> BI **partition**(BI first, BI last, P pred);	N (N/2 swaps)
template<class BI, class P> BI **stable_partition**(BI first, BI last, P pred);	N *Swaps:* O(NlogN)

Table B.3 Sorting algorithms

Function	Complexity
template<class RI> void **sort**(RI first, RI last);	O(NlogN)
template<class RI, class Compare> void **sort**(RI first, RI last, Compare comp);	O(NlogN)
template<class RI> void **stable_sort**(RI first, RI last);	$O(N(logN)^2)$
template<class RI, class Compare> void **stable_sort**(RI first, RI last, Compare comp);	$O(N(logN)^2)$
template<class RI> void **partial_sort**(RI first, RI middle, RI last);	O(NlogN)
template<class RI, class Compare> void **partial_sort**(RI first, RI middle, RI last, Compare comp);	O(NlogN)
template<class II, class RI> RI **partial_sort_copy**(II first, II last, RI result_first, RI result_last);	O(NlogN)
template<class II,class RI,class Compare> RI **partial_sort_copy**(II first, II last, RI result_first, RI result_last, Compare comp);	O(NlogN)
template<class RI> void **nth_element**(RI first, RI nth, RI last);	O(N)
template<class RI,class Compare> void **nth_element**(RI first, RI nth, RI last, Compare comp);	O(N)

Table B.4   Sorted search and merge algorithms

Function	Complexity
template<class FI, class T> FI **lower_bound**(FI first, FI last, const T& value);	O(logN)
template<class FI, class T, class Compare> FI **lower_bound**(FI first, FI last, const T& value, Compare comp);	O(logN)
template<class FI, class T> FI **upper_bound**(FI first, FI last, const T& value);	O(logN)
template<class FI,class T, class Compare> FI **upper_bound**(FI first, FI last, const T& value, Compare comp);	O(logN)
template<class FI, class T> pair<FI,FI> **equal_range**(FI first, FI last, const T& value);	O(logN)
template<class FI,class T, class Compare> pair<FI,FI> **equal_range**(FI first, FI last, const T& value, Compare comp);	O(logN)
template<class FI, class T> bool **binary_search**(FI first, FI last, const T& value);	O(logN)
template<class FI, class T, class Compare> bool **binary_search**(FI first, FI last, const T& value, Compare comp);	O(logN)
template<class II1, class II2, class OI> OI **merge**(II1 first1, II1 last1, II2 first2, II2 last2, OI result);	O(M*N)
template<class II1, class II2, class OI, class Compare> OI **merge**(II1 first1, II1 last1, II2 first2, II2 last2, OI result, Compare comp);	O(M*N)
template<class BI> void **inplace_merge**(BI first, BI mid, BI last);	O(NlogN)
template<class BI,class Compare> void **inplace_merge**(BI first, BI mid, BI last, Compare comp);	O(NlogN)

Table B.5   Set operations

Function	Complexity
template<class II1, class II2> bool **includes**(II1 first1, II1 last1, II2 first2, II2 last2);	O(M+N)
template<class II1, class II2, class Compare> bool **includes**(II1 first1, II1 last1, II2 first2, II2 last2, Compare comp);	O(M+N)
template<class II1, class II2, class OI> OI **set_union**(II1 first1, II1 last1, II2 first2, II2 last2,OI result);	O(M+N)
template<class II1, class II2, class OI, class Compare> OI **set_union**(II1 first1, II1 last1, II2 first2, II2 last2, OI result, Compare comp);	O(M+N)
template<class II1, class II2, class OI> OI **set_intersection**(II1 first1, II1 last1, I2 first2, II2 last2, OI result);	O(M+N)
Template<class II1, class II2, class OI, class Compare> OI **set_intersection**(II1 first1, II1 last1, II2 first2, II2 last2, OI result, Compare comp);	O(M+N)
template<class II1, class II2, class OI> OI **set_difference**(II1 first1, II1 last1, II2 first2, II2 last2, OI result);	O(M+N)
template<class II1, class II2, class OI, class Compare> OI **set_difference**(II1 first1, II1 last1, II2 first2, II2 last2, OI result, Compare comp);	O(M+N)
template<class II1, class II2, class OI> OI **set_symmetric_difference**(II1 first1, II1 last1, II2 first2, II2 last2, OI result);	O(M+N)
template<class II1, class II2, class OI, class Compare> OI **set_symmetric_difference**(II1 first1, II1 last1, II2 first2, II2 last2, OI result, Compare comp);	O(M+N)

Table B.6   Heap operations

Function	Complexity
template<class RI> void **push_heap**(RI first, RI last);	O(logN)
template<class RI, class Compare> void **push_heap**(RI first, RI last, Compare comp);	O(logN)
template<class RI> void **pop_heap**(RI first, RI last);	O(logN)
template<class RI, class Compare> void **pop_heap**(RI first, RI last, Compare comp);	O(logN)
template<class RI> void **make_heap**(RI first, RI last);	O(3*N)
template<class RI, class Compare> void **make_heap**(RI first, RI last, Compare comp);	O(3*N)
template<class RI> void **sort_heap**(RI first, RI last);	O(NlogN)
template<class RI, class Compare> void **sort_heap**(RI first, RI last, Compare comp);	O(NlogN)

Table B.7   Minimum and maximum algorithms

Function	Complexity
template<class T> const T& **min**(const T& a, const T& b);	constant
template<class T, class Compare> const T& **min**(const T& a, const T& b, Compare comp);	constant
template<class T> const T& **max**(const T& a, const T& b);	constant
template<class T, class Compare> const T& **max**(const T& a, const T& b, Compare comp);	constant
template<class FI> FI **min_element**(FI first, FI last);	N−1
template<class FI, class Compare> FI **min_element**(FI first, FI last, Compare comp);	N−1
template<class FI> FI **max_element**(FI first, FI last);	N−1
template<class FI, class Compare> FI **max_element**(FI first, FI last, Compare comp);	N−1
template<class II1, class II2> bool **lexicographical_compare**(II1 first1, II1 last1, II2 first2, II2 last2);	min(N,M)
template<class II1, class II2, class Compare> bool **lexicographical_compare**(II1 first1, II1 last1,II2 first2, II2 last2, Compare comp);	min(N,M)

Table B.8 Permutation algorithms

Function	Complexity
template<class BI> bool **next_permutation**(BI first, BI last);	O(N/2)
template<class BI, class Compare> bool **next_permutation**(BI first, BI last, Compare comp);	O(N/2)
template<class BI> bool **prev_permutation**(BI first, BI last);	O(N/2)
template<class BI, class Compare> bool **prev_permutation**(BI first, BI last, Compare comp);	O(N/2)

Table B.9 Numeric algorithms

Function	Complexity
template<class II, class T> T **accumulate**(II first, II last, T init);	O(N)
template<class II, class T, class BOP> T **accumulate**(II first, II last, T init, BOP op);	O(N)
template<class II1, class II2, class T> T **inner_product**(II1 first1, II1 last1, II2 first2, T init);	O(N)
template<class II1, class II2, class T, class BOP1, class BOP2> T **inner_product**(II1 first1, II1 last1, II2 first2, T init, BOP1 op1, BOP2 op2);	O(N)
template<class II, class OI> OI **partial_sum**(II first, II last, OI result);	N–1
template<class II, class OI, class BOP> OI **partial_sum**(II first, II last, OI result, BOP op);	N–1
template<class II, class OI> OI **adjacent_difference**(II first, II last, OI result);	N–1
template<class II, class OI, class BOP> OI **adjacent_difference**(II first, II last, OI result, BOP op);	N–1

Function Objects and Adapters

Function Objects

All standard function objects are adaptable inasmuch as they define the argument and return types required by the function object adapters. They do this by deriving from either `unary_function` or `binary_function`. See Chapter 15 for more information.

Table C.1   Arithmetic operations

Operation	Cardinality	operator() returns:
plus	binary	x + y
minus	binary	x − y
multiplies	binary	x * y
divides	binary	x / y
modulus	binary	x % y
negate	unary	−x

Table C.2   Comparisons

Operation	Cardinality	operator() returns:
equal_to	binary	x == y
not_equal_to	binary	x != y
greater	binary	x > y
less	binary	x < y
greater_equal	binary	x >= y
less_equal	binary	x <= y

Table C.3 Logical operations

Operation	Cardinality	*operator () returns:*
logical_and	binary	x && y
logical_or	binary	x ll y
logical_not	unary	!x

Table C.4 Negators

Object	Cardinality	*operator () returns:*
unary_negate(pred)	unary	!pred(x)
binary_negate(pred)	binary	!pred(x,y)

Table C.5 Binders

Object	Cardinality	*operator (x) returns:*
binder1st(op, value)	unary	op(value, x)
binder2nd(op, value)	unary	op(x, value)

Table C.6 Function pointer objects

Object	Cardinality	*operator (x...) returns:*
pointer_to_unary_function(f)	unary	f(x)
pointer_to_binary_function(f)	binary	f(x,y)

Table C.7 Member function pointer objects

Object	Cardinality	*operator (...) returns:*
mem_fun_t(pmf)	unary	ptr2obj->pmf()
mem_fun1_t(pmf)	binary	ptr2obj->pmf(x)
mem_ref_t(pmf)	unary	&obj->pmf()
mem_ref1_t(pmf)	binary	&obj->pmf(x)

Function Object Adapters

Function object adapters are function templates that transform one adaptable function object along with optional arguments into another adaptable function object.

Table C.8   Negaters

Adapter	Returns:
not1(unary_pred)	unary_negate(unary_pred)
not2(binary_pred)	binary_negate(binary_pred)

Table C.9   Binders

Adapter	Returns:
bind1st(bop, val)	binder1st(bop, val)
bind2nd(bop, val)	binder2nd(bop, val)

Table C.10   Pointers to functions

Adapter	Returns:
ptr_fun(R (*pf)(A))	pointer_to_unary_function(pf)
ptr_fun(R (*pf)(A1, A2))	pointer_to_binary_function(pf)

Table C.11   Pointers to member functions

Adapter	Returns:
mem_fun(R (T::*pmf)())	mem_fun_t(pmf)
mem_fun(R (T::*pmf)(A))	mem_fun1_t(pmf)
mem_ref(R (T::*pmf)())	mem_ref_t(pmf)
mem_ref(R (T::*pmf)(A))	mem_ref1_t(pmf)

Annotated Bibliography

The following books are, in my opinion, the *crème de la crème*. These are the classics that are unquestionably worth your while. For a more complete list, see the C/C++ Users Journal Web Site, http://www.cuj.com. Each entry is annotated with descriptive qualifiers from the following list:

Qualifier	Meaning
INTRO	Introductory
INTMD	Intermediate
ADV	Advanced
REF	Reference Material
DESIGN	Illustrates OO Design
IDIOMS	Covers Idioms/Patterns

The C Practitioner's Booklist

FEUER, ALAN R., *The C Puzzle Book*, 2nd ed. Englewood Cliffs, NJ: Prentice-Hall ESM, 1989. ISBN 0-13-109926-4. Represents a rite of passage all C programmers should undergo. Although somewhat esoteric and abstract, the author rigorously tests your mastery of important concepts. [INTMD, REF]

KERNIGHAN, BRIAN W., and RITCHIE, DENNIS M., *The C Programming Language*, 2nd ed. Englewood Cliffs, NJ: Prentice Hall, 1988. ISBN 0-13-110362-8. The quintessential reference. Essential catechism for all C folks. [INTRO, INTMD, ADV, REF]

KOENIG, ANDREW, *C Traps and Pitfalls*, Addison-Wesley, 1989, ISBN 0-201-17928-8. Uniquely Koenig, an expert who really knows how to communicate. He elucidates dark corners and "gotchas" that so many never notice. Concise, readable, and indispensable. [INTRO, INTMD, ADV, REF]

PLAUGER, P. J., *The Standard C Library*. Englewood Cliffs, NJ: Prentice-Hall, 1991. ISBN 0-13-131509-9. Without peer. This book provides the needed polish for mastering C. [INTMD, ADV, REF]

PLUM, THOMAS, *Learning to Program in C*, 2nd ed. Plum Hall, 1989. ISBN 0-911537-08-2. [INTRO]

————, *C Programming Guidelines*, 2nd ed. Plum Hall, 1989, ISBN 0-911537-07-4. [INTRO, INTMD, REF, DESIGN]

PLUM, THOMAS, and BRODIE, JIM, *Efficient C*, Plum Hall, 1985. ISBN 0-911537-05-8.

Few people understand C as well as Tom, and his books couple that expertise with sound software engineering principles. His books are now a little dated (mostly pre-ANSI C), but the principles are timeless. [INTMD, ADV, DESIGN]

The C++ Practitioner's Booklist

CARGILL, TOM, *C++ Programming Style*. Addison-Wesley, 1992. ISBN 0-201-56365-7. One of the very best on proper use of classes and objects in C++, as well as tricks of the trade. (Reviewed in the *C/C++ Users Journal*, April 1993). [INTMD, DESIGN, IDIOMS]

CLINE, MARSHALL, and LOMOW, GREG, *C++ FAQs*. Addison-Wesley, 1995. ISBN 0-201-58958-3. Probably the best text for daily use in the workplace. Amazing depth in covering good solid engineering practice. Only dopes overlook this one. [INTMD, ADV, REF, DESIGN, IDIOMS]

COPLIEN, JAMES, *Advanced C++*. Addison-Wesley, 1992. ISBN 0-201-54855-0. The one and only truly advanced text. Way ahead of its time. Rich in design idioms. For power users only. [ADV, DESIGN, IDIOMS]

ECKEL, BRUCE, *Thinking in C++*. Upper Saddle River, NJ: Prentice-Hall, 1995. ISBN 0-13-9177094. By far the best way to study C++. A tutorial work of art. (2nd edition to appear). [INTRO]

HENRICSON, MATS, and NYQUIST, ERIK, *Industrial Strength C++*. Upper Saddle River, NJ: Prentice-Hall, 1997.ISBN 0-13-120965-5. Concise and readable style guide for real-world C++ programming. [REF, DESIGN, IDIOMS]

KOENIG, ANDREW, and MOO, BARBARA, *Ruminations on C++*. Addison-Wesley, 1997, ISBN 0-201-42339-1. For me, this is about the best book I own on C++. (Reviewed in the *C/C++ Users Journal*, April 1997). [INTMD, ADV, DESIGN, IDIOMS]

LIPPMAN, STANLEY, *C++ Primer*. 2nd ed. Addison-Wesley, 1991. ISBN 0-201-16487-6. Excellent tutorial for beginners. Very thorough. (3rd Edition to appear). [INTRO]

MEYERS, SCOTT, *Effective C++*. 2nd ed. Addison-Wesley, 1998. ISBN 0-201-92488-9.

———, *More Effective C++*. Addison-Wesley, 1996. ISBN 0-201-63371-X.

Two of the best books by far. Concise chapters on specific implementation issues. [INTMD, REF, DESIGN, IDIOMS]

STROUSTRUP, BJARNE, *The C++ Programming Language*. 3rd ed. Addison-Wesley, 1997. ISBN 0-201-88954-4. The "K&R" of C++, but a much better read (no offense intended). The most thorough coverage of C++ available. [INTRO, INTMD, REF]

———, *The Design and Evolution of C++*. Addison-Wesley, 1994. ISBN 0-201-54330-2. The standard text on C++ history and philosophy from its designer. Explains why C++ is the way it is. A must-read. [INTMD, ADV, IDIOMS]

Index